STUD

RALPH A. GRIFi
ER.

—

30

CARDIGANSHIRE AND THE CARDI, *c.*1760–*c.*2000

Trevor Fishlock, *Talking of Wales* (London, 1976), p. 62.
By permission of Gren Calendars Ltd.

CARDIGANSHIRE AND THE CARDI, *c.*1760–*c.*2000

LOCATING A PLACE AND ITS PEOPLE

by

MIKE BENBOUGH-JACKSON

*Published on behalf of the
University of Wales*

CARDIFF
UNIVERSITY OF WALES PRESS
2011

www.uwp.co.uk

British Library Cataloguing-in-Publication Data
A catalogue record for this book is available from the British Library.

ISBN 978-0-7083-2394-6
e-ISBN 978-0-7083-2395-3

Printed by CPI Antony Rowe, Chippenham, Wiltshire

SERIES EDITORS' FOREWORD

Since the foundation of the series in 1977, the study of Wales's history has attracted growing attention among historians internationally and continues to enjoy a vigorous popularity. Not only are approaches, both traditional and new, to the study of history in general being successfully applied in a Welsh context, but Wales's historical experience is increasingly appreciated by writers on British, European and world history. These advances have been especially marked in the university institutions in Wales itself.

In order to make more widely available the conclusions of original research, much of it of limited accessibility in postgraduate dissertations and theses, in 1977 the History and Law Committee of the Board of Celtic Studies inaugurated this series of monographs, *Studies in Welsh History*. It was anticipated that many of the volumes would originate in research conducted in the University of Wales or under the auspices of the Board of Celtic Studies, and so it proved. Although the Board of Celtic Studies no longer exists, the University of Wales continues to sponsor the series. It seeks to publish significant contributions made by researchers in Wales and elsewhere. Its primary aim is to serve historical scholarship and to encourage the study of Welsh history.

CONTENTS

ACKNOWLEDGEMENTS

Living on the wrong side of the Teifi, I soon became aware of the judgements being made about Cardiganshire and the Cardi. On crossing the bridge to go to work, however, the people did not appear that different. Some might say that if my summer job was as a waiter, rather than as a 'wash-up boy', I would have noticed that the tips were both less frequent and less generous than elsewhere. In my first year at university, I was introduced to Edward Said's *Orientalism* during a sociology seminar. Some years later, when I was contemplating a topic for a Ph.D. proposal, I realized that there was a less exotic, occidental 'other' on my door step. So, my first acknowledgement is to the difference, and *différance*, of Cardiganshire and the Cardi.

Many people have helped me refine my initial interest in the representational history of Cardiganshire and its inhabitants. My initial supervisor, Professor Anne Borsay, encouraged me to explore ideas and concepts which were used in the social sciences. Without these academic tools, it would have been impossible to cut through the thicket of representations which I was collecting, let alone organize them. After Anne left the University of Wales, Lampeter, Professor Peter Borsay became my supervisor. Peter encouraged me to contextualize my research and advised me on how the historical significance of Cardiganshire and the Cardi could be demonstrated. Anne's and Peter's patience and generosity channelled my enthusiasm and helped me to appreciate the historian's craft.

The recommendations and commendation of my external examiner, Professor Rob Colls, together with his work on the Geordie, mean that I am doubly indebted to him; although I am still a little disappointed that he did not sample a bowl of *cawl* on his journey across Wales to examine my thesis. Later, the series editors helped to turn the thesis into a book.

Their amendments and suggestions enabled me to clarify the arguments contained in this study. Indeed, their guidance, particularly that provided by Professor Ralph Griffiths, has meant that I have learned much from putting this book together.

I am also indebted to others who have given me ideas, information and support. Peter Borsay introduced me to Neil Evans, whose good humour and generosity (with ideas, facts and coffee) eased my way into Welsh history; it was Neil who pointed me in the direction of the Gren cartoon 'Cardi buys a round'. Neil arranged a meeting with Professor Ieuan Gwynedd Jones who listened to my ideas, instantaneously provided me with a list of titles to chase up, then descended to the basement and emerged with some more sources. Working with Neil and Dr Paul O'Leary on a research project broadened my knowledge of Welsh history and microfilm readers. Dr Bill Jones, and occasionally his wife Val, have ferried me across the Teifi on trips to the National Library of Wales. As well as helping me gather information, these journeys took the edge off the sense of isolation which often assails researchers. I am grateful to a number of good lecturers who have taught me at undergraduate and postgraduate level, especially Ieuan Thomas at Glamorgan and Professor Chris Williams at Cardiff. My former and present colleagues at Liverpool John Moores University have supported me with their camaraderie, humour and counsel. They accepted a lowly Notts Co fan into the capital of football, even though he did not take up the red (sorry, Frank) or the blue (apologies, Ron). The staff at libraries and archives in Bangor, Aberystwyth, Lampeter, Carmarthen, St Fagans, Cardiff, Liverpool and London have helped me on innumerable occasions by retrieving, reserving and pointing me towards material. In particular, I am grateful for the permission to use Horsfall-Turner's map of Cardiganshire which was granted by the National Library of Wales. I would also like to thank Gren Calendars Ltd for permission to use the cartoon for the frontispiece of this volume. R. D. Jones, James Marvin Morgan and William H. Richards responded to my call for information in the press and on the radio, and I wish to thank them for providing me with other representations of Cardiganshire and the Cardi.

Most importantly, I would like to thank my wife, Shân, and my parents. Ivy and Michael have supported me over the years and during that time demonstrated an admirable ability to put up with a child whose interest in the past became a career; although it did not turn out to be palaeontology as I predicted some thirty-two years ago. Shân has lived with a historian. That alone is worthy of commendation. She has helped me focus on my work and reacquaint myself with the present.

ABBREVIATIONS

BUL	Bangor University Library
BPP	British Parliamentary Papers
C	*Cambrian*
CN	*Cambrian News*
CTA	*Cardigan and Tivyside Advertiser*
CJ	*Carmarthen Journal*
CAS	Carmarthenshire Archive Service
CA	Ceredigion Archive
NLW	National Library of Wales
W	*Welshman*
WG	*Welsh Gazette*
WM	*Western Mail*

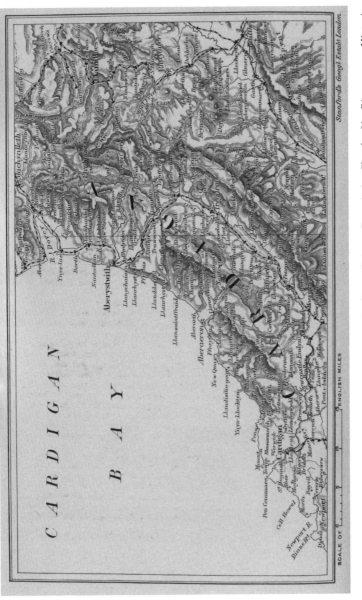

E. R. Horsfall-Turner, *Walks and Wanderings in County Cardigan: Being a Descriptive Sketch of its Picturesque, Historic, Antiquarian, Romantic and Traditional Features* (Bingley, 1902). By permission of Llyfrgell Genedlaethol Cymru / The National Library of Wales.

I

INTRODUCTION: LOCUS AND FOCUS

Places and people are frequently categorized. After catego-rization they are often employed as ideological implements, palpable examples that reinforce world-views. At times, rival representations signal sociocultural conflicts. At others, unchallenged interpretations indicate cultural dominance or subjection. Such representations help us to appreciate the 'mechanisms by means of which a group imposes (or attempts to impose) its conception of the social world'.[1] This book explores issues that could relate to any geographical area or group of people and applies them to a particular locus – the Welsh county of Cardigan, presently Ceredigion, during the modern period. Representations of Cardiganshire provide a rich vein for those interested in the way a place and a group of people have been engaged because the county has been regularly marked out as being peculiar. Perceived difference attracted commentary; as Edward Said noted in relation to the Orient, '"strong" ideas' tend to congregate around that which is perceived as different.[2] This book is a 'repre-sentational history', which has been recently defined as an approach that focuses on 'the ways in which meanings and understandings are constructed in society through cultural exchange'.[3] As such, it treats perceptions of Cardiganshire and the Cardi as historical phenomena worthy of study in their own right.

The guiding concept of this study is that of 'location'. It needs to be stressed that the use of this word in a meta-phorical way differs significantly from its common usage. In the latter, every physical entity has a location. In the

---

[1] Roger Chartier, *Cultural History: Between Practice and Representations*, trans. Lydia G. Cochrane (Cambridge, 1988), p. 5.

[2] Edward W. Said, *Orientalism: Western Conceptions of the Orient* (London, 1978), p. 22.

[3] Brian Maidment, *Dusty Bob: A Cultural History of Dustmen, 1780–1870* (Manchester, 2007), p. 12.

metaphorical sense, however, the notion of location goes from being solid to fluid; it is based on how people position the place on mental maps and chronologies. As 'identity remains unintelligible unless it is located in the world', places and peoples often come to embody values.[4] This is achieved by locating places and people on a spectrum of qualities. Therefore, when a group or place is designated as possessing some quality it is always, either explicitly or implicitly, in relation to other places. Representations of the county and its inhabitants (often nicknamed Cardis) are regularly placed in four locations.[5] Two of these – past and future – are related to time. The former interprets a place or group as typifying the past. The latter detects signs of a desirable future. Conversely, the third and fourth locations – centre and margin – figuratively pertain to space. These locate the inhabitants or place as being at the centre of specific values or far removed from them. Besides these locations, there are instances of naming the county and its inhabitants that often serve to emphasize one or more of these locations. The categories, clarified below, are not narrow, and contain much diversity within them. Nevertheless, all these locations are imbued with sentiments stimulated by a place and a people or, rather, by the idea of a place and a people.

The locus of this study may be limited to one county, but the focus is on the way representations of places and people may be permeated by the beliefs of particular groups. Investigations of the meanings attributed to places could be applied to other settings, from continents to villages. All places are located, metaphorically as well as spatially. They are placed in relation to central concerns that take aspects of their actuality, such as a prevalent trade – as was the case of the south Wales mining valleys – and make use of them. For that reason, the focus will be on the arrangement of a place in relation to other places, peoples and times. Cardiganshire,

---

[4] Peter L. Berger and Thomas Luckmann, *The Social Construction of Reality* (London, 1966), p. 174.

[5] This is an example of 'grounded theory' which 'seeks to develop an apt framework out of the materials themselves and hence it is necessarily more pragmatic and flexible than adherence to a pre-existing theory'. Ludmilla Jordanova, *History in Practice* (London, 2000), p. 70.

the locus, will be studied in order to demonstrate the ways in which a place can be culturally mapped. It has been argued that the 'connotations' of Geordie 'are very different from those of the Londoner, Mancunian or indeed Tynesider'.[6] The nuances evoked by each of these groups vary considerably. Yet this study, while seeking to understand the peculiar associations induced by a place, posits a structure on which these dissimilarities may be contrasted. For it is only through such constructions of difference that places obtain their particularity. This consideration of Cardiganshire opens up a field of connotations in which other places and people are located. After outlining the value of this enquiry and the materials used in its compilation, the remainder of this chapter will examine the locus and focus in greater detail.

More investigations are needed into the ways whereby the mental patchwork of divisions within Wales have been culturally composed. An observation that the south of England has not been adequately inspected as 'a series of attitudes and expectations' applies equally to Welsh regions.[7] Works on economic, social and cultural issues have, of course, noted distinctions in terms of economics and language use.[8] But these have not been related to the way in which people constituted these areas psychologically, that is, the 'ontology of groupness'.[9] How people have distinguished areas and groups, and the purpose served in defining themselves and others, are subjects worthy of examination. Historians note perceived differences, but tend not to study them. Divides are referred to, often jestingly, before being overshadowed by other matters.[10] Such fissures and designations of difference,

---

[6] P. Lewis, 'Region and class: an introduction to Sid Chaplin (1916–86)', *Durham University Journal*, 85, 1 (1993), 105–9, 107.

[7] J. R. Lowerson, 'Editorial preface', *Southern History*, 1, 1 (1979), 9–10, 9.

[8] For an example of economic activity seen as the determinant of identity, see Neil Evans 'Regional dynamics: north Wales, 1750–1914', in Edward Royle (ed.), *Issues of Regional Identity: In Honour of John Marshall* (Manchester, 1998), pp. 201–25, 218.

[9] Eric Storm, 'Regionalism in history, 1890–1945: the cultural approach', *European History Quarterly*, 33, 2 (2003), 251–65, 251. Also see Celia Applegate, 'A Europe of regions: reflections on the historiography of sub-national places in modern times', *American Historical Review*, 114, 4 (1999), 1157–81, 1174.

[10] Allusions to the Cardi's reputation for money making at the expense of the consumer are, for instance, made by Geraint H. Jenkins, *The Foundations of Modern*

however, demand consideration if an attempt to piece together how people have, and indeed do, make sense of the world is to be made. This study selects one of these manifold divisions, the cultural demarcation of Cardiganshire and the Cardi, and shows how the county and its inhabitants have found their way into the popular consciousness. Yet the study can be related to, and indeed depends on, many distinctions. Therefore, the ways in which Wales as a whole has been seen and used forms part of this investigation.

In 1964 the American critic Marius Bewley observed that cultural history required 'a firmly held criterion of relevance'.[11] It is necessary to comment on the reasons why the materials, which provide the foundation of this enquiry, have been selected. There has been an attempt to avoid limiting the range of commentators. Thus the study forms a cumulative biography of the county, one that at times contains contending voices. The ways in which Cardiganshire has been located are scattered throughout many sources and often emerge in the form of a brief allusive comment. This necessitated the inclusion of a range of material in Welsh and English, such as local and national newspapers, ballads, memoirs, travel accounts, government reports, manuscripts and novels. The examination has been able, therefore, to avoid as much as possible dependence upon a limited range of commentators, which is likely to skew studies of representations. Even so, views from those from outside the county predominate, especially in the late eighteenth and early nineteenth centuries. To attempt to compensate for this, when possible representations from both inhabitants and outside sources were considered: how the inhabitants saw and how they were seen. Images derived from these 'internal' and 'external' sources enable cultural changes in more than one sector to be traced, as 'each is chronically implicated in the other in an ongoing dialectic of identification'.[12] Taking into account a range of perspectives

Wales: Wales, 1642–1780 (Oxford, 1993), p. 77, and Kenneth O. Morgan, Rebirth of a Nation: Wales, 1880–1980 (Cardiff and Oxford, 1981), p. 6.

[11] Marius Bewley, 'Temptations of the cultural historian', The New York Review of Books, 19 (November 1964), 19–21, 19.

[12] Richard Jenkins, Rethinking Ethnicity: Arguments and Explanations (London, 1997), p. 47.

poses its own problems, however. There is a risk that the opinions will remain fragments disconnected from one another and, more importantly, their milieu. Adequate appreciation of these representations demands that the various locations are related to one another and their context in a multilayered discussion. The four categories of location used here, together with the part played by naming, bring these strands of opinion closer together. In addition, this enquiry considers the relationship between place and concepts such as nation, class and, to a lesser extent, gender, but avoids presenting a one-dimensional analysis that unduly prioritizes the relationship between any one of them and the place.[13]

Eschewing an exclusively local approach, this volume will look at how substantial ideas wash against, interact with, and emerge from one area. In sum, it is a local history with one foot in the local and the other amongst the concepts that have been used to categorize the county.[14] Studying a repeatedly dissimilated place such as Cardiganshire brings to the fore the ways in which difference is defined and deployed. Simone de Beauvoir recounted how she and Jean-Paul Sartre believed that 'in order to understand something about mankind, it was necessary to scrutinise extreme cases'.[15] Depictions of Cardiganshire often provide 'extreme cases' of a perceived identity marked out from others and used in discourse. Not all places have been used by commentators as often as Cardiganshire has, but all demarcations rely on specific means of differentiation which the acute example of Cardiganshire can elucidate. Social scientists have long recognized the importance of looking in the past to identify those markers that distinguish groups. Michael Hechter and Margaret Levi stated that: 'The explanation of all these puzzles [arising from 'markers'] must lie in the realm of history.'[16] The 'puzzle' of Cardiganshire's distinctiveness and the issue of distinction in general are addressed in this study.

[13] These suggestions were among those made by Adrian Jones in 'Word *and* deed: why a *post*-poststructural history is needed, and how it might look', *Historical Journal*, 43, 2 (2000), 517–41, 525.

[14] George Sheeran and Yanina Sheeran, 'Discourses in local history', *Rethinking History*, 2, 1 (1998), 65–86, 82; J. D. Marshall, *The Tyranny of the Discrete: A Discussion of the Problems of Local History in England* (Aldershot, 1997), p. 80.

[15] Maurice Cranston, *Sartre* (Edinburgh, 1962), p. 23.

[16] Michael Hechter and Margaret Levi, 'Ethno-regional movements in the West',

A history concerned with the way in which a place has been perceived cannot overlook aspects dealt with in more common histories, such as shifts in economic activity, political allegiance or the area's social make-up. Attention must be paid to what people made of these structural shifts; hence this book relates discourse to the historical context that provided the materials with which people constructed their perspective. Definitions were produced by those who, for various reasons, claimed to know the essence of the place and its populace. Many have claimed to discern the quintessence of Cardiganshire and these attempts to explain or deploy the place illustrate how their ideologies employed and determined the county's image.

Divisions *within* Cardiganshire are occasionally found in accounts, and there remains scope for studies of what Eugen Weber described as 'the psychic distance between one village and another' in the county.[17] But the emphasis of this investigation is on the ways in which the county as a whole has been conceptualized, because it has been these countywide generalizations that have been deployed in wider debates. It is interested in the selection and omission of particular aspects of the county that were deemed to represent Cardiganshire – the way in which a multifarious reality was reduced and used – rather than the definition of more local distinctions.[18]

The ideas, images and objects used in the ascription or declaration of identity are explored in this book. Location, as an organizing concept, is an attempt to move the issue of identity away from an oversimplified statement of fact or a superficial recognition of diversity, to an examination of how definitions are used and articulated. Mediated descriptions of the past, and indeed the present, are all we have. Traditions, ranging from food to language, have featured

Ethnic and Racial Studies, 2, 3 (1979), 262–74, 262.

[17] Eugen Weber, *Peasants into Frenchmen: The Modernization of Rural France, 1870–1914* (London, 1976), p. 49.

[18] An indication of the perceived differences within the county was given by Thomas Jones in *Leeks and Daffodils* (Newtown, 1942), p. 188. Also see J. Geraint Jenkins, *Ceredigion: Interpreting an Ancient County* (Llandysul, 2005), pp. 10–12. For the way in which visitors constructed hierarchies of value within the county, see M. Benbough-Jackson, 'Ceredigion and the changing visitor gaze, c.1760–2000', *Ceredigion*, 14, 3 (2003), 21–41.

in these depictions and their symbolic use will be considered here. There is value in tracing how and when traditions
emerge because they point to changes in society 'which
are otherwise difficult to date'.[19] Traditions associated with
places provide examples of 'lived experience' that could be
evoked for the purposes of 'political expediency'.[20] Indeed, it
is not so much a case of traditions being invented as the use
to which carefully selected elements of these traditions have
been put.

Each act of locating Cardiganshire produced an encounter
between ideas and places. Peter Burke's instruction that 'a
cultural history centred on encounters' needs to contain 'a
variety of tongues' is adopted in the following pages.[21] Even
then, the very nature of the historical record means that
many sections of society have not left their impression of the
area until late in the period, if at all. Insights into the way the
county has been located are restricted to those who wrote or
whose judgments were recorded. These 'interested parties'
deserve to be studied for their own sake as they helped to
shape, and were shaped by, dominant currents of thought,
yet it must be borne in mind that they amount to a fraction
of those who would have seen the county, lived in it or interacted with its inhabitants. Occasionally, other voices, that
would not usually have left a testimony, do enter the historical record and their contribution is highlighted. In this
wide-ranging study, representations will often be referred to
as being located on mental maps and chronologies. From
these a more extensive map and larger timescale will be
outlined. Before exploring the five components of cultural
location, Cardiganshire's physical location and composition
will be outlined, and the periods of enquiry that structure
the following chapters will be explained.

[19] Eric Hobsbawm, 'Introduction: inventing traditions', in Hobsbawm and
Terence Ranger (eds), *The Invention of Tradition* (Cambridge, 1983), pp. 1–15, 12.
[20] David Hopkin, 'Identity in a divided province: the folklorists of Lorraine,
1860–1960', *French Historical Review*, 23, 4 (2000), 639–82, 642.
[21] Peter Burke, *Varieties of Cultural History* (Cambridge, 1997), pp. 211–12.
Also see Robert F. Berkhofer, Jr, *Beyond the Great Story: History as Text and Discourse*
(Cambridge, MA, 1995), pp. 170–201.

Locus

Cardiganshire's appearance on a map has been described as a 'smooth, sea-lion curve'.[22] More prosaically, in an Edwardian textbook written by one of the county's leading educationalists, its outline was likened to that of a boot.[23] Those maps based on the Gall-Peters rather than the Mercator projection, though, suggest a less elongated form. As with all shapes, the county is defined by its border. The prominent physical features that mark Cardiganshire's perimeter have encouraged writers to emphasize its isolation.[24] While it could be argued that such descriptions underestimate similarities and contact with other areas, these geographical markers have provided the county with more discernible boundaries than many other counties. The county lacks a western neighbour; a late Victorian publication for children mentioned that it looked to the west.[25] This side faces Cardigan Bay; opposite it, some eighty miles away, is the Irish county of Wexford. Cardiganshire is a maritime county, its coastline being over fifty miles in length. The people's relationship with the coast – whether through smuggling, fishing, trade or tourism – pervades Cardiganshire's history. Although the county lacks deep, natural harbours, the coastline is dotted with settlements, from Ynyslas in the north to Cardigan in the south. This coastal strip is predominantly influenced by south-westerly winds and has milder winters than inland areas. Despite observations about summer visitors wearing mackintoshes, the more clement winters experienced there helped contribute to the development of resorts.

Cardiganshire's southern boundary, mainly formed by the Teifi river, separates the county from two southern neighbours – Pembrokeshire and Carmarthenshire.[26] Unlike the

---

[22] Julian Barnes, *England, England* (London, 1998), p. 5.

[23] D. J. Saer, *The Story of Cardiganshire* (Cardiff, 1912), pp. 1–2.

[24] For example, see John Edward Lloyd, *The Story of Ceredigion* (Cardiff, 1937), p. 1.

[25] Anon., 'Siroedd Cymru: II Ceredigion', *Cymru'r Plant*, 8 (1899), 47–51, 47.

[26] For a scholarly account of the river, see Richard J. Moore-Colyer, *The Teifi: Scenery and Antiquities of a Welsh River* (Llandysul, 1987). For a survey of the county's physical characteristics, see David B. James, *Ceredigion: Its Natural History* (Bow Street, 2001).

northern parts of the neighbouring counties to the south
and the rest of Cardiganshire, the southern segment of the
county contains a band of settlements.[27] The lower part of
the river's course, from Llandysul through Newcastle Emlyn
and on to Cardigan, is known as 'Tivyside' – Tivy being the
anglicized form of the river's name. This area was identified with the landed and leisured portion of society in the
nineteenth and early twentieth centuries.[28] Indeed, it is
important to acknowledge that areas, in this case a sub-
region of three counties, were often most readily defined as
a social entity for the elite.[29] But this patrician and, as the
spelling of Tivyside shows, anglicized stratum was complemented and later ousted by the predominantly Liberal
middle class and farmers who provided services and products in the towns. For many in the north of Pembrokeshire
and Carmarthenshire, the nearest major market towns would
have been in Cardiganshire. Charles Phythian-Adams has
identified the importance of drainage basins in the formation of a region's economic and cultural characteristics, and
'Tivyside' illustrates how it 'becomes possible to be techni-
cally resident in a county and yet be "looking" in an opposite
direction'.[30]

The river, which stems from Llyn Teifi near the remains of
Strata Florida abbey, does not constitute the entire southern
boundary of the county. On reaching Lampeter, the border
zigzags across sparsely populated land. It meets the Tywi as
this river leaves the Llyn Brianne reservoir. The old county of
Brecon shares a border with Cardiganshire, which is defined
by the young Tywi, and runs for some twelve miles before

[27] The importance of small towns – defined as places with a population of 10,000
or fewer – in Cardiganshire was especially noticeable in 1901 when over 25 per cent
of the population was estimated to have resided in them. See Stephen A. Royle, 'The
development of small towns in Britain', in Martin Daunton (ed.), *The Cambridge
Urban History of Britain*, vol. 3: *1840–1950* (Cambridge, 2000), pp. 151–84, 171.

[28] See H. M. Vaughan, *The South Wales Squires* ([1926] Carmarthen, 1988).

[29] David Eastwood, *Government and Community in the English Provinces, 1700–1870*
(Basingstoke, 1997), p. 93.

[30] Charles Phythian-Adams, 'Introduction: an agenda for English local history', in
C. Phythian-Adams (ed.), *Societies, Cultures and Kinship, 1580–1850: Cultural Provinces
and English Local History* (Leicester, 1993), pp. 1–23, 15. Equally, for many in
Cardiganshire, Carmarthen could play a greater role in their lives than Aberystwyth;
see Myra Evans, *Atgofion Ceinewydd* (Aberystwyth, 1961), p. 41.

meeting Radnorshire. After ten miles, another old county
border, that of Montgomeryshire, is shared for some twenty-
seven miles. Even in this deserted region, people were aware
of the boundary between Cardiganshire and its neighbour;
one traveller noted crossing a 'small brook' that separated
the two counties.[31] This highland district, known as the
Pumlumon plateau, forms part of the Cambrian Mountains
and many rivers, notably the Severn and the Wye, originate
here. Described as one of the most deserted parts of Wales,
this border district is mainly over a thousand feet above sea
level – its highest peak being just under two and a half thousand feet. It forms a ridge between Cardiganshire and eastern
Wales. Even though the highland has been traversed for the
sake of commerce and leisure for many years, it features in
the gallery of images used to illustrate Cardiganshire's isolation. Lucien Febvre maintained that human perceptions
alter boundaries, and subtle shifts in emphasis given to this
physical feature, and that of the Teifi, that reflect the way
Cardiganshire has been located culturally will be addressed
in this book.[32] The border then curves westwards towards the
Dyfi Estuary. This stretch of water separates Cardiganshire
from Merioneth. At this point the county is at its narrowest.

These boundaries of the modern county are much the
same as those of the ancient kingdom of Ceredig. Yet
there were some minor changes in the modern era, such
as the shifting status of parts of St Dogmaels to the south,
that have been overlooked by some who stress the antiquity of the county border.[33] Significant changes that would
have split Cardiganshire were proposed during the 1960s.
These provoked responses from inhabitants of the county,
and reveal contrasting perceptions of the area, which are

---

[31] William Fordyce Mavor, *A Tour in Wales and through Several Counties of England
. . . Performed in the Summer of 1805* (London, 1806), p. 74.

[32] Lucien Febvre, *A Geographical Introduction to History*, trans. E. G. Mountford
and J. H. Paxton (London, 1925), p. 18. For a study of the various ways in which a
geographical feature has been perceived, see Klaus Plonien, '"Germany's river, but
not Germany's border": the Rhine as a national myth in early nineteenth-century
German literature', *National Identities*, 2, 1 (2000), 81–6.

[33] Thomas Lloyd, Julian Orbach and Robert Scourfield, *The Buildings of Wales:
Carmarthenshire and Ceredigion* (London, 2006), p. 3. For a summary of these alterations, see Gerald Morgan, *Ceredigion: A Wealth of History* (Llandysul, 2005), pp. 18–19.

explored in chapter VI. From 1974, the county, together with the counties of Pembroke and Carmarthen, formed Dyfed. Despite some resentment, it retained its borders and identity as a district within the county. The district was christened 'Ceredigion', a title that was retained when county status returned in 1996. Emphasis placed on the county's borders by those who locate Cardiganshire will figure in this book and contribute to a rich symbolic tapestry that also includes emblems from within the county.

A number of rivers and streams cut across Cardiganshire. Their valleys are focal points, and woollen mills have used their fast-flowing waters as an energy source. Before assuming its status as county border, the youthful Teifi, for example, runs through Pontrhydfendigaid and passes Tregaron. A stretch of bog land called Cors Caron lies between these settlements. It has in the past, like other marshlands in the county such as Cors Fochno to the north, provided fuel in the form of peat. A route, known as Cefn Cardis (Cardis' Ridge), formerly used by cattle drovers and migrant workers heads eastwards from Tregaron.[34] To the west is the River Aeron. Alongside the young river is Llangeitho, a focus of Calvinistic Methodism. The river enters Cardigan Bay at Aberaeron after having passed through land now often associated with the poet Dylan Thomas who named his daughter, Aeronwy, after it.[35] The Aeron originates in an upland area to the north called Mynydd Bach (Small Mountain). Part of this area, unlike most of western Cardiganshire, is 1,000 feet above sea level.[36] Another river flowing from Mynydd Bach is the Wyre. After a relatively straight course it enters the sea near Llanrhystud. Further north are two major rivers: the Ystwyth and the Rheidol. Lead mines, which took their toll on fish stocks, were situated in both valleys. In its twenty-two-mile course, the Ystwyth passes the remains of lead mines at Cwmystwyth and the renowned scenery of the former Hafod estate before joining the Rheidol at Aberystwyth, the

---

[34] John Williams-Davies, '"Merched y Gerddi": mudwyr tymhorol o Geredigion', *Ceredigion*, 8, 3 (1978), 291–301, 294.

[35] Paul Ferris, *Dylan Thomas: The Biography* (London, 1977), p. 185.

[36] For a history of the area, see Evan Jones, *Y Mynydd Bach a Bro Eiddwen* (Aberystwyth, 1990).

county's largest town. The Rheidol has harvested praise for its scenery, especially when it is joined by the Mynach at Devil's Bridge. From here a route used by the drovers went down to Cwmystwyth and eventually to the markets of Birmingham. On the map, the county may have appeared to be looking westward, but, in the main, its commercial interests faced east.

These physical features and the human activities around them – religious buildings, schools and livestock – have contributed to the way Cardiganshire has been located in people's minds. Broader meanings were formed from these materials as they spawned images that conveyed ideas. The degree to which these images were, to quote Peter Borsay in his study of the changing image of Bath, 'inextricably bound up with social and political forces, of which they were both a product and part', will be returned to throughout this study.[37] Many of these natural and human features were not unique to the county. Mountains, chapels and schools, for example, have all been used to symbolize Wales. Yet, at times, these general symbols gave an additional level to the county image without submerging its own particularity.

Interpretations of Cardiganshire and the Cardi do not adhere to strict periods. Unlike physical confrontations and negotiations, symbolic ones cannot be easily dated. A combination of cultural, demographic and economic currents have been taken into consideration before selecting the periods into which this book is divided, and they consequently follow conventional chronological partitions. These may be somewhat crudely categorized as: an era of economic upsurge that contributed to particular utilitarian and Romantic views of the area (c.1760–1830); the relationship between amplified secular and religious discourses of improvement and the county (1830–70); interactions between the county's declining population, combined with an increased interest in the past, and representations of Cardiganshire and the Cardi (1870–1914); a time of political division brought about by the challenge of socialism

---

[37] Peter Borsay, *The Image of Georgian Bath, 1700–2000: Towns, Heritage and History* (Oxford, 2000), p. 324.

together with international conflict and their impact on
the location of the county and its inhabitants (1914–45);
and the influence of heightened consumerism, in-migra-
tion and technological change on images of Cardiganshire
and its inhabitants (1945–2000). Although their origins
are not traceable to a specific year or the pen of any individual, distinct representations may be detected during these
periods. At the start of each chapter the features of the era,
which provide the lens through which both place and people
are seen, are outlined before an analysis of the ways in which
Cardiganshire and the Cardi have been located. Such an
approach could be described as a chronological history of
representations seamed with themes.

Concentrating on certain temporal envelopes enables
closer attention to be paid to the relations between contemporaneous interpretations. Purely theoretical chapters
would involve combining diverse perspectives that would
have benefited from being more closely related to contemporaneous contrasting interpretations. Arguably, running
contrary, relatively contemporaneous ideas together is
better suited than a separation of theoretical strands that are
then segmented chronologically. Moreover, a chronological
approach draws attention to emergent voices. The surfacing
of views about Cardiganshire from various sources, be it
government publications from the early Victorian period or
autobiographies written in the latter part of the twentieth
century, mark significant shifts in the nature of public, widely
diffused images. Accordingly, the nature and type of sources
contribute to the periodization adopted by this investigation. Most importantly, a chronological approach cultivates
an appreciation of the layers of images and attitudes that are
called upon, rejected or ignored at certain times. A study
that concentrated on a narrower period would do less justice
to the subject matter's kaleidoscopic character. This is important because if one thing is 'given' about representations it is
that they are never static.

The broad-brush approach has been influenced by some
seminal investigations of regional representations and how
they alter over time. Robert Colls's study traced a shift in
the way the north-eastern pitman was depicted from the

intemperate to the respectable and then to the victim in just over a hundred and fifty years. Gareth Stedman Jones's essay on the London Cockney and John Belchem's on the Merseyside Scouser also noted changes and ambiguities in both the image of a city and its denizens.[38] In one respect, this study differs from these in that it investigates a predominantly rural area. A more substantial difference between the present study and the above mentioned lies in its focus on descriptive categories. Whereas the other studies were predominantly conducted from the perspective of social history, this examination focuses on ways in which Cardiganshire and the Cardi have been endowed with meaning. The categories deployed in the practice of cultural location will now be addressed.

FOCUS

Naming

Raymond Williams identified the changes in the use of words such as class, art and culture that suggested general shifts 'in our characteristic ways of thinking about our common life'.[39] While not encompassing the range covered by words such as culture, an indication of how people imagined the area may be found in the names they used. A variety of names, including nicknames and official names, together with the principal meanings attached to them, will be considered in this study. Names may inform cultural historians about relationships between people and the way a place is conceived. Care should be taken, however, because the same word might well mean different things. Negative stereotypes have been appropriated and used as badges of distinctiveness. For

[38] Robert Colls, *The Collier's Rant: Song and Culture in the Industrial Village* (London, 1977); Gareth Stedman Jones, 'The Cockney and the nation, 1780–1988', in David Feldman and Gareth Stedman Jones (eds), *Metropolis London: Histories and Representations Since 1800* (London, 1989), pp. 272–324; John Belchem, '"An accent exceedingly rare": Scouse and the inflexion of class', in Belchem and Neville Kirk (eds), *Languages of Labour* (Aldershot, 1997), pp. 99–139. Also see Derek B. Scott, 'The music-hall Cockney: flesh and blood, or replicant?', *Music & Letters*, 83, 2 (2002), 237–59; Krisztina Fenyő, *Contempt, Sympathy and Romance: Lowland Perceptions of the Highlands and the Clearances during the Famine Years, 1845–1855* (East Linton, 2000); Philip Payton, *The Making of Modern Cornwall: Historical Experience and the Persistence of 'Difference'* (Redruth, 1992).

[39] Raymond Williams, *Culture and Society, 1780–1950* (London, 1958), p. xiii.

instance, a survey describing trends in the regional identity of the southern USA by James C. Cobb identified the ways in which southern whites had adopted previously critical epithets like 'redneck'.[40] Moreover, those who are included in a name may vary. The Cardi provides an example of this, as seen in chapter III where the use of the name as shorthand for someone who hailed from a rural area is explained.

Names often represent the interests of a specific group in abridged form. More innocently, they may be limited because they are the product of that group's cultural horizons; despite this, they are useful because they indicate how perceptions have been formed. Groups of people and their work are often conflated in the names. The name 'cotton balls', given to holidaying workers on the Isle of Man in the nineteenth century, is one example of the part work plays in the creation of group images.[41] Names are used to classify things, and acts of categorization reflect the mind of the classifier. Naming has significant implications since a word or series of words may influence how others see a person or group of people. In turn, names may determine how the named see themselves. Even though the statement 'you are what you are named' is somewhat fanciful, it cannot be denied that naming plays a pivotal role in the formation of perceptions and the efficacy of their transmission.[42] When historians investigate 'traditions which increase, or diminish people's concern and respect for one another', the implications of naming need to be considered.[43]

Changes in what was regarded as the defining component of a group can be detected through alterations in the name applied to that group. Noting transformations in the structure of any society can tell us much about altered conditions;

[40] James C. Cobb, 'An epitaph for the North: reflections on the politics of regional and national identity at the millennium', *Journal of Southern History*, 66, 1 (2000), 3–24, 12.

[41] John Belchem, '"The playground of northern England": the Isle of Man, Manxness and the northern working class', in Neville Kirk (ed.), *Northern Identities: Historical Interpretations of 'The North' and 'Northernness'* (Aldershot, 2000), pp. 71–86, 71.

[42] Frank Nussel, *The Study of Names: A Guide to the Principles and Topics* (Westport, CT, 1992), p. 5.

[43] C. Behan McCullagh, *The Truth of History* (London, 1998), p. 306.

studying changes in the way particular groups are named complements this by revealing that conditions were deemed definitive. Names supply a convenient hook on which several characteristics and objects associated with a place and people can be hung.[44] In some instances, names remain constant while the associations they arouse fluctuate as a result of cultural currents. To be typically English at the end of the 1930s necessitated the recognition of a considerably 'different set of values and beliefs' from forty years earlier.[45] Being English, therefore, changed with prevailing concerns, but these cannot be traced easily to specific causes. Amidst the whole panoply of factors that influence notions of 'being of' a particular country or place, we need to be aware of those contending or dominant interests that championed a particular reading of a people and a place. For a long time, a range of images and behaviours usually related to the 'governing elite' determined notions of Englishness. This investigation will look at changes in what it meant to 'be of' Cardiganshire and suggest possible reasons for these transformations.

When a name acquires popular currency, this indicates its applicability or usefulness for the named, the namer or both. A name has to resonate among a certain number of people in order to become widely used. Any consideration of naming must include those who name as well as those who are named. In fact, self-ascription may take the form of adopting a name coined by outsiders. This appears to have been the case with the name Geordie used to describe people from the north-east of England and Tyneside in particular.[46] The import attached to a name may provide examples of how groups have been located in relation to various ideas. Bestowing names on others is often driven by the need to distinguish them or oneself. Fernand Braudel observed, in a French context, that the 'vital thing for every community is to avoid being confused with the next tiny "patrie", to

---

[44] Athony Giddens, *Sociology* (Cambridge, 1997), p. 582.

[45] Judy Giles and Tim Middleton, 'Introduction', in Giles and Middleton (eds), *Writing Englishness 1900–1950: An Introductory Sourcebook on National Identity* (London, 1995), pp. 1–12, 6.

[46] Robert Colls and Bill Lancaster, 'Preface', in Colls and Lancaster (eds), *Geordies: Roots of Regionalism* (Edinburgh, 1993), pp. x–xv, xi.

remain *other*.[47] The namer attributes particular aspects to the named. Not all of these are necessarily overtly judgemental; they could simply define someone as coming from a place. But specific ways of thinking about an area or its people often come together with the name used.[48]

Instances of self-definition also need to be taken into consideration. Yet self-styled names should not necessarily be taken as being a more genuine reflection of a group's character than those originating from the outside. They, too, are sometimes the products of interested parties keen to assign a particular characteristic to a people. The same issues of who provides or promotes particular names and meanings remain relevant. Again, it is the variable nature of these self-images that is of interest here. Questions of why and how they are deployed need to be asked. There is a need to proclaim difference only when the different are being met or addressed. The times covered by this investigation saw ongoing changes in transportation and trade that provided a canvas on which to paint larger distinctions. Differences between villages and towns persisted, but with urban growth other broader distinctions arose. It has been observed that 'since the variety of cultures lies in their juxtaposition, they exaggerate themselves and each other'.[49] Industrialization and urbanization enabled further exaggeration, spread by an expanding media, to be made between places and people. Accents and dialects were given names that represented places and people in the popular consciousness. John Langton underscored the significance of regional names and their links with different ways of speaking English in the nineteenth century. He argued that they 'gave both a justification for and a means of displaying a hotter pride in regional identity'.[50]

[47] Fernand Braudel, *The Identity of France*, vol. 1: *History and Environment*, trans. Siân Reynolds (London, 1988), p. 41.

[48] For some Welsh examples, see Myrddin ap Dafydd (ed.), *Pigion Llafar Gwlad 4: Llysenwau* (Llanwrst, 1997), pp. 82–93.

[49] Anthony P. Cohen, *The Symbolic Construction of Community* (Chichester, 1985), p. 115.

[50] John Langton, 'The industrial revolution and the regional geography of England', *Transactions of the Institute of British Geographers*, new ser. 9, 2 (1984),

In addition to distinguishing one group from another, self-definition brings together those included in the name. This was most noticeable when groups gathered together outside their place of origin, sometimes in formal societies, thus marking themselves off from those around them. But comparable expressions of similarity through conscious acts of naming were made in the area itself. On occasion, local newspapers foster identification with localities. Activities carried out in the place could, either formally or informally, be given the name of the area and serve to rally pride. In this manner, an assemblage of things, ideas, individuals and beliefs may be bound up in a name. So to be of a specific place means more than being resident or from there. In the same way, negative interpretations of a product, as was the case with the illustrious 'Brummidgem goods' from Birmingham, could colour an area's image. Names stimulate feeling, as demonstrated by the reaction of an Anglesey historian in 1940. The nickname 'Moch Môn' was usually translated into 'Anglesey Pigs', but the historian contended that 'moch' actually meant 'quick' or 'ready', and was deemed an 'honourable term'.[51] Nicknames bring perceived characteristics even closer to the fore. As will be noted in chapters V and VI, reactions against their pejorative associations indicate social tension and regional rivalry.

A consideration of naming introduces and highlights themes that will be explored in greater detail during the analysis of the four locations in which Cardiganshire and its inhabitants have been positioned. For that reason, naming has a section to itself in each chapter in which dominant and contending pronouncements will be outlined. What is more, different phases, during which there occur alterations in the meanings attached to the same name, adoptions of new names, or the reinvigoration of old names, will be identified. The extent to which they mark important points in the history of the way Cardiganshire has been perceived will also be addressed. As naming often suits the needs of the namer,

145–67, 162. Also see Michael Freeman, 'The industrial revolution and the regional geography of England: a comment', ibid., 507–12.

[51] Lucy Williams, 'Factors in the culture of pre-railway Holyhead', *Anglesey Society and Field Club Transactions*, 8 (1940), 93–9, 93.

when the motive to name changes so do the names, or what they imply. Fluctuations in the relationship between namer and named, and the ways they come together to make or contest meaning, will be considered.

Past
Groups of people or places are sometimes depicted as being representative of the past. These descriptions of areas or groups as being typical of the past are not simply factual, however, because they involve judgements about what constitutes the past. Prevailing concerns are unveiled when some aspect of the past is applied to a space. Criticizing these beliefs as partial or inaccurate only takes us so far in understanding their uses. Their omissions are instructive, but should serve as the starting point for an enquiry into the needs they fulfilled. Moreover, classifying something as being representative of the past contains within it an implicit definition of the present. Interpretations of any given time can be glanced through what it is thought to be leaving behind.

   In part, this study is concerned with the ideological use of the past. Those who place things in the past, even if they do not have an obvious programme, have an interest in doing so. Instilling the past and its remnants with value involves condemnation as well as commendation. This interested use of the past is most commonly associated with those who disliked aspects of modernity. The Welsh educationalist O. M. Edwards, for example, saw industry and urbanization as posing a threat to the quintessence of Wales.[52] To be placed in the past by Edwards was to be honoured; though, of course, his favoured past, where wives 'wove and spun' instead of gossiping all day, was a particular past, as indeed all pasts are.[53] Such outlooks led to the championship of some areas, where change was gradual, above others. The kind of past venerated depends on a country's context. It has been noted that for Irish cultural nationalists, 'the spirit of the essential Irish nation was located . . . in the period

[52] See Emlyn Sherrington, 'O. M. Edwards, culture and the industrial classes', *Llafur*, 6, 1 (1992), 28–41.
[53] O. M. Edwards, 'Stray leaves', *Wales*, 3 (1896), 1–6, 1.

before colonization'.[54] Those who locate places in the past often overlook similarities with neighbours and dependence on areas possessing 'modern' characteristics. The variegated nature of a place's past is frequently simplified in what amounts to a pursuit of difference. Yet connections and changes constitute every area's past.[55] The simplifying projections developed by various positions shed light on their fears and foes.

Catherine Brace linked power and selected characteristics of place in her work on the Cotswolds. Those who employ ideological concepts, such as Englishness, seek out and attach the immaterial concept to material signs, thereby enhancing the legibility of their message. Images of Cotswold stonework and gardens were used as healthy aesthetic opposites to modern influences.[56] This study will estimate the degree to which aspects of Cardiganshire and its population functioned as a vehicle by which national discourses could gather additional momentum. Nevertheless, in terms of mental location, places are multidimensional and they have been related to the past in assorted ways. A dominant interpretation may be rejected or ignored. In time, forceful images wither and new ones take their place. The unfurling of this process in the case of the Cardi character-type is paid especial attention in chapters IV to VI. Variations in the way Cardiganshire and the Cardis have been located in the past highlight the variegated nature of cultural and political contests over time.

Most assessments of the way places are deemed more 'authentic' than others are founded on what one cultural historian has described as the 'publicly presented past'.[57] Other ways of expressing the relationship between the past and a place or group of people have operated, however. Being located in the past might well entail disparagement.

[54] Christopher Chul Morash, *Writing the Irish Famine* (Oxford, 1995), p. 63.

[55] Doreen Massey, 'Places and their pasts', *History Workshop Journal*, 39 (1995), 182–92, 183.

[56] Catherine Brace, 'Gardenesque imagery in the representation of regional and national identity: the Cotswold Garden of Stone', *Journal of Rural Studies*, 15, 4 (1999), 365–76, 366; *eadem*, 'Looking back: the Cotswolds and English national identity, *c.*1890–1950', *Journal of Historical Geography*, 25, 4 (1999), 502–16.

[57] Michael Kammen, *In the Past Lane: Historical Perspectives on American Culture* (New York, 1997), p. xii.

Successive modernizing and reforming impulses, both religious and secular, surface in the period covered by this study.
So, far from being a commendation, being located in the
past could denote disapproval. A negative view of past things
has provided a rhetorical platform from which to emphasize the benefits of progress. Cardiganshire has been looked
upon in this way on numerous occasions, and the dynamics
of these negative past locations are examined in this book.
Historians should be as aware of these hypercritical observations as those more familiar complimentary assessments.
Yet these two aspects, praise and derision, of locating people
or places in the past are similar in that they originate with,
and are expressed by, those who seek to change or promote
certain actions and reactions. Those 'texts, practices, and
people [that] struggle against each other' in the social arena
need to locate people and places in the past in order to gain
some advantage by claiming to know the past.[58]

Specific objects or activities given value by commentators need to be considered. Often the evidence for a place,
a county or any other area as being representative of the
past originates in a handful of images that are then magnified and come to stand for the area as a whole. Therefore,
in addition to identifying those positions that benefit from
locating places and groups in the past, this approach will
consider how local institutions, personifications, everyday
objects and settings are drawn upon when the place and its
people are located in the past. Points at which these entities
attain symbolic value reveal shifts in cultural perceptions.
The emphasis placed on the Cardi as an emblem of the past,
notably in the second half of the twentieth century, and the
selection of a broth (*cawl*) as an embodiment of the county
and the past in the late nineteenth century are among
the instances scrutinized in this study. Such designations
founded on food and clothing are significant indicators of
the way people interpreted the social world.[59] Some places

[58] 'Truth, power, self: an interview with Michel Foucault, October 25 1982', in
Huck Gutman, Patrick H. Hutton and Luther H. Martin (eds), *Technologies of the Self:
A Seminar with Michel Foucault* (London, 1988), pp. 9–15, 14.

[59] Joe Moran, 'History, memory and the everyday', *Rethinking History*, 8, 1 (2004),
51–68.

have been ascribed a closer relationship with the past than others. The description of the American South as being '*against* the historical tide' could also be applied to other areas.[60] In order to convey this difference, those who posit it utilize objects, behaviours and images. Furthermore, some inhabitants of an area may welcome their location in the past. Marks of poverty or peripherality, such as *cawl*, could be transformed into something of worth. It has been argued that Scottish Highlanders welcomed being part of the 'Primitive Picturesque' because 'it set them apart, giving them an air of importance which masked their comparative poverty'.[61]

Inhabitants of an area themselves might locate the soul of their locality in the past. This raises the question whether the oft-invoked self-defining 'other' is always a contemporary presence. Self-definition need not rely on the contrast provided by a different culture, gender or race. After examining Maori culture, Anne Salmond suggested an alternative interpretation of how identity is constituted. Instead of being defined against a present-day opposite, Maori identity was established by reference to their ancestors.[62] Accordingly, the yardstick of tradition and ostensible past standards may be applied to the present. This tendency is by no means exclusive to the locus of Salmond's study. Loss or dilution of past identity is a common theme in both national and regional contexts in the British Isles. In the case of Cardiganshire, it will be noted how demographic decline during the last third of the nineteenth century contributed to this outlook. The factors that need to be brought to bear on studies of identity formation were summarized by Marshall Sahlins: 'Divinities or enemies, ancestors or affines, the "others" are in various ways the necessary conditions of a society's existence.'[63] The

---

[60] Peter Gray, *Southern Aberrations: Writers of the American South and the Problems of Regionalism* (Baton Rouge, 2000), p. 499.

[61] Murray G. H. Pittock, *Celtic Identity and the British Image* (Manchester, 1999), pp. 39–40.

[62] Referred to in Anthony P. Cohen, *Self Consciousness: An Alternative Anthropology of Identity* (London, 1995), p. 129.

[63] Marshall Sahlins, 'Goodbye to tristes tropes: ethnography in the context of modern world history', in Robert Borofsky (ed.), *Assessing Cultural Anthropology* (New York, 1994), pp. 377–95, 387.

ancestors need not be literal; previous habits and manners also pattern the relationship between a locale and its past.

Future
This investigation is not restricted to an assessment of a single future vision. Instead a variety of expressions, each as contestable and malleable as those that focused on the past, are examined. Concentrating on statements that look towards the future open up another perspective on the way in which groups and places have been culturally fashioned. Like other locations, each future location conveys a particular understanding of a place and a people that contributes to our appreciation of its role in public consciousness.

An American visitor to mid-nineteenth-century England affords an example of future location: 'Everything in England is at a quick pace. They have reinforced their own productivity by the creation of that marvellous machinery which differences this age from any other age.'[64] Though referring to the present – technology and national character – the commentator was associating these impressions with a future; it was all going somewhere and was being applauded for its future potential. Panoramic observations like this were not the only ways in which places and people could be located. It was not esoteric or limited to the ostensibly detached observer from abroad. William Davies's history of the Carmarthenshire market town of Llandeilo, published in 1858, illustrates how the future image of England and the English painted above permeated other minds. Davies's interest in the past was combined with hopes for the future, yet enterprise was not expected to come from the town's Welsh population. 'The Celt by nature is not a seller', he remarked. Instead Welsh towns often required 'a *Sais* [English man], a man of spirit, intelligence, and thrift', who acted upon opportunities that made money.[65] Potential was located in the archetypal Englishman who became synonymous with material advancement. By the same token, the typical Celt was located in the past. The two locations were

[64] R. W. Emerson, *English Traits* (Boston, 1856), p. 160.
[65] William Davies, *Llandeilo-Vawr and its Neighbourhood* (Llandeilo, 1858), p. 173.

founded on their mutual contrasts. As this example shows, the attribution of momentum to a group or nation provided an influential cultural marker.

Specific ideas direct the way in which the future is invoked; this is most obviously the case in utopian projections. However, similar meanings can be attached to contemporaneous activities. By claiming that something represents desirable change, particular activities are being singled out. Claiming to know what constitutes a preferred future is as potent a form of knowledge as claiming to discern the meaning of the past. 'Nothing gives greater importance or credibility to a moral or political value than ... that it is an essential element of historical movement from past through present to future.'[66] Ideas about a required future have often determined the prospect from which places and people are viewed. They also provide part of the framework with which people understand their world. Belief in the capable '*Sais*' was founded on the potential of this energetic type of person to act as a prime mover and further changes already occurring at that time. Events, institutions, groups, all of these could be harnessed to notions of what the future could and should be. At any one time, however, there could be conflicting future locations and these conflicting futures illuminate tensions between world-views.

The category 'future' has been preferred to 'progress' in this study because it possesses fewer connotations of inevitable improvement. Although master narratives have been integral to the future location of many geographical areas and groups of people, and terms such as progress are regularly used, it is important that less explicit expressions of historical processes are not overshadowed by them. Adhering to strict interpretations of schools of progress would limit the scope of this study because future locations were not always driven by explicit philosophical visions. Ideas might well come from a sense of local pride, competitiveness, or a desire to assuage material want, as much as the articulation of a future vision. Perhaps this could be described as progress with a small 'p'. Further, with its less grand connotations,

---

[66] Robert Nisbet, *History of the Idea of Progress* (London, 1980), p. 4.

future embraces shorter periods of time, including the lives
of individuals. Local trajectories may correspond with intellectual movements and designs for grand progress, but are
equally likely to be governed by the pressing concerns of the
everyday. As will be seen in an examination of Cardiganshire
societies during the interwar years, the Cardi was associated
with personal advancement. Places and people can be clad
in so many possible futures that the connotations of progress
seem too restrictive. It is possible that progressive aspects
were attributed to something that would be reckoned dated
elsewhere.

A common type of future location takes a past-like place
inhabited by unambitious people and recommends ways in
which they are able to be drawn into a favourable future. It is
the relationship between a potential future and a place that
generates the future location here, rather than a people who
possess a key to the future. It differs from a past location in
its emphasis on prescription rather than description. Those
who urged the adaptation of new agricultural techniques
during the late eighteenth and early nineteenth centuries,
whose recommendations are examined in chapter II, provide
an example of this variety of location. Generally, there is a
missionary-like impetus to these future locations. They focus
on symbols of progress that need to be introduced to the area,
or attributes to be instilled into its inhabitants. This variety
of future location is founded on potential present-day benefits; its course is not governed by any 'chiliastic endpoint'.[67]
In the main, the future aspect is directed towards material,
technological or commercial gain, with mental well-being
and contentment considered corollaries of this. Such ideas,
however, may not have been commonly accepted.

All the same, adding value to a place through improvements can play a fundamental part in contributing to
pride in an area that extends beyond those who initiated
the change, as seen in the desire to keep pace with other
places. To be behind may be a source of shame and embarrassment. For inhabitants of Cardiganshire, the designation

---

[67] Margarita Mathiopoulos, *History and Progress: In Search of the European and
American Mind* (New York, 1989), p. 382.

'old-fashioned' or its equivalent became, on occasion, something to shake off as much as preserve. Various material things such as the railway, that former epitome of 'modernity's future orientation', have been distinguished as essentials for advancement.[68] Following an externally generated pattern for development need not, therefore, breed resentment. An area or group of people might well seek distinctiveness through a commonly accepted definition of advancement. In Wales during the two decades after the Second World War, for example, a symbol of progress, especially when compared to the interwar years, was provided by economic renewal – '"New South Wales" became for a while a Welsh as well as an Australian concept'.[69] A sense of partaking in development, of affiliating an area or group of people to improvement, may contribute to self-descriptions based on the desire to gain, seek or maintain a position of leadership among competing regions or groups. A group's standing may often be related to the degree to which they are thought to embody advancement.

Symbolic competition between areas need not be restricted to a comparison of technical or material features. A future location could be articulated in intellectual or spiritual terms. Some of these expressions are compensatory, an attempt to balance economic or political power elsewhere. But the material and the spiritual should not be strictly separated. They both claim to be moving onwards in a better direction, away from a recent or distant past. A future focus is a rhetorical technique that places importance on an area and, more specifically, on what that area represents. In effect, it sets a place and a people apart. The notion of individual progress, moreover, cannot be divorced from ideas about the area from which the people came. It is possible for ideas of improvement to be attached to groups within a place. A profession may be depicted as moving forward in terms of wealth or cultural significance. The mid-Victorian northern tradesman, whom Elizabeth Gaskell's Mr Thornton

[68] Ian Carter, *Railways and Culture in Britain: The Epitome of Modernity* (Manchester, 2001), p. 16.

[69] Rob Humphreys, 'Images of Wales', in Trevor Herbert and Gareth Elwyn Jones (eds), *Post-War Wales* (Cardiff, 1995), pp. 133–59, 138.

described as looking upon life 'as a time for action and exertion', provides one case of the way in which a group may be depicted as active, as making a future.[70] These vanguards show how individual progress is likely to be linked to a group that then, in the next link of the chain, is related to a place. There may be as many vanguards as there are causes to which an idea of the future is attached: cultural movements, religious beliefs, political visions or even ethnic strains could be called upon to illustrate and validate specific ideas.

Centre
Whereas the locations outlined above are based on temporal comparisons, spatial factors govern the positioning of a place and its people as a centre. A central location is founded on a contemporary comparison. The notion that the Welsh lower orders were made of a stronger moral fibre than their English equivalents is an example of this location. Expressed in the mid-nineteenth century travel accounts and government reports examined in chapter III, this opinion identified the concentration of a quality in one place and its relative scarcity in another. At face value, these statements of centrality are one-dimensional. On closer inspection and contextualization, however, these locations are based on a collection of attitudes that are encapsulated in a comparison designed to promote a world-view.

The terms 'centre' and 'margin' are not synonymous with the more commonly used expressions of 'core' and 'periphery'. They refer to perceptions rather than the uneven distribution of wealth and influence over a spatial area that is conveyed by the latter pair, but the four concepts are complementary. Evident differences between places provoked responses that played a role in distinguishing entities. It has been noted that at a time of industrial and commercial expansion during the modern period there were a 'multiplicity of new cores and peripheries'.[71] Just as there were numerous economic cores, many centres of moral, social

---

[70] Elizabeth Gaskell, *North and South* ([1855] Harmondsworth, 1995), p. 326.
[71] Keith Robbins, *History, Religion and Identity in Modern Britain* (London, 1993), p. 246.

or spiritual qualities have existed. When people defined places or groups as being a centre of positive features they were constructing a map of qualities that overlaid the core and periphery. Taking these views into account enables us to get closer to how people have experienced their world. The geographer Emrys Jones observed that by adding 'perception to the core-periphery model . . . you begin to get nearer the world in which people live'.[72] By considering instances when Cardiganshire has been deemed a centre of values, we add something to the differences usually expressed in terms of wealth and influence, and highlight the correspondences and conflicts between these two scales. Being perceived as a centre of certain characteristics requires measurement against other places thought to have less of the qualities in question. Centrality involves the mental concentration of particular ideals in a place.

Location at the centre of positive characteristics may be contested; centres are often open to ridicule and attacked. Some interwar Anglo-Welsh writers, notably Caradoc Evans, questioned the idea of the Cardi as a moral centre. Their efforts to 'relocate' a centre to the margin of desirable values will be among the issues considered in chapter V. Essentially, claims to identify a centre are founded on expressions of exclusivity or concentration of certain qualities that may be questioned. Competition for centrality takes the form of claims to morality, bravery and intelligence, among others. As with other mental locations, symbols play an important part in claims to centrality. By assembling these symbols and assertions, superiority in some facet can be declared and displayed. Values are attributed to characteristics and items that not only distinguish one place from another through a regional 'characteristic culture', but claim to possess something more than another area does.[73] In addition, a mutual dependence on difference may also arise. An example of this has been uncovered in a study of Lancashire and Yorkshire whose 'rivalry should . . . be seen as an internal feature

[72] Emrys Jones, 'Where is Wales?', *Transactions of the Honourable Society of Cymmrodorion 1994*, new ser. 1 (1995), 123–34, 125.

[73] T. S. Eliot, *Notes Towards the Definition of Culture* ([1948] London, 1962), pp. 53–4.

of a single cultural system, not as proof that there are two separate ones'.[74] Although sharing many similar features and historical links, these two English counties have been frequently set in opposition. A similar dynamic, founded on contrasting centres, can be seen in the history of Welsh counties and regions. To take one example, some emphasized Cardiganshire as an alternate centre to Cardiff; the motivations behind this contrast are explained in chapter VI.

A number of topics could influence symbolic relationships between Cardiganshire and other geographical areas. Issues of representing Welshness, urban and rural divides, class, gender and modernity will be considered in this examination of contrasts. Perceived centres do not necessarily correspond to a single county or a country. For a late Victorian praising the common folk of southern Pembrokeshire, the values he identified there were common to the English, but not to the Welsh. Consequently, in contrast to 'the Welshman our Little Englanders are good horsemen and bold sailors'.[75] General ideas associated with a larger geographical area or belief system may be located in small corners. When looking at the claims surrounding a geographical centre we also need to consider the reasons *why* claims were made. At one time and among some people, sailors and horsemen were thought typically English and not Welsh, for example. These cultural mid-points could cause offence to others. The issue of England's monopolizing the ocean-going image could provoke assertions from the Welsh who demanded that their contribution be acknowledged. As a maritime county, Cardiganshire provided a base from which these responses could be launched.[76] The claim and counter-claim of being an important place, a centre of some quality, is able to reveal something of the concerns and attachments that predominated at any one time.

[74] Stephen Caunce, 'Regional identity in Lancashire and Yorkshire: hunting the Snark', *Journal of Regional and Local Studies*, 20, 1 (1999), 25–50, 27.

[75] Edward Laws, *The History of Little England Beyond Wales, and the Non-Kymric Colony Settled in Pembrokeshire* (London, 1888), p. 417.

[76] For example, see *CTA*, February 1946, 1; O. M. Edwards, *Yn y Wlad: Troeon Crwydr Yma ac Acw yng Nghymru* (Wrecsam, 1932), p. 37.

Personal characteristics prompt assertions of cultural centrality. Some Victorians, such as Thomas Hardy, maintained that the 'essence of individuality' lay in the provinces.[77] This suggests that something different, and less tangible, than regional pride in specific fields is being alluded to. The mental make-up of a population is being commended rather than a particular act or product that originates from the area. The perception of a group's spirit contributes towards many claims of distinctiveness. It has been argued that: 'Most of England's thirty-nine counties have a recognisable identity and will be said to have their own particular characteristics and distinctive inhabitants.'[78] While this statement is not wholly inaccurate, there are a few outstanding county types. All counties have recognizable features, but some are referred to in discourse and considered centres of certain qualities more often than others. The question as to why some counties are reducible to a type while others are not intrigued a contributor to a 1948 publication, *The English Counties Illustrated*, who remarked that 'no one dreams of saying [that somebody] has distinctive Middlesex qualities, as we say that a man is "very Yorkshire"'.[79] Like Yorkshire, Cardiganshire has been selected as typifying specific qualities and manners. Indeed, the Yorkshire man and the Cardi have been hailed as epitomes of a provincial authenticity that cosmopolitan locales lack. The opposite of the characteristic provinces was a dull uniformity, a lack of distinction that mid-twentieth-century Middlesex, overshadowed then consumed by the metropolis, could represent.

In spite of these attempts to ground qualities in specific geographical settings, centrality is relative and flexible. More than one place or group of people can stand for a value. Although any single nation's cultural pantheon may not represent every corner, the ideals thought to reside there are transferable to other areas and groups. On a European scale,

---

[77] Robin Gilmour, 'Regional and provincial in Victorian literature', in R. P. Draper (ed.), *The Literature of Region and Nation* (London, 1989), pp. 51–60, 56.

[78] Peter Childs, 'Places and peoples: nation and region', in Mike Storry and Peter Childs (eds), *British Cultural Identities* (2nd edn, London, 2002), pp. 35–72, 53.

[79] Sidney Dark, 'Middlesex', in C. E. M. Joad (ed.), *The English Counties Illustrated* (London, 1948), pp. 43–50, 50.

the 'localism, egalitarianism and autonomy' embodied in the peasant has been considered a 'humanising force' in the face of government's expanding role.[80] A group, in this case peasants, has been located as a centre of specific, desirable qualities. Independence and self-sufficiency are respected characteristics that develop individuals by purportedly removing them from dependence on others. These centralities are frequently gendered, as the reference to the 'he' who is a typical Yorkshire 'man' indicates. The Cardi has likewise generally assumed a male form. So while at the same time as asserting qualities such as independence, frankness and simplicity, these centres could reinforce or perpetuate the association between the male and the public face of a place. These boundaries drawn around the centre are instructive.

Another variety of centrality that also illustrates its elasticity relates to the fact that parts of a nation may be supposed to epitomize the values of the nation as a whole. In fact, the centre of a nation or nation-state is sometimes located in a part of it that does not necessarily correspond to any geographical definition of a spatial centre.[81] These statements of centrality, to be the heart of a nation, tell us something about dominant interpretations of nationhood. To be a centre there must be a margin, and giving precedence to a particular part of a country involves omitting much of what it is held to embody. Parts of the United States of America, such as New England, have thought 'of the nation in terms of itself'.[82] In addition, this prioritizing does not always originate from the selected area itself. This can be seen in the way the Alsatian village became endowed with 'patriotic symbolism' after the First World War and took on the guise of the archetypal French village.[83] Charles Manning Hope Clarke warned against the dangers of putative national

---

[80] Salvador Giner and Eduardo Sevilla-Guzman, 'The demise of the peasant: some reflections on ideological inroads into social theory', *Sociologia Ruralis*, 20, 1–2 (1980), 13–27, 23.

[81] See Pyrs Gruffudd, 'Prospects of Wales: contested geographical imaginations', in Ralph Fevre and Andrew Thompson (eds), *Nation, Identity and Social Theory: Perspectives from Wales* (Cardiff, 1999), pp. 149–67, 166.

[82] Frederick Jackson Turner, *Frontier and Section: Selected Essays of Frederick Jackson Turner* (Englewood Cliffs, NJ, 1961), p. 144.

[83] Laird Boswell, 'From liberation to purge trials in the "Mythic Provinces":

characteristics, namely the idea of Australian 'mateship', which was 'created and used to support . . . political and cultural movements'.[84] The uses and application of these centres deserve to be examined further by historians, and this study will investigate those interests that benefited from attributing essential values to Cardiganshire and the Cardi.

Margin

Investigating the marginal provides a means of assessing changes on a number of levels, from manners to politics. When a place is considered to be on the margin it is removed from qualities deemed desirable. Opinions that marginalize or centre an area or its inhabitants ensure that nations will never be culturally uniform; the hierarchical nature inherent in the location of value means that differences will continue to be asserted. Yet the type of characteristics selected as markers of marginality do change. Ideas of places or people being on the edge cannot be dismissed as irrelevant because they form part of people's mental furniture, their actions as well as their attitudes. Every time another group is referred to, in speech or print, as possessing less of a desirable quality than another, a message is being conveyed and received. Being removed from sense or rationality provides one common example of how people are located on the edge. This can be seen in those stories about villages, towns and regions full of stupid people that have been 'rife in English folklore' and that of other countries.[85]

Other instances when groups are located on the edge stem from their perceived transgression of norms. The other group is thought to have contravened ethical principles; they are untrustworthy and work against the interests of the community. Jews, a particularly vilified group, provide an instance of this. Bryan Cheyette, in his investigation of how Jews have been represented in English literature, described

recasting French identities in Alsace and Lorraine, 1918–1920', *French Historical Studies*, 23, 1 (2000), 129–62, 132.

[84] Charles Manning Clark, 'Re-writing Australian history', in T. A. G. Hungerford (ed.), *Australian Signpost: An Anthology* (Melbourne, 1956), pp. 130–43, 136.

[85] K. D. M. Snell, 'The culture of local xenophobia', *Social History*, 28, 1 (2003), 1–30, 10.

the widely held view of them as 'unassimilable cosmopolitans who possessed an international wealth which eroded national boundaries and traditions'; they were often located far from the centre of national values.[86] Yet there are other norms or expectations that need not be founded on national interests. Distance from decency, generosity and other preferable traits may be located in groups that share the same religion and nationality as their detractors. A collection of proverbs about Yorkshire, gathered at the end of the eighteenth century, reveals how inhabitants and migrants from a county were thought to lack polite attributes. One of these includes a description of a Yorkshire man's coat of arms consisting of a fly (because he will 'tipple with everybody'), a flea (because he will 'bite everybody') and a magpie (due to his tendency to 'chatter with anybody'). Often swiftly dismissed as stereotypes, such statements inform us of attitudes and divides. Abstractions and exaggerations are culturally significant.[87]

As the coat of arms proverb demonstrated, many features contribute towards a place or group being deemed marginal. Locating something at the edge is based upon feelings of discomfort or offence and touches on those broad acres, such as sound, smell and taste, that interest some cultural historians. A group's perceived manners, be it ignorance or crassness, could be used to demonstrate how they were on the edge of civility or style. Take, for instance, one twentieth-century description of English Midlanders: '[They were] our equivalent of the Irish; dull, slow, invariably fat and middle aged and created by God to come and annoy us and be made fools of.'[88] No matter how crude this is, it still constitutes a delineation that is accepted or rejected and plays a part in the way in which the image of an area or group is composed. As tangible images of marginality spread, it is likely, as has been

[86] Brian Cheyette, *Constructions of 'the Jew' in English Literature and Society: Racial Representations, 1875–1945* (Cambridge, 1993), p. 157.
[87] Francis Grose, *A Provincial Glossary with a collection of Local Proverbs and Popular Superstitions* (2nd edn, London, 1790), 'Yorkshire', p. 2 (unnumbered). For the significance of generalizations about regions made in fiction, see K. D. M. Snell (ed.), *The Regional Novel in Britain and Ireland, 1800–1990* (Cambridge, 1998).
[88] John Field, 'The view from Folkestone', in Ralph Samuel (ed.), *Patriotism: The Making and Unmaking of British National Identity*, vol. 2: *Minorities and Outsiders* (London, 1989), pp. 3–8, 5.

remarked about the image of the Irish in Victorian Britain, to be set 'into a more or less rigid category to which there were no exceptions that mattered'.[89] Even so, this study of the Cardi points towards the relatively short-lived nature of some of these markers of marginality. Like other acts of location, those that placed the Cardi on the margins of cultural acceptability were products of, and provide insights into, particular historical circumstances, tastes and strains.

Instances of Cardiganshire and the Cardi being located on the edge are fragmentary; there are few treatises on 'Cardi-bashing'. Therefore, the negative images will not be taken out of context, but neither should they be passed over, as they are useful indicators of social tension. It is likely that there have been numerous unrecorded oral comments that located the inhabitants, or those that hailed from the area, on the margin. By chance, some opinions are recorded that provide chinks of light in a cavern of unrecorded connotations. Taken together, and related to other locations, a network of corresponding and competing images are able to be made out. The close relationship between centre and margin can be seen in the figure of the Jew, a centre of financial knowledge and yet the edge of putative human values of generosity. Designating something as marginal rarely depends on a single feature or source; it is an image compounded of selected features and is triggered by circumstances.

The interrelationship between centre and margin is seen in the designation, made by the interwar artists described as 'English Modernists', of southern England as cosmopolitan and consequently removed from true Englishness. In judging the hub of new industries and a magnet for northerners as somehow less English, the centre was placed to the north, illustrating how the categories of centre and margin depend on one another. When looking at Cardiganshire as a centre we also consider the margin against which it is defined. On the occasions when Cardiganshire was described as being isolated from certain values, it was in relation to a centre elsewhere. This range of perceptions, like those that 'implicated

[89] L. P. Curtis, Jr, *Anglo-Saxons and Celts: A Study of Anti-Irish Prejudice in Victorian England* (Bridgeport, CT, 1968), p. 40.

London as a whole with cosmopolitanism', reveal the variety of expressions made in struggles to assert meaning and value.[90] Bestowing marginal locations reinforces a sense of self-importance. So, when tracing the way Cardiganshire and the Cardi have been located on the margins, the self-images of the placers will be highlighted. A very broad definition of marginality is used in this investigation, but this is necessary as it allows us to detect the many fine strands running through representations of a locality.

Acts of location need to be traced over time if we are to understand their meaning and appreciate their use. By tracing patterns in the way Cardiganshire and its inhabitants have been located, this book will indicate when and why some images dominated. The ensuing five chapters investigate the intersection of naming and the four locations within specific time frames. These chronological divides will inform each other and generate revealing contrasts. From the latter part of the eighteenth century to the start of the twenty-first, there has been a range of portrayals, each of which contributes to the discordant narrative running through this biography of a contested place. The concluding chapter compares Cardiganshire with other areas and people that have accrued value in modern times. In doing so, the prevalence of these organizational categories and the positions that deploy them will be demonstrated. There remain many other peoples and places whose instrumental value in buttressing positions has yet to be inspected.

[90] Michael Saler, 'Making it new: visual modernism and the "Myth of the North" in interwar England', *Journal of British Studies*, 37, 4 (1998), 419–40, 427.

II

VISITS AND ADVICE, c.1760–1830

Cardiganshire was a poor part of the kingdom. At the same time, however, the county contributed to the British economy. Long-standing trade links, such as the export of cattle and pigs, grew with the demand generated by an increasing population.[1] In 1795, John Aikin's survey noted that although the county's 'towns are of little consequence', its exports included black cattle that were sent to Kent and Essex, pigs and salt butter to Bristol and barley and oats to Liverpool.[2] Some industrial activities, notably lead mining and the export of copper to the Swansea valley for smelting, were carried out in the county. As this was a time of religious awakening, there were also exports of a spiritual nature. The influence of the county's leading Methodist preacher, Daniel Rowland of Llangeitho, was such that at the end of the eighteenth century many Welsh people were described as 'Rowlandists'.[3]

Contact with elsewhere and the knowledge of changes that were taking place beyond the county's borders led to comparisons being made between Cardiganshire and other places. From the 1750s onwards, industrial developments in south-east Wales, particularly the band of ironworks running from Blaenafon in Monmouthshire to Hirwaun in Glamorgan,

[1] P. Deane and W. A. Cole, *British Economic Growth, 1688–1959* (Cambridge, 1962), p. 8. Between 1750 and 1831, two English cities which the county supplied with produce, Liverpool and Bristol, grew from 22,000 to 202,000 and 50,000 to 104,000 respectively. B. R. Mitchell and P. Deane, *Abstract of British Historical Statistics* (Cambridge, 1962), p. 24; Rosemary Sweet, *The English Town: Government, Society and Culture* (Harlow, 1999), p. 3.

[2] J. Aikin, *England Delineated; or, a Geographical Description of Every County in England and Wales* (3rd edn, London, 1795), p. 379. Two previous editions published in 1788 and 1790 do not note these trade links.

[3] J. Evans, *Letters Written During a Tour through North Wales in the Year 1798, and at Other Times* (London, 1800), p. 413. Also see Eryn White, 'The people called "Methodists": early Welsh Methodism and the question of identity', *Journal of Welsh Religious History*, new ser., 1 (2001), 1–14.

added to the long-standing distinction between parts of Wales formerly based on agricultural activity – pastoral or arable. The pull exerted by industrial growth in the south-east on the imaginations and movements of people influenced experiences and perceptions.[4] In the British context, also, the area displayed some distinctive structural features. Non-coastal transport networks were poor, and disparities between the region and genteel holidaymakers' places of origin were frequently remarked upon.[5] Nonetheless, distinct advances in accessibility, compared with the first decade of the century, were already being noted by the 1820s.[6]

Throughout this period people came to Cardiganshire for the purpose of leisure. A fashion at the time to view peripheral areas ran alongside less aesthetic motivations, such as the desire to bathe and socialize. The Romantic inclination provided one of the lenses through which visitors viewed the county. Characterized by its praise of the natural and unfettered, it conferred qualities on Cardiganshire and its inhabitants just as it did on one of its better-known geographical focal points, the Lake District. Wordsworth's 'sweet shire of Cardigan' provided a convenient setting for the poem 'Simon Lee: The Old Huntsman', first published in 1798.[7] A poor retired Somerset huntsman reputedly inspired the verses. The choice of Cardiganshire as a setting demonstrates how it came to stand for rusticity and poverty.[8] Although the county could not supply a surfeit of the sublime, it possessed other features, notably a simple peasant population, the

[4] The following seemingly improbable example sheds more light on the imagined divide than on reality: 'To the people of Cardiganshire the glow of the furnaces of Dowlais, which they could see in the night sky from their hill-tops, symbolized a kind of hell', in Gwyn Williams, *The Land Remembers: A View of Wales* (London, 1977), p. 185.

[5] 'Aberystwyth, in 1787', in George Eyre Evans (ed.), *Cardiganshire* (Aberystwyth, 1903), pp. 3–5.

[6] G. J. Freeman, *Sketches in Wales; or a Diary of Three Walking Excursions to that Principality* (London, 1826), p. 28. For the evolution of the road network in northern Cardiganshire, see Dewi Davies, 'The early years of the Turnpike Trust in Cardiganshire: evidence from the minutes of Aberystwyth District', *Ceredigion*, 14, 3 (2003), 7–19. Other developments in this period are noted in Moelwyn Williams, *The South Wales Landscape* (London, 1975), pp. 211–12, 240–1.

[7] In William Wordsworth, *The Poetical Works of William Wordsworth*, ed. Thomas Hutchinson (Oxford, 1996), pp. 378–9.

[8] Mary Moorman, *William Wordsworth: A Biography* (Oxford, 1957), p. 383.

antithesis of the restrictive order imposed by civilization. This interplay between the county and romanticism's 'shared palette of imagery' will be traced in this chapter.[9]

Other contemporary ideas found sustenance in Cardiganshire. Those who thought that reason should illuminate both the mind and the dark corners of the nation found this part of Wales useful. A place removed from the main currents of change was ripe for improvement. Rational activities like scientific farming and commerce, alongside thought unhindered by tradition, were suggested as means to enhance the land, releasing its populace from the vicissitudes of nature. The Enlightenment of the latter part of the eighteenth century, with its 'contrast between knowledge, reason or science and ignorance, prejudice and superstition', was founded on the belief that the rational mind could solve the numerous problems besetting humanity. With its poverty and superstition, Cardiganshire presented a fair number of these problems.[10] For some, then, the area was useful for what it retained, for others for what it might become. No single perspective dominated accounts at this time; often these positions exist in the same narrative. In turn, they interacted with other outlooks and helped commentators to locate the county on a mental map.[11]

The image of the county at this time was a comparatively limited one. Those who wrote about the area hailed from a small literate group, mainly composed of outsiders. Their descriptions were a complex of comparisons with places and people in Wales, Britain and occasionally beyond. The common people of the county were seen as passive, part of the county's structure responding to the environmental constraints wrought by nature and peripherality. For some, these individuals presented an instance of what should be

---

[9] Maynard Solomon, 'Some romantic images of Beethoven', in Thomas Pfau and Robert F. Gleckner (eds), *Lessons of Romanticism: A Critical Companion* (Durham, NC, 1998), pp. 225–43, 228.

[10] Christopher J. Berry, *Social Theory of the Scottish Enlightenment* (Edinburgh, 1997), p. 2.

[11] Contrasting ways of seeing Wales in eighteenth-century literature are considered in Moira Dearnley, *Distant Fields: Eighteenth-Century Fictions of Wales* (Cardiff, 2001). Also see Andrew Davies, '"The reputed nation of inspiration": representations of Wales in fiction from the romantic period' (Ph.D. thesis, University of Wales, Cardiff, 2001).

changed, for others a moral lesson for the less than grateful lower classes of England. These arguments reflected the mindsets of those making them, including hard-headed improvers and idealists with less of a Utilitarian bent.

Nonetheless, glimpses of more popular, locally generated or widespread images are afforded. Various tangible items, from bread to horses, were coupled with the area and regularly used when locating it. Towards the end of the period, newspapers offer another source from which representations can be garnered, although the depth and range of their coverage is limited when compared with the newspapers published from the 1830s onwards when financial restrictions on their production were reduced.[12] Indeed, the want of representations originating from the area distinguishes this time from later periods, there being comparatively little in the way of religious periodicals and government reports. Yet existing examples indicate how useful a peripheral area like Cardiganshire was for various inclinations and prejudices. Fundamental to these schemas was the identification of difference, and this can be seen in the way the county and its inhabitants were named.

NAMING

During the years covered in this chapter, the word 'Cardi' appears only occasionally in printed sources. Nevertheless, it can be surmised that the term was widely used at this time. There was a reference to it in the first Welsh language weekly, *Seren Gomer*, in 1820.[13] This early example was not directly associated with any particular characteristics that would accompany the name in later years; rather, it indicated a person's place of origin. A character, Sioni Gardi, forms part of a morality tale illustrating the intemperance and violence of miners. One of a number of men working in Merthyr Tydfil identified by nickname, Sioni Gardi's role consisted of getting beaten by Gitto Gelli-Deg after claiming

---

[12] Aled Gruffydd Jones, *Press, Politics and Society: A History of Journalism in Wales* (Cardiff, 1993), pp. 61–3.

[13] Siencyn ap Tydfil, 'Buchedd Gitto Gelli Deg yn yr wythnos gadw', *Seren Gomer*, 3ydd gyf., 3 (1820), 163–4, 163.

that he could fill a coal tram faster than Gitto. Sioni was a migrant industrial worker and the existence of this nickname suggests the importance of migration in the fashioning of appellations; the name may well have been coined in order to identify the Cardi away from home. Sioni, and his real-life equivalents mentioned in the press, contrast with the respectable, sober figure that dominated later representations of the Cardi.[14] Then again, like Sioni Gardi in 1820, they were being employed as a moral example.

Twm Shon Catty by T. J. Llewelyn Prichard, first published in 1828 with subsequent editions in 1839 and 1873, aired the nickname more frequently than did any other publication. After returning from London, in the 1820s Llewelyn Prichard lived in Aberystwyth. He was, however, living in his native Breconshire when he completed his first version of the novel. References to distinct styles of clothing in the Welsh counties were combined with judgements about the character of the people, which will be considered later. In the book a female servant from Cardiganshire is referred to as 'Cardy' and there is a 'Cardy angler'.[15] Llewelyn Prichard's book was partly targeted at the Welsh market – a twentieth-century Cardiganshire author noted how popular the book was in the county.[16] The use of the term in what has been hailed as the 'first Welsh novel' undoubtedly carried the nickname to other places.

Unlike future visitors, travellers at this time did not refer to Cardis, although there were allusions to attributes that later contributed to clearly defined representations of the county-type. Such paucity demonstrates the limitations of only taking visitors' accounts into consideration and ignoring the press and works of fiction. This is not to say that those who passed through the county did not deem its inhabitants to be in any way distinctive. Rather, the absence of a distinct name, in widespread use, suggests that the area's otherness had not acquired the currency it would later have among visitors from further afield. Perhaps Llewelyn Prichard's novel contributed somewhat to this later cultural prominence.

[14] For instance, see *C*, 20 July 1811, 1, and 9 October 1830, 3.
[15] T. J. Llewelyn Prichard, *Twm Shon Catty* (Aberystwyth, 1828), pp. 51, 289.
[16] Evan Jones, *Cymdogaeth Soar-y-Mynydd* (Abertawe, 1979), p. 10.

Names other than Cardi were applied to Cardiganshire's populace. Lewis Morris, the Anglesey antiquarian who lived in the north of the county from 1742 until his death in 1765, used the word 'Cardigonian' in a letter written to William Vaughan in 1754.[17] Morris was not favourably disposed towards the people, wealthy or poor, whom he met in his role as deputy steward of the Crown manors in the county. Yet his comments appear to have extended beyond personal pique in their range and nature. He referred to the lead miners, many of whom would have been migrants, as being 'a mixture of all nations and languages, like Babel' and castigated the local gentry for their poor knowledge of the Welsh language. In 1742, he contrasted the high standard of Welsh spoken in Montgomeryshire with that of 'the inhabitants of Aberteivi [Cardiganshire]'.[18] Morris often noted the standard and type of Welsh spoken in different parts of the country.[19] In so doing, he used geographical and administrative divides – counties and north/south – to define areas where, by his yardstick, good or poor Welsh was spoken. This comparison brings to light the ways in which the counties of north and mid-Wales could shape Cardiganshire's location. Although south-east Wales played an especially significant role in the cultural location of the county, other 'others', so to speak, figured in Cardiganshire's representational history.

In an agricultural survey published towards the end of the Napoleonic Wars, Walter Davies mentioned 'Cardiganians'.[20] An unattributed source, cited in his report, addressed his letter to 'My Caredigion'. Davies, a poet and antiquary like Morris, gave a footnote to explain this term of address to his readers at the Board of Agriculture: 'Literally, beloved friends. *Ceredigion* is the Welsh name of the tract of country now called from it, the county of Cardigan.'[21] In this explanation, Davies took the opportunity to bring the county's

[17] Hugh Owen (ed.), *Additional Letters of the Morrises of Anglesey (1735–1785)* (London, 1947), pp. 254–5.

[18] Ibid., p. 110.

[19] For example, see J. H. Davies (ed.), *The Letters of Lewis, Richard, William and John Morris, of Anglesey*, 2 vols (Aberystwyth, 1909), vol. 2, p. 237.

[20] Walter Davies, *General View of the Agriculture and Domestic Economy of South Wales*, 2 vols (London, 1815), vol. 1, p. 278.

[21] Ibid., vol. 2, p. 361. The choice of Ceredigion over Cardiganshire or sir

original Welsh name to the attention of his English readers, thus raising their awareness of a distinct Welsh heritage at a time when the English Cardiganshire or its literal Welsh translation *Sir Aberteifi* would have been more common. At other times Walter Davies used the appellation 'Dimetian', a Roman name for the tribe that occupied south-west Wales, and it was later used to distinguish the counties of Carmarthen, Cardigan and Pembroke from the 'Silurian' counties of Glamorgan and Monmouth.[22] Founded on agricultural rather than industrial difference, this distinction was an important one in this period. Another less common name for Cardiganshire based on geographical differences was 'Shir Aber Noeth'. The word 'noeth' literally translates as bare or stark, a reference to the barren nature of the county's upland. This title was used, for example, in an anonymous account of a native's return visit to the county in the middle of the eighteenth century, and it also included a description of the poor, some of whom, no doubt, were migrant forerunners of Sioni Gardi.[23]

Travel writers in the early nineteenth century also used classical terms when describing south Wales. Thomas Evans in his *Walks through Wales*, published in 1819, divided the kinds of cottages found in south Wales according to the racial descent of their builders, including the 'Dimetae' whose dwellings were 'not unfrequently of a declining posture'.[24] In a study of travel literature, Charles L. Batten Jr remarked that this allusion to classical geography was a characteristic of mid- to late eighteenth-century British travel literature.[25] Its perseverance into the early nineteenth century in descriptions of Wales is, therefore, worthy of note; it illustrates how classical terms implied that Wales was somehow older than England.

Aberteifi among Welsh men of letters can also be seen in J. H. Davies (ed.), *The Letters of Goronwy Owen (1723–1769)* (Cardiff, 1924), p. 24.

[22] Davies, *General View*, vol. 2, p. 283.

[23] J. H. Davies, 'Daniel Rowland: contemporary descriptions (1746 and 1835)', *Cylchgrawn Cymdeithas Hanes y Methodistiad Calfinaidd*, 1 (1916), 52–7, 53.

[24] Thomas Evans, *Walks through Wales* (London, 1819), pp. 61–2. For two items (the 'Welch plough' and cart) believed to distinguish Demetian Wales, see Charles Hassall, *General View of the Agriculture of the County of Pembroke* (London, 1794), pp. 18–19.

[25] Charles L. Batten Jr, *Pleasurable Instruction: Form and Convention in Eighteenth-Century Travel Literature* (Berkeley, 1978), pp. 116–18.

Furthermore, the Demetian/Silurian divide indicates that there were perceived similarities between the three western counties compared with their more prosperous eastern neighbours. Walter Davies, in the second volume of his survey of south Wales agriculture, distinguished between styles of 'cottage horticulture' in the south-east and south-west, the former demonstrating greater aptitude for cultivating plants than the latter.[26] These east and west comparisons were more apparent than those of north and south in writing during this period. The differentiations were based on the cultivation of nature; in this respect, tribal names explained differences noted on the ground. Classically educated surveyors utilized past divides to emphasize present ones.

PAST

Most characteristics used to mark out Demetian Wales, such as isolation and poverty, were structural indicators of difference. Along with these, however, were observations about the behaviour of the area's population that dwelt on superstition and other unenlightened manners. Some local people and visitors used the continuity of primitive ways to attack religious bodies that they opposed. Others called upon scientific explanation to dispel superstition. These comments about primitive acts and ideas located the area in the past. Distinguishing Cardiganshire from the rest of what was generally held to be a superstitious country is not straightforward; much of what was said about Wales could apply to representations of Cardiganshire and vice versa. Both the county and country were located in the past by several commentators.[27] However, explanations for the existence of these beliefs were based on isolation from progressive currents. Distance from enlightened areas was believed to explain the prevalence of superstition. Among Welsh counties, therefore, the remote county of Cardigan provided a

---

[26] Davies, *General View*, vol. 2, p. 2.

[27] Samuel Jackson Pratt, *Gleanings through Wales, Holland, and Westphalia*, 2 vols (London, 1795), vol. 2, p. 127; Elizabeth Isabella Spence, *Summer Excursions through Parts of Oxfordshire . . . and South Wales* (2nd edn, London, 1809), p. 176. For superstitious beliefs in this period, see Russell Davies, *Hope and Heartbreak: A Social History of Wales and the Welsh, 1776–1871* (Cardiff, 2005), pp. 357–75.

prime example of how isolation nurtured beliefs. The county was also part of what was considered a particularly superstitious region, the bishopric of St Davids. In 1780 Edmund Jones, a Nonconformist minister from Monmouthshire, thought 'Carmarthenshire, &c' was the district where varieties of ghostly visitations occurred that were unheard of in his native county.[28] Cardiganshire was part of this cultural region marked by the existence of traditional customs and beliefs, often judged typical of the Welsh. Some commentators expressly singled out the county as an area in which superstition was more widespread than in others.

One of the strongest critics of these tendencies in late Georgian Wales was Samuel Rush Meyrick, lawyer, antiquary and author of Cardiganshire's first history, published in 1808. Meyrick connected a belief in the supernatural with the less wealthy portion of the county – the 'lower order of people in Cardiganshire are uncommonly superstitious'.[29] The majority of the county's population, therefore, was regarded as not being imbued with reason. Natives of the county, that Meyrick was only too keen to praise for its antiquities, were also linked to popish practices that were in turn associated with pagan ideas. In his history he focused on these tendencies, that he conflated with Methodism, when describing the behaviour of local people. In the main, the inhabitants are depicted as easily swayed by emotion, an attribute that explained the persistence of pagan, Catholic and Methodist ways; this combination formed a genealogy of error. Published three years before the Calvinistic Methodists broke with the Church of England, this account emphasized the loss of reason incurred by preachers who worked 'upon the infatuated, and inflamed imaginations' of the people.[30] By consigning Methodism to a disreputable past, any progressive interpretation of the movement could be countered.

---

[28] Edmund Jones, *A Relation of Apparitions of Spirits in the Principality of Wales* ([Trevecca (?)], 1780), p. 35. For more on the author, see John Harvey's 'Introduction', in John Harvey (ed.), *The Appearance of Evil: Apparitions of Spirits in Wales* (Cardiff, 2003), pp. 1–38.

[29] Samuel Rush Meyrick, *The History and Antiquities of the County of Cardigan* (London, 1808), p. 55.

[30] Ibid., p. 49. Compare with Henry Penruddocke Wyndham, *A Gentleman's Tour through Monmouthshire and Wales in the Months of June and July, 1774* (London, 1775), p. 108.

Influenced by his dislike of Methodism, Meyrick's delineation bore the mark of what J. C. D. Clark called the Anglican 'confessional state'.[31] Even so, notions of a highly superstitious people permeated other representations of Cardiganshire's population. In 1826, Thomas Jenkins, who later became an accomplished craftsman, began keeping a diary. It owed its conception to an unusual, poltergeist-like incident involving a vibrating candlestick and a disappearing pair of socks that occurred when he was thirteen. Before relating this bizarre occurrence, Jenkins wrote: 'I am not prone to superstition although living in, I should think, the most superstitious part of the country.' At that time he was residing at Brynymaen in Cardiganshire. He also related that he had been instructed by his parents not to believe in stories about supernatural creatures 'which are so prevalent a source of terror in many a secluded locality to this day'.[32] According to the antiquarian and surgeon George Lipscomb, who travelled through Wales in 1799, even less isolated parts of the county, such as the county town of Cardigan, were permeated with old ways. From his being baffled by a maid polishing a door with what he understood to be blood, Lipscomb made the generalization that the Welsh are 'obstinate cherishers of superstition'. That was the only way he could explain this strange activity because the maid 'engaged in this extraordinary employment' fled when he attempted to question her.[33] It is significant that Lipscomb unhesitatingly explained this practice in terms of superstition, indicating its use as a *deus ex machina* and capable of explaining any unintelligible behaviour encountered by a traveller. Locating a practice like this in the past enabled the visitor to categorize and 'know' the unusual.

George Lipscomb was not alone in seeing such practices as part of the Welsh disposition. Revd John Evans detected

[31] J. C. D. Clark, *English Society, 1688–1832: Ideology, Social Structure and Political Practice during the Ancien Régime* (Cambridge, 1985), p. 411.

[32] D. C. Jenkins (ed.), *The Diary of Thomas Jenkins of Llandeilo, 1826–1870* (Bala, 1976), p. 1.

[33] George Lipscomb, *Journey into South Wales . . . in 1799* (London, 1802), p. 175. Generalizations evoked by daily tasks and pertaining to late nineteenth-century Holland are noted by Simon Schama, *The Embarrassment of Riches: An Interpretation of Dutch Culture in the Golden Age* (London, 1988), p. 3.

the 'unbounded credulity' of the Welsh in his tour through south Wales during 1803. He listed belief in holy wells and charlatans masquerading under the title 'Water doctors' as symptoms of this national naivety.[34] Joseph Hucks, reflecting on the Welsh during a tour undertaken some nine years before Evans, noted that 'the disposition of the people is strongly blended with superstition'.[35] Observations made in Cardiganshire, therefore, contributed to a conceptual distinction between a backward Wales and a developed England, the latter embodied in its educated inhabitants. A guide to Aberystwyth published in 1816 demonstrates how this national division was played out in Cardiganshire itself. Contact with visitors was thought to have improved local manners. This was a connection 'which other towns in Cardiganshire, situated more inland, have not the opportunity of experiencing'. Criticism of old ways was not universal, however. Inhabitants of the town still demonstrated 'many Welsh customs, which, they imagine, and perhaps with great reason, cannot at present be changed for better'.[36] Among these less offensive traditions were funerals that were better attended than those in England. Beliefs could be changed through example and, in the same way, lack of sustained contact would lead to the perpetuation of habits. In this guide to Aberystwyth, however, we are also given an indication of valued traditions, showing how not all activities were frowned upon. This is an important caveat in any broad summation of this period as one in which tradition was thought of as merely an impediment to moral and intellectual development.

The more secluded and hilly areas were, as the Aberystwyth guide pointed out, the places that harboured old beliefs. Much of Cardiganshire therefore provoked comment about superstition. While J. M. Golby and A. W. Purdue noted that 'Britain in 1800 was a country where superstitions abounded', some areas, such as Cardiganshire, were deemed more prone than others to hold on to beliefs and this distinction played

[34] J. Evans, *Letters Written during a Tour through South Wales* . . . (London, 1804), p. 438.

[35] Alun R. Jones and William Tydeman (eds), *Joseph Hucks: A Pedestrian Tour through North Wales in a Series of Letters* (Cardiff, 1979), p. 60.

[36] J. Stephenson, *The Aberystwyth Guide* (Aberystwyth, 1816), pp. 47–8, 67–9.

an important part in its location in the past.[37] Evans wrote
that 'in Cardigan and its borders the belief in canwyll corf,
or the *corpse candle* is greatly magnified and extended'.[38] After
distinguishing the county in this way, he offered a scientific
explanation for this phenomenon based on the phosphores-
cent quality of the area's peaty soils. Meyrick also suggested
an explanation for the 'knockers' believed by miners in
the north of the county to direct them towards metals. He
contended that it was 'in all probability from the oozing
of the waters through the fissures underground, though
the common people ascribe it to supernatural agency'.[39]
Demystification of supernatural visitations like these inferred
that believers in apparitions were behaving in a manner
contrary to reason, while at the same time emphasizing the
explainer's rationality. A whole system of belief, strongly associated by both writers with Cardiganshire, was being located
in the past fears and primitive machinations of minds unac-
quainted with the scientific laws governing the natural world.

As is often the case in portrayals of the 'other', the faults
identified are the opposites of the critics' presumed virtues
and their plans for improvement. Lack of enterprise among
inhabitants was a notable criticism in representations of
Cardiganshire's populace and became a truism among those
who advocated progress. While praising the land and its isolation, Benjamin Heath Malkin expressed reservations about
the effect this distance had on people's minds. Cherished
habits could, he argued, bar any improvement from taking
effect. Lack of contact with elsewhere had 'a strong tendency
to fix the manners of the people'.[40] This stagnant area, bereft
of any refreshing tides, led him to question whether such an
'indolent' people could be captured by the 'spirit of emigration', even if they could speak English. These were a people
rooted to the land. Initiative was wanting in Cardiganshire
because the people were locked into manners and customs

[37] J. M. Golby and A. W. Purdue, *The Civilisation of the Crowd: Popular Culture in
England, 1750–1900* (2nd edn, London, 1999), p. 134.
[38] Evans, *Tour through South Wales*, p. 440.
[39] Meyrick, *History and Antiquities*, p. 93.
[40] Benjamin Heath Malkin, *The Scenery, Antiquities, and Biography of South Wales*
(London, 1804), p. 322.

from a previous era, and this had repercussions beyond adherence to fanciful beliefs. Malkin described a people devoid of motivation when he observed that the 'greatest fault imputed to the common people by their superiors is the want of due regard to their own interests, without which they are never likely to be industrious'. The target here was not sloth, because they were 'faithful servants to their employers', but, rather, a lack of forethought. 'It is the uniform answer to every suggestion, with respect to the duty of labouring beyond their present, and saving for their future necessities, that they are sure to do well if Providence will take care of them.' This mentality that shackled them to their environment was part of an 'unthrifty argument' that was 'characteristic of the poor in general, and not peculiar to those of Cardiganshire; but in the more populous and dissipated parts of the country, it proceeds from a disposition to spend all they get; here from an indifference about getting anything'.[41]

Malkin's separation of the lack of thrift in urban areas, brought about by wastefulness, from the passivity of Cardigan-shire's predominantly rural population is informative. Even when critical of the rural poor, moral condemnation is placed more heavily on those ostensibly squandering opportuni-ties in progressive towns. Malkin praised the faithfulness of Cardiganshire's poor to their masters, but this was not enough for them to be held a centre of virtue. Relying on providence was clearly not sufficient; the compliant peasants needed to take steps to improve their circumstances. In the past, nature may have instilled superstitions and fatalism, but this time had passed. An account from a correspondent of the *Cambrian* in 1817, who had spent some time in 'the upper parts of Carmarthenshire and in Cardiganshire', described the extent to which the poor were at the mercy of the elements. An improvement in the appearance of the crops had 'considerably enlivened the peasantry, whose countenances have assumed a smile of anticipation that their privations are now nearly at an end'.[42] These poor people were not freed from what, in 1829, Thomas Carlyle called 'rude Nature'; they had yet to benefit

    [41] Malkin, *Scenery, Antiquities, and Biography*, p. 325.
    [42] *C*, 26 July 1817, 3.

from the 'resistless engines' that guaranteed mankind's tran-scendence over nature.[43]

This rare account of the emotional condition of the labouring population renders an image of a people, latter-day Demetians, whose increasing population was placing an ever greater strain on the land, as dependent on the whims of nature as were their forebears. Such accounts, with their focus on fate and the fatalism of the area's inhabit-ants, did not address the role that those in authority could play in improving their condition. The onus was on those who languished in the past. This opinion was not the only one, as revealed by a manuscript sent by Thomas Lloyd of Cilgwyn to the Board of Agriculture, which published it *sans critique*.[44] Yet even those who sought to deliver improvement in, for example, the form of inoculation described their difficulty in coaxing this population to partake of the fruits of medical advancement. Timeless nature, inscribed in the minds of those who depended on it, impeded attempts at improvement.[45] When commentators wished to express their frustrations at the inertia around them, they described the people as embodying the characteristics of the past.

FUTURE

Old beliefs frustrated those bent on agricultural improve-ment. At the start of the nineteenth century the politician and agricultural innovator Thomas Johnes of Hafod related his irritation at not knowing how many heads of sheep he had. This information was denied him because the shepherds believed that counting the livestock was unlucky.[46] In order to combat this and other oddities, the innovators promoted

[43] Thomas Carlyle, 'Signs of the times', in Alan Shelston (ed.), *Selected Writing* (Harmondsworth, 1971), p. 64.

[44] CAS, CDX/632/2, manuscript copy of 'An agricultural survey of Cardiganshire' by T. Lloyd (1793), fos 10–11.

[45] David Howell, *The Rural Poor in Eighteenth-Century Wales* (Cardiff, 2000), p. 19. William Fordyce Mavor made this observation while travelling in northern Cardiganshire, *A Tour in Wales and through Several Counties of England . . . Performed in the Summer of 1805* (London, 1806), p. 61.

[46] Richard J. Moore-Colyer (ed.), *Land of Pure Delight: Selections from the Letters of Thomas Johnes of Hafod, Cardiganshire (1748–1816)* (Llandysul, 1992), p. 152.

reforms to enhance the county's prospects. Such plans need to be put in the context of the time. It has been noted that in the agricultural domain 'the process of change was speeded up' from around 1760.[47] Although the degree of success achieved by these propagandists has been questioned, the present enquiry is concerned with the way in which they envisaged the path to the future. Part of this encouragement in Cardiganshire, as elsewhere, took the form of 'bounties' dispensed by the county's agricultural society, founded in 1784 – the third county agricultural society to be formed in Wales. Johnes, who had moved to Hafod a year before its establishment, was fundamental in setting up this organization. His example coloured other perceptions of an improved Cardiganshire. In a description of the county published in 1810, Thomas Rees wrote that if 'other land proprietors of mountainous districts' followed the example set by the master of Hafod, 'these hitherto barren wastes might be converted into rich and productive forests'.[48]

Transforming the land meant transforming its inhabitants. Malkin mentioned that Johnes sought to inculcate 'a more manly and industrious spirit' among the people.[49] The county's population needed to develop those characteristics usually found in 'cultivated countries'.[50] A lack of vitality rendered them less 'manly', less able to impose their will on their surroundings. The absurdity of continuing in the present manner was put in a similar way elsewhere: Archibald Grant of Monymusk was aghast at the prospect of Aberdeenshire's 'strong lubberly fellows . . . knitting stockings' in 1760.[51] In this way a particular vision of the future could be called upon as a means to re-establish the natural order of things, while at the same time effecting change. The opinions Johnes held regarding his tenants influenced other representations of Cardiganshire's population. This

[47] Pamela Horn, 'The contribution of the propagandist to eighteenth-century agricultural improvement', *Historical Journal*, 2, 2 (1982), 313–30, 313.

[48] Thomas Rees, *A Topographical and Historical Description of Cardiganshire* (London, 1810), p. 400.

[49] Malkin, *Scenery, Antiquities, and Biography*, p. 326.

[50] Benjamin Heath Malkin, *Essays on Subjects Connected with Civilization* (London, 1795), p. 238.

[51] James E. Handley, *Scottish Farming in the Eighteenth Century* (London, 1953), pp. 132–3.

produced a profoundly different sort of Cardi than in later representations. Edinburgh-educated Johnes contrasted the energetic, progressive Scotsmen with his tenants. At this time, attributes accredited to the Scots were akin to those later identified in the Cardi.[52] The potential to weave a better future was located in the Scottish pioneers of improvement. Inculcating the characteristics embodied by the Scots in the native populace would, therefore, advance the county.

Johnes and other reformers were contending against what Pierre Bourdieu described as a 'system of dispositions – a past that survives in the present and tends to perpetuate itself into the future by making itself present in practices', thus ensuring their continuity. These behaviours ensconced in the agricultural practices carried out in the area were 'the product of history' that needed to be remedied if productivity and the standard of living were to improve.[53] Notions of improvement were transfigured when set against these unproductive ingrained manners. In his *A Cardiganshire Landlord's Advice to his Tenants* (1800), which was translated into Welsh for his own tenants, Johnes intended to reform the peasantry. He began his manual by stating his 'long and ambitious desire for improving your condition'. But not everything was to be changed; for example, he was 'very happy' that the local population preferred light carts to wagons. Many other features were, however, not acceptable. He wished to 'imprint' in the minds of his tenants the importance of intelligent cropping that would include a fallow period so as not to exhaust the ground. This advice on cropping concluded with the statement that he was 'determined . . . to put an end to this destructive system'. The issue of cattle was put in even starker terms:

> I know there is a very strong prejudice against any sorts of cattle in this county except Black Cattle. They are said to be hardier, and that the English Drovers will not purchase any other – I am satisfied the first objection is false, and doubt the other.[54]

---

[52] Moore-Colyer, 'Introduction', in *A Land of Pure Delight*, pp. 1–75, 4.

[53] Pierre Bourdieu, *Outline of a Theory of Practice*, trans. R. Nice (Cambridge, 1977), p. 82.

[54] Thomas Johnes, *A Cardiganshire Landlord's Advice to his Tenants* (Bristol, 1800), pp. 3, 54–5, 73.

Such counsel was couched in terms of a forward-looking rational mind brought to bear on the embedded traditions of Cardiganshire's rural dwellers.

Cardiganshire was being judged in terms of its contribution to the nation. This was a significant yardstick that would often be applied to the area in both a Welsh and a British context, and during war and peace. After describing the 'uniform sterility' about him in the south of the county, John Evans remarked: 'no wonder after this that the farmer is very little different from the peasant, and that the pride and sinews of a country, an industrious and respectable yeomanry, does not exist'. Evans pursued the description beyond material want to the psychological condition of the populace: 'common people throughout this county are not only poor, but appear completely dejected, as if they had given up every ray of hope of being otherwise'.[55] This state is related purely to the environment and the effects of the conflicts with France, not to any innate lack of initiative. In this we can see optimistic Enlightenment notions of how reason could improve all people, that there were no inherent weaknesses, only those remnants of the past and environmental circumstances that could be corrected through the application of intelligence. If the means for the people to improve themselves were made available and adopted, he thought that they would be as hard working as any other. Like Malkin and Johnes, this representation compared the county's population with an incarnation of improvement outside, in this case an upright and diligent class of farmer. Without this type the area would lack the stock upon which nations depended. This analysis concluded that the area was not contributing to the nation; it was atrophying for want of leadership. A letter describing features of Burgundy society in the late 1780s conveys some of the values that were invested in the concept of the yeoman in contemporary thought. Certain restrictions on the times when local landowners could begin pressing grapes were called 'absolute vassalage' by the author, who finished with a comparison noting that 'the yeomen of England [would] rise in tumultuous uproar' at such impositions.[56] A limited

[55] Evans, *Tour through South Wales*, p. 327.

[56] James St John, *Letters from France to a Gentleman in the South of Ireland*, 2 vols (Dublin, 1788), vol. 2, p. 182.

definition of liberty and freedom, prerequisites of progress, was ensconced in the mind of the yeoman.

Transportation was another measure of advancement that impinged on representations of this isolated county. In a letter to the *Cambrian*, a local man proposed the construction of a canal from Swansea 'to the borders of Cardiganshire'. This was a theme – the introduction of new communication links – that recurred in proposals to advance the area.[57] The county was constantly being urged to adopt activities or innovations that were common elsewhere. Malkin, for instance, decried the failure to utilize the county's mineral reserves. The metal riches beneath Cardiganshire would, he argued, lie untapped until the 'spirit of enterprise, and the hand of industry' extracted it. These two lodestars of improvement were, however, confined to 'a few inhabitants of the higher order; and as they are generally men of landed property and ancient family their attention is turned to agricultural, rather than commercial improvement'.[58] Nonetheless, he had seen among the gentry some potential, an embryo from which the county's commercial prospects could develop. In fact, there was evidence of this in the enhancement of Aberaeron harbour and the establishment of a planned settlement there by the landlord, the Revd Alban Gwynne, and his son from 1807.[59] When a place is related to the future, these potential or actual vanguards – Scots, yeomen or lesser gentry – are central to the vision. Like Johnes, Malkin failed to take the physical factors behind much of the area's lack of commercial prospects into account. Yet confident affirmations of advancement needed vanquishable foes; locating a place or group in a favourable future involved stressing achievable potential, not intractable limitations.

---

[57] *C*, 17 May 1817, 3.

[58] Malkin, *Scenery, Antiquities, and Biography*, p. 318.

[59] The establishment of planned village communities in peripheral areas also occurred in Scotland and Ireland. See R. G. Rodger, 'The evolution of Scottish town planning', in George Gordon and Brian Dicks (eds), *Scottish Urban History* (Aberdeen, 1983), pp. 71–91, 82–3, 86; Susan Hood, 'The significance of the villages and small towns in rural Ireland during the eighteenth and nineteenth centuries', in Peter Borsay and Lindsay Proudfoot (eds), *Provincial Towns in Early Modern England and Ireland: Change, Convergence and Divergence* (Oxford, 2002), pp. 241–61, 251–4.

A letter written in 1770 by John Paynter, a lead-mine manager from Derbyshire who held a life lease of Hafod, provides an early example of proposals to develop the county. It also illustrates the use of comparisons with other places thought to epitomize advancement or backwardness, a common feature when mentally positioning Cardiganshire on a temporal scale. The letter, addressed to Robert Lance, secretary to the Society for Promoting Manufacture and for Employing the Poor in the counties of Pembroke and Cardigan, contained numerous suggestions. Paynter was irked because Cardiganshire, itself ideally situated for manufacturing wool, was 'obliged to dispose of every ounce [of wool] to *foreigners*; that is to the counties of Montgomery and Merioneth, where it is manufactured'. Much of his ire was directed at the nine-tenths of the people who 'will not work without compulsion'; to be rid of the 'idle poor', a 'load upon the industrious few', was vital. He made a comparison with Holland, where, he argued, they had done away with 'beggars', thereby enhancing the prospects of hard-working people whose income was being absorbed by the poor rate.[60] He likewise fulminated against working farmers. Akin to Johnes after him, he ridiculed their cropping methods and primitive equipment: 'The plows also with which they perform this bungling operation . . . are like to those which the wild Irish of old used to tye to horse's tails.' A want of enterprise could be detected in manufacture and agriculture, both of which, he stressed, must advance together 'for the improvement of this neglected county'. In addition, he was concerned how visitors to the sea, many of whom were 'persons of distinction' (before the railway, Aberystwyth mainly attracted the upper classes), saw the area. He remarked that these notables '*will have it* that this remote county of ours is a desert' but wanted them to be '*surprised* to find it a paradise'. Bringing about this transformation from perceived and present desert to future paradise required leadership, yet the tillers of the soil could not provide it.[61]

[60] Pieter Spierenburg, 'Imprisonment and the family: an analysis of petitions for confinement in Holland, 1680–1805', *Social Science History*, 10, 2 (1986), 115–46.

[61] NLW, Noyadd Trefawr 1678, letter from J. Paynter to Robert Lance (1770), fos 2, 6, 3, 12, 13.

The local press placed similar emphasis on certain sections of society which were thought to be capable of cultivating the germ of development. Evidently, these constitute dominant themes in the projection of Cardiganshire's desired future. Reports of entertainments organized by Thomas and James Lloyd of Bronwydd, a substantial estate situated between Llandysul and Newcastle Emlyn, stressed how the improvement of horses could develop the county and enhance its reputation. In August 1813 races were held on the coast at Penbryn. A year later the event was moved inland near Llandysul, and this event was again described in 1815.[62] Inspired by these accounts, a local newspaper extolled the benefits that would accrue from breeding horses. It did this with reference to that section of society which John Evans had championed a decade earlier: 'We learn with pleasure that the Cardiganshire races . . . have already had the effect of exciting a laudable competition amongst the yeomanry of the county in the further improvement of the breed of these useful and noble animals.'[63] The connection between the county and horses continued in future years, providing Cardiganshire with another distinguishing mark, a source of pride and sometimes of concern about the loss of its reputation in this field.

Towards the end of 1815 a correspondent covering the end of term at two of the county's grammar schools, Ystrad Meurig and Lampeter, expressed a similar sense of optimism concerning the district's future. Further, this source sums up the provenance of the majority of depictions from this period. As the idea of a liberal education was encouraged, the reporter believed that the wealth of the county as a whole would increase with it. Progress in Scotland was cited as proof of this causal relationship.[64] Once again,

[62] *CJ*, 6 August 1813, 3; ibid., 15 July 1814, 3; ibid., 11 August 1815, 3.
[63] Ibid., 29 July 1814, 3. The connection between horses and ideas of improvement can also be found in Davies, *General View*, vol. 2, p. 278:

> Improvements in the breed, which takes place rapidly, and the present great advance in the price of good horses of every description, are of themselves sufficient *inducements* for a less shrewd people than the Cardiganians are in general, to pay greater attention to the rearing and management of horses.

[64] *CJ*, 29 December 1815, 3.

therefore, we see the interrelationship between representations of Cardiganshire and Scotland, this time, however, not
so much in despair but in hope. Evidently, the high regard
in which 'Scotch knowledge' was held elsewhere in the
British Isles had reached Cardiganshire, although it should
be added that, on occasion, it could be a two-way process as
Walter Scott's son Charles was sent to Lampeter grammar
school.[65] Yet the gravitational pull of the northern partner in
this cultural exchange was reasserted when Charles's former
tutor, Archdeacon John Williams, departed to Edinburgh
University in 1824. Tellingly, the role of education in
furthering the lives of the less privileged, and the central role
played by non-Anglican institutions, was not emphasized by
most commentators. Their ideas of the future were generated by a predominantly Anglican, English-speaking and
landowning minority.

Centre

Charges against the inert mentality of Cardiganshire's
population need to be set against other definitions of the
place and its people. Different facets of the same area could
be prioritized, thus casting it in a very different light. The
residents of the county's uplands attracted the attention of
many visitors who used them to make a moral point. They
balanced the worldly corruption and lassitude perceived
among other groups, and comparisons were made with
greedy and ungrateful lower orders elsewhere. Mountain
dwellers were cast as symbols of rectitude. Economic interests
contributed to this trope. Impressions of seasonal migrants
'from the mountainous parts of Wales ... mostly from
Cardiganshire', who assisted in the collection of the harvest
in Herefordshire, were contrasted with that English county's
labouring poor. During 1794 the latter were rebuked by John
Clark in an account he wrote for the Board of Agriculture.
Clark, a resident of Builth, Breconshire, called for the enclosure of land to remove 'the means of subsisting in idleness'.[66]

---

[65] J. G. Lockhart, *The Life of Sir Walter Scott* (London, 1906), p. 399.
[66] John Clark, *General View of the Agriculture of the County of Hereford* (London, 1794), p. 29.

Another volume about Herefordshire's agriculture, written by an Englishman who resided in the county, described the seasonal migrants as being temperate and industrious. Although the author did not note the religious inclinations of the migrants, their manners were possibly a result of their stout Calvinistic Methodism. Such traits meant that they avoided 'the society of our natives'.[67] Though not without fault – they were said to be 'easily irritated and easily pleased' – these generally complimentary perceptions of migrants from Cardiganshire were, by and large, influenced by views of other groups. In other words, many of Herefordshire's inhabitants were removed from the values the commentators desired. Future points of contact would play an even greater role in locating positive values in the Cardi.

Travel writers were struck by the fact that impoverished upland dwellers did not display discontent. A shepherd employed as a guide by Malkin, while he was travelling from the north of the county to its centre in 1803, lived in a 'wretched hovel'. All the same, the visitor thought that he 'appeared content'.[68] Given this apparently harmonious relationship with a rugged environment, these Welsh highlanders provoked reflection on the corrupting effect of comfort. Mountaineers were not primitives in need of reform, they were contemporary models that others should emulate. During his tour, Evans paid special attention to 'poor huts' occupied by 'peaters and shepherds'. From this dreary scene, three children, 'almost in a state of nudity', rushed out followed by their mother, 'a stout, fresh coloured woman'. Visitors to the Lake District also depicted upland women in a way that linked sturdy frames with mountainous surroundings.[69] Evans then described the dwelling in detail. The few objects inside included a couple of 'stones with a plank across them [that] served as a chair'. Yet there was none of 'the misery and filth observable in the dwellings of the English poor' who earned between four and six times as much a week. The floor of 'native rock' was evidently

<hr />

[67] John Duncumb, *General View of the Agriculture of the County of Hereford* (London, 1805), pp. 64–5.

[68] Malkin, *Scenery, Antiquities, and Biography*, p. 386.

[69] For instance, see William Gell, *A Tour in the Lakes 1797 by William Gell*, ed. William Rollinson (Otley, 2000), p. 7.

'regularly swept' and 'all appeared in order'.[70] Evans had not introduced his readers to a noble savage in the Rousseauan sense, but to a domesticated one demonstrating virtues of good housekeeping and piety in adverse conditions – a moral centre away from the temptations of commercial areas. His impression of upland Cardiganshire presented an image of innate goodness with which the English lower orders could be traduced. Although Evans dismissed superstitious beliefs prevalent in the county, there were aspects of the place that he vaunted, a contrast that demonstrates the adaptability of mental locations.

George Lipscomb also praised inhabitants of the mountainous north and east of the county. Unlike Evans, however, Lipscomb made no overt critical comparison with the English poor. Instead, he drew on this desolate region to illustrate how people could, despite living in poor conditions, demonstrate that 'attachment which binds men to their native wilds' and enabled them to override 'the allurements of curiosity, and the temptations of emigration'.[71] Similar concern was expressed by others in the early decades of the nineteenth century, such as a vicar from Aberdare who was alarmed at 'the mania for emigration' from poverty-stricken Cardiganshire to the North American continent. Many comfortable members of society could not comprehend the desire of the poor to leave their 'sweet home'.[72] The wider world did, however, intrude into this arcadia. A shepherd related how a 'recruiting sergeant' tempted his eldest son, through the promise of 'a large bounty', to join the military and set sail for the West Indies.[73] In this peaceful setting, among a shepherd with his hundred sheep and no rent to pay, the intrusion of war was made all the more tangible. Lipscomb, the son of a naval surgeon, was among the war weary (during his Welsh tour the short-lived second coalition against France was faltering). The tale illustrated the capacity of war to disturb even one of the remotest parts

---

[70] Evans, *Tour through South Wales*, pp. 348–9.
[71] Lipscomb, *South Wales*, p. 149.
[72] George Eyre Evans, *Lampeter* (Aberystwyth, 1905), p. 181.
[73] Lipscomb, *South Wales*, p. 156.

of the kingdom, and the ways in which the highlands could stand for a blissful, vulnerable innocence.

The mountaineers were depicted as people who were free from the vices that the upper sections of society detected in the swelling population beneath them. In fact, the Welsh as a whole were frequently regarded as being a natural, unaffected people. They were not alone in this and joined a range of favoured types, which included Scottish Highlanders, whose preferment demonstrated unease with demographic and societal changes.[74] These interpretations were selective as they focused primarily on those from the hilly districts, which allowed contrasts with industrial or lowland environments to be made easily. Occasionally, individuals were selected for praise and the visitor saw in their actions features thought to typify the nation as a whole. The Revd Richard Warner, for instance, described meeting a one-armed fisherman in Cardiganshire. He discovered that the man had lost his arm as a result of a mining accident, but despite this impediment he could throw a fishing line of about 'twenty-two yards in length'. Warner employed him as a guide to Hafod. Afterwards Warner offered a 'small gratuity', which '*surprised*' the guide 'for he exhibited another instance of Welsh disinterested kindness'. Together with an admiration of the fisherman's adaptability, there was praise for his helpfulness and unassuming character, that were described as national characteristics. The region selected by Evans, Lipscomb and others for comment encapsulated the virtues of the common Welsh identified by Warner in an account of his first journey through Wales in 1797, the same journey during which he met the one-armed angler. The lively Welsh character was contrasted with the 'torpor and dejection which characterise the labouring poor of our own country'. This was because the self-reliant Welsh 'continue to act as nature dictates'.[75] Warner's comments echo concerns about the indolent, poor-law-dependent agricultural labourers of southern England most notably expressed in the Revd Thomas Malthus's essay published a year after Warner's first tour.

[74] See Ian Carter, 'The changing image of the Scottish peasantry, 1745–1980', in Raphael Samuel (ed.), *People's History and Socialist Theory* (London, 1981), pp. 9–15.
[75] Richard Warner, *A Walk through Wales in August 1797* (2nd edn, Bath, 1798), pp. 66–73, 184.

Qualities attributed to the mountaineers of Cardiganshire were not considered unique to them. In the above quotation, Warner was celebrating an isolated area between Machynlleth and Bala. Those living in remote parts of Cardiganshire were, however, part of a strip of western Wales that proved an invaluable reference point in the mental map for those, many of whom were clergymen, who sought a geographical centre of qualities. These meritorious features were summed up by the naturalist Revd William Bingley as an 'innocence and simplicity of character, unknown in the populous parts of our country'.[76] Yet he cautioned that these virtues were eroded when the Welsh lived near roads, because this tempted them to cheat visitors. By contrast, the mountaineers, owing to their distance from the corrupting influence of commerce, were the antithesis of these opportunist profit seekers. Although not unique to Wales, the universally applied division between the north and south of Wales meant that Cardiganshire presented a centre of virtue in the context of south Wales. Furthermore, the county's lack of routes to Ireland, such as the 'swindler'-ridden high road to Holyhead mentioned in one of Thomas De Quincy's essays, could help explain why the county was looked upon as a centre of virtue.[77] Romantic notions of nature, and suppositions about the corrupting influence of trade, were reinforced by scientific opinion about the mountaineers. In 1820, the Welsh academic Revd Thomas Price, in a note on the 'causes affecting the mental character', reported the increased 'buoyancy of spirits and alertness of mind' experienced in 'mountainous regions' compared with the lowlands, where 'a more refined and artificial state of society' eroded these characteristics.[78]

The rest of Cardiganshire's population could not be as neatly categorized. Even so, other uncomplicated country dwellers served the moral arguments of those keen to chastise human failings. When observing peasant folk on the way to

---

[76] Revd W. Bingley, *North Wales Delineated from Two Excursions* (2nd edn, London, 1814), p. 488.

[77] T. De Quincey, *The Confessions of an English Opium Eater and Other Essays* (London, 1906), p. 108; also see Pratt, *Gleanings*, vol. 1, p. 96.

[78] T. Price, *An Essay on the Physiognomy and Physiology of the Present Inhabitants of Britain* (London, 1820), p. 123.

market, travellers remarked on their admirable simplicity.[79] The market days held at Aberystwyth offered a sojourner in the town an opportunity to reflect upon country folk. Henry Wigstead, recalling a tour through Wales in 1797, described a market numerously attended by 'nymphs and swains from an extensive vicinity . . . happiness beams in every countenance, and rural felicity may, perhaps, raise some portion of envy in the passing emigrant children of fashion and dissipation'.[80] Once again the location of positive features was founded on a comparison, on this occasion with fashionable visitors to the town. This moral application of a simple country existence also figures in the accounts of the Franco-American Louis Simond. While touring the same area, namely the coastal road from Cardigan to Aberystwyth, Simond described how the country people gave his company a 'friendly nod' as they drove along. A description of the women as 'uncommonly good-looking' reiterated the author's pleasant impression of these rural folk. These observations were very different from his views of bustling Falmouth and the inordinate wealth seen in Bath, where 'half of the inhabitants do nothing the other half supplies them with nothings'.[81] While travelling through Cardiganshire observers could see that very few of the inhabitants did nothing, and the work that was done involved providing necessities not fancies.

Morality divided Wales into various parts, too. While some of these were based on statistics related to lawfulness, often founded on the comments of visiting great sessions judges, others touched on everyday characteristics such as clothing.[82] Clothing acquired moral significance as cotton came to replace flannel among the lower orders. This led to anxieties about the distinction 'between different ranks' being

[79] For example, see E. Donovan, *Descriptive Excursions through South Wales and Monmouthshire*, 2 vols (London, 1805), vol. 2, p. 201.

[80] Henry Wigstead, *Remarks on a Tour to North and South Wales in the Year 1797* (London, 1799), pp. 49–50.

[81] Louis Simond, *Journal of a Tour and Residence in Great Britain during the Years 1810 and 1811*, 2 vols (Edinburgh, 1815), vol. 1, pp. 213, 1, 15.

[82] For example, see *C*, 17 September 1808, 3; *CJ*, 16 April 1813, 3. David J. V. Jones remarked that contemporaries believed that industrial areas of Wales in the early nineteenth century 'lacked controls and offered temptations', *Crime in Nineteenth-Century Wales* (Cardiff, 1992), p. 112.

imperilled.[83] In *Twm Shon Catty*, Llewelyn Prichard used putative differences in the behaviour and clothing of female inhabitants to differentiate parts of Wales. In this manner, the morality and conduct of women were used to delineate areas; dissolute women meant a dissipated place. Women from Cardiganshire, for example, were said to scorn 'the sluttish garb and bare feet of the Glamorganshire maiden'. Distinctions were also made between the 'abominable pride' of a vain Pembrokeshire woman, who preferred 'leathern shoes', and the humble Cardiganshire maid, named Cardy, who wore 'honest clogs'. This lady's positive features were also evinced when she brewed authentic Welsh ale and refused to wear 'cotton prints' instead of her native clothes.[84] Without these opposites, claims to moral and national centrality could not have been made. In this case, the divide was not merely between Siluria and Demetia, but also between the counties of Pembroke and Cardigan. Cardy's virtues were heightened when contrasted with more than one undesirable feature. Pritchard's part in the elevation of an unsullied county, and his awareness of the tension between the whimsical nature of fashion and the simple essence of national identity, can be seen in his 1824 guide to Aberystwyth. He hoped that the 'singular novelty' of 'Welsh Trowsers', made and coloured in the same way as gowns and petticoats in Cardiganshire and Merioneth, would enhance 'patriotic and economic virtues' despite originating from the 'caprice of fashion'. If, thought Prichard, the county militia would adopt these dark blue 'cossack-cut' trousers with thin red stripes then something akin to the symbolic resonance of tartan could be attained.[85]

All the above ways of locating Cardiganshire and the Cardi took into consideration assorted actions and impressions founded on morality and nationality. But singular events place claims to centrality on a national stage. This was especially true if an area was thought to be upholding the

[83] *CJ*, 23 May 1834, 3. Also see Beverly Lemire, 'Second-hand beaux and "red-armed belles": conflict and the creation of fashions in England, c.1660–1800', *Continuity and Change*, 15, 3 (2000), 391–419, 410–12.

[84] Prichard, *Twm Shon Catty*, pp. 47–50.

[85] T. J. Llewelyn Prichard, *The New Aberystwyth Guide* (Aberystwyth, 1824), pp. 180–1.

interests of a nation state in peril. One occasion, influenced by discourses of patriotism, that profoundly influenced depictions of Cardiganshire's population came in the wake of the attempted French invasion of the British Isles in 1797. In a study of images relating to Wales, the art historian Peter Lord detected a shift in the visual representation of the Welsh after the French forces were repelled. After defending the nation state, the Welsh were depicted as reliable people, like John Bull.[86] The Cardiganshire militia, formed in 1760, had played an important role during the invasion. Concomitant with the change in portrayal observed by Lord was a patriotic prose tribute written by Theophilus Jones under the pseudonym 'CYMRO'. This essay, published in 1799, marked out the county's population by inflating their physical stature to correspond to the part they had played during the episode: 'The size and general height of the labouring inhabitants of Cardiganshire seem to have something peculiar. They are mostly thick set . . . brave, determined and resolute as the French desperadoes who lately landed on their coast can attest.'[87] Jones's emphasis on the common people's contribution to this venture was especially pertinent, as the French had expressed hopes that the poor would rebel. What better centre of loyalty than those the enemy had hoped to win over, but who, when the time came, remained faithful?

The representation of a place and its people depends on how far they fit into the mental locations cherished by observers. In the case of Jones it was allegiance to the state; with Llewelyn Prichard it was the maintenance of distinctions between ranks. For all commentators, images of the county's population served as rhetorical tools that they used to strengthen their ideological positions. By 1830, there were many representations that placed the county at the heart of positive values, notably as a counter to groups in other places. With increasing industrial activity and urban development, Cardiganshire's

---

[86] Peter Lord, *Words with Pictures: Welsh Images and Images of Wales in the Popular Press, 1640–1860* (Aberystwyth, 1995), p. 72.

[87] CYMRO, 'Cursory remarks on Welsh tours or travels', *Cambrian Register*, 2 (1799), 421–54, 426. For an investigation of this historian's opinions on English travel writers, see Hywel M. Davies, 'Wales in English travel writing, 1791–8: the Welsh critique of Theophilus Jones', *Welsh History Review*, 23, 3 (2007), 65–93.

role as a focal point for specific ideals persisted. Proclamations of centrality, however, shared cultural space with less positive representations.

MARGIN

Lawlessness contributed to cultural marginality, especially at times when external and internal threats were magnified. In addition, observers could locate the county on the margin in terms of taste and convenience. It has been argued that 'no Welsh county was more disturbed in the late 1810s than Cardiganshire'.[88] The predominant difficulties faced by the small farmers of the county included land hunger brought about by a rising population, the absence or inapplicability of new methods of farming and the problems stemming from geographic and climatic conditions.[89] For poorer farmers, increased enclosure of common land at the end of the eighteenth century restricted free grazing on upland pastures. Discontent among these groups, and the even less fortunate agricultural labourers, sometimes took the form of disturbances in north Pembrokeshire and Cardiganshire in 1820.[90] On a number of occasions the county, where recorded serious crime was rare, could be transformed into a troublesome corner of the kingdom. Depictions of the county during this period, when trade in contraband goods was at its height, manifested concerns about both potential and actual disorder. Propriety had not, as yet, gained the upper hand in representations of the county.

Grievances presented by property owners to central government contain representations of the lower ranks. A 'meeting of the gentlemen, free holders and inhabitants of the county of Cardigan' held at Aberaeron in 1816 passed a number of resolutions designed to make Parliament aware of

[88] D. J. V. Jones, 'Distress and discontent in Cardiganshire, 1814–1819', *Ceredigion*, 5, 3 (1964–7), 280–9, 280.

[89] Between 1801 and 1831 the county's population is estimated to have risen from 42,956 to 64,780, John Williams, *Digest of Welsh Historical Statistics*, 2 vols (Cardiff, 1985), vol. 1, 12.

[90] For example, see D. Williams, 'Rhyfel y Sais bach', *Ceredigion*, 2, 1 (1952–5), 39–52; D. J. V. Jones, *Before Rebecca: Popular Protests in Wales, 1793–1835* (London, 1973), pp. 16–17, 48–9.

their plight. They did this by stressing the 'ripening seeds of insubordination' among unemployed labourers, a substantial part of a distraught population. Many in the assemblage would have benefited from the reductions in taxes and duties, called for in order to ease the 'distress, misery and exhaustion of the county'. Grievances specifically targeted taxes on products 'carried coastwise which is so detrimental to the agricultural and coasting trade of this county and so contrary to all the maxims of political wisdom'. Particular emphasis was placed on the removal of duties on coal and culm brought to the county by sea.[91] Tellingly, the meeting stressed the county's loyalty during the war with France, an allusion to the contribution made by people from the county, members of the 81st regiment of foot (The Loyal Lincoln Volunteers), at Maida in southern Italy.[92] By drawing attention to the county's fidelity during times of conflict, the slide towards insubordination was believed to stem from desperation rather than opposition to the state. Geographical isolation, punishing navigation laws – annulled with respect to coastal trade only in 1854 – and a restive population all served to place Cardiganshire on the edge of order. Presumably, the reduction of duty would have also eased the problem of smuggling along the county's shore.

Perceptions of Cardiganshire's coastal population loomed large in unfavourable descriptions of the county. This constituency stood in contrast to the robust but docile mountaineer. Evaluations of the former group were based on a number of factors ranging from criminal acts to the psychological make-up of certain occupations. The reasons why they were regarded as being distant from pleasing characteristics and behaviours shed light on the issues that aroused disquiet among people in authority. Smugglers and those who plundered shipwrecks were frequently denounced in the press. The opportunity that the sea afforded the less wealthy exercised many respectable minds and led to a considerable portion of the county and its population being tainted. At this point in the history of Cardiganshire's image there were

[91] *CJ,* 29 March 1816, 3.
[92] Direct reference to this battle, fought on 4 July 1806, was made in another statement of Cardiganshire's grievances in *CJ,* 17 May 1816, 3.

people whose activities substantially qualified its portrayal as a moral core; they added a sinister tinge to the inhabitants of the county, just as the wreckers did in Cornwall.[93] At Llanon in 1806 some 200 smugglers attacked excise officers 'with the most savage fury, assailing them with large stones'. There were eighty 'fraudulent maltsters in and about this village, who never pay any duty to the government'. Others evidently supported them in order to make up the number reported to have attacked the officers.[94] These were acts that broke the law and harmed the interests of the nation: the newspaper reporting the incident mentioned the total revenue lost by the government every year through smuggling. Notwithstanding the difficulties involved in assessing the quantitative impact of smuggling, it was a major presence in representations of the county's inhabitants.

Those prone to dishonourable conduct could, moreover, affect relations between countries. Late in 1816, a French vessel was lost near Aberporth. Local people collected part of the ship's cargo of French wine, and 'the outrageous conduct of the country people' was censured. Moreover, the French consul intended to make a report of the incident to the British government. The event was a cause of national as well as local embarrassment.[95] Another paper reported the incident at greater length; together with its cautionary rhetoric – eleven of the looters experienced an '*untimely death* in consequence of making free with the wine' – the damning language used to locate these people on the margins can be discerned. 'It is with deep concern that we have to report the late lawless . . . depredations . . . an immense number of the peasantry of the neighbourhood who had assembled on the beach were guilty of depredations highly disgraceful to a civilised country.' The irresponsibility of the mob was contrasted with the conscientiousness of Colonel Price, of Pigeonsford, and the customs men who protected the cargo.[96] Men in authority had risked their lives to protect

[93] Simon Trezise, 'The Celt, the Saxon and the Cornishman: stereotypes and counter-stereotypes of the Victorian period', *Cornish Studies*, 8 (2000), 54–68, 59.

[94] *C*, 22 February 1806, 3.

[95] Ibid., 18 January 1817, 3.

[96] *CJ*, 20 December 1816, 3.

the intemperate from themselves. The county's notoriety for illicit coastal trading lived on for many years in the tales about the eighteenth-century smuggler Siôn Cwilt, whose name was given to a part of Cardiganshire known as Banc Siôn Cwilt.[97] This individual was just one of many who bene-fited from flotsam and illegal imports.

The sense that enough local people were involved to merit the comprehensive condemnation of the 'country people' and 'the peasantry' in the press is supported in travellers' observations. These conveyed the impression of a geograph-ically isolated area many of whose inhabitants profited from crime. Living near such a convenient location for landing illicit goods meant that such activities were part of the fabric of life. During the course of a day's ride, Mavor drew atten-tion to the prevalence of smuggling around Aberaeron and the shores of Cardiganshire generally. There were notices on many doors signifying 'a dealer in prohibited commod-ities', and these signs were composed of 'characters more rude and uncouth even than the Egyptian which . . . deform the signs of the citizens of London'.[98] Part of Mavor's impres-sion of outlandishness possibly arose from the fact that the notices were written in Welsh. For Mavor, whose publications included *The English Spelling Book*, published two years before his Welsh expedition, the style and nature of the lettering he saw played an important part in confirming the 'other-ness' of a people. Writing at about the same time, Evans commented that New Quay offered shelter to a 'nest of smugglers'. Unlike Mavor, he suggested that this illicit trade, which he maintained was the main form of commerce on the Cardiganshire coast, corrupted the farmers living nearby, who were seduced by 'the hopes arising from this fraudulent species of gain' and neglected their farms. Evans cited cases of cattle being employed for the purpose of moving smug-gled goods rather than the 'cultivation of the soil'.[99]

Besides criminal activity, there were unfavourable inter-pretations of the mentality of those who lived or earned their

[97] See Gillian Clarke, *Banc Siôn Cwilt: A Local Habitation and a Name* (Newtown, 1998).

[98] Mavor, *Tour in Wales*, p. 53.

[99] Evans, *Tour through South Wales*, p. 332.

livelihoods on the coast. An indication of the stress placed
on the coast's ability to challenge stability is provided by an
adventure story, possibly autobiographical, about the esca-
pades of two men in Africa published in the 1780s. The
author, David Lowellin, recalled how his parents moved
to an estate they had inherited 'between Aberystwyth and
Cardigan'.[100] Growing up among people who were inclined
to talk about 'distant parts' inspired a *wanderlust* that never
abated. If the mountaineers reflected concepts of order,
then these coastal parts were often comprehended as places
of motion and instability. This lack of rootedness troubled
those interested in the moral condition of the common
people, and these commentators turned their attention to
those who lived off the sea. A contributor to Walter Davies's
View of Agriculture, referred to as C.D., described the tension
between the farming and fishing communities arising from
the fishermen's improvidence and failure to participate in
agricultural work: 'Where fishermen nest together, they
seldom assist much in expediting our harvest work; for they
seldom aim at a higher independence than living well for a
week, and then starve for the winter.' It was not surprising,
therefore, that the county's coast, whose two main ports
were among the most significant in south Wales at the time,
should gain repute as a place where the desired standards
were found wanting.[101]

One of the most critical accounts produced by a visitor to
the county at this time duly pointed out the fishermen. This
differentiation was all the more significant because it came
from a commentator who praised the Welsh people. On his
journey along Cardiganshire's southern coast during his
second tour of Wales in 1798, Warner, a seasoned traveller
who also wrote up tours of south-west England and Scotland,
claimed to be conscious of the moral failings present in
what he described as 'colonies of fishermen'. The influence
of their occupation on their manners set them apart from

[100] David Lowellin, *The Admirable Travels of Messieurs Thomas Jenkins and David
Lowellin through the Unknown Tracts of Africa* (London, 1786), pp. 5–6.
[101] Davies, *General View*, vol. 2, p. 296; 'Shipping of Wales 1814/1815', *Cambrian
Register*, 3 (1818), p. 340. These estimates put Cardigan and Aberystwyth ahead of
Swansea and Pembroke in terms of both registered ships and tonnage.

the upright ideals he espoused. They, Warner intoned, 'live on the irregular profits of their precarious profession . . . Those whose gains are uncertain, are seldom characterised by habits of economy.' He added that few of these seafarers spoke English, but this was where similarities with other Welsh people ended. Warner stressed that they, 'unlike their countrymen, are not only dull and heavy, but exhibit none of that civility of manners and kindness of heart which render the Welsh character in general so estimable'. This is a rare example of values typically associated with the Welsh being used to judge evidently Welsh-speaking people themselves. He suggested that the nature of their occupation with its lack of certainty diminished their ability to behave responsibly. These characteristics were quite different from those Warner described when in the mountainous parts of Wales. Moulded by their profession, the fishermen are in a sense rejected from the mental set employed by Warner when classifying the Welsh. The patterns of behaviour imbued through a life at sea had, in Warner's opinion, taken them away from what typified their country, namely the mountains and the cultivation of the land.[102]

Perceptions of towns and villages were central in accounts of the area. When, for instance, Malkin was unable to find a pair of shoes in Cardigan, he was struck by the lack of services in a county town and this served to emphasize the whole county's distance from comfort and convenience. Visitors from most parts of Britain would have found Cardiganshire's towns wanting in some respect or other; a comparison of Welsh towns in 1830 revealed that Cardiganshire did not possess an abundance of grocers, bookbinders or physicians. These impressions may have been exaggerated by the visitors' inexperience of hardship or want, but they were relayed among others as evidence of marginality and came to fix the county's image. Moreover, there is some

---

[102] Richard Warner, *A Second Walk through Wales* (Bath, 1799), pp. 328–9. Miners were another section of Cardiganshire's population who were differentiated in physical and behavioural terms – 'robust, athletic' and of 'no religion' not like the 'honest labourers': Anon., *Cambrian Register*, 2 (1799), 386–89. 387. Some four years later Evans also noted the appearance of the inhabitants of the same village, Pontrhydfendigaid, calling them 'a stout and athletic race': *Tour through South Wales*, p. 354.

indication that those less accustomed to comfort than some of these travellers located the county in a similar, if less well-documented, way. According to Richard Gough, in his additions to William Camden's *Britannia* published in 1789, the beef of Cardiganshire was 'greatly inferior to that of Monmouthshire, whose inhabitants give this county the nickname of the "Devil's Grandmother's Jointure"'.[103] This vivid image became a point of reference for those who visited the county. In 1824, one tourist observed that the county was 'deservedly branded with the nickname of the Devil's Grandmother's Jointure'.[104] The phrase also reveals how a structural feature assumed a symbolic nature; the lack of meat on cattle resulting from scanty herbage served to identify the area as a whole, to set it apart in the popular consciousness from the more prosperous south-east of Wales. Such judgements contributed to the creation of equivalence, the county becoming synonymous with want.

Food added to the county's reputation in other ways. In fact, it appears that Cardiganshire's inhabitants were themselves aware of these defining characteristics and that on occasion this knowledge influenced their behaviour. Captain Jenkin Jones of the Royal Navy kept a diary of a visit to his forefathers' county in 1819. While having a meal in a public house at Bow Street, he was given 'wheaten bread' by his host instead of the 'barley-meal' he wished for because the host considered it more suitable for 'shentle folks to eat'. At the end of the eighteenth century, Frederic Morton Eden detected a 'strong prejudice against rye-bread' in southern England, and Jones's host may well have known about, and acted on, this preference for wheat over other grains. Barley bread was part of a culinary boundary that defined Cardiganshire; the county would for some time be known by the appellation 'gwlad y bara barleys' (the land of barley bread). Jones noted that getting mistaken for a gentleman

[103] Malkin, S*cenery, Antiquities, and Biography*, p. 408; Harold Carter, 'The growth and decline of Welsh towns', in Donald Moore (ed.), *Wales in the Eighteenth Century* (Swansea, 1976), pp. 47–62, 58–9; William Camden, *Britannia . . . Enlarged by Richard Gough*, 3 vols (London, 1789), vol. 2, p. 526.

[104] NLW, Glynne of Hawarden, B/57, 'A journal of a tour through south Wales and the border counties' (1824), fo. 32.

was most unusual because if he were twenty miles out of London he would, owing to his weary appearance and jaded clothes, be seen as anything but a gentleman. Different standards of assessing a gentleman, and the food a man of that standing should eat, in north Cardiganshire and London provided an indication of the poverty of the area through which he was travelling.[105]

Comparisons with isolated islands indicate how visitors conceptualized Cardiganshire as a place removed from norms. A traveller noted in his diary that bread was 'made and baked *in a frying pan*'. The whole experience, he exclaimed, was reminiscent of *Robinson Crusoe*. The relation of this county, with its different language and strange customs, to places on the other side of the world tells us something about the potency of this metaphor for strangeness. From the 1770s onwards, the voyages of Captain Cook, which 'had a huge impact on the British imagination', joined Defoe's tale of a stranded European in people's symbolic galleries. These provided filters through which Cardiganshire was imagined and experienced, although as illustrated by Lipscomb's reaction to a strange sight he fell upon as he approached Hafod, Defoe's vision was the one most often referred to in the context of Cardiganshire: 'Here were half a score *Welch* boys, dressed in almost black cloths, dancing round a fire of switch, in a field; a group which brought to my mind the idea conveyed in Robinson Crusoe's adventures, of the savages at their revels.'[106]

The strange and outlandish was often deemed disreputable and base, especially when the commentator adhered to 'the discourse of civilization and barbarism that informed the

---

[105] NLW, MS 785A, Captain Jenkin Jones, 'Tours in England and Wales' (1819), fo. 75; Frederic Morton Eden, *The State of the Poor*, 3 vols (London, 1797), vol. 2, 526. Also see J. T. Barber, *A Tour throughout South Wales and Monmouthshire* (London, 1803), pp. 123–4. R. Elwyn Hughes explains shifts in the consumption of different varieties of bread in Wales in *Dysgl Bren a Dysgl Arian: Nodiadau ar Hanes Bwyd yng Nghymru* (Talybont, 2003), pp. 157–94.

[106] NLW, MS 786A, Captain Lloyd, 'A tour in England and Wales' (1827), fo. 23; Kathleen Wilson, 'The island race: Captain Cook, Protestant evangelicalism and the construction of English national identity, 1760–1800', in Tony Claydon and Ian McBride (eds), *Protestantism and National Identity: Britain and Ireland, c.1650–c.1850* (Cambridge, 1998), pp. 265–90, 279; Lipscomb, *South Wales*, p. 125.

Scottish Enlightenment'.[107] An account by Richard Vaughan Yates, son of an eminent Unitarian minister in Liverpool, employed similar language to that used to describe barbarous peoples from beyond the British Isles. As he left the county, he observed changes in the landscape and the fertility of the soil. This sense of entering and leaving a very different land featured in other travel accounts. Captain Lloyd, on entering Machynlleth, thought it had 'a more respectable appearance than the towns [Lampeter and Tregaron] we have seen lately'.[108] On entering Tregaron, Yates was struck by its primitiveness. The people appeared 'to be in a state bordering on barbarism in their dress, their habitations and their manners, which are extremely rude'. On moving south to Lampeter, he found a similar type of people who 'still had the same semibarbarous appearance' as those in Tregaron. It is significant that Yates compliments the inns he visited in both towns. The comforts they offered evidently mitigated the unpleasantness of the locals. A sense of relief can be detected when he recorded that, on the road to Llandeilo and the Tywi Valley of Carmarthenshire, the 'country and state of agriculture improved'.[109] This more fertile scene, which included numerous estates with their cultivated grounds, made Yates feel that he had entered a place bearing the characteristics of society and culture. Later, during the 1840s, the importance Yates placed on the symbiosis between landscape and morality was put into effect when he founded a public park in Toxteth, Liverpool. Analogous attempts to improve the morality of commoners during the early and mid-Victorian era influenced the ways in which Cardiganshire and the Cardi were located; these will be among the discourses explored in the following chapter.

---

[107] John Gray, *Post-Liberalism: Studies in Political Thought* (New York, 1993), p. 328.
[108] NLW, MS 786A, fo. 23.
[109] NLW, MS 687B, Richard Vaughan Yates, 'A tour in Wales' (1805), fos 128–9.

III

INSPECTION AND INTEGRATION, 1830–1870

Connections between Cardiganshire and elsewhere increased between 1830 and 1870. After the arrival of the railway during the 1860s, more people visited the area. Expectations of increased trade were high – one ballad foresaw flourishing fairs in the county's interior.[1] These were also the 'glorious years of shipbuilding' on the Cardiganshire coast, partly stimulated by the new pier at New Quay, constructed in 1837.[2] Woollen manufacture in the southern part of the county and lead mining in the north developed, too. Both industries profited from urbanization and industrialization; lead was required for buildings and industries, and wool to clothe their occupants and workers. By the mid-1840s these products were mentioned in descriptions of the county's economy.[3] Accordingly, the county shared the optimism that characterized the time. A witness testifying before an inquiry into the Rebecca riots was asked whether the county's condition had improved in the past twenty years. He responded: 'Formerly, twenty years ago . . . you saw the women walking around without shoes and stockings, but now you never see such an occurrence in this part of the country.'[4] Nonetheless, there was considerable pressure on the land as the county's population increased, peaking at 73,441 in 1871, a figure only surpassed 130 years later.[5] Emigration and education

[1] NLW, Baledi, J. D. Lewis, 32, David Jones, 'Manchester and Milford Railway', p. 4. For other manifestations of railway excitement in the county, see *CJ*, 3 February 1854, 3, and *Yr Eurgrawn Wesleyaidd*, 49 (1857), 306.

[2] G. Ivor Thomas, 'The growth and decline of Cardiganshire shipbuilding from 1740–1914 with special reference to Llansanffraid', 2 vols (M.Phil. thesis, University of Wales, Lampeter, 1994), vol. 1, 161–225.

[3] Thomas Dugdale, *Curiosities of Great Britain*, 11 vols (London, [1845]), vol. 3, p. 380.

[4] BPP, XVI (1844), *Report of the Commissioners of Inquiry for South Wales* (London, 1844), p. 239.

[5] John Williams, *Digest of Welsh Historical Statistics*, 2 vols (Cardiff, 1985), vol. 1, p. 12.

were means of alleviating this and both contributed to the way Cardiganshire was located mentally.[6]

Depictions of Cardiganshire produced in the middle of the nineteenth century were different, though not dissociated, from those of the previous period. Concerns with order and development took on a different character. At this time, Wales possessed its own version of the 'condition of England question'.[7] Consequently, representations of the county's inhabitants were often set against disturbances and social questions. Those who contributed to parliamentary publications brought a more systematic reforming agenda to bear on the county than the advice contained in the ruminations of earlier observers. These 'key instruments of the moral revolution of the nineteenth century' signalled the emergence, from around 1830, of the increased economic and political confidence of the middle classes.[8] One proposed solution, that reflected the economic context and opportunities of the age, was that native monoglots should learn English. Notions of improvement, while apparent in the earlier period, were now asserted confidently. This improvement involved integration, marching along a road with English signposts.[9]

While government reports sought to ascertain the area's social condition, those concerned with spiritual advancement expressed apprehension about the persistence of old beliefs or immoral habits. From the 1830s a 'great shift towards

[6] For the county's poor, see Michael Birtwistle, 'Pobl y tai bach: some aspects of the agricultural labouring classes of Cardiganshire in the second half of the nineteenth century' (MA thesis, University of Wales, Aberystwyth, 1981), and A. M. E. Davies, 'Poverty and its treatment in Cardiganshire, 1750–1850' (MA thesis, University of Wales, Aberystwyth, 1968). For migration to England during this period, see Colin G. Pooley, 'Welsh migration to England in the mid-nineteenth century', *Journal of Historical Geography*, 9, 3 (1983), 287–306.

[7] Ieuan Gwynedd Jones noted a shift in focus during the 1830s when there was 'a realization [of] the potential for revolution in the coalfield towns and villages': *Mid-Victorian Wales: The Observers and the Observed* (Cardiff, 1992), p. 5.

[8] Philip Corrigan and Derek Sayer, *The Great Arch: English State Formation as Cultural Revolution* (Oxford, 1986), p. 124. Also see L. Goldman, 'The origins of British "Social Science": political economy, natural science and statistics, 1830–1835', *Historical Journal*, 26, 3 (1983), 587–616, 590.

[9] Gwyneth Tyson Roberts concluded that many Welsh people followed the culture of progress that characterized early and mid-Victorian Britain, *The Language of the Blue Books: The Perfect Instrument of Empire* (Cardiff, 1998), p. 237.

nonconformist and radical culture' occurred in Wales.[10] The county contained substantial concentrations of the main denominations, including two with a very different ethos, the Calvinistic Methodists and the Unitarians. Agendas of spiritual and physical improvement that distinguish this period took aspects of Cardiganshire to illustrate what was good and bad. Furthermore, the 1859 revival which originated in the county, albeit with a transatlantic impetus, added to the area's religious reputation. As the stature of Nonconformity grew, Cardiganshire contributed to, and was shaped by, this motif of Welsh identity.[11]

There was a significant expansion in the amount of printed material from 1830, and its origin in Wales for a Welsh readership means that there need be less reliance on visitors' accounts. The output of the denominational and secular press multiplied as antiquarian and literary publications such as *Y Brython*, started in 1858, joined religious journals such as the Independents' *Y Diwygiwr*, established in 1835. Though this growth brings new voices to notice, with their own ways of locating the county, it still amounts to a somewhat limited range of opinion. However, definitions of what the locators opposed provide an insight into alternative views of society. Influential individuals, espousing perspectives on Cardiganshire and the world in general, found a channel in these publications. Moreover, during these forty years the number of newspapers increased, like the short-lived *Demetian Mirror* of 1840 and the more enduring *Welshman*, first published in 1832. Government reports, notably those on education and agricultural employment, despite their ostensibly objective methods, also offer a source of opinion and perception. These reports included local witnesses whose perspectives enlarge the range of locations and augment others in which the county was placed.

[10] Prys Morgan, 'Wild Wales: civilising the Welsh from the sixteenth to the nineteenth Centuries', in Peter Burke, Brian Harrison and Paul Slack (eds), *Civil Histories: Essays Presented to Sir Keith Thomas* (Oxford, 2000), pp. 265–83, 282, 279. Also see David Russell Barnes, *People of Seion: Patterns of Nonconformity in Cardiganshire and Carmarthenshire in the Century Preceding the Religious Census of 1851* (Llandysul, 1995).

[11] For the language that characterized this period, see Paul O'Leary, 'The languages of patriotism in Wales, 1840–1880', in Geraint H. Jenkins (ed.), *The Welsh Language and its Social Domains, 1801–1911* (Cardiff, 2000), pp. 533–60.

NAMING

The literature of the time does not present us with a congregation of Cardis. There are the occasional references and the term appears in an account of a journey from Lampeter to Teifi Pools in the Unitarian publication *Yr Ymofynnydd*, published in 1868, but this is a trickle compared with later cataracts.[12] The name was also used in an essay about the 1865 election contest in Cardiganshire between two Liberal candidates, Sir Thomas Lloyd and David Davies. When speaking of the county's electorate, the word 'Cardis' personifies the 'common man' of the county. In defending the suitability of David Davies, who was not born in Cardiganshire, the author asked whether the Cardis would prefer a man born in the county or one who could put butter on their bread and a side of pork under their roofs.[13] With the expansion of the electorate, as a result of the 1884 Reform Act, the use of the word in political debate increased. The account of the 1865 contest thus presages a more widespread utilization of the name in a political context.

As stated earlier, this relative dearth of the cognomen did not indicate the absence of distinctiveness because the term was evidently in use in everyday speech. Two representations of the county's inhabitants that mention the term Cardi as being used in the middle of the nineteenth century come from the Edwardian era. The first originates from an unpublished manuscript describing the 'Cardy carts' that sold meat and butter to the iron towns of Glamorgan and Monmouthshire. The second comes from the memories of a native of the Vale of Glamorgan who recollected harvest gangs from Cardiganshire.[14] Such reminiscences indicate that the term was comparatively common. It is also significant that both accounts relate to contact with people from Cardiganshire in south-east Wales that was founded on trade and seasonal migration. These recollections imply that people of the south-east applied the name to traders and

[12] Anon., 'O Lanbedr i Lyn Teifi', *Yr Ymofynnydd*, 3ydd, gyf. 1 (1868), 265–9, 267.

[13] Anon., 'Etholiadau Ceredigion a Meirionydd', *Y Traethodydd*, 20 (1865), 488–512, 499.

[14] NLW, MS Maybery 1884, Transcripts of John Lloyd 'Cardy Carts' [*c.*1906], fos 1–2; *Glamorgan Gazette*, 18 August 1911, 5.

migrants. Contact with difference impelled naming. A name conveniently allowed other qualities to be located easily in the Cardi.

A significant aspect of these two accounts in relation to naming lies in the suggestion that the term was not necessarily used just to describe those from the county of Cardigan. These hints at the term's wider catchment area, which included adjacent parts of Carmarthenshire, indicate that the term was a convenient way to bracket those who came from part of west Wales. Thus, attributes assigned to the Cardi were not restricted to the county; the cultural region perceived by those from south-east Wales was not restricted to an administrative area. The Vale of Glamorgan source recalled that the name 'Cardies' was 'bestowed by local people upon those immigrants' who were 'men from Cardiganshire and Carmarthenshire'. Likewise, in the account of the 'Cardy carts', the relater describes a 'large trade by means of the Cardy carts in dressed pigs and in casks of butter from Cardiganshire and west Carmarthenshire'. Both examples reveal how an administrative area could be used as shorthand for a group that spilt over boundaries. While these seasonal migrants and tradesmen may have identified themselves on the basis of their village or parish, those living in the south-east of Wales drew another, broader distinction.[15] Contact meant conflation.

Other descriptions of the county's inhabitants may signal difference. Expressions like 'Cardiganshire man', for instance, demonstrate some delineation that could express county pride in an individual's achievements. Counties built their own collection of notables embodying certain desirable or entertaining characteristics, such as the 'Cardiganshire Crimean heroes' of 1855.[16] Towards the end of the 1860s two collections of county notables were published.[17] The fact that most were associated with religion indicates the influence of

---

[15] The word was also used in the middle of the nineteenth century simply to describe anyone from the countryside. See J. Howell, 'Adgofion boreu oes, gan mwyaf yn fy nghysylltiad a Merthyr', *Y Geninen*, 19 (1901), 212–15, 212.

[16] *CJ*, 12 October 1855, 3.

[17] Benjamin Williams (Gwynionydd), *Enwogion Ceredigion* (Caerfyrddin, 1869); Griffith Jones (Glan Menai), *Enwogion Sir Aberteifi: Traethawd Buddugol yn Eisteddfod Genedlaethol Aberystwyth, 1865* (Dolgellau, 1868).

a largely non-aristocratic sector that assumed cultural leadership at this time. They herald a self-assurance and cultural assertiveness that flowered after 1870.

Less distinguished ambassadors of the county also existed. For many people the individuals mentioned in newspaper reports may have been more significant than any minister or missionary. Two soldiers stationed in Cardigan in 1843 during the Rebecca disturbances fell for 'beautiful Cardiganshire lassies'. In order to forestall their prospective marriages, their commanding officer sent them inland. On going to say goodbye to his belle, one soldier found her marrying a local blacksmith.[18] Seven years later a three-day ploughing match took place near Kidwelly, Carmarthenshire, that was described as 'Cardiganshire against the rest of South Wales'. Although the successful contingent from Cardiganshire hailed from near the border town of Newcastle Emlyn, the reporter concluded that the whole county of 'Cardigan may well be proud of her ploughmen as none but the most skilful and experienced would have had the slightest chance on such ground'.[19] While we cannot access the opinions held by those who have not left a record of their sense of belonging, the identification of people as being of a county, by others, both within and outside the area, indicates how groups were defined. Naming indicates apparent differences from outsiders, whether military swains or competitors in a ploughing match. The texture of these perceived and actual differences is examined below.

PAST

Considerable attempts were made to remove the stain of superstition in mid-nineteenth-century Cardiganshire. Expressions of criticism had, of course, existed before the 1830s, but with the increase of religious and secular publications from around this date the criticisms mounted. These increased calls for improvement and the middle classes' abhorrence of ignorance led to an increasing emphasis

---

[18] *CJ*, 4 August 1843, 3.
[19] Ibid., 15 February 1850, 3.

on the anachronistic nature of superstition. In *Cambrian Superstitions*, W. Howells wrote of the 'march of intellect' that had reassured the peasantry that the dark posed no threat to them. While admitting that the subject of his book still existed in corners of Wales, Howells described these as being 'like a little snow congregated into corners and already beginning to melt before the all-powerful sun'.[20] Some of these corners were identified in Cardiganshire and contributed to the representation of its inhabitants; a letter to *The Times* in 1858 described the 'unscientific natives of these wild Welsh hills'.[21] These spots persisted far longer than Howells thought; in the years covered by the following chapter such corners may be seen less as impediments to improvement, but as harmless, even valuable, traditions.

The notion that isolated parts harboured belief in the supernatural was often applied to Cardiganshire as a whole. To some, like Thomas Roscoe, the county was seen as being especially prone to this tendency. Unlike several native commentators, Roscoe, a literary man, expressed astonishment but was not overly critical. Roscoe, like Howells, was of the opinion that the 'familiar superstitions of Wales were becoming gradually fainter and fainter', yet added that 'it is notorious that in this county [Cardiganshire] they are more rife than in almost any other in Wales'.[22] Such was the prevalence of this irrationality that even educated people had some belief in the supernatural, contradicting widely held opinion that education dispelled credulity. Nonetheless, public expressions of belief in the supernatural by the educated were not forthcoming. There was an intellectual argument, voiced by, among others, the politician Henry Richard, who was born in Tregaron, that belief in the supernatural could engender belief in God.[23] Yet the number of exasperated comments made by professionals, especially medical men and ministers, from and about the county indicate that many

[20] W. Howells, *Cambrian Superstitions* (London, 1831), pp. 7–8.
[21] Reproduced in the *Aberystwith Observer*, 20 November 1858, 1.
[22] Thomas Roscoe, *Wanderings and Excursions in South Wales* (2nd edn, London, 1854), p. 48.
[23] Henry Richard, *Letters on the Social and Political Condition of the Principality of Wales* (London, 1866), pp. 33–4.

members of the middle classes were defining themselves in terms of progress and regress. Superstition contradicted the 'English idea of progress by means of science' that engaged the minds of the Victorian middling sorts.[24]

In an age when science and industry were in the limelight, geographies of the supernatural drew boundaries around people and spaces, metaphorically locating them in a shadowy past. Places like the Forest of Dean were described in similar ways, categorized as harbouring old customs by Welsh commentators keen to counter the slight that Wales alone was backward.[25] Therefore, Cardiganshire was one place among many where 'superstition prevails' and did not fit the template of progress that was increasingly used at a time of unprecedented industrial growth.[26] The professional classes sought to dispel belief in strange phenomena. Unlike earlier dismissals, these were not proclaimed in travel accounts but in public and reproduced in the local press. In 1851 a medical doctor, H. Bell, gave a lecture at the Aberystwyth Literary, Scientific and Mechanics Institution on 'spectral illusions and popular superstitions'. In concluding, 'a light was shown, which had the power of giving an extremely cadaverous appearance to the countenance'.[27] The fact that Bell included the word 'popular' in the title of his lecture illustrates how the partnership of superstition and the people of Cardiganshire continued well into the nineteenth century.

Not all comments on old beliefs were overtly critical. Some were expressed in a wry manner, although in so doing they contributed to the broad censure of such customs through highlighting their absurdity. A newspaper report entitled 'Welsh law' referred to the 'credulity' of a woman from Ystumtuen who sought the help of a 'quack doctor' to cure her sick son. After claiming to have identified a curse, he recommended that the son's best trousers be buried and as they rotted the boy would recover. Despite following this procedure, the son died. While in Aberystwyth on a hiring

[24] G. M. Young, *Victorian Essays* (Oxford, 1962), p. 113.
[25] *CJ*, 21 January 1848, 3. Also see Mr and Mrs S. C. Hall, *The Book of South Wales, the Wye and the Coast* (London, 1861), p. 6.
[26] BPP, XXVII (1847), *Reports of the Commissioners of Inquiry into the State of Education in Wales, Part II*, p. 64.
[27] *CJ*, 10 January 1851, 3.

fair day – a time when residents of remote areas entered the town in some numbers – the mother saw the charlatan wearing her son's trousers. The mother got the trousers back, much to the amusement of many onlookers. It was, the report concluded, an example of 'Welsh law'.[28] This tale illustrated both the gullibility and tenacity of the woman from the outlying district and the basic, out-of-court, justice meted out. Both were very much the product of what was seen as a primitive, simple view of the world. In order to appreciate the range and pervasiveness of the way in which certain beliefs and those holding them were located in the past, humorous accounts like this need to be put alongside more serious comments. Newspapers were a means whereby the voice of reason criticized examples of erroneous notions in out-of-the-way places.[29] As a result, this means of communication, which displayed 'instances of human folly', contributed to the mental grid on which people positioned places.[30]

Denominational periodicals were eager to distance themselves from old customs thought to originate in a pagan or papist past. They reveal how general perceptions of the county's adherence to superstition, such as those offered by Roscoe, were broken down into more particular, localized representations. A correspondent to the Anglican publication *Yr Haul* reported how the inhabitants of Borth, in northern Cardiganshire, visited the 'ddewines o Glandwr' (wise woman of Glandwr) whenever a person or animal was ill. Respectable inhabitants were, the writer assured his readers, doing their utmost to eradicate the practice.[31] Some denominations established a local moral hierarchy based on the professed absence of primitive beliefs in their own area. The Unitarians asserted that the district in the south of the county where they were concentrated was free of superstition. Calvinistic Methodists, by contrast, were reported to have consulted wise men, and the irony of educated men

---

[28] Ibid., 29 November 1839, 3.

[29] Also see *Demetian Mirror*, 15 August 1840, 5, which described a 'sorcerer' standing trial in Aberystwyth whose activities, and those 'ignorant creatures' who believed him, were proclaimed disgraceful 'in the present day'.

[30] See Owen Davies, 'Newspapers and the popular belief in witchcraft and magic in the modern period', *Journal of British Studies*, 37, 2 (1998), 139–65, 149.

[31] *Yr Haul*, cyfres newydd, c.n., 4 (1853), 238.

asking those without learning for information was emphasized.[32] In short, absence of credulity indicated progress
along the road to both civilization and piety. Yet reports in
these journals reveal the durability of the beliefs they wished
to erase. Symbols of advancement, like the railway, could be
incorporated into a superstitious thought-world. Tangible
features of progress could not immediately eradicate the
beliefs of a people whose minds were located in the past.
Belief in a curse laid upon the mansion of Maesyfelin by Rees
Prichard, the vicar of Llandovery, in the seventeenth century
was revived by Lampeter people to explain the deaths of
three men working on the railway. Significantly, the vicar of
Lampeter stated that it was 'y werin', or ordinary people, who
still believed in the old curse and implied that a considerable
section of the population held the belief in the mid-1860s.[33]
With this portion of the county deemed susceptible to the
pull of past ways, the area as a whole could likewise be designated backward.

Campaigns against superstition were even waged by
publications that sought to preserve Welsh traditions. The
Cambrian Journal aimed to 'bring down the mythical and
superstitious to the practical, real and historical, and thus to
elicit truth . . . to take from magic its pretended supernatural
character'.[34] Another journal concerned with Welsh antiquities, *Y Brython*, published a short drama about superstition
in the county that shows how particular aspects of the past
were prioritized. Set in a farmhouse that is being visited by
children who sing songs in order to receive *calennig*, a New
Year's gift, the play is based on dialogue between three characters: the owners of the farmhouse – Tomos and his wife
Sian – and their guest Dafydd. Tomos dismisses the fanciful
beliefs indulged in by the other two, particularly his wife,
who believes that luck will ensue if someone bearing a
particular name is the first to be seen on New Year's Day. Yet
Tomos was not averse to *calennig*; indeed, he contrasts the
children's practical request for gifts of food with the others'

[32] *Yr Ymofynnydd*, 1 (1847), 22–3.
[33] Anon., 'Eisteddfod Aberystwyth', *Yr Haul*, Cyfres Caerfyrddin, c.c., 9 (1865), 336–8. 337.
[34] G. W., 'Superstition', *Cambrian Journal*, 7 (1861), 42–4. 42.

ideas. Moreover, this patriarchal farmer defended the tradition as a way of ensuring that the poor acquire food. Sian,
on the other hand, expressed irritation at their nonsensical
verses and the amount of food they are being given. Dafydd
and Sian were warned that if they do not divest themselves
of their beliefs they will stand out like white crows among an
enlightened people.[35]

Instructive fictional examples were echoed at election time.
Figures of authority were locating aspects of Cardiganshire
in the past and calling for their removal. An address given by
John S. Harford at the Aberystwyth assembly room in 1849
contained the instruction that ignorance created by isolation
could be reduced only when all parts of the kingdom evolved
together. The prospective representative for the county's
borough seat extolled the benefits of 'free and congenial
intercourse with Great Britain'. Knowledge, Harford maintained, dispelled fear. Lightning that had always caused
alarm was now 'harmless, at the touch of Science, in the
form of electricity'. Accordingly, science was believed to free
mankind from fear of both the natural and the supernatural.
The reflections of this prospective MP were no doubt stimulated by the system of telegraphic communication that was
initiated and expanded rapidly in the first twenty years of the
period covered in this chapter. Communication was imperative, but distance combined with linguistic differences, both
pronounced in the case of Cardiganshire, impeded this flow
of information.[36] The eradication of other peculiarities, such
as forms of community justice, would surely follow closer
integration. Until then, however, the place and the majority
of its people would remain located in a gloomy past.

The potency of the county's location in the past lay in its
ubiquity. Bodies as well as beliefs could become a metaphor
for backwardness. This process of connecting bodies with
environments, that characterized some of the comments
made by early visitors of a Romantic disposition, was given
a bleaker aspect by a local physician, Richard Williams, in

---

[35] Ieuan Gwenog, 'Dydd Calan yn Ngheredigion', *Y Brython*, 3 (1860), 10–13.

[36] J. S. Harford, *Address Delivered in the Assembly Room of Aberystwyth on October 18th,
1849* (Bristol, 1849), p. 13. On p. 14, the need for English to be taught is stressed: 'In
Cardiganshire it is computed that only 3,000 persons out of 68,766 speak English.'

the late 1830s. His notebook, containing a blend of moral condemnation and suggestions for reform, epitomizes the professional classes' assessment of the county's less fortunate inhabitants. The doctor investigated childbirth in the northern part of Cardiganshire and noted how unremitting toil and the whim of the seasons led to people being physically moulded by their surroundings. After criticizing the rate of illegitimacy in Wales, and describing how barley bread dominated the diet, Williams gave a detailed picture of the peasant women. Females in the district start out as others – 'young women are well formed and not inferior in good looks to their English neighbours' – but they reverted to primitive, animal form through contact with agricultural work: 'the women grow up short with thick legs, strong muscular and coarse features'. Those who entered domestic work, where some knowledge of English was often required, retained 'their natural comeliness'.[37] It was only through removal from the 'drudgery' central to rural life that their innate womanliness could be maintained. A comely appearance came from securing positions in 'genteel families'. The comparison with 'English neighbours' is telling. Cultivation was epitomized by what was on the other side of Offa's Dyke. Achievement of potential on a national or individual scale came from something that was far removed from the ancient employments, beliefs and traditions that characterized the area.

FUTURE

Distinctions based on advancement or backwardness preoccupied contemporaries. Given that Cardiganshire was relatively isolated from currents of change compared with many other parts of Wales, there was, possibly, an added pressure on the county's inhabitants to be seen to take steps towards the widely accepted conception of the way forward. The importance placed on refuting common notions of the

---

[37] NLW, MS 12165E, R. Williams, 'Parturition in Cardiganshire', fo. 15. See Emyr Wyn Jones, 'Medical glimpse of early nineteenth-century Cardiganshire', *National Library of Wales Journal*, 14 (1965–6), 253–75, for a transcript of this manuscript and information about Richard Williams.

county's inherent backwardness is conspicuous in a report on the Cardigan Agricultural Society's annual exhibition of 1855. It was hoped that this demonstration of agricultural improvement would negate the 'oft-repeated sneer that Cardigan is a century behind every other town or locality in the Principality'.[38] This consciousness of others' opinions, in this case within a Welsh context, coloured the aspirations of many. It would be mistaken to assume that the location of the county in relation to the future noted in the preceding chapter was limited to those who wrote about it. Even so, the mid-Victorian heyday was a time of industrial expansion, which altered the nature of available comparisons. Representations of Cardiganshire touched on matters agricultural, industrial, educational, and the need to improve communications. Moving towards a relatively clearly defined future was of great import. Material advancement might come in the form of entrepreneurs and machines but, first, ideas about what constituted advancement needed to be diffused and adopted.

Aspirations for the county reflected comments made by Karl Marx when, in the 1860s, he surveyed Britain's industrial ascendancy and its influence on the rest of the world: 'The country that is more developed industrially only shows, to the less developed, the image of its own future.'[39] Likewise, many in and outside Cardiganshire sketched the county's future in the light of industrial and commercial activities in the southeast. Some commentators, therefore, emphasized the area's reputation as a mineral district. Lead extraction peaked in the years before 1870, so the claims were not over fanciful. They do, however, betray the influence of dominant interpretations of development. Opportunities to pronounce that Cardiganshire was 'a mining county' were eagerly grasped as this title added dignity and denoted a contribution to British industrial capacity. A subscription initiated by a school in the county for the families of those who died in the Hartley colliery disaster of 1862 prompted the comment that

[38] *CJ*, 10 August 1855, 3.
[39] Karl Marx, *Capital: A Critical Analysis of Capitalist Production*, ed. Friederich Engels, trans. Samuel Moore and Edward Aveling, 2 vols (New York, 1901), vol. 1, p. xi.

Cardiganshire 'as a mining county would naturally be considered forward in so laudable an undertaking'. Identification as a county with potential was even more explicit at times of celebration. Later that year, the planned exhibition of lead ores at the World's Fair in London by the company Messrs Taylor – 'whose successful enterprise in Cardiganshire mining is so well known' – was seen as grounds for pride in the county's products.[40] The 'thousands of visitors' viewing these 'splendid specimens' would be seeing a link between Cardiganshire and industrial progress.

For some a prosperous future depended on attracting people from beyond Cardiganshire's borders. This idea was not novel, but there was a growing interest in the seaside among the middle classes during the mid-Victorian era and it was hoped that the county's less well-known beaches would absorb part of this demand.[41] In 1852, 'a Cardiganshire man' condemned the 'shocking indifference of the Cardiganshire people to the improvement of their county'. He was incensed at the failure to exploit the commercial potential of numerous coastal villages, including Tresaith, Llangrannog and Aberporth. Less refined country folk were using these beaches, but this was part of the problem. These people were blocking a potential, more prosperous future. On arriving at these 'small healthy watering places' he found that they were 'frequented mostly by labouring people and farmers, and sometimes some of the better orders, but very few'. Improving the roads was the means whereby the plebeian local contingent could be replaced, or at least overlain. Similarly, a letter from 'A Tourist' recounted shock on finding that a place with such 'a fine share of sand' as New Quay had been so little known and contained 'a greater proportion of sailors among the inhabitants than you generally meet even in a seaport'. The reason for this situation could be found, the writer concluded, in there being only one appallingly neglected road leading to the place. To enhance the county's commercial fortunes a different kind of visitor would have

---

[40] *W*, 31 January 1862, 5; ibid., 21 March 1862, 5. Cf. *Cardiff and Merthyr Guardian*, 8 December 1855, 6.

[41] John K. Walton, *The English Seaside Resort: A Social History, 1750–1914* (Leicester, 1983), p. 25.

to be attracted by means of a substantial improvement of the roads.[42]

The theme of opening up an excluded area suffused accounts of the county in the press and even poetry. Both these sources intimate how people invested hope in the changes around them. Rees Jones (Amnon), from the south of the county, wrote 'Prophwydoliaeth y Baledwr' (The Balladeer's Prophesy), which appeared in a collection of his work published in 1848, four years after he died. It demonstrates the hold that anticipated headway in material matters had on the inhabitants of the county. In addition, it provides an example of how ideas about the future held by the less affluent differed from those who, for example, sought to refashion the beaches. Both broadly shared ideas about how Cardiganshire needed to develop, contact with the outside being key. However, Jones's vision, which included a number of radical political expectations, spoke of primary concerns, such as an extension of trade through the ports of New Quay and Aberaeron, and the possibility of a 'tram-road' to the former. Jones wanted the less wealthy to benefit from the cheaper coal that these developments were expected to bring, and hoped that they could then say farewell to the messier forms of fuel previously relied on such as gorse, ferns, peat and wood.[43] Those tangible benefits wrought by changes in technology and commerce, expressed in Jones's poem, were repeated over thirty years later in a report on the condition of female and child agricultural workers. In this, the agricultural labourers of the county found a champion in the person of J. Henry Tremenheere, a barrister and the younger brother of the prominent inspector and royal commissioner Hugh Seymour. Responding to complaints made by farmers about the poor 'efficiency' of Cardiganshire's agricultural labourers, Tremenheere wrote that this was due to a lack of sustenance, not to any deficiency of will. When employed in other occupations, such as building railways, their potential was fully realized.[44] This suggests that general symbols of

[42] *W*, 3 September 1852, 3; ibid., 27 August 1852, 3.

[43] Rees Jones (Amnon), *Crwth Dyffryn Clettwr* (Caerfyrddin, 1848), pp. 45–8, 47.

[44] BPP, XIII (1870), *Commission on the Employment of Children, Young Persons, and Women in Agriculture Third Report* (1867), p. 52.

progress, such as trains, could be related to the fortunes of groups at the lower end of the social scale. For some, a better future meant cheaper and cleaner fuel for warmth and light, or perhaps more money to buy extra food. These humble aspirations founded on fundamental needs meant that, to some extent, notions of improvement were common among different classes.

Before the arrival of the railway, there was anxiety that poor transport links between Cardiganshire and elsewhere would condemn the county's inhabitants to a limbo where opportunities would pass its inhabitants by. Opposition to this modernizing imperative was rare. A letter to the *Carmarthen Journal* in 1839 expressed support for a new road between Carmarthen and Cardigan, stating that it would benefit the sale of lime and coal in this 'now unfrequented country'. Cardigan town was so 'utterly isolated from all markets at present, that it might be said to be entirely secluded from the commercial world'. Less explicit fear about isolation can be perceived in the sense of relief that greeted the establishment of a regular steamer between Cardigan and Liverpool in 1841. Two benefits from this service mentioned in the account included the swifter procurement of goods from Birmingham and Manchester, and a means to travel from London via Liverpool in under twenty-four hours. Not everyone welcomed the arrival of goods from elsewhere, however. In 1845 there were complaints from tradesmen against the 'gentlemen ordering their tea, groceries, spirits, etc from England'. Such voices were rare, but this is unsurprising since such protestations would not have been in keeping with the general sense of jubilation that pervaded the press.[45]

Alongside expressions of the county's future potential founded on industry and communications was the complementary issue of education. This period was characterized by an increased awareness of the need to further educational provision, as exemplified by the tentative beginnings of state

---

[45] *CJ*, 22 November 1839, 3; ibid., 25 June 1841, 3; ibid., 24 January 1845, 3. Ship launches were significant social occasions drawing hundreds of spectators; see D. J. Davies, *Hanes, Hynafiaethau, ac Achyddiaeth Llanarth, Henfynyw, Llanllwchaiarn a Llandyssilio-Gogo* (2nd edn, Caerfyrddin, 1930), p. 78.

funding in 1833 and the symbolically significant establishment of a government Educational Department in 1856.
Education was to play a significant part in the canon of Welsh
cultural tendencies, and commentators who described the
mental landscape of Cardiganshire have magnified this. In
the period considered here, however, this trait had yet to
assume the symbolic presence it acquired during the latter
part of the century when education became one of the
brightest lights in the constellation of qualities associated
with the Cardi. Yet the emergence of education as a defining
attribute of the county and of rural Wales in general can be
seen by the middle of the nineteenth century. It could be
argued that this amounted to a compensatory mechanism
because at the time education and religion were desirable markers of a group's worth; both provided a civilizing
and progressive counterpoise to the primitive image of the
area. Whatever the reason, this value placed on education
nurtured positive representations, even among those who
had little sympathy for other Welsh characteristics.

Education and the promise of its rewards were used to
locate a group in relation to the future, primarily because it
led to greater engagement with the outside world. We need
to ask how this reputation was deployed in definitions of the
social world. Just as claims to be a mining county bolstered the
area's reputation by locating it alongside regions of material
progress, so education enhanced a place's standing culturally. Those interested in cultivating minds, such as the vicars,
solicitors, magistrates and chairmen of quarter sessions who
gave evidence to investigations carried out in the late 1840s
and 1860s, made judgements that were influenced by their
hopes and experiences. However, what matters most in a
consideration of the way a place and its people were located
is the way that these judgements were formulated and used.
On the whole, the witnesses presented an interpretation of
the county that impressed external inspectors who in turn
often invoked differences between rural and industrial Wales
or between Wales and other parts of the British Isles. Self-
definition as a forward-looking people was combined with an
external definition, and the latter provided a conduit for this
representation to be transmitted. An instance of the former

can be seen in the evidence provided by G. H. Thomas, a schoolmaster of a National School in the north of the county, to Tremenheere in the late 1860s: 'Welsh children . . . have a great desire to better their position, and their parents, particularly those residing in the agricultural districts, are very desirous of giving them the advantages of education.'[46]

Similar opinions had been voiced some twenty years previously to the Commission of Inquiry into the State of Education in Wales. John Hughes, a land agent, believed that 'the poorer classes have a strong disposition to learn', particularly in the more isolated inland districts. His points were similar to those made in other testimonies, including those from Aberaeron provided by a Calvinistic Methodist minister, a draper and a merchant that described how 'the people desire better education, and see the want of it more and more; many who send their children to sea are anxious that they should first learn to write. This feeling is increasing.'[47] The interest expressed in education by those intending to go to sea was repeated in *Yr Haul*, which reported, no doubt with some denominational self-satisfaction, the gratitude expressed by sailors for the education they had received at the National School established at Aberporth.[48] By cultivating sailing skills or learning English to enter domestic service, the individual previously wedded to less fruitful enterprises could multiply their opportunities. If female, they could become like the attractive figures identified by Richard Williams. Tradition did not feature strongly in the aims of education; cultural goods such as education were geared to personal and national progress.[49]

There were, however, elements of control amidst the good intentions of those who sought to provide education. Many reformers wanted to advance certain aims that, despite their coinciding with the aspirations of personal progress held by

[46] BPP, XIII (1870), 129.
[47] Ibid., XXVII (1847), 79, 80.
[48] M.T., 'Aberporth ac addysg', *Yr Haul*, c.c., 12 (1868), 389.
[49] For life chances and their role in social change, see R. Dahrendorf, *Life Chances: Approaches to Social and Political Theory* (London, 1979). One native of the county, whose brothers set up a school during this period, described a hunger ('newyn') for knowledge; see Ruth Jones, *Atgofion Ruth Mynachlog, sef Ruth Jones, Brynsilio, ger Synod, Ceredigion* (Llandysul, 1939), p. 10.

less influential people, included attempts to influence 'the patterns of thought, sentiment and behaviour of the working class'.[50] This is seen in comments made by Thomas Williams, a clerk to magistrates for the Lampeter Division in the late 1840s, that although 'farm girls' acquired good biblical knowledge at Sunday schools, their morality was none the better for it.[51] That said, images of a pious, though still far from ideal, population served another purpose. They could be located against others from outside the area who were deemed to have less of a penchant for learning. Jellinger C. Symons's opinions, published after his inspection of the state of education in the county, encapsulate this Janus-faced interpretation that chastised the somewhat rude inhabitants of Cardiganshire whose prospects were limited by the Welsh language, before contrasting them favourably with industrial populations. Although they were 'ignorant', they ardently sought education and 'their natural capacity is of a high order'. Symons then made a distinction between different parts of Wales when he remarked that these qualities of desire and natural ability were to be found 'especially in the Welsh districts'.[52] They were, to a degree, looking forward in this life and to the next.

It appears that the sole reason for observers locating potential in the population lay in the inhabitants' acquaintance with the scriptures. It was the provision of Sunday schools in the county that was given as the most likely explanation for scriptural knowledge, though these were often deemed practically worthless in implanting technical understanding. Notwithstanding this caveat, biblical knowledge displayed by the common folk impressed Symons. After attending a Calvinistic Methodist Sunday school in Aberystwyth, he wrote: 'The book of Deuteronomy would hardly have been selected in any other part of the kingdom as a subject of Sunday school reading.'[53] Such remarks, especially when made by those with influence, were important in constructing an impression of a

[50] Richard Johnson, 'Educational policy and social control in early Victorian England', *Past and Present*, 49 (1970), 96–119, 119.
[51] BPP, XXVII (1847), 75–6.
[52] Ibid., 65–6.
[53] Ibid., 154.

people with nascent potential. Their physical location, away from concentrations of population, and more importantly their religiosity, enabled both local and external inspectors to weigh up their potential and come to a positive judgement. Those corporeal embodiments of progress, namely industry and towns, might have lain outside the county's borders, but a cultural spring was detected within that beckoned development. This promise tied in with another location in which the county and its inhabitants were placed, that of being a centre of virtue.

CENTRE

Perceptions of Cardiganshire contributed to an image of the Welsh that gained prominence during the Victorian era. In the minds of many contemporaries, features that embodied Wales were identical to facets thought to typify Cardiganshire; often the two were taken to be synonymous. These were selective images, ones that gained a hold in people's minds because they corresponded with prominent themes in contemporary discourse. Apprehension about the state of morals and the prospect of disorder shaped the county's image and that of Wales. It could be said that the positive picture of the quiescent Welsh owed more to the observers' fears and prejudices than to any inherent goodness. Echoes of the earlier ideals that the romantically inclined found in the county's population can be detected, but prevailing concerns tailored the values located in Cardiganshire. Most notably, the middle classes were preoccupied with orderliness when they described places. They employed an orderly opposite to feared forces of disorder and immorality. This assemblage of symbolic opposites resulted in the desired and the undesired being given physical locations. Wales, of which Cardiganshire was taken as an exemplary part, was represented as the converse of urban concentrations. In order to distance these symbolic centres of orderliness, the dissonance between mental and physical locations evoked by the Rebecca disturbances, for example, had to be either eschewed or explained.

Prominent individuals, whose expressions could find a place in print, tended to endorse a specific idea of the county; a lyrical expression of this was provided by the radical Independent from Carmarthenshire, David Rees, who extolled the special, unembellished (*diaddurn*) style of religion that existed in Cardiganshire in an essay published in 1857.[54] Some idea of why the county was located at the centre of particular virtues can be discerned in comments made by the historian and Independent minister, Thomas Rees, before the Royal Institution of South Wales at Swansea in 1864. In an effort to tally the mental image of the Welsh as inherently well behaved with the behaviour of those living in the 'coal and iron districts', Rees noted the arrival of the Irish, English and Scots. In essence, what might geographically be in Wales was not wholly of it. To find the 'very commend-able habits' displayed by the native character, he averred, one had to look towards 'the agricultural districts' or areas where Welshmen constituted the majority of industrial work-ers.[55] Differentiation along these lines automatically imbued Cardiganshire with value as both a national and a moral centre. These sentiments mirror the beliefs and actions of Lady Llanover, a Welsh cultural nationalist and advocate of temperance who, in order to acquire native Welsh speakers, introduced people from the county to her Monmouthshire estate: a kind of cultural infusion as opposed to Thomas Johnes's earlier idea of an economic boost to Cardiganshire through the importation of Scotsmen. The opinions of Lady Llanover, who visited Aberystwyth in 1848 and noted how she enjoyed communicating with the Welsh-speaking population there, contributed to an accretion of educated opinion that favoured the area.[56]

Using respectability to categorize places served many purposes. Each contributed to the widely held perception of the county as superior to other places. It was periodically used to convey the calm of what had become the county's largest town, Aberystwyth. Even during the relatively quiet period between the strife of 1830–2 and the disturbances

[54] D. Rees, 'Taith yn Sir Aberteifi', *Y Diwygiwr*, 22 (1857), 8–15, 8.

[55] Thomas Rees, *Miscellaneous Papers on Subjects Relating to Wales by Thomas Rees, D.D.* (London, 1867), p. 14. Also see BPP, XXVII (1847), 63.

[56] Maxwell Fraser, 'Sir Benjamin and Lady Hall in the 1840s. Part II: 1846–1849', *National Library of Wales Journal*, 14 (1965–6), 194–213, 200.

that resulted from the rebuff to the Chartist petition in 1839, the peacefulness of this town was underscored in relation to other areas. In his New Year's speech heralding 1838, the mayor complimented the town's inhabitants for their 'good behaviour during the Christmas week' and stated that no town could compare to it in the whole United Kingdom.[57] As a resort town, the need to present an orderly image and to reassure visitors that the lower orders were not as bad as many may have conceived concerned municipal leaders. The local press aided them in this by, for instance, publishing a letter from a self-proclaimed tourist in 1837. After praising many features of the town, the author turned to what 'most arrested my attention'. This key attraction of the town was 'their [the 'lower classes'] moral conduct and peaceable demeanour'. The measure of this well-behaved popula-tion was two features that would be repeated in numerous depictions of what constituted a good common people, namely, work – 'mechanics and labourers [were] vigilantly at their work on week days' – and piety – 'on Sundays, in no place I have ever been at, have I seen divine worship so well attended'.[58]

More pressing was the occasional need to create distance from those troublesome activities near or in the county. Protecting an orderly image required considerable effort during the Chartist troubles in eastern Wales. This was espe-cially the case when the 12th (East Suffolk) regiment of foot left for Llanidloes in 1839. While at Aberystwyth, the *Carmarthen Journal* remarked, the troops behaved well. But on their arrival the 'respectable inhabitants' were said to have expressed surprise that the town was considered potentially dangerous. When they found that they were 'bent inland, every brow was restored to its wonted brightness'.[59] There was a comic element attached to the arrival of troops bound for Llanidloes that served to call attention to Aberystwyth's uprightness. The paper recalled how the troops were anxious, thinking that the crowd gathered to watch their

[57] *W*, 5 January 1838, 3.
[58] *CJ*, 1 September 1837, 3.
[59] Ibid., 17 May 1839, 3.

arrival at the quayside were Chartists.[60] The press employed similar distancing techniques during the Rebecca troubles four years later. It was stated that English newspapers tended to exaggerate the disturbances and that Aberystwyth was in a 'peaceable and well-ordered neighbourhood'.[61]

There were other changes in the way the county was located at the centre of moral worth founded on a preoccupation with the minds and actions of the working classes. The reputation of the county, and of others in Wales, for being peaceful had been expressed before. Yet growing onus was placed on the people themselves, whereas earlier accounts in newspapers tended only to praise those in authority for maintaining order. In 1833, the *Welshman* reported at length the compliments bestowed by the judge at the spring assizes at Cardigan. It is important to note the judge's location of the county as special even when compared with the rest of Wales. The county's character was enhanced by high-ranking individuals who concluded that Cardiganshire was a particularly law-abiding component of a lawful Wales, especially when worries about the condition of the working classes were widespread. On being met with no prisoner to try, the judge remarked: 'This seldom happens . . . I recollect one instance of this nature once happened in the county of Westmoreland . . . Your county forms a great contrast, even with the rest of this principality.'[62] Reports about the provision of education in the county also presented it as a peaceful part of the country.[63] Judges like Sir Edward Vaughan Williams who visited Cardiganshire, which was part of the Carmarthen assize circuit, contributed to the area's reputation with the following comments made after hearing that there were no prisoners for trial: 'This is the tenth year I have had the honour of being one of the major judges, and it is the first time such an event has occurred to me.' Praise was lavished on the county, especially as it had an increasing population and was experiencing greater economic activity than before. The press stated that this absence of serious crime demon-

[60] Ibid., 30 August 1839, 3.
[61] Ibid., 21 July 1843, 3.
[62] *W*, 22 March 1833, 3.
[63] BPP, XXVII (1847), 63.

strated 'the honesty and morality' of the lower orders that was 'highly creditable to the county; particularly when it is considered that Cardiganshire as a mineral and agricultural district is progressively developing itself, and it is generally at such a period that men violate the laws of the country'.[64] Cardiganshire had broken the assumed law that increased commercial activity and population growth led to increased criminal activity.

The lead miners in the north of the county, moreover, shared this respectable reputation. In 1865, a publication on the working classes in Wales proclaimed that the lead miners of Cardiganshire were literally a shining example for all other workers to follow. Although doubtless influenced by the fact that it was entered in an eisteddfod held at Aberystwyth, this contemplation of the condition of the labouring population demonstrates the instructive role that representations of the county's population played. Many of these miners, it was noted, hailed from surrounding areas, as craftsmen realized that they could earn more in this employment. Thus, the alien contingent was low. They were praised for their clean, tidy abodes and neat clothing. The author distinguished them from the miners and iron workers of south-east Wales, chiefly on the grounds that Cardiganshire's miners owned their homes. Workers in the south-east could more easily afford to buy their homes because they earned more, but chose not to do so.[65] Negative assessments of those employed in the coal and iron districts as being 'very improvident and extravagant in their habits' were also made in the *Cambrian Journal* at about this time.[66] Such comparisons, founded on perceived differences in behaviour between Cardiganshire and the south-east, would significantly contribute to the formulation of the image of the Cardi and give the impression of the areas being virtual polar opposites. A study of Manchester brickmakers during the 1860s noted how contemporaries portrayed them as a group existing on the lower steps of 'the

[64] *W*, 30 July 1852, 3.

[65] Ceredig (O. Ap Harri), *Y Dosbarth Gweithiol yng Nghymru* (Caerfyrddin, 1865), pp. 67–8.

[66] G. Edwards, 'Education in Wales and the proposal for founding a Welsh university', *Cambrian Journal*, 10 (1864), 73–104, 80.

ladder of civilisation'; this position was attributed to their not being 'integrated into Liberal society'.[67] By the same token, the miners of south-east Wales were ranked lower on this scale than the miners of Cardiganshire. These acts of location indicate the qualities that the middle ranks desired, particularly at a time when the working classes were yet to be formally included in the body politic.

General remarks about an area's morality were, at times, complemented by more detailed observations of the people. In these we see some of the details that went into making certain areas more likely to be deemed centres of worth than others: notably the perceived link between scarcity and morality suggested by the remark that, despite earning more, the workers of the south-east were less wise with their money than the home-owning miners of Cardiganshire. These judgements touched on concerns about the concentration of the working classes, the allurements of towns and the fallibility of human nature. They also overlooked contrary evidence. Yet, in doing so, they presented a powerful, easily absorbed image that carried weight. The picture of poverty presented by Thomas Turner in an account of a journey from Gloucester to Aberystwyth, privately published in 1840, captured the way in which dearth, industry and devoutness were combined in the minds of many observers. When travelling through Cardiganshire, Turner focused on things like shoddy dwellings, dung heaps, stagnant puddles and the intermingling of children, pigs and fowl. When seen around their homes, the inhabitants' dress matched the squalid surroundings. On Sundays, market days or holidays, however, 'the cottagers, especially the females, with their clean national costume, look neatness itself'. Turner evidently thought that these improvements in appearance were more than cosmetic and revealed the quintessence of these simple people because he added that they were not 'deficient in industry; an adult loiterer, either male or female, is hardly ever encountered'.[68] Contrasts between 'cheerful, hard feeding mountaineers' and the 'croaking consumers of beef, bacon, pudding, and

---

[67] Richard N. Price, 'The other face of respectability: violence in the Manchester brickmaking trade, 1859–1870', *Past and Present*, 66 (1975), 110–32, 110.

[68] Thomas Turner, *Narrative of a Journey . . . July 31st to September 8th, 1837* (London, 1840), pp. 30–1.

ale, in England' were made by Roscoe while travelling in Cardiganshire, and both sets of opinion indicate how food, mental outlook and work were woven together to form patterns of difference on which moral judgements were based and imparted.[69] The priority in any assessment was compliance with certain norms and any variation from these was overlooked in the effort to sculpt an ideal.

If religious observance provided a fount of respectability, then the findings of the 1851 religious census pertaining to Cardiganshire suggest that the county was full to the brim with this quality.[70] These findings were gathered against a backdrop of disappointment about the overall low level of seating and attendance, particularly in the urban areas of England. Small actions, such as that of the Cardigan ship owners who did not charge for carrying Bible Society Bibles, and the donations collected in the 'Bible Box' at the port, reinforced this positive impression.[71] Temperance, a cause that gathered pace from the 1830s, was also associated with the county. An account of mistaken identity published in the *Welshman* during 1844, and set 'in a Cardiganshire town', demonstrates how the press adopted and conveyed county images. Under the heading 'Father Matthew in Wales', it was noted that the Irish 'father of teetotallers' was due to arrive in the town, but a man bearing his likeness arrived before him and caused some consternation when he ordered whisky and a 'Havannah cigar'. A 'Cardiganshire town' provided an ideal 'dry' backdrop for a comical story about a 'wet' visitor: the epicure was a 'portly gent from one of the midland counties of England'.[72] In a county dominated by Calvinistic Methodists, who were 'by far the strongest advocates of temperance', it was not surprising that a correlation between the county and abstinence was formed. Three years prior to the mix-up over Father Matthew, twenty-eight chapels in the county switched to unfermented wine.[73]

[69] Roscoe, *Wanderings*, p. 45.

[70] For example, the county provided five of the thirty districts with the most religious accommodation in England and Wales. See BPP, LXXXIX (1852–3), *Census of Great Britain, 1851. Religious Worship. England and Wales. Report and Tables*, p. ccxcvi.

[71] *Y Drysorfa*, 22 (1852), 104.

[72] *W*, 31 May 1844, 2.

[73] W. R. Lambert, *Drink and Sobriety in Victorian Wales, c.1820–c.1895* (Cardiff, 1983), pp. 137, 123.

Cultural markers, such as those that differentiated the expectant abstainers from the weighty Englishman, also contributed to the establishment of distinctiveness and acquisition of value in south-east Wales. D. T. Alexander recalled that the 'servant girls employed at Aberdare in the fifties were Carmarthenshire and Cardiganshire girls, and nearly every one of them wore the old Welsh tall hat'. Contemporaries from the county took this item of clothing to be a marker of place, too, as E. Herber Evans, while an apprentice at a shop in Rhydlewis in the 1850s, wrote of 'the tall hats of Cardiganshire women'.[74] Others, however, recalled further markers drawn from conduct and bodily appearance that placed the Cardi at the centre of positive qualities. By this means they either symbolically marginalized other groups or simply elevated people from Cardiganshire. In these accounts, estimation as well as description is evident. An account of seasonal migrants employed in agricultural work in the Vale of Glamorgan included details of their piety, and remarked that 'the way of their living among us was a lesson in thrift' because they saved most of their earnings to take home. In order to save money they also walked to the Vale of Glamorgan instead of using the railway.[75] These acts, when interpreted positively, contributed to the commendable image of the Cardi. In the light of the relative affluence present in the observers' region and prevalent moral codes, practices born of poverty were interpreted in moral terms. Furthermore, the anonymous relater compared the west Walians with other seasonal workers from western England and Ireland. The 'Cardies', despite their habit of chewing tobacco in church, were contrasted favourably with the English whose bad language 'was not fit for ears polite'.

[74] D. T. Alexander, *Glamorgan Reminiscences* (Carmarthen, 1915), p. 39; H. Elvet Lewis, *The Life of E. Herber Evans, D.D. From his Letters, Journals, etc.* (London, 1900), p. 34. It was said that hatters from Cardiganshire 'produced most of the high hats worn in South Wales': Sir Leonard Twiston Davies and Averyl Edwards, *Welsh Life in the Eighteenth Century* (London, 1939), p. 8.
[75] A similar point about cheap travel was made about women carrying their clogs while walking to work in London during the early decades of the nineteenth century, in D. Edwardes, *Reminiscences of the Rev. D. Edwardes* (Shrewsbury, 1914), p. 17. For the saving rather than spending mentality of Cardiganshire farmers, see *C*, 8 February 1840, 3.

Unlike the Cardis, the English workers were said to visit taverns on Saturday nights and to make 'the roads hideous with their orgies'. The Irish were also cast in an unfavourable light. Unlike the west Walians, the Irish came over in families, the wives hatless and the children without shoes and whose feet 'would be torn and bleeding from treading the stubbles'. The remark about the hatless Irish women may indicate some of the significance placed upon the hats worn by females from west Wales. Debauched Englishmen and neglectful Irish provided two counterpoints for the careful 'Cardies'.[76] Prudent behaviour, similar to that of the agricultural seasonal migrants, was noted in 1840 by the ironmaster G. S. Kenrick, who detailed how workers from Cardiganshire returned with their earnings to their home county. The most significant feature of this piece, though, is the implicit association of the migrants' behaviour with what was thought typically Welsh. Kenrick declared that 'the Welsh are frugal' and illustrated this point with reference to the practices of the seasonal workers from the county. For many individuals of high social status, certain aspects of Cardiganshire conveyed an idea of Wales as a whole.[77]

Another point of contact with the iron districts that prompted distinctive representations originated with the farmers who delivered pig meat and butter to these areas in the mid-nineteenth century. A manuscript describing the 'Cardy carts' that, before the arrival of railways, visited towns in the industrial valleys during the early autumn and winter months illustrates the characteristics thought to define the 'Cardys' – another variant spelling of the name. As with the previous descriptions, money played an important role in this portrait. Exchange and retention of cash contributed as much as religion to many visions of the Cardi. Each of the carts was purported to have returned to west Wales with up

---

[76] *Glamorgan Gazette*, 18 August 1911, 5. The shock of marrying a slovenly woman is expressed fittingly from the perspective of a staid Cardi in a ballad, Welsh Folk Museum, Evan Jones Collection, 2035/78, T. M. Jones, 'Can newydd sef achwyniad Sion Morris Griffith y Cardi, o herwydd iddo briodi gwraig anrefnus'.

[77] G. S. Kenrick, 'Statistics of the population in the parish of Trevethin (Pontypool) and at the neighbouring works of Blaenavon, in Monmouthshire, chiefly employed in the iron trade and inhabiting part of the district recently disturbed', *Journal of the Statistical Society of London*, 3 (1840), 366–75, 370.

to £35. Yet these individuals were not marked out by money alone. The cart itself, with its light wheels and sides, the latter open with low upright turned rails, was 'foreign'-looking in Breconshire. The horse was also different: 'a Cardy horse was a breed of itself', which the author, the antiquarian John Lloyd, described as being 'light and slingy, fourteen hands or a little more in height, a good free walker, and capable of going long distances without tiring'. The author described the driver in a similar way. He was distinguished as being physically 'of that spare and lathy breed of men' found on the borders of Carmarthenshire and Cardiganshire.[78] Physical differences came hand in hand with an evident admiration for the Cardi's enterprise and determination.

Work was an important component in assertions of centrality. An account published in a Unitarian journal reveals how labour played a part in the symbolic competitions waged by people from different places. Most of the Unitarian's report was concerned with historical and literary matters; however, a brief allusion to the inhabitants of the county offered an opinion on the perceived character of the Cardi. After describing the tons of peat cut from Tregaron bog, lying ready to be taken home for fuel, the author remarked that they provided the medicine that helped the Cardis ward off colds. He then added that this showed the care they took to make things secure. This fleeting comment presages later portrayals of the cautious Cardi. Although not making any substantial generalization about the character of the population, it suggests vigilance brought about by a struggle with the elements. Perhaps more significantly, the author remarks that the scene before him, miles of peat drying on the hillsides, is something with which to counter the bragging of the Glamorgan men. This brief statement hints at the perceived pride of Glamorgan, a centre of Welsh industry and population at the time, and responds to it with an image of industry from peripheral Cardiganshire.[79] The rhetorical jostling between these counties reflected

[78] NLW, MS Maybery 1884, fo. 1. For contemporary accounts of the trade, see *The Silurian*, 22 October 1842, 2, and John Murray, *A Handbook for Travelers in South Wales and its Borders* (London, 1860), p. xxiv.

[79] Anon., 'O Lanbedr i Lyn Teifi', *Yr Ymofynydd*, 3ydd gyf., 1 (1868), 265–9, 267–8.

differences between them, particularly in the spheres of industry and wealth, that seeped into later representations.

MARGIN

By contrast, some articulations located Cardiganshire and its people on the margin of desired values. A number of these have been considered in the section that explored the ways in which the county was located in the past. Yet there were other means whereby the county could be slighted that were not expressed on a strictly temporal scale. Despite the county's physical location, far from the social tensions of industrial Britain, its representation was affected by what many commentators perceived to be deficiencies in the Welsh psyche. These shortcomings included a want of practicality and vigour or, as one contemporary scholar put it, a lack of 'foresight and perseverance'.[80] Perhaps these impressions stemmed from rural areas being distant from hives of industry, and the ability of the latter to capture the imagination of contemporaries, thereby forging their definition of work. Moreover, those who generally defended the moral reputation of the county acknowledged these features.[81] General perceptions of the Welsh as possessing less nous than the English were combined with concerns about the morality of the lower classes. Both interpretations appear to contradict the image of the hard-working Cardi and the religious environment of Cardiganshire. These accounts thus highlight the relativity of cultural locations. Particular experiences and concerns led to different images being emphasized; notions of industrious harvesters in the Vale of Glamorgan coincided with doubts about the determination of the Welshman. Despite this ambiguity, each particular location had unambiguous uses. What is more, some texts specifically criticized the county or a type of inhabitant that was often held to represent it. In these instances the faults identified were not those of the Welsh but of the Cardi. Notwithstanding the volume of positive comments, natives as

[80] NLW, MS 933, Thomas Stephens, 'The working men of Wales' (1852), fo. 189–90.

[81] For example, see Rees, *Miscellaneous Papers*, pp. 19–21.

well as outsiders occasionally mentally located Cardiganshire some distance away from positive values.

Macroscopic views that summed up Cardiganshire as a centre of moral worth need to be set against microscopic observations. The former sketched out an ideal invariably defined against groups or areas outside the county. The latter, however, reveal gaps that existed between generalizations about a moral county and specific concerns. This was not simply a contrast between a simplified image and a complicated reality. Those who reproached aspects found in the county were still selecting features and locating qualities, or their absence, in the population. They show how categorizing principles founded on mentality and morality led to the common people of Cardiganshire being figuratively distanced from standards set by moral arbiters. These acts of location were primarily motivated by a desire to reform and, while this study is not concerned with the institutional mechanisms whereby this regulation was enforced or attempted, it does point towards the 'other' within the county, that is to say, those whose actions did not match the predominantly pious and orderly depiction of Cardiganshire. Hence there were many who, despite residing in the county, were deemed to be not of it.

In 1849, the Society for Promoting Christian Knowledge printed an edifying biography of a man from Cardiganshire, David Lloyd of Hafod Fach. Yet this account of a pious individual, printed in both Welsh and English, did not reflect an idea of the county as a whole. It was, in fact, the tale of an exception: a Welshman who lived according to ideals spurned by most of his compatriots. To make his ways more attractive to the intended audience, Lloyd's affluence, attained after years of hard work, was stressed. He also cultivated his own garden – a commonly accepted indicator of industriousness. Part of this publication was directed at perceived deficiencies in the Welsh way of raising children. The protagonist, who enjoined obedience with the rod, presented a model that the Welsh, who were often heard asking their children if they would 'like' to do something instead of telling them, would do well to follow. In addition to this, the Welsh were exhorted to 'take care of their time' (*cymmeryd gofal o'ch amser*). During his life, Lloyd, who was said to be seventy-five years old at the time of publication, used every minute to advance his earnings and knowledge. Generally, though, time 'is sadly wasted by the Welsh'. This call to work harder corresponded to the image of the Cardi that was forming at the time in southeast Wales and in the minds of some travel writers. Still, E. W. Payne, the author of this tract and a Christian reformer whose other publications included a description of the Black Country, did not consider this a distinguishing characteristic of the county's inhabitants. Indeed, this rare female commentator's impression of the Welsh was applied to all parts of the country, including those who lived next to the model of Christian discipline promoted by this publication.[82]

It appears that the projection of a negative image of the Welsh onto the inhabitants of Cardiganshire permeated the thoughts of many educated people. At a time when Britain was vaunted as the workshop of the world, rural dwellers did not comply with ideas of efficiency. When compared with the epitome of a regulated workforce, many concluded that there was something lax about the Welsh. A decade after the virtual hagiography of David Lloyd was published, a contributor to the journal of the Cambrian Archaeological Association referred to the faults of the principality's natives in a manner reminiscent of E. W. Payne. Once more, the setting was Cardiganshire and a portion of the county was chosen as the embodiment of qualities thought absent in the surrounding area. Somewhat ironically, given the symbolic confrontations between the Cardi and the Irishman that were to feature in later instances of location, the exceptions in this case were the descendants of ancient Irish settlers who lived in the parish of Llanwenog in the south of the county. The 'restless energy' of these people was contrasted with the general 'apathetic and spiritless bearing' of their Welsh neighbours.[83] This antiquarian afforded a very different perspective of the natives of the Teifi Valley from those who saw characteristics like determination and enterprise embodied in the butter

[82] E. W. P[ayne]., *Memoir of David Lloyd of Hafod Fach, Cardiganshire* (London, 1849), pp. 6, 10, 18, 26, 30.

[83] D.J., 'The Gwyddyl in Cardiganshire', *Archaeologia Cambrensis*, 3rd ser., 17 (1859), 306–7, 307.

and bacon sellers who hailed from that area. Both, however, signify the pivotal role that assumptions based on productivity and endeavour played in the way groups were culturally located at this time.

As noted earlier, Symons praised the Welsh-speaking areas in his assessment of the educational state of the region he surveyed. The observations made by witnesses living in the county, however, identified an absence of desirable qualities in significant segments of the county. These were not so much blanket condemnations of the county as selective ones that identified bothersome components. In doing so, they were applying similar moral yardsticks to those who drew the broader geographical distinctions between counties or countries, the only difference being that these mental maps were on a smaller scale. Thomas Lloyd, from Cardigan, revealed distinctions within the county that highlighted those from 'remote places' who were naturally ignorant of biblical matters. Likewise, Joshua Davies, a schoolmaster from the same town, distinguished between the teachers in 'country places' and those in towns on the basis of his experience of children who had come to Cardigan from the interior of the county.[84] Some twenty years later, Tremenheere contrasted the upland districts with the towns in terms that reflected his and others' comprehension of what constituted beneficial work. Within the county there was a perceived divide between towns, where cultivated gardens were more prevalent and 'the wives of cottagers may be seen . . . carrying their baskets of vegetables and fruit to the market town or hawking them about from house to house', and the hill farms where the children led a 'wild and solitary life . . . among the hills in idleness and listlessness'.[85] From a consideration of these conceptual distinctions, it is evident that the county's towns were defined against more remote areas within the county where such qualities were lacking. This was a reversal of positions compared with many earlier accounts that commended those who lived in the uplands. Whereas urban concentrations of working people in other places sometimes provoked trepidation, Cardiganshire's small towns were understood to

[84] BPP, XXVII (1847), 82.
[85] Ibid., XIII (1870), 53–4.

benefit the county's social fabric. These comments reflect a belief in what has been described as 'the power of adjacent associations'. By their residing closer to the educated and cultivated, the manners and condition of the lower orders could be improved.[86]

There were some sections whose activities, rather than their indolence, aroused greater concern. The opportunities offered by a life at sea meant that sailors were still occasionally designated as a troublesome group within the county, though not to the degree that Warner and Evans suggested at the end of the eighteenth and early in the nineteenth century. While there were undoubtedly members of that group who conformed to respectable norms – as described in a study of the Aberaeron seafaring community – the brisk coastal trade offered an opportunity for those fleeing legal sanctions.[87] In 1851, one of the county's magistrates described 'a common practice' carried out by some young men. When these lawbreakers 'knew they were going to sea by the next tide', they would use the night of their departure 'to commit every kind of destructive and disgraceful outrage'.[88] These comments imply that such activities were common, and contrast with the praiseworthy reports given by visiting judges. Accounts of smuggling continued to feature in reports about the Cardiganshire coast as they had done in the early nineteenth century. The degree of conflict, from both the nature and frequency of reports, seems to have dissipated, however. In addition, the papers did not implicate as broad a spectrum of the county's population as before.[89] As smuggling declined, so one of the reasons for this maritime county's obtaining a marginal position in geographies of respectability faded. Besides, the margins of lawfulness were increasingly located in industrial centres.

---

[86] Joseph W. Childers, 'Observation and representation: Mr. Chadwick writes the poor', *Victorian Studies*, 37, 3 (1994), 405–32, 428.

[87] David Lewis Jones, 'Aberaeron: the community and seafaring, 1800–1900', *Ceredigion*, 6, 2 (1969), 201–42, 221.

[88] *W*, 18 April 1851, 3.

[89] *CJ*, 2 March 1849, 3, related that hundreds of people had collected wheat washed ashore from a sunken ship; ibid., 22 June 1832, 3, reported how smuggled alcohol injured legal traders.

Compared with the period discussed in the previous chapter, the lower orders were not perceived as such a threat. Even so, they were still seen by many of the middle classes as a problem. Instead of locating them away from lawfulness, they were depicted as existing in a behavioural realm remote from those standards which their social superiors expected. Accordingly, they needed to be guided, and encouraged to think and to act in particular ways. This stress on reforming activities came at a time when the lower orders were encouraged to discard superstitious ideas. The latter placed them in a negative past, while the former positioned them on the margins of morality. Both branches of this attempt to reform made use of the local press. Through their emphasis on a working population prone to immorality, these moral arbiters effectively located the majority of the county at some psychological distance away from moral fortitude. This was similar to the approach used by commentators who singled out the miners as spendthrifts, or the English peasant as a carping glutton. Concern was primarily directed towards the behaviour of women. The respectable element within the county set up a 'society for the promotion of morality among the lower classes' at Cardigan in 1850 that declared its intention not to employ any female as a domestic servant who was 'guilty of the gross immoralities unfortunately so prevalent in this country'.[90] After the magnetism of revivals had waned, movements away from chapel attendance in the county led to correspondents sketching scenes of trivial, though not depraved, activity. The reputation that the county had when viewed from a distance and compared with many other places was perceived by many within Cardiganshire who felt that their preferred cultural pattern was not being realized. The same worries about behaviour were replicated within the county, and given its reputation for religiosity they were perhaps given added emphasis. One person complained how the Whit Monday holiday in Cardigan had declined from a day in which many attended the 'Pwnc' (a competition that tested religious knowledge) in various chapels to one where people placed bets for ridiculous items like 'a bottle of pop'

[90] Ibid., 10 May 1850, 3.

at the pony races. In similar vein, a reporter from Lampeter depicted the town's peasants and mechanics as idling around the streets and villages. His suggestion for moral improvement was not attendance at chapel but 'manly' cricket.[91]

There were other ways in which the county's inhabitants could be figuratively put on the margin, some of which did not owe their origin to a respectable reforming schema. An example of scarcity being used to label the county is supplied by a conversation that George Borrow had after he had crossed into Carmarthenshire. On hearing a man welcoming him to 'Shire Câr', Borrow replied: 'I suppose you mean Shire Cardigan?'. He was corrected. 'Shire Cardigan! … no indeed; by Shire Câr is meant Carmarthenshire. Your honour has left beggarly Cardigan some way behind you.'[92] This comment provides a rare example of Cardiganshire's being demarcated by people living on the border.[93] Furthermore, such differentiation on the border reveals how cultural markers based on adjoining areas operated at the same time as those founded on contrasts with the south-east. Unfortunately, neither Borrow nor his acquaintances made any more of this definition of county characteristics. Yet it provides a clear case of the county being defined by its poverty.[94] Such distinctions were also touched on in the observation that 'the distance from which these materials are brought renders lime a dear article of manure to the farmers of Cardiganshire, so they

[91] Ibid., 1 June 1866, 5; ibid., 27 June 1845, 3.

[92] George Borrow, *Wild Wales* ([1862] Llandysul, 1995), p. 496.

[93] Lack of acquaintance with Welsh may explain why there was little more said about this image of Cardiganshire. Borrow could communicate in the language, but others met those who 'neither speak nor understand a word of English', Joseph Onwhyn, *Onwhyn's Welsh Tourist* (2nd edn, London, 1853), p. 128.

[94] An indication of how poverty came to define the county's inhabitants, and migrants from the county in particular, can be found in a comparison made between them and the rural poor who moved from Anglesey to mainland north Wales in the middle of the nineteenth century: W. J. Gruffydd, *Hen Atgofion* ([1936] Llandysul, 1964), pp. 35–6. That scarcity and simplicity were not always viewed as virtues, even among men of the cloth, can be seen in the comments made in a letter written in 1859 by Rowland Williams, then professor of Hebrew and vice-principal of St David's College, Lampeter, about 'a Cardiganshire service', in which the rural vicar used a 'pocket knife' to cut the bread: *The Life and Letters of Rowland Williams D.D. with Extracts from his Note Books*, ed. by his wife [Ellen Williams], 2 vols (London, 1874), vol. 1, pp. 392–3. A 'Cardy parson' who did not clean his 'hoofs' irritated W. Williams of Aberpergwm, NLW, Aberpergwm (1), 903, fo. 1.

use it very sparingly'.[95] Farmers in the east of Cardiganshire obtained their lime from Carmarthenshire, and this interaction conceivably contributed to their reputation for financial prudence. These practices imposed by environmental conditions contributed to a way of living sparingly that was then given symbolic form in the image of the mean Cardi and 'beggarly Cardigan', or a penny-wise and frugal figure in whom many positive values were located. In sum, actual conditions led to contrasting interpretations.

An awareness of financial gain among simple peasants clashed with the idea of Welsh generosity held by the traveller and fisherman John Henry Cliffe. Disappointed preconceptions about a people lead to them being vigorously judged by their own supposed standards. The setting for this loss of innocence was a wretched cottage, heated by turf and located in what Cliffe called the 'great desert of Wales' between Tregaron and Llandovery during the 1840s. The rude setting did not offend him; rather, he was upset on being asked to pay a sum of one and a half shillings for the bread and cheese his company had received. Cliffe related how they 'felt hurt and surprised at the demand, so contrary to the time-honoured observance of Cambrian hospitality'.[96] Some twenty years later, this same virtue was said to exist in the very hills where Cliffe's company had parted with their money.[97] Cliffe may have met the exception or have come across this acquisitiveness elsewhere, but this experience alludes to the picture of the parsimonious inhabitant of the county that was to surface in later representations of the Cardi. Distance from sought-after qualities, such as generosity, was identified by William Cobbett in the kind of people who lived in 'beggarly parts', namely pastoral, upland areas.[98]

---

[95] Samuel Lewis, *Topographical Dictionary of Wales*, 2 vols (London, 1833), vol. 1, p. y.

[96] John Henry Cliffe, *Notes and Recollections of an Angler* (London, 1860), p. 221. Like his brother, Charles Frederick Cliffe defined the county by its 'barren' hills: *The Book of South Wales, the Bristol Channel, Monmouthshire and the Wye* (2nd edn, London, 1848), p. 300.

[97] 'The inhabitants of these hills are remarkably kind hearted to strangers: it is a pleasure to them to do acts of kindness': John Rowlands (Giraldus), *Historical Notes of the Counties of Glamorgan, Carmarthen and Cardigan* (Cardiff, 1866), p. 87.

[98] William Cobbett, *Rural Rides*, 3 vols ([1830] London, 1930), vol. 3, pp. 880–1.

These behavioural distinctions founded on environmental conditions evidently contributed to negative portrayals, but caution with money was praised as frugality by most observers at this time. Female domestic servants in the county, for example, were chastised for not putting the money spent on 'gaudy tawdry dress' in the savings bank.[99] Prominent features on the mental maps of these casual but vocal inspectors were other failings of the human condition, such as a lack of religious attendance, illegitimacy, idleness and vanity. This reflected their interest in a respectable, sedate population. Nonetheless, we need to be aware of other ways in which the ordinary people of the county could be located on the edge, and the idea of close-fisted rural dwellers would, in time, overshadow the unrespectable in descriptions of the county that focused on its faults. Cardiganshire and the Cardis were different, but in a Wales whose population still included a large rural segment and a shared language, this particularity had not yet condensed into the type that took shape during the following forty years.

---

[99] *Aberystwith Observer*, 1 October 1859, 1; ibid., 8 October 1859, 1.

IV

DECLINE AND ELEVATION, 1870–1914

As symbols, Cardiganshire and the Cardi acquired greater prominence during the years covered in this chapter. Concurrently, Cardiganshire's population fell at a time when both the British and Welsh populations were increasing; this was the first decrease in residents since figures were recorded in 1801.[1] Between 1881 and 1891 the county's population plunged by almost 11 per cent – from 70,270 to 62,630 – while the same decade saw the Welsh population as a whole increase by 13 per cent. The coal valleys of south-east Wales attracted many from the county, and its own extractive industries declined. Long-standing comparisons between these areas thus acquired a new dimension. The comparison could be made on a wider scale as each census during this period indicated that Britain's population was increasingly concentrated in urban areas.[2]

Other trends altered the county's structure and heightened its distinctiveness. Coastal trade declined in the latter part of the nineteenth century; its partial nemesis, the railway, also facilitated the exodus. Yet the county's woollen industries waxed after the First World War; therefore, decline was not absolute. There was, however, a downturn in the county's agricultural sector in the final decades of the nineteenth century. Although this period is best known as a testing time

---

[1] J. W. Aitchison and Harold Carter, 'The population of Cardiganshire', in Geraint H. Jenkins and Ieuan Gwynedd Jones (eds), *Cardiganshire County History*, vol. 3: *Cardiganshire in Modern Times* (Cardiff, 1998), pp. 2–3. For an indication of Cardiganshire's age structure and that of its neighbours, see John Langton and R. J. Morris (eds), *Atlas of Industrializing Britain* (London, 1986), pp. 17, 19.

[2] John Williams, *Digest of Welsh Historical Statistics*, 2 vols (Cardiff, 1985), vol. 1, p. 12; C. M. Law, 'The growth of urban population in England and Wales, 1801–1911', *Transactions of the Institute of British Geographers*, 41 (1967), 125–43. Brief accounts of this movement can be found in J. Griffiths, *Profiad ar y Môr* (Tonypandy, 1908), pp. 11–17; Dan Jones, *Atgofion Llafurwr i Ieuenctyd Cymru* (Bow Street, 1956), p. 29.

for arable farmers, a decline in the prices of livestock, dairy produce and wool affected Cardiganshire's predominantly pastoral farms. Prices received in the mid-1870s would not be reached again before 1914.[3] Bleak language has been used to describe these circumstances.[4] In a diatribe against the rates charged by railways to carry local produce, for example, the *Cambrian News* described how local industries were 'gradually being exterminated'. Such interpretations support Fernand Braudel's assertion that progress, though 'marching with great strides throughout the land, turns out to have changed one *pays* more than its neighbour, or perhaps to have changed it in a particular way, creating a new difference which becomes a new cleavage'.[5] Railways, previously a harbinger of progress, became another reminder of peripherality.

Alongside these economic and demographic changes, others of a cultural and political nature contributed to the county's symbolic standing. Some symbols were, however, passing away or being challenged. Anxieties were expressed about the county's ability, given the drop in agricultural prices, to maintain its reputation for breeding fine horses. Others mourned the loss of Cardiganshire's title as the foremost pig producer in Wales. But at the time this obituary to past eminence was being composed the county assumed leadership in a number of cultural, non-agricultural, contexts.[6] A university college was established at Aberystwyth in 1872. In its first eight years this college received some 313 students, 117 of whom came from Cardiganshire.[7] Five interme-

---

[3] David W. Howell, *Land and People in Nineteenth-Century Wales* (London, 1977), pp. 8–9. Also see J. Llefelys Davies, 'The diary of a Cardiganshire farmer, 1870–1900', *Welsh Journal of Agriculture*, 10 (1934), 5–20, 20.

[4] David Jenkins, '"Cardiff Tramps, Cardi Crews": Cardiganshire shipowners and seamen in Cardiff, c.1870–1950', *Ceredigion*, 10, 4 (1984–7), 405–29, 421; *Y Brython Cymreig*, 20 May 1892, 2–3.

[5] *CN*, 2 January 1885, 4; Fernand Braudel, *The Identity of France*, vol. 1: *History and Environment*, trans. Siân Reynolds (London, 1988), p. 41. For other changes in the county's make-up during this 'remarkable and traumatic period', see Gareth Williams, 'The disenchantment of the world: innovation, crisis and change in Cardiganshire c.1880–1910', *Ceredigion*, 9, 4 (1980–3), 303–21, 317.

[6] *CN*, 11 March 1881, 2; *CTA*, 9 June 1899, 5.

[7] Henry Austin Bruce, *Lectures and Addresses by the Right Hon. Henry Austin Bruce* (London, 1901), p. 345.

diate schools were established in the county in the ten years after the Intermediate Education Act of 1889. It was largely through these institutions that the county developed its reputation for learning. At the same time, the enfranchisement of a section of the population, mainly tenant farmers and farm labourers, after the Representation of the People Act of 1884, combined with the introduction of the county council in 1889, secured a Liberal hegemony that became another of the county's most identifiable characteristics.

Anthony P. Cohen has noted the way in which decline and integration are converted into symbolic forms that stress difference.[8] It could be argued that during the period covered by this chapter the county was elevated symbolically as it declined and altered structurally. While Cohen was interested in the ways in which symbols defined small-scale communities, the concern here is how the county was used symbolically in argument and in contrast with other places. At this time, the county attracted more interest from within and outside Wales because it could be evoked as being different from the world into which it was being increasingly drawn, thereby becoming a valuable tool of dissimilation. Earlier contrasts were accentuated by the growing number of English speakers in south-east Wales, particularly from the turn of the century onwards. Additionally, a more positive interest was being taken in traditional custom. This appears to have been a reaction to those modernizing forces encouraged earlier in the century. Moreover, the extension of the franchise led to ruminations about what constituted a good citizen.[9] For various reasons, people were making use of the county as never before, and they had a greater range of media by which to do this. In tracing shifts in location during this period, there is less dependence on travellers' accounts, a limited press or solely denominational publications.

---

[8] Anthony P. Cohen, *Symbolic Construction of Community* (Chichester, 1985), p. 44.

[9] At the start of the twentieth century the number of Welsh speakers is estimated to have fallen to below half of the population for the first time; see J. Aitchison and Harold Carter, *A Geography of the Welsh Language 1961–1991* (Cardiff, 1994), p. 41; Richard Dawson, *The British Folklorists: A History* (London, 1968), pp. 392–441; Julia Stapleton, 'Political thought and national identity in Britain, 1850–1950', in Stefan Collini, Richard Whatmore and Brian Young (eds), *British Intellectual History, 1750–1950: History, Religion and Culture* (Cambridge, 2000), pp. 245–69, 245.

This phase in the county's representational history was distinguished by the development and establishment of a local press. The *Cambrian News* and the *Cardigan and Tivyside Advertiser*, both of which originated in the 1860s, enlarged to meet the needs of the county's literate and enfranchised population. The *Welsh Gazette* and *Y Cardi* joined them in 1899 and 1902 respectively. Through their reports, editorials and letters, these papers provide examples of how the county and its inhabitants were mentally located. In addition to these internal representations of the county there were those originating outside the area, such as government reports, travel accounts and national newspapers. On the Welsh level, there was a burgeoning cultural nationalism, many of whose exponents found the rural areas a suitable canvas for their ideas. This was expressed in publications such as *Wales* and the *Red Dragon*. These perspectives imbued the area with symbolic worth and demonstrate how those in positions of influence continued to evoke the county. Concluding this chapter at the commonly used watermark of 1914 does not signify that this date constituted a radical break in the area's representational history. However, the interwar years saw a realignment in Wales and the British Isles. Contrasts between the county and other places continued in nature but a heightened class element, among other things, added a new layer to the palimpsest of representations.

NAMING

Travel writers began to use the term 'Cardi' specifically in the late nineteenth and early twentieth centuries. Why the Cliffes and Borrow, for instance, did not mention the Cardi, but later writers from around the turn of the twentieth century did so, is puzzling. Natives of Cardiganshire had found a new role in visitors' accounts. They had been delineated from the end of the eighteenth century, but now they were becoming a type. Increased migration from the county may well have heightened awareness of this particular group. Yet the Cardi figure satisfied precise needs. True, migration would have made the Cardis and their characteristics better known, but it was the selection of precise features for varied ends that enabled the name to gain currency. In representations, naming signified a personalization of a hitherto varied population. Whereas before the mountaineers, peasants, seamen and scholars had been tinted with difference but not banded together in accounts of erudite visitors, now the Cardi began to be used as a term that supposedly encompassed the entire population. Many of the qualities previously identified, such as frugality and religious adherence, were still coupled with the Cardi type. Yet outsiders were using the people of Cardiganshire far more explicitly than before; naming defined them against what lay beyond.

The use of the term in print by the Welsh and the people of Cardiganshire themselves also increased. In 'Cofion Cardi' (A Cardi's memories), a comparison between neighbourhood physicians, who used traditional remedies, and professional medical practitioners of the twentieth century favoured the former. This typifies how Cardi ways were a shorthand for a preferred past. Indeed, six years after these memories were published, a struggle took place between two brothers from Cardigan, who used herbs to treat cancer sufferers, and sceptical medical authorities.[10]

In Lampeter, at the beginning of the twentieth century, an ostensibly local paper entitled *Y Cardi* was established. A list of distributors identifies those who, by buying the paper, in all likelihood defined themselves as Cardis. Not surprisingly a number of these subscribers lived in places such as Dowlais and Tonypandy in Glamorgan that had attracted many migrants from Cardiganshire. The paper demonstrates attachment to a name and implies that a bond existed between people from the county when they were in a new environment. Contributors to newspapers and journals were more likely to use the name, too. There were variations, like that made by a correspondent to the *Welshman* in 1882 who used the nom de plume 'North Cardi'.[11] On its own, the prevalence of the name does not tell us much about how the

[10] Cardi, 'Cofion Cardi', *Y Geninen*, 19 (1901), 191–4, 192, 193; T. Llew Jones and D. Wyn Jones, *Cancer Cures or Quacks? The Story of a Secret Herbal Remedy* (Llandysul, 1993), pp. 19–20.

[11] *Y Cardi*, 3 January 1902, 2; *W*, 11 August 1882, 5. Also see Allen Raine, *A Welsh Witch: A Romance of Rough Places* (London, 1902), p. 248.

Cardi was mentally located. This is to be found in the layers of meaning applied by both the natives of the county and outsiders. Increased use of the name means that more acts of location can be traced and related to one another.

Ways in which the name could be used and received can be seen in three examples from the closing decades of the nineteenth century. Two of these originated on the border with Carmarthenshire, the area that spawned the seasonal migrants and traders originally christened Cardis by the inhabitants of south-east Wales. A meeting to investigate the 'Welsh Fasting Girl', Sarah Jacob, was opened by a north Walian, John Griffith, who stated that 'he was not a Carmarthenshire man, nor was he a "Cardi" (laughter)'.[12] This amusement expressed by the thirty or forty farmers and tradesmen assembled at the Eagle Inn, Llanfihangel-ar-Arth, indicated the humorous connotations of the word. At a time when printed sources do not offer a surfeit of jokes, such glimpses indicate that the term had a humorous aspect before the jokes arrived in printed form. Also, this occurrence offers a far sharper definition of the name – that is, one that was founded on county borders – than that applied by the inhabitants of the south-east, as noted in the last chapter.

Familial pride in the achievements of fellow Cardis can be seen in an 1893 newspaper report from Llandysul: 'Cardis to the front! The president of the international Unitarian Congress at the world's fair Chicago, will be the Rev. Jenkin Lloyd Jones, a native of Llandysul.'[13] This use of the term when a native of the county achieved something of significance in the wider world is important. The nickname focused on the county and reflected onto it the success of the individual. The use of Cardi as a term by another expatriate can be seen in the diary of Joseph Jenkins. While he sojourned in Australia in 1880 he looked for gold with 'David Evans, and another Cardiganshire man, David Jones'. The latter sent a few specks of gold back home and composed a humorous *englyn* that began 'Tri Chardi'n chwilio'r aur' (Three Cardis

[12] Robert Fowler, *A Complete History of the Case of the Welsh Fasting Girl* (London, 1871), p. 36.
[13] *CJ*, 17 February 1893, 8.

looking for gold).[14] The name communicated fellowship, pride and humour. Yet it was not the only means by which natives of Cardiganshire were distinguished.

At events, prominent individuals often used the term 'Cardiganshire man'. Reasons for this being preferred to Cardi may lie in the more formal nature of these occasions, suggesting that those of higher status shied away from a word with common associations. During St David's day celebrations at Aberystwyth in 1879, the Revd T. A. Penry considered 'it a great honour that the Bishop was a Welshman, and, moreover, a Cardiganshire man (hear, hear, and applause)'.[15] He was referring to the bishop of St Davids, William Basil Jones, who was born in England to an English mother, but whose father was from Llangynfelyn, Cardiganshire. Fourteen years later, the politician Sir George Osborne Morgan voiced similar pride at an indirect relationship with the county when, during the unveiling of Henry Richard's statue at Tregaron, he stated that his own father was 'a Cardiganshire man'.[16] There was kudos in claiming some association with a county renowned for its religiosity and Liberal political tradition. These associations further amplified this image, which matched the aspirations and value systems held by many contemporaries. The reasons for the importance accorded an area can be found in a consideration of those who bore or emphasized its name. In the following sections the constitution of this symbolic weight and the purposes it served will be examined.

PAST

The persistence of traditions became the more noticeable by their decline elsewhere; deep-rooted beliefs were also less likely to be deemed a threat to the well-being of society. A change in the perspectives of observers and a reduction in the role played by these beliefs in the lives of people led to major changes in the county's location. Moreover, features

[14] Joseph Jenkins, *Diary of a Welsh Swagman*, ed. William Evans (Victoria, 1975), p. 100.
[15] *W*, 7 March 1879, 3.
[16] *CJ*, 25 August 1893, 8.

other than old customs linked the area to a positive past. Characteristics of the social world, such as personal interaction in trade or certain foodstuffs, took on symbolic stature. Taken together, these diverse traditions gave the county a reputation for preserving the old and representing Wales that was itself frequently defined in terms of the past.

People interested in customs were eager to identify those places in which they continued. In 1871, Mary Curtis, a governess and landscape painter from east London who spent time on the Carmarthenshire coast, published a description of folk customs. Like many during this time of increased urbanization, Curtis recorded folk customs because she felt they were becoming extinct. She noted that, although the traditions were passing away, some areas were less prone to this decline than others. She was especially interested in wedding traditions and noted how 'in Cardiganshire the old wedding customs are thoroughly kept up'.[17] Given its reputation for holding onto old ways, the county could either be described as backward or hailed as an important counterweight to ongoing change elsewhere, as seen in a letter to the *Cambrian News* in 1877. After detailing encroaching metropolitan influences in the county's coastal towns – that included 'recent importations of cockney slang' – the author called on Welshmen to 'protect the youth of old Cymru [Wales]' from corruption.[18] Traditions, including the way people spoke and acted, were being threatened. 'Old Wales' served as a symbol against the multitude of changes and Cardiganshire provided a good example of this psycho-geographical concept.

Even belief in the supernatural was viewed positively. This significant shift can be seen in a collection of folklore published by the traveller and linguist Jonathan Ceredig Davies. Davies observed that fairy lore had 'almost died out in those districts which I visited . . . though I found a few new fairy stories in Cardiganshire'.[19] It is noteworthy that a place could produce fresh material for this collector; it seemed that a crucial component of the past lived on there.

[17] Mary Curtis, *The Antiquities of Langharne and Pendine* (London, 1871), p. 76.
[18] *CN*, 18 May 1877, 2.
[19] Jonathan Ceredig Davies, *Folklore of West and Mid-Wales* (Aberystwyth, 1911), p. vii.

Cardiganshire's relative remoteness insulated it from the breezes of modernity. The advance of rationality, promulgated in the mid-nineteenth century, was not called upon to banish traditions as it had been earlier. Expatriates contributed to this valorization of tradition that, in turn, enhanced the county's image.[20] Fear that distinctiveness would be sacrificed through advancement motivated these efforts to conserve.

Certain entities and objects associated with the county did not have to be particularly old in order to gain significance. Some had been commonplace barely half a century earlier, but owing to substantial alterations in the social fabric they acquired added meaning. Cardiganshire was deployed to counter the less salubrious aspects of modernity. The latter were often embodied in urban lower classes, such as the 'London hucksters and their coarse sons and stupid wives and daughters', who were castigated by antiquarians visiting south-eastern Cardiganshire in the 1870s. They expressed relief that such characters had not yet penetrated this sanctuary where locals immersed in folklore catered for their needs.[21] The dependable, traditional sons of the soil may also have served to offset those organized, restless rustics who, from the 1870s, were turning to Unionism.[22]

The 'Welsh character sketches' series, mainly written (under the pen-name Ap Adda) by Charles Wilkins, the Gloucestershire-born author of a history of Merthyr Tydfil and founder of the *Red Dragon* journal, exemplifies how people with particular interests adopted a place and its inhabitants, using them as a piece on an ideological chessboard. The journal, published in the rapidly expanding coal metropolis of Cardiff, which gained city status in 1905, focused on south Wales and drew its contrasts to change from rural areas, notably Cardiganshire. In sum, it encapsulated the interest shown by late nineteenth-century British commentators, such as W. H. Hudson, in 'survivals from

[20] NLW, MS 15467C, Minute book of 'Cymdeithas Genedlaethol Cymry Manceinion', 1900–11, fo. 84 [1906].
[21] W. G. Smith, 'A holiday in Cardiganshire', *Bye-Gones*, 4 (1878–9), 111–12, 111.
[22] R. Jefferies, 'The labourer's daily life [1874]', in R. Mabey (ed.), *Landscape with Figures: An Anthology of Richard Jefferies' Prose* (Harmondsworth, 1983), pp. 40–63, 48.

a rural past'.[23] Such interest in the roots of a nation often betrays concern about modern-day pests attacking its leaves. The *Red Dragon* included portraits of a 'Cardiganshire butterman' and the 'Cardiganshire herring dealer'. It related how the former fell victim to the railways and the 'commercial traveller'. Yet, thanks to the railway, some Cardiganshire people settled down to open a shop in the valleys, thus 'leavening the village race of mixed nationalities with the bluff and sturdy Cardiganshire element'. This interest in healthy rural stock introduced to urban areas reflected apprehensions about racial degeneracy and the debilitating effects of urban life.[24] It also exhibits how contemporary beliefs were asserted in 'nostalgic' pieces. Wilkins's sketch of the fish dealer, whose booming voice echoed the sea where he earned his livelihood, equated health with denizens of this predominantly rural county.[25] In these sketches, enterprising, relatively recent, healthy alternatives to urban decay are presented. Above all, they were personifications of individuals and individualism, grounded in tradition and counteracting impersonal, modern forces. The concluding comment about the butter dealer contrasted his leisurely manner with the 'commercial' trader 'who sends his goods by rail, and a vast amount of business is done without any representative at all, simply by letter and telegram'.[26] This commemoration was a symptom of alienation from face-to-face contact with the producers of goods. Such topics, from degeneration to modes of purchasing goods, anchored the county in a positive past.

There were similarities between the ideas of the Arts and Crafts movement and some uses of the county. While the vernacular traditions of Cotswold locksmiths and furniture makers charmed this English movement, rural crafts

[23] Paul Rich, 'The quest for Englishness', in Gordon Marsden (ed.), *Victorian Values: Personalities and Perspectives in Nineteenth-Century Society* (London, 1990), pp. 211–25, 218.

[24] Ap Adda, 'The Cardiganshire butterman', *Red Dragon*, 2 (1882), 160–2, 162; Daniel Pick, *Faces of Degeneration: A European Disorder, c.1848–c.1918* (Cambridge, 1989), p. 209. Also see T. F. Tout, 'Welsh shires: a study in constitutional history', *Y Cymmrodor*, 9 (1888), 201–26, 217.

[25] Ap Adda, 'The Cardiganshire herring dealer', *Red Dragon*, 5 (1884), 76–8, 77.

[26] Ap Adda, 'Cardiganshire butterman', 162.

in Cardiganshire attracted similar sentiments in Wales. A theme running throughout the 'Welsh character sketches' was the praise of home industry, small-scale craft trade and shops as set against mechanical, large-scale production. Wilkins observed that the 'old Welsh stocking knitter' with her independent industry was to be found in Caron parish, Cardiganshire. Like the other sketches by Wilkins, individual craftsmanship was a victim of fashion and the 'assimilation of English' practices.[27] Modest shops in the county were also praised and used to criticize larger-scale retail enterprises across the Atlantic. The Revd Owen Griffith, who from 1889 edited a Baptist monthly in the USA called the *Day Light*, visited Wales in the 1880s. His home, Utica, New York, was the location of F. W. Woolworth's first shop in 1879, and this may well explain Griffith's comment about a small shop in Llandysul, 'Mae siopau hen-ffasiwnol yn llawer mwy dymunol na rhai ysblenydd diweddar' (old-fashioned shops are much more pleasant than the splendid recent ones).[28] During this period many aspects of Welsh life, such as small shops, were deemed to represent the past and the county provided a superabundance of these.[29]

Types of food thought to exemplify the past merged into the county's image. These were common in rural parts but came to be especially connected with Cardiganshire in many minds because of its predominantly agricultural character. Food had distinguished the area in earlier periods, but only at a time when the intelligentsia were exalting familiar national roots were simple dishes complimented instead of being located at the margins of culinary taste. The reputation that the county acquired for making *cawl* (a meat broth, usually of bacon or dried beef with vegetables) was particularly noticeable. Nothing could have been as far removed from cultivated affectedness than what was, in effect, a main course in the form of soup. Against a backdrop of substan-

---

[27] Ap Adda, 'The old stocking knitter', *Red Dragon*, 5 (1884), 271–3, 272. Some of these characters appeared in an earlier publication by Charles Wilkins, *Tales and Sketches of Wales* (Cardiff, 1879), pp. 252–5.

[28] Owen Griffith, *Naw Mis yn Nghymru* (Utica, 1887), pp. 178–9.

[29] Wirt Sikes, *Rambles and Studies in Old South Wales* (London, 1881), pp. 202–3; *Bye-Gones*, 8 (1886–7), 139; *Encyclopaedia Britannica*, 29 vols (Cambridge, 1910–11), vol. 5, pp. 320–1.

tial increases in the importation of food from the 1870s, however, this dish attained almost totemic status. It was called 'the Cardiganshire dish' in one man's memoirs and A. G. Bradley thought it 'a Cardiganshire speciality'. An idea of why so much value was placed on this meal can be detected in the comments made in the second report of the Royal Commission on Land in Wales and Monmouthshire, published in 1896. Witnesses before the commission noted how the less wealthy inhabitants of Cardiganshire depended on this broth. Converting a source of sustenance born of necessity into something imbued with extra social meaning, the report remarked how 'the art of making an excellent soup is not yet extinct' in Cardiganshire despite its unfashionable status among the Welsh middling sorts. This link between the county and food was one of many ways by which the county became known as a cultural *Pura Walia* towards the end of the nineteenth century, a time when changes in available food and the means to procure it were redefining the symbolic value of many victuals. Indeed, what was seen as a Cardiganshire dish in this period soon assumed status as a Welsh dish, thus effecting a transition from regional to national reputation similar to that experienced by the Yorkshire pudding.[30]

A bond between traditional foods and the county could, however, lead Cardiganshire to acquire a negative as well as a positive timbre. The 'bwyd plaen' (plain food) was not eulogized by all. Given that the weight of opinion about Cardiganshire's pastness was largely positive, it is important to remember that contrary readings, the result of comparisons with other sorts of food, existed. The biography of the renowned Independent minister Kilsby Jones contains

[30] For figures on food importation, see Peter Mathias, *Retailing Revolution: A History of Multiple Retailing in the Food Trades based upon the Allied Suppliers Group of Companies* (London, 1967), pp. 30–1; David Williams, *Y Wladfa Fach Fynyddig* (Dinbych, 1963), p. 76; A. G. Bradley, *Highways and Byways in South Wales* (London, 1903), p. 248; BPP, XXXIV (1896), *Second Report of the Royal Commission on Land in Wales and Monmouthshire* (London, 1896), pp. 633, 636; see Jennifer Stead, 'Prodigal frugality: Yorkshire pudding and parkin, two traditional Yorkshire foods', in C. Anne Wilson (ed.), *Traditional Food East and West of the Pennines* (Edinburgh, 1991), pp. 143–86. Different valuations of barley and white bread in the last decades of the nineteenth century are noted in Hettie Glyn Davies, *Edrych yn Ôl: Hen Atgofion Bentref Gwledig* (Lerpwl, 1958), p. 22.

a reference to 'caws Cardi' (Cardi cheese). Such was the solidity of this cheese, it was credited with preventing beer getting to the heads of Kilsby and his fellow students from Neuadd-lwyd, near Aberaeron. This kind of cheese, dry, hard and made from skimmed milk, was also called farmer's cheese – presumably because the more profitable cream would have been sold.[31] Butter from the district was referred to in less than complimentary terms, too. Articles by a farmer cautioning fellow farmers in west Wales not to over-salt their butter were published in the press. In fact, the area seems to have earned a reputation for this practice and the arrival of foreign butter at more reasonable prices led to a decline in its consumption among the 'gwŷr Morgannwg' (men of Glamorgan) who now had an alternative to the salty and expensive product from the west. The butter market consequently declined and became another illustration of past practices. For some, it was emblematic of a time when consumers were obliged to comply with the mercenary profit-making motives of the farmers, who reputedly stored butter over the winter to sell in the spring when the product was scarce and expensive.[32]

Given these frequent acts of locating the county in relation to the past, it was not surprising that the area found itself defined by the past in fiction. The popular novels of Allen Raine, and equally importantly the responses to them, encapsulated the prevailing image of Cardiganshire. They also reveal those forces against which it was defined. Born in Newcastle Emlyn, on the Carmarthenshire border, Raine, the daughter of a solicitor, later moved to England. Most of her novels, such as *Where Billows Roll*, based on her prize-winning essay at the 1894 Caernarfon eisteddfod, were set

[31] Dan Davies and William Thomas Hughes, *Atgofion Dau Grefftwr* (Aberystwyth, 1963), p. 9; John Vyrnwy Morgan, *Kilsby Jones* (Wrexham, 1897), pp. 185–6; Huw Jones, *Cydymaith Byd Amaeth*, 4 vols (Llanrwst, 1999), vol. 1, p. 210; BPP, XXXVII (1894), *Minutes of Evidence taken before the Royal Commission on Land in Wales and Monmouthshire*, vol. II (London, 1894), p. 332. Another reference to 'Cardiganshire cheese' can be found in John Griffith, 'Daniel Rowlands of Llangeitho', *Red Dragon*, 2 (1882), 1–8, 2. The inhabitants of the county were also named after this product; see Huw Evans and Marian Davies, *'Fyl'na Weden I': Blas ar Dafodiaeth Canol Ceredigion* (Llanrwst, 2000), p. 44.

[32] *W*, 14 March 1879, 6; J. Islan Jones, *Yr Hen Amser Gynt* (Aberystwyth, 1958), p. 47.

in little seaside villages, modelled on the village of Tresaith where she spent part of her life. The role that Cardiganshire's past location played in her books is conveyed in a scrapbook containing reviews and letters published in newspapers from 1897 to her death in 1908. Raine herself wrote that 'modern ways are beginning to rob life of its romance and picturesqueness even here'. A reviewer noted that 'here we have a rural Wales that is slowly passing away', while others stressed the 'simple lives of the Cardiganshire peasantry'. A large part of her success – over two million copies of her novels had been issued by 1909 – was due to her settings being so easily associated in the public mind with the past when there was so much concern about its passing. This symbolic union, which found its conduit in Raine's stories, was moulded by feelings of unease in the face of 'modern ways'. Such tendencies influenced definitions of Wales, and further embossed Cardiganshire with a mark of genuine Welshness. In a letter sent in 1906 to the collector of folklore Jonathan Ceredig Davies, Princess Sapieha asked him to 'put together all the old customs and superstitions of Cardiganshire. It is the most truly Welsh part of Wales, and it is such a pity they are not put down.' This rather exotic enthusiast for the county developed her interest through her first marriage to one of the county's major landowners, the fifth earl of Lisburne. Her comment indicates how conceptions of region and nation intersect.[33]

The county was a useful backwater where features previously considered backward were praised as traditional. This happened only after Cardiganshire had been shorn of the unsettling or threatening aspects of the past. Yet this was only one of the myriad representations generated by those utilizing images of the county and its inhabitants. If, on one level, Cardiganshire was a useful mental museum piece, on another it served as a model of progress. The county's distinctiveness, which was particularly marked during this era, resulted from an amalgamation of apparently contradictory mental locations.

<hr />

[33] CAS, Beckingsale 61/5, scrapbook, fos 1, 3, 5; Allen Raine, *Where Billows Roll: A Tale of the Welsh Coast* (London, 1909), p. ii; Jonathan Ceredig Davies, *Life, Travels and Reminiscences of Jonathan Ceredig Davies* (Llandewi Brefi, 1927), p. 169. Also see Sally Jones, *Allen Raine* (Cardiff, 1979).

FUTURE

Cardiganshire appealed to a number of people who spoke about a desired future. For some, the county was at the forefront of democracy's march; still more applauded its contribution to education; and a few celebrated the material successes, usually earned outside the county, of the Cardis. A study of the Cotswolds at this time summarized their portrayal as being 'incontiguous, set apart and remote in time from contemporary England'.[34] By contrast, Cardiganshire was central to many people's ideas of a future Wales because it incarnated self-improvement and independence. Unlike earlier periods, the actions of the county's people assumed greater significance in discourse. This did not reflect the experiences or proclivities of all of Cardiganshire's inhabitants; instead the links with a desired future echoed particular notions of advancement. Calling Cardiganshire 'the premier Liberal and Nonconformist county of Wales', as did one contributor to the *Daily News* during the Irish Home Rule crisis of 1886, involved positioning the county at the vanguard of 'freedom', in opposition to Unionist repression.[35]

An association between categories of people and political ideas was touched on by Belchem in his study of the Scouser and in Stedman Jones's work on the Cockney. Both linked the evolution of their respective types to their entry into the political nation, through the acquisition of the vote, and to the context in which they were then deployed in political argument.[36] Some comparisons can be made between these English urban types and the Cardi in form if not in substance. The relationship between the Liberal Party and the county was crowned by the county council election of 1889, which returned few of the landowners who had sat at the quarter

---

[34] Catherine Brace, 'Looking back: the Cotswolds and English national identity, c.1890–1950', *Journal of Historical Geography*, 25, 4 (1999), 502–16, 502.

[35] *Daily News*, 7 June 1886, 5.

[36] John Belchem, '"An accent exceedingly rare": Scouse and the inflexion of class', in John Belchem and Neville Kirk (eds), *Languages of Labour* (Aldershot, 1997), pp. 115–16; Gareth Stedman Jones, 'The Cockney and the nation, 1780–1988', in Gareth Stedman Jones and David Feldman (eds), *Metropolis London: Histories and Representations since 1800* (London, 1989), p. 316. Also see D. Ben Rees, *Hanes Plwyf Llanddewi Brefi* (Llanddewi Brefi, 1984), p. 209.

sessions.[37] This progressive image, with all groupings benefiting from the demise of privilege, can, of course, be
debated. After all, Tom Richards, a historian of early modern
Wales, recollected that in the 1880s his father was concerned
that the land he rented would be snapped up by a wealthy
Aberystwyth merchant or an ambitious ('uchelgeisiol') Cardi
from London. Differentials in terms of wealth and opportunity plainly continued. And detractors of the new Welsh
optimism, such as a 'Welsh correspondent' for *The Times*,
made much of these inequalities in their critiques.[38]

All the same, the complexities of power and influence in
post-landlord-dominated Cardiganshire did not lessen the
usefulness of the Cardi as a Liberal lodestar, and as an indicator of the contemporary distribution of cultural influence.
A meeting at New Quay in 1884, calling for the extension of
the franchise, embodied the individualism and questioning
of authority then widely held to typify the radical Cardi.
Morgan Evans of Oakford, in seconding a motion criticizing
the House of Lords for rejecting a bill to extend the franchise,
said that 'Providence had not blessed the eldest sons of Peers
with higher intellectual powers than those of ordinary men'.
Indeed, the fact that Tom Richards could rise from his background and help his parents financially indicates some reality
behind the image. This egalitarian, though individualistic,
facet of the Cardi was soon to be jostled through comparison
with broader communitarian principles emanating from
industrial workers and their advocates. For a brief period,
though, representations of the Cardi advanced with radical
Liberalism as it sought 'to expel the remnants of aristocratic
privilege'.[39] A contrast between an aristocracy of title and an
aristocracy of talent lent this county and its figureheads a
progressive hue, but one that faded when a comparison was
made with those who called for egalitarianism.

[37] Kenneth O. Morgan, 'Cardiganshire politics: the Liberal ascendancy, 1885–
1923', in *Modern Wales: Politics, Place and People* (Cardiff, 1995), pp. 216–50, p. 249.
[38] Tom Richards, *Atgofion Cardi* (Aberystwyth, 1960), p. 21; *The Times*,
25 September 1890, 8.
[39] *CJ*, 5 September 1884, 2; Jose Harris, *Private Lives, Public Spirit: Britain, 1870–
1914* (Harmondsworth, 1994), p. 189. For an insight into the thoughts of a radical
Liberal at this time, see CA, ADX/168, pocket book and farmers' diary, 1889, of
Morgan Evans JP, Oakford, Llanarth.

One incident in 1890 sheds considerable light not only on how the Cardi was deployed in political debates but also on how widespread the notion of the independent-minded Cardi had become. A year after the Liberal-dominated county council had been elected, a dispute began between Liberal councillors and the 'magisterial representatives on the police committee' over the appointment of a new chief constable. This took on national importance when the Conservative home secretary, Henry Matthews, later created Lord Llandaff in 1895, became involved. The man chosen by the joint committee was a Nonconformist who had previously held the post of sergeant in the force. Those Tories opposed to this new appointee, who had been chosen over two senior contenders, contacted Matthews and this led to the home secretary refusing to approve the appointment. Considerable attention focused on the county, which was also the scene of anti-tithe activity at this time, and comments in newspapers from outside the area were reproduced in the local press. These external reports pictured the people of Cardiganshire as democratic pioneers. Further, they embodied these qualities in the Cardi personality, linking positive personal traits like independence and determination with a progressive political outlook. In this democratic 'David versus governmental Goliath' struggle, the Liberal *Liverpool Mercury* declared that Matthews's refusal to accept the appointment would not 'terrify the "Cardie" for their pluck and prowess are recognized throughout the Principality'. The county's high proportion of freeholders explained the 'sturdiness and independence of the people'. Other papers, like the *Caernarvon Herald*, coupled the Cardi with tenacity when it mentioned that they would 'fight like bulldogs'. Some drew parallels with the Social Democratic Federation disturbance in Trafalgar Square on 13 November 1887. The press alluded to Matthews as 'the hero of Trafalgar Square [who] will discover that they ['the men of Cardigan'] are a little different from the Cockneys'; outraged Liberals, it would seem, were more tenacious than upstart socialists.[40] The issue was resolved

[40] *CN*, 5 September 1890, 5. In 1892 it was noted that the issue summed up differences between Liberal county councils and the Conservative government; see W. O. Brigstocke, 'Welsh county councils', *The Welsh Review*, 1 (1891–2), 485–92, 487.

when the controversial appointee, Chief Constable Evans, died in October and Matthews accepted Howell Evans, a Nonconformist from Llanelli, as his successor.

Personal progress through education went hand in hand with this democratic ideal, an ideal that drew comparisons with the USA. An American visitor complimented Welsh 'educational ideals' when she called them 'popular and progressive, with something of the so-called American spirit in them'.[41] In this respect, Cardiganshire once again served to illustrate a feature often related to Wales, particularly Nonconformist rural Wales. A stress on education was not unique to the area, but for many the county was foremost among Welsh counties in espousing education. This enabled a counter-stereotype to the ignorant rural dweller to develop. It is impossible to gauge the significance of this alternative figure among rural or urban people, but its appearance, utilization and amplification indicate its cultural value. When the Aberdare Commission on Welsh education was formed, it was noted by the vice-principal of Lampeter, the Revd William Harrison Davey, that two out of the five Welshmen on it were 'Cardiganshire men' (Henry Richard and John Rhys) and 'a third was a Cardiganshire man once or twice removed' (Lewis Morris). Davey went beyond these individuals, however, and noted 'that for a long time there had been a strong feeling in Cardigan, in pushing the sons of Cardigan men into an intellectual position, and the effect had been a large impulse given to education for many years'.[42] Hopes for educational progress were placed in a British context. In 1877, the college at Aberystwyth was expected to add a 'little leaven' to the Welsh that would enable them to compete on equal terms with not only the English, but the Scots and Irish as well. Later that year an editorial in the *Cambrian News* expressed concern that Englishmen were more afraid of competing for positions of influence with Scots than with Welshmen.[43]

[41] Jeannette Marks, *Gallant Little Wales: Sketches of its People, Places and Customs* (London, 1912), p. 16. For similar instances of American praise for Welsh 'independent spirit' and love of 'liberty' at this time, see Owen Jones 'The land of his birth', in B. D. Thomas (ed.), *Frederick Evans D.D. Ednyfed: A Memorial* (Philadelphia, 1899), pp. 9–19, 12, and Revd R. E. Williams, *Glimpses of Wales and the Welsh* (Pittsburgh, 1894), p. 57.

[42] *W*, 3 March 1882, 5.

[43] *CN*, 20 April 1877, 5; ibid., 21 December 1877, 5.

Thus, the nations of the British Isles were ranked in terms of assertiveness, with commentators often finding the Welsh wanting. In redressing the balance, Cardiganshire provided not only the locale for institutions; it also provided a 'type' of person to accompany them.

Behind the cultural significance accorded to education was the notion of individual self-improvement. As a result, individual progress became entwined with the county's progressive image, typifying an important part of Cardiganshire's story. One among many was Lewis Edwards (d.1887), the founder of what became a theological college at Bala. His lowly origins served to illustrate what could be done, thus tapping into people's aspirations, if not for themselves then for their children. Individual narratives like that surrounding Edwards were applied on a more general, county level, as seen in the comments of Jenkin James, the county's director of education, in 1911. Cardiganshire 'is not rich in mineral resources, like some other counties in Wales. But poor though it is in other respects, Cardiganshire is rich in raw material for the teaching profession.'[44] The production of teachers, like preachers earlier, fed local pride and gave representations of its inhabitants a momentum that was lacking in the periods covered in the preceding chapters: seasonal migrants, although praised by many, lacked the status of later exports. Although unable to contribute to the industry that fuelled the empire – something that the counties of Glamorgan and Monmouth could claim to do – the county could contribute, and therefore compensate with, a cultural quality. Pride generated by the county's teachers was similar to value placed on distinctive products. This is especially so when the products, be they goods or people, are exported elsewhere and, therefore, seen by others. This

[44] Jenkin James, 'Education in Cardiganshire: elementary and higher', in J. Ballinger (ed.), *Aberystwyth and District: A Guide Prepared for the Conference of the National Union of Teachers, 1911* (Aberystwyth, 1911), p. 243. Also see NLW, MS 16352D, original MS of D. J. Saer's *The Story of Cardiganshire* (1912), fo. 64. Other occupations associated with the county contributed to this reputation. For example, in an obituary to mark his death in 1913 the poet, journalist and seaman David Williams was described as being typical of men from the shores of Cardiganshire who were not satisfied until they had become masters of their own ship: CA, ADX 504 3/2, David Williams collection, obituary Bethesda Chapel. Also see *The Druid*, 14 April 1910, 5.

process could be seen as a group's identity being preserved and amplified during interaction with other groups; products effectively became ambassadors that could reflect positively, or negatively, on their place of origin.

Education was a concept that was used to transform a limited past into an open future. J. J. Williams was a minister, born in Talybont, Cardiganshire, who moved to Glamorgan as a young man, but his poems often featured the county of his birth. 'Gloch yr Ysgol' (The School Bell) demonstrates how education was presented as a means to escape hardship. In the third verse, the poet harked back to a time when the children's fathers were young, when there was no sound of the school bell and life was difficult. The final verse reassures the children that, although learning in lessons can be difficult, it is the way to improve one's life.[45] Education did not elevate most of the rural population, so such poetry might be seen as betraying 'a spirit of self-congratulation and complacency [that] prevailed among those who formed educational policy'.[46] Yet the attitude represents the success of those for whom the educational system presented opportunities. It was these – the professionals, large farmers and shopkeepers – who articulated most of the progressive images of Cardiganshire. They were demonstrating their achievements, binding their own narrative to that of the county.

Unlike education and religion, entrepreneurial spirit and the Welsh were rarely conflated. In 1875, a Breconshire poet, Rhys Davies, encapsulated this sentiment in 'John Jones and John Bull'. He called for the Welshman to 'let progress be stamped on thy banner', by being more economically assertive like the English and 'shrewd canny Scotty'.[47] Nonetheless, the Cardi provided a counter-type to the figure of the unambitious Welshman. One individual who did

[45] J. J. Williams, 'Gloch Yr Ysgol', in J. James (ed.), *Gemau Ceredigion* (Caerdydd, 1914), pp. 11–12.

[46] Robert Smith, *Schools, Politics and Society: Elementary Education in Wales, 1870–1902* (Cardiff, 1999), p. 261.

[47] R. Davies, *Sketches in Wales* (Brecon, 1875), pp. 128–30. The strident chorus reads:

Now John Jones awake from thy slumbers
'Tis time thou should'st alter thy tones
The fact is, we all must admit it
There's no speculation in Jones.

much to locate this germ of initiative in the Cardi at the turn of the twentieth century, and who continued the trend for men of the cloth to champion the industrious Cardi, was J. Myfenydd Morgan, then Anglican vicar of St Dogmaels who had served in churches in Glamorgan and Anglesey. Morgan demonstrated how the striving sons of Cardiganshire could be epitomes of material progress. In starting his essay about the poet Ioan Mynyw of Tregaron, Morgan stated that the county was one that has contributed significantly to the development ('cynnydd') of Wales. In addition, Morgan acknowledged that the county was received differently in various parts of Wales, its inhabitants being called 'Hwntws' by northerners and 'Cardies' by southerners, and occasion-ally attracting unfair judgement. Even so, Morgan concluded that it is hard to think of anybody as capable of wrestling with – and conquering – material difficulties as were the people of Cardiganshire.[48] This portrait of a people battling their way out of poverty was instanced as proof of Welsh entrepreneurialism during 1898 in a study entitled *Welsh Characteristics*, by W. J. Wallis-Jones, a student at Aberystwyth. There was evidently a desire to link Wales with progress at this time, to stress that the people were contributing to the upkeep of the British state. In the chapter 'Welsh industry and ingenuity', Wallis-Jones cited the industriousness of the small farmer, stating that 'the Cardiganshire small farmers are the most typical of this class'. Progress was identified with the Cardi, who became a pendant of advancement adorning the Welsh nation. Although taken as 'typical', Wallis-Jones intimated that Cardis are exceptional. On going to south Wales as professionals or businessmen, for example, 'their shrewdness, perseverance and industry raise them to the most honourable positions in municipal and social life'.[49]

The activities of west Walians in the London dairy trade, that grew with an increased demand for milk from the mid-1870s, became a particularly common symbol of success. They appear in a novel published in 1898, where one of their number possessed that contemporary prized item 'a

[48] J. Myfenydd Morgan, 'Ioan Mynyw', *Y Traethodydd*, 55 (1900), 183–90, 183–4.
[49] W. J. Wallis-Jones, *Welsh Characteristics* (Pencader, 1898), pp. 48–9. Also see Saer, *Story of Cardiganshire*, fo. 66.

gold watch in his pocket' when visiting his birthplace.[50] The
notion that Welsh talents deserved the largest stage – London
– featured in Welsh political thought.[51] Success for others in
non-political activity outside Wales, such as the clergymen in
London extolled in the pages of *Y Cardi*, attained a similar
if less singular aura to that of the Welsh politicians who
stormed London, notably Lloyd George.[52] Despite moving
and thriving in England, these scions of progress were often
praised for maintaining Welsh ways. They provided an alternative to the caricature of Dic Sion Dafydd, who shed his
Welshness in England; the successful Cardi was formulated
as an inverse Dic Sion Dafydd. In endeavouring to raise
more funds from the natives of Cardiganshire to secure the
National Library at Aberystwyth, J. H. Davies described a
trip to London and the sum of £1,500 raised there. Davies
stated that this money had come from those men from
Cardiganshire who had 'gone up to London without a penny
in their pockets' and were 'working hard to earn a little
bread and a little money wherewith to enable them to come
back to Cardiganshire to live'. They exemplified patriotism
and self-improvement, qualities that Davies accentuated to
bestir the denizens of Aberystwyth to part with more than the
£1,200 they had hitherto contributed. Somewhat ironically,
the very depopulation that was felt by one Edwardian local
historian to keep 'the rate of improvement at a standstill'
enabled inhabitants of the county to be regarded as icons of
advancement.[53]

Many of those who located future potential in aspects of
Cardiganshire and its people, whether at home or outside
the county, based their projections on key virtues that those
from the county were held to possess. Locating these qualities involved implicit or explicit comparisons with other

[50] John Finnemore, *The Custom of the Country: An Idyll of the Welsh Mountains*
(London, 1898), p. 28. See P. J. Atkins, 'The retail milk trade in London, *c*.1790–
1914', *Economic History Review*, 33, 4 (1980), 522–37. Also see Emrys Jones, 'The age
of societies', in Emrys Jones (ed.) *The Welsh in London* (Cardiff, 2001), pp. 55–87.

[51] John Davies, *The Green and the Red: Nationalism and Ideology in Twentieth-Century
Wales* (Aberystwyth, 1982), p. 8.

[52] J. Ceredig Jones, 'Pregethwyr Sir Aberteifi yn Llundain', *Y Cardi*, 2 May 1902, 4.

[53] *Welsh Gazette*, 4 May 1905, 5; E. Davies, *Hanes Plwyf Llangynllo* (Llandysul, 1905),
p. 176.

places not so much founded on perceptions of past or future but on spatial concentrations of value. Kinds of cultural location interact with and reinforce one another other, each providing a different evaluative energy to bear on the social world. This interaction was especially noticeable when development was linked to moral worth.[54]

CENTRE

Contemporary accounts illuminate symbolic relationships between the county, Wales and the rest of Britain. Some parts of Wales, such as Cardiganshire, contributed more to its national image than others. As mentioned earlier, ideas about the past led to the nation's essence being found in the least modern practices and places. Other ways of identifying Wales and promulgating values existed, however, that were not expressed in relation to the past or future, and Cardiganshire played a part in this as well. According to Arjun Appadurai, nations 'have their special sites of sacredness, their special tests of loyalty and treachery, their special measures of compliance and disorder'.[55] From the late nineteenth century onwards, concerns about national efficiency would add urgency to these assessments. However, Cardiganshire passed many of the tests set by national leaders and disseminators of culture identified by Appadurai.

Positive features defined as particularly Welsh were specifically linked to the Cardi as never before. Although the county itself was home to a dwindling population, Cardiganshire's human exports contributed to a greater symbolic presence than that of any other Welsh county and, indeed, more than most English counties. Cardis emerged as a rural Welsh type that was contrasted with the Welsh industrial population and the less tractable Irish. This template of the ideal citizen, obedient but not servile, was not peculiar to Cardiganshire. A bundle of similar virtues can be seen in 'Rochdale Man' and 'Manchester Man', 'the respectable self-helping,

---

[54] Stefan Collini, 'The idea of "character" in Victorian political thought', *Transactions of the Royal Historical Society*, 35 (1985), 29–50, 41.

[55] Arjun Appadurai, 'The production of locality', in R. Fardon (ed.), *Counterworks: Managing the Diversity of Knowledge* (London, 1995), pp. 204–25, p. 213.

self-educating working man with his cooperative society, savings bank and chapel'.[56] The Cardi's respectable representation differed from that of the trustworthy Lancastrian not only in being exclusively based on a county rather than a particular town, but in affording an alternative Celtic type to the troublesome Irishman. In sum, the county-type took on the characteristics of the Society for Promoting Christian Knowledge's hero David Lloyd mentioned in the previous chapter. It is important, therefore, to add the Cardi to the two Welsh figures identified by R. Merfyn Jones. He traced the replacement of the mountaineer-type of Welshman, whom Romantics lauded in Cardiganshire during the late eighteenth and early nineteenth centuries, by the miner who was 'personified either as proletarian hero or lumpen threat'.[57] This shift from primitive to industrial Wales threw up another type that embodied respectability and was, unlike the miner, either personified as a respectable hero or, as will be seen in the following section, a grasping capitalist. Cardiganshire was not the only place that produced these categories, but it was the only Welsh county that was overtly linked to them.

Frugality was the characteristic most commonly connected to the Cardi. Many attributed this feature to rural dwellers, in particular to farmers. Yet at this time it was also deemed a typically Welsh trait by, for example, the campaigner for the female franchise Frances Power Cobbe. In an article in the *Cornhill Magazine*, she contrasted the 'wine to-day, water tomorrow' attitude of the Irish with 'prudence', the 'distinguishing characteristic' of the Welsh. This feature meant that Wales produced more professionals from the 'sons of small farmers' than did other parts of Britain. For those who saw virtue in self-reliance and thrift, this feature of the Welsh was praised and found undiluted among inhabitants

---

[56] Michael E. Rose, 'Rochdale man and the Stalybridge riot: the relief and control of the unemployed during the Lancashire cotton famine', in A. P. Donajgrodski (ed.), *Social Control in Nineteenth-Century Britain* (London, 1977), pp. 185–206, 185. The biography of the 'Manchester man' has yet to be written, although Gary S. Messinger dedicates a chapter to him, which includes a section on the 'Manchester woman', in *Manchester in the Victorian Age: The Half-Known City* (Manchester, 1985), pp. 173–92.

[57] R. Merfyn Jones, 'Beyond identity? The reconstruction of the Welsh', *Journal of British Studies*, 31, 4 (1992), 330–57, 331.

of Cardiganshire. In his letters to *The Times*, J. E. Vincent, a barrister and propagandist for the landlords of Wales, observed that the majority of 'Welshmen are born dealers and excessively keen at a bargain, and the Cardiganshire men can do something more than hold their own with any of their brethren'.[58]

His judgement, and that of many others, was probably influenced by the penny-postage-stamp system of saving introduced by the postmaster-general, Henry Fawcett, one of whose avowed aims was to use the post office as a vehicle to encourage thrift. In 1880, the county was one of those chosen to try the system. Local newspapers reported the success of the experiment, citing examples of enormous increases in accounts opened since the new regulations had been introduced. The *Carmarthen Journal* reported how new accounts at Aberystwyth post office had increased tenfold since the scheme began. Fawcett's book, *The Post Office and Aids to Thrift*, was hailed by the *Cambrian News* as a most useful publication that ought to be translated into Welsh. Of all the counties where this system of saving was tested, Cardiganshire was hailed as the one that responded with the most interest to the savings scheme, which enabled £10 to purchase government stock at 3 per cent interest 'and safer than the bank of England'.[59] This 'value in the eyes of others' would be welcomed and taken as a badge of pride in the county's perceived character.[60]

Other elements of respectability, such as independence and hard work, were attached to the county's population. If Cardiganshire was a centre of such traits then its antipode was, once again, Ireland. In 1886 the *Country Gentleman*

[58] F.[rances] P.[ower] C.[obbe],'The Celt of Wales and the Celt of Ireland', *Cornhill Magazine*, 32 (1877), 661–78, 677; J. E. Vincent, *Letters from Wales* (London, 1889), p. 162.

[59] Leslie Stephen, *Life of Henry Fawcett* (5th edn, London, 1886), p. 414; *CJ*, 22 October 1880, 3; *CN*, 11 February 1881, 5. Also see *Swansea Boy*, 12 November 1880, 11.

[60] Philip Abrams, *Historical Sociology* (Shepton Mallet, 1982), p. 251. An example of this praise can be found in *The Times*, 7 September 1895, 11, where F. J. Ceste from Chester noted how the 'people of Cardiganshire' are well-known for their 'self-denial'. Also see BPP, XIV (1893–4), *Royal Commission on Labour: The Agricultural Labourer Volume II (Wales)* (London, 1893), p. 58.

magazine ran an account of the Tivyside hunt that was
reproduced in the *Welshman* newspaper. A behavioural
gap – the Irish 'toil not, neither do they spin', the Welsh
'loyal, contented people, both toil and spin'– reflected the
concerns of the readership of magazines like the *Country
Gentleman* that felt that the Irish threat, no doubt heightened
by Gladstone's conversion to Home Rule in 1885, needed
a symbolic counter-type. Cardiganshire folk, very different
in language but faithful Protestants who paid their rent on
time, provided this. Furthermore, the reception of this praise
illustrates how such opinion was taken on board unquestion-
ingly. The *Welshman*, a Liberal paper, noted that 'no loyal
Welshman can fail to feel proud' after reading this publication. Such public commentary amplified opinion and, in all
likelihood, engendered it.[61]

The use of this antithesis was not restricted to country
gentlemen; if that had been so then the location of value
would not have carried much weight. Educationalists dissem-
inated this dichotomy as well. In 1911, the magazine *Wales*
contained an article by T. Darlington, a school inspector, that
contrasted the cultured intellect of the Welshman with the
irrepressible nature of the Irishman. Through locating qualities in the typical Welsh rural dweller, of whom the Cardi
was deemed representative, the Welsh intelligentsia could
declare their nation's maturity. Darlington illustrated the
difference by comparing the 'Cardiganshire farmer [who]
will thrive where a Connaught peasant would starve'.[62] A
similar theme was pursued by E. M. Wilmot-Buxton, author
of textbooks for children, in a guide to Wales published the
same year as Darlington's article. These sentiments reflect
prejudices about the Irish and reveal the extent to which
the positive stereotype of the Cardi helped those who held
these negative views of the Irish to impart their ideas. Despite
physical similarities, Wilmot-Buxton stressed that the mental
composition of the two could not have been more dissim-

[61] *W*, 16 January 1886, 3. Another example of favourable comments about the
county, on this occasion from the Liberal *Daily Chronicle*, being reprinted in the local
press can be found in *CTA*, 20 September 1895, 8.

[62] T. Darlington, 'The Cymric element in the English people', *Wales*, 1 (1911),
361–8, 367.

ilar; the 'Cardy' 'differs in the fact that he is very industrious and independent'.[63] These brief, but significant, eulogies composed in honour of Cardiganshire's inhabitants were not simply descriptions: they broadcast values. Some idea of the origin of the ideas circulated by Darlington and Wilmot-Buxton can be found in the letters of J. E. Vincent over twenty years earlier. His agenda, an attempt to disprove the accusations made against landowners by Nonconformist radicals in north-east Wales, necessitated overlooking the county's own similar, if less virulent, tradition. Vincent found solace in two of the county's characteristics: its tendency to produce Anglican ministers and its 'abundance of small freeholders'. Vincent identified other accumulations of freeholders in Wales, such as in Anglesey, but nowhere does he find them 'so marked and distinct a class as in Cardiganshire'.[64]

It was this group, seen as a crucial component of a vital nation, on which the county's praiseworthy image in this period was founded. Many of the public intelligentsia who were alarmed by, among other things, demands from the unskilled urban workers saw the small landowner with a stake in the country as an antidote to reckless democracy. William Owen Brigstocke, a landowner and Liberal with radical leanings, expressed this opinion before the Royal Commission on Land in Wales and Monmouthshire. After saying how he thought there were more freeholders in the county than in any other in England or Wales – a fact that he credited to an increase in land purchases from around 1875 – Brigstocke observed that such a class was 'a very good thing for the state; when a man has an interest in the state, in theory he is supposed to be a better citizen'.[65] Newspapers in south Wales transmitted similar observations.[66]

Again, it is important to stress the variety of ways in which Cardiganshire was thought to be the centre of some values. It was this variety, the very scope of contrasts with other places and people, that underpinned its location. As well as the

[63] E. M. Wilmot-Buxton, *Peeps at Many Lands: Wales* (London, 1911), pp. 71–2.

[64] Vincent, *Letters*, p. 160.

[65] BPP, XL (1895), *Minutes of Evidence taken before the Royal Commission on Land in Wales and Monmouthshire Volume III* (London, 1895), p. 393.

[66] *Cardiff Times*, 16 January 1897, 1.

topical concerns mentioned above, there were others that echoed the comments made earlier in the century about differences between Cardiganshire and more commercial and industrial areas. An unnamed man, who shared a railway carriage from Carmarthen to Pencader with a Unitarian minister from Dowlais in the mid-1880s, demonstrated how this difference between east and west Wales could be conveyed. The man on the Manchester and Milford loco-motive criticized everything connected with the 'gweithiau' (literally the 'works', a name for the industrial valleys). He thought the people of Glamorgan were less trustworthy than the 'Cardis', that the former could not work half as well as the latter and that all was good in Cardiganshire and bad in Glamorgan. He even asserted that the horses of Cardiganshire were swifter than their Glamorgan counterparts.[67] Issues of respectability appear to have played a fundamental part in the distinction between two ideas of Wales, embodied by the counties of Cardigan and Glamorgan, and this is all the more noteworthy when the extensive contact and migration between the two places are taken into account. Differences in social and economic structure had, for some, rendered the two places asunder. For many the former was the essence of respectable Wales. By contrast, Glamorgan had earned the unenviable appellation of 'Black Glamorgan'.[68]

As in earlier periods, religion contributed to the moral distinctions between areas. Yet such distinctions were accen-tuated by social changes in other places. A place is often given the accolade of centre or finds this title being reinforced as a result of changes elsewhere. What is more, moral associations were composed of mutually reinforcing layers encompassing a range of denominations and a panoply of ideas about what constituted Wales. The elevation of the county also drew on events, statistics, individuals and impressions of land-scape. In their work on Welsh Nonconformity, published in five volumes between 1871 and 1891, Rees and Thomas held Cardiganshire to be one of the most Nonconformist

[67] W. J. Davies, 'O Ddowlais i Sir Aberteifi', *Yr Ymofynydd*, c.n., 11 (1886), 135–8, 138.

[68] J. Littlejohns, *Pamphlets for the People No. 1: Black Glamorgan* (Swansea, 1901).

and religious counties in the kingdom.[69] Towards the end
of nineteenth century concerns about increasing seculari-
zation were more widespread than they were in the middle
of the century, and this gave additional resonance to their
opinion. In addition, Cardiganshire would have been further
distanced from its shadow, 'Black Glamorgan', by its ecclesi-
astical exports to positions in the established Church. The
part these played in fostering the county's reputation as
a centre of religious conviction is seen in comments made
by John Rhys, then fellow of Merton College, Oxford, at
Ystrad Meurig grammar school on prize-giving day in 1872:
'It was a well known fact that almost all . . . of the North
Wales clergy were *Hwntws* (South Walians) . . . and of those
again the greatest number might safely be said to be natives
of Cardiganshire.'[70] The exports from Cardiganshire, celebrated by Rhys, were especially significant because they
contributed to the revival of the Anglican Church in Wales
during the late nineteenth century.[71] At the same time, ministers who worked in north Wales provided the foundation
for a less lauded occupational stereotype. Some northern
Nonconformists depicted these men, who were praised by
those gathered at Ystrad Meurig, as being somewhat alien.
As a child in Edwardian Merionethshire, O. M. Edwards
believed that Cardiganshire was somewhere in the middle of
England. This was owing to the parson who hailed from that
county who spoke only English in public.[72] In all likelihood,
this feature would have marked the parson out in the eyes of
a few adults as well.

The county's religious reputation was underscored by
the revival of 1904–5, whose leader, Evan Roberts, underwent a spiritual experience at a meeting in Blaenannerch,

[69] Thomas Rees and J. Thomas, *Hanes Eglwysi Annibynol Cymru*, 5 vols (Lerpwl, 1871–91), vol. 4, p. 81.
[70] *CJ*, 2 August 1872, 2. Also see *Swansea Boy*, 14 September 1883, 4; *South Wales Daily News*, 13 January 1910, 4.
[71] Owain J. Jones, 'The Welsh church in the nineteenth century', in D. Walker (ed.), *A History of the Church in Wales* (Penarth, 1976), pp. 144–63, 162.
[72] Owen Edwards, *Clych Atgof: Penodau yn Hanes fy Addysg* (Wrecsam, 1933), pp. 32–3. A ballad by John Jones (Jac Glan y Gors, 1767–1821), highlights the moral shortcomings of the Cardiganshire vicar: BUL, Cerddi Bangor 24 (123–4), 'Person Sir Aberteifi' [n.d.].

near Cardigan, that motivated him to commence evangelical preaching. This, together with the memory of the 1859 revival (a book about the event was published in 1909) gave the county a forceful Nonconformist character that could, depending on one's denominational standpoint, either complement or partially obscure the county's Anglican tradition. Figures cited in the Report of the Royal Commission on religious organizations in Wales, published in 1910, support this qualitative impression. In a discussion about the impact of the decline in rural populations on chapel building, the case of Cardiganshire was cited. Despite a decline in population of some 13,000 between 1871 and 1901, the number of chapels in the county had risen by forty-seven. At a time when the 'spiritual welfare of the people' troubled the commissioners, a county like Cardiganshire could serve as a beacon that shone on less acceptable areas. Emphasis on this indicator of morality was all the more important because a general decline in crime, widely held to have taken place from the late nineteenth century, had taken some of the novelty away from the county's reputation for obedience; indeed, it is noteworthy that visiting judges were less effusive in their compliments. A change in available contrasts meant that a previously key element in depictions of the county faded somewhat.[73] Religiosity, however, ensured that Cardiganshire's reputation for morality did not disappear.

Interpretations of the county's topography were woven into positive judgements about the area, thus making the judgements appear to be part of the natural order rather than the product of opinion. This link between general definitions, individual character and geographical qualities gave weight to accounts that located Cardiganshire at the centre. Publications such as *Cymru* and *Cymru'r Plant* asserted

[73] J. J. Morgan, *The '59 Revival in Wales* (Mold, 1909); BPP, XIV (1910), *Royal Commission of the Church of England and other Religious Bodies in Wales and Monmouthshire Volume I* (London, 1910), pp. 128, 5; George Grosvenor, 'Statistics of the abatement of crime in England and Wales, during the twenty years ended 1887–1888', *Journal of the Royal Statistical Society*, 53 (1890), 377–419. Local newspapers still reported the relative lack of crime, but not as boldly as in the mid-Victorian period: *CTA*, 3 February 1899, 4. Also see the comments of E. Williams, chief constable for the county, in his contribution, 'Crime in Wales', to T. Stephens (ed.), *Wales To-day and To-morrow* (Cardiff, 1907), pp. 174–5, 174.

notions of Wales and Welshness, providing the nation with a readily identifiable heart. In so doing, of course, they had to render other places as peripheral. At the start of the twentieth century, W. T. Parry, from the University of Wales's southern college at Cardiff, wrote an account of a tour during which he sketched old houses and visited places of religious interest. On his second day in the county, he found that the landscape set the area apart from south-east Wales. From the hills above Tregaron he described a panoramic view that, he believed, revived the spirit of those who, like himself, had left the deep valleys of Glamorgan where he lived with only a little of the earth and even less of the heavens within sight. Here was land with no sign of industry, the home or birthplace of important religious figures and where the Welsh language was common.[74]

This very perception of the southern valleys as being removed from nature – in other words, from its Welshness or true nature – led to Cardiganshire acquiring an enhanced reputation as a national centre. When trying to explain how the mental divergence between parts of Wales occurred, these cultural implications, the corollary of changes in society, need to be considered. This focus on perceived elemental aspects of Welshness is illustrated in the mental topography of the poet Edward Thomas, who rendered similar word images about the essence of England. London-born Thomas, who had studied history at Oxford under O. M. Edwards, editor of the nation-defining journals *Cymru* and *Cymru'r Plant*, hoisted the area's landscape above others in his 1905 book *Beautiful Wales*. The 'heart' of Wales was located in 'peaty Tregaron', near where Parry enthused about the view. Thomas located the 'soul' of Wales 'on Plynlimmon itself'.[75] It was as if the muscles or hands were represented by the south-east and the inner qualities, heart and soul, were secreted in the rural west. As a summary of the county in *Cymru'r Plant* exclaimed,

[74] W. T. Parry, 'Dau ddiwrnod yng nghanolbarth Sir Aberteifi: yr ail ddiwrnod', *Cymru*, 21 (1901), 268–74, 273.
[75] Edward Thomas, *Beautiful Wales* (London, 1905), p. 28. In 1910, Thomas wrote to his friend and proofreader, Gordon Bottomley, that he had spent a fortnight in 'the wild part of Cardiganshire', *Selected Letters*, ed. R. George Thomas (Oxford, 1995), p. 60.

Cardiganshire was defined as the most patriotic and Welsh of counties – 'y fwyaf gwladgar a Chymreig o siroedd Cymru'. Conversely, an account of Glamorgan took pains to point out that, despite its not being as clean as other counties, it did have many pious workers.[76]

Of course, the effect that these mental locations had on the public mind cannot be measured precisely. Nonetheless, they were the preponderant ones in the public sphere. Previous traditions that located morality and prudence in Cardiganshire and its population were sharpened and announced to a greater extent. Contrasts between parts of Wales based on occupation and topography were relayed in the local press. One example of these contrasts, published in 1893, espoused the health-giving properties of the coast in a poem. Entitled 'Gwbert on the sea', it contra-positions industrial and rural Wales in an endeavour to entice visitors:

> Come ye from Rhondda's Vale
> Weary and worn and pale
> from striving town and city far
> Come seek repose at Nature's bar.[77]

Health, nation and beauty were combined in the scenery of Cardiganshire, but such a conjunction overlooked as much as it included: where, for example is the 'worn and weary', though probably less 'pale', agricultural worker? Presumably, in addition to shattering the image of rural well-being, rural labourers were not the intended recipients of such publicity. Contrasting representations of the county located Cardiganshire on the edge of the qualities considered in this section: there was sickness in the land, and religion, respectability and education did not guarantee a just society. Beneath the vocal championing of Cardiganshire's tradition, its contribution to certain types of progress and its raised symbolic stature, there were other voices from within and without the county that contested or contradicted images of the county, voices that often took the 'worn and weary' farm worker into account.

[76] Anon., 'Siroedd Cymru: II Ceredigion', *Cymru'r Plant*, 8 (1899), 47–51, 51; ibid., 'Siroedd Cymru: I Morgannwg', 15–18, 18.
[77] *CJ*, 18 August 1893, 8.

Margin

From the late Victorian period onwards, substantial portions of Cardiganshire's population were defined as naive, ignorant or unfashionable country dwellers. Other criticisms foreshadow those that evolved during the interwar years. These noted the reputed grasping, non-communal character of the county's business class, and indicated an increased concern about social justice. The process of differentiating the county from other areas or groups, and the intellectual and social trends identified with them, served further to distinguish Cardiganshire, although probably not in a manner to the liking of all its inhabitants and certainly not those who championed its perceived virtues. By locating Cardiganshire on the edge, commentators were adding more pieces to the mosaic that makes up the county's representational history.

Cardiganshire was thought to contain people who would be out of place in the world beyond. These comments matched the county's geographically marginal position to the minds of its inhabitants. This distancing from the centres of fashion and thought was not new, but in an increasingly urban context the means by which the county's inhabitants could be distanced from these centres had altered. Despite being exaggerations, these comments indicate how cultural differences were often expressed in an urban/rural framework and may, indirectly, explain why so much pride was taken in the achievements of those successful migrants who countered this image. Those who assign marginality always assume their own centrality, a certainty about their own ways. These urban views of the Cardi were doubtless buttressed by a contemporary context, namely 'the process of urbanisation [that] peaked and levelled out in the years just before 1914'.[78] In addition, the following examples point out how humour, often based on people in situations they do not comprehend, contributed to representations of peripheral people.

Emma Mary Thomas, who used the nom de plume Marie Trevelyan, was a well-travelled native of Llantwit Major in the

---

[78] F. M. L. Thompson, 'Town and city', in F. M. L. Thompson (ed.), *The Cambridge Social History of Britain, 1750 –1950*, vol. 1: *Regions and Communities* (Cambridge, 1990), pp. 1–86, 70.

Vale of Glamorgan. Her *Glimpses of Welsh Life and Character* contains 'stories' purporting to illustrate Welsh people's love of leeks. One of these, about a 'Cardiganshire lover [who] took his sweetheart to the National Eisteddfod at Swansea', reveals ways in which the Cardi was perceived as being different from other Welsh people, marked out by accent, habit and expectation. First, the man's speech, which Trevelyan littered with hyphens – 'He-er's-a-greet-town' – is described as being 'the drawling tone prevalent in Cardigan'. The place and pace of speech are linked again when she described him as 'the slow Cardigan man'. At the eisteddfod the couple request 'two-basins-of leek-proth (broth)'. On being told, by the amused waiter, that this could not be procured even if more money was offered, the couple leave, surprised that such meals are not to be found 'in-thiss-pig (big)-town-of-Swaaneee'.[79] It is significant that the innocent couple display their ignorance at an eisteddfod. For Thomas and those from whom she heard this tale, the rural dweller, regarded by many at the time as the source of Welsh culture, seems out of place where this very culture was being celebrated. This is because the gap noted here is between the slow country dweller and the town, here was the Cardi who stayed at home.

A similar reading of Cardiganshire's population, which sets a greenhorn figure on social as much as physical *terra incognita*, is preserved in a song called 'Taith y Cardi o Landyssul i Lundain, yn ystod pa un y daeth i gyffyrddiad a'r Widw Fach Lan' (A Cardi's journey from Llandysul to London, during which he meets the Fair Little Widow). It was published in north Wales (Llanrwst), south-east Wales (Aberdare) and Cardiganshire (Llandysul itself), thus tapping into a widespread conception of the Cardis and possibly their ability to laugh at notions of themselves. The sibilant accent of the young Cardi, who is travelling to the capital to collect money bequeathed to him by his wealthy uncle, forms part of this parody of innocence and acquisitiveness. The train provides the meeting point between the naive man and the wily world. Cardi relates the tale in a mix of English and Welsh,

---

[79] Marie Trevelyan, *Glimpses of Welsh Life and Character* (London, 1893), pp. 395–6.

describing how a young woman, holding a baby, engages him in conversation: 'Dystawrwydd [silence] wass broken by my purty companion.' After shedding tears while telling him about her husband's death, she makes an excuse to disembark at a station, promising to return, and leaving the Cardi holding the baby. The train continues, Cardi finds his money, ticket and watch stolen; the baby is a dummy. Any sympathy felt for the dupe is mixed with an awareness of the value he places on material things, like his waistcoat: 'Nice silk wastgat, too, John Jones Teilwr make before I wass go from home, iss, yndeed, there you.' This fancy does not depict the Cardi as wholly removed from the world, oblivious to its trappings. Indeed, we see something here, and in other songs from the area such as 'Y March Glas' (The Grey Horse), of what Eugen Weber identified as a liking for things originating from the nation's capital, *articles de Paris*, among the rural population of France in the same period.[80] Instead, what separates the country dweller from those outside in this song is vigilance in the wider world, whose very riches the Cardi desires. At the end of his tale, the deceived man stressed the dangers beyond the confines of home: 'Now, boys of Llandyssul, now mind you take warnin; mind you the widows who do cry like rain.'[81]

Such images of the Cardi were not based on a deficiency of capital. The leek-loving couple was willing to pay a substantial amount for their preferred meal and the duped young man was not poor. These were distinctions based on the perceived mentality of the rural inhabitant, and there were doubtless many more expressions of this than those recorded in printed sources.[82] Besides distinctions based on actions, there were descriptions that distinguished Cardiganshire people on

[80] Eugen Weber, *Peasants into Frenchmen: The Modernization of Rural France, 1870–1914* (London, 1976), p. 7.

[81] BUL, Cerddi Bangor 25 (145), 'Taith y Cardi o Landyssul i Lundain, yn ystod pa un y daeth i gyffyrddiad a'r Widw Fach Lan' (Aberdare, 1904/1906), pp. 2, 4; a popular song in the county mentions a well-fitted coat from a London tailor, *Cardiganshire Antiquarian Society Transactions*, 6 (1929), 1–2.

[82] R. D. Jones of Aberdare, for instance, recalled his father saying how Cardis travelling back to visit relatives insisted on crossing wooden bridges on foot as they believed that 'the weight of the train full of passengers would be too much for the viaducts' (ex inf., 8 September 2002). Also see *Tarian y Gweithiwr*, 2 Mai 1912, 1.

the basis of their appearance. A guide to the county by E. R. Horsfall-Turner, a Yorkshire man who married a native of the county, noted the visibility of Cardiganshire folk. His book was applauded by J. Myfenydd Morgan, a defender of the Cardi, for nowhere attempting to 'scorn and despise the "Cardies"' – a comment that suggests that negative impressions of the Cardi were common.[83] Nonetheless, as well as listing notables and historic sites, the author delineated holidaymakers at New Quay and this vignette reveals distinctions within the Cardi clan based on style of dress. He observed that the men from farming communities wore 'clod-hopping boots and large misfit suits piloting along, proud in possession, their giggling round-faced sweethearts dressed like grandmothers'.[84] These rustic couples, while preferable to the sickly miners, compare unfavourably with the smart wealthy milk dealers originally from the county who returned to holiday at the resort; perhaps these were the kind of successful Cardis with whom Morgan identified. Similarly, Trevelyan thought that the women of Cardiganshire looked unlike other Welsh women, although she stressed their physique as well as their dress, distancing these unsophisticated country females from genteel society. 'Cardiganshire women', Trevelyan related, 'are for the most part thick-set and short of stature'.[85] This condescending view of rural people, which echoes the observations considered in the previous chapter, came from a cosmopolitan perspective. It could be argued that it was the county's misfortune to be caught between this snobbery and other judgements that, for quite different reasons, appeared to contradict more favourable estimations of the county and its inhabitants.

Astute observers noted the dissonance between different impressions of Cardiganshire. The travel writer A. G. Bradley did not attempt to explain the division but provided an intriguing overview, briefly addressing opinions about the

[83] *CTA*, 27 March 1903, 6.

[84] E. R. Horsfall-Turner, *Walks and Wanderings in County Cardigan: Being a Descriptive Sketch of its Picturesque, Historic, Antiquarian, Romantic and Traditional Features* (Bingley, 1902), p. 119.

[85] Trevelyan, *Glimpses of Welsh Life*, p. 168.

county that were not commonly expressed in contemporary printed sources:

> Other Welshmen look at him ['the Cardy'] as a somewhat distinct specimen of their family, and with a mixture of respect and the other thing, that I cannot quite define and do not wish to. In some ways he is the Paddy of Wales, in others quite the opposite.

Cardiganshire's reputation for producing professionals was noted, and he remarked upon the apparent inconsistency between this and what he had heard from Welshmen who considered the 'Cardy' to be 'less imaginative and of a coarser fibre than his neighbours, having somewhat of the clod about him'.[86] It is possible that Cardiganshire's isolation contributed to this variety of Cardi. O. M. Edwards wrote a history, *Wales*, published two years before Bradley's book, in which he observed that the county's 'definite geographical unity [was] mirrored in the strongly marked characteristics of its people'.[87] At this point in time, then, two perceptions of the county's inhabitants were vying for position in the cultural arena. Both were, of course, separate measures of a variegated reality, in which successful exports and poor provincials coexisted. Yet this ambivalence intrigued commentators, and in future differing representations of the Cardi would recur, albeit modified according to prevalent circumstances, bewildering those travel writers who were in search of a convenient, universal image of Cardiganshire's inhabitants.

Contrasting summations of Cardiganshire before the First World War were also noted in the county's press. These comparisons usually accompanied criticisms of a section of Cardiganshire society whose individual progress and centrality in discourse about the area were set against less favourable features. In sum, there was an internal struggle of ideas about what the county should be. Poor health and housing drew the attention of many as concerns about the quality of the British population multiplied. The county's reputation, propagated by the achievements of individuals in business, education and the ministry, contrasted with the

[86] Bradley, *South Wales*, p. 212. Bradley's interest in the county intruded into *Highways and Byways in North Wales* (London, 1898), pp. 419–20.

[87] O. M. Edwards, *Wales* (London, 1901), p. 318. Also see J. Hugh Edwards, 'Interviews with Welsh leaders: Ellis J. Griffith MP', *Welsh Review*, 1 (1906), 19–21, 19.

findings of Dr J. Arthur Rees, the medical officer for the southern division of the Aberystwyth Poor Law Union. These positive images were turned against those who fostered them, exposing what was thought to be neglect and hypocrisy; in effect, the local press located those widely held to represent the county negatively. A *Cambrian News* editorial from 1912, entitled 'How the poor live', observed that 'Cardiganshire is a county where religion, political intelligence, education and business acuteness prevail', before going on to contrast this with Rees's 1911 report. The death rate for this part of the county, inflated by 'chest complaints' and poor housing, was all the more astounding because it exceeded the birth rate and related to a place where the person-to-acre ratio was favourable; such space was usually linked with healthy conditions. These figures were embarrassing when set against attributes that epitomized the county. They fed disenchantment with the Liberal Nonconformist ethos, with its emphasis on individual rather than collective advancement. As well as calling for increased attention to sanitary conditions from 'the people themselves', the editorial censured the Church and chapels for their lack of concern.[88] One man's memoirs captured the irony of an attentive Nonconformist conscience that coexisted with deprivation when he recalled the absence of clean water at his school while temperance was being taught for one period a week, 'thus proving that officialdom had its priorities mixed'.[89]

In addition to the juxtaposition of mortality and morality in Cardiganshire, comparisons were made with other places. Health statistics, such as the county's relatively high death rate, were, in part, a symptom of its structural peripherality, as an ageing population predominated when the younger and healthier people moved away. In 1907, the *Western Mail* related details of a report by the county's medical officer, Dr Evan Evans, under the heading 'The White Plague in Cardiganshire'. The county's overall death rate of 16.9 per thousand compared unfavourably with the combined English and Welsh average of 15.4. Furthermore, the county was

[88] *CN*, 24 May 1912, 5. The paper also highlighted instances of poor living conditions in the late nineteenth century: see ibid., 11 July 1890, 5.

[89] James Williams, *Give Me Yesterday* (Llandysul, 1971), p. 20.

'notorious' for its high levels of phthisis: 2.1 deaths per thousand, compared with 0.64 in the Rhondda valleys, and 1.25 in England and Wales as a whole. The want of a 'communal conscience' in country areas became all the more noticeable during the interwar years.[90] Emphasis on living conditions instead of its successful components opened up a new critique, one that included condemnation of the county's business and cultural leadership. After surveying the Board of Education report for 1914, the *Welsh Outlook* highlighted the extent of dental disease in the county, asking 'What is Cardiganshire doing? Will not some retired milk-seller remove this reproach from the mouths of the children of his native county?' The rates of tuberculosis are considered and the exasperated tone continued: 'cannot the Schools of Divinity at Aberystwyth and Lampeter devote some attention to cleanliness as well as to godliness?'[91]

The county's declining population was linked to the issue of health, and it was also discussed with reference to sections of the county that were ostensibly emblems of respectability and progress. Criticisms, that predated Caradoc Evans's invective by some forty years, were directed at a bogus morality that suffused the county's chapel-dominated villages and small towns. Editorials in the *Cambrian News*, probably penned by John Gibson, its editor between 1873 and 1915, thought that frustrated human needs encouraged people to move from country to town. Gibson, a professed lover of liberty, expressed concern that the county's political Liberalism was not accompanied by liberal attitudes. It was removed from the values of freedom that he cherished. 'Individuality' was too often treated as 'eccentricity', and 'villagers decide whether the bereaved exhibit the required manifestations of grief'.[92] This latter point countered a potent symbol, that of the large funeral, used to encapsulate the religiosity and community spirit of rural west Wales. Deadening conformity came from the very practices that contributed to the county's reputation as a centre of positive values. Although, the editorial

[90] John Davies, 'The communal conscience in Wales in the inter-war years', *Transactions of the Honourable Society of Cymmrodorion 1998*, new ser., 5 (1999), 145–60, 160.

[91] *Welsh Outlook*, 2 (1915), 44.

[92] *CN*, 16 January 1885, 4.

conceded, there were positive points about the countryside, the opportunities offered by loosening the shackles produced by 'differences of wealth, culture, ancestry and position' were an incentive to migrate, especially when combined with the likelihood of increased wages.

Internal denominational squabbles, expressed in a diatribe published by the Calvinistic Methodist journal, *Y Goleuad*, exposed many negative interpretations that set the county apart. Local Calvinistic Methodists condemned the principal of Aberystwyth's University College, the Revd Thomas Charles Edwards, for attending athletic sports held at the institution in the early 1880s. A response in *Y Goleuad* was directed at those ministers who opposed college athletics, and widened its condemnation to the county as a whole. This commentary managed to shift the county's position from a centre of respectability to a periphery where probity is virtually non-existent. It achieved this by turning what many espoused as positive motifs, such as a keen business sense and religiosity, into features that separated the area from certain norms. Entitled 'Cardiganshire and religious discipline', the piece attributed all the county's faults to the influence of the Calvinistic leadership. It presented a substantial list of charges, including poor morality among the people as evidenced by the number of children conceived out of marriage. Commercial life was berated, too, with the whole county being described as a nest of fraud and covetousness. This attack prompted a reaction from a native of the county working with the *Western Mail*. The response of 'Non con Quill' was an attempt to move the county from the periphery back to the desired centre of respectability. A long list of the county's religious leaders was noted, starting with contemporary figures before moving to fathers of Nonconformity like Daniel Rowland. Indeed, the whole county is elevated, the 'grave charges' of *Y Goleuad* being deemed unfair because they had been applied to 'a county popularly considered the most religious in Wales and freest from crime'. This struggle to locate Cardiganshire indicates how far the county was engraved in the popular consciousness and the risks that came along with its reputation for uprightness.[93]

[93] *Y Goleuad*, 21 May 1881, 9; *WM*, 30 May 1881, 3. Also see *Pontypridd Chronicle*, 2 July 1881, 2.

Unfortunately for defenders of the county's honour like 'Non con Quill', there were other pockets of opinion that placed the Cardi some distance from positive values. One man remembers how, on moving to the Rhondda in 1895, he was informed that Cardis were overly ambitious: if a Cardi got his foot into any room he would soon be sitting on the chair near the fire. Such ambition – demonstrated by 'colonies' of people from south Cardiganshire and north Pembrokeshire who set up shops in the Rhondda from the 1880s – became increasingly distant from the values espoused by many in the mining valleys, especially during times of widespread distress. The gap between the Liberal ideal and a more egalitarian view of society was debated within Cardiganshire's borders. However, as the struggles of the working classes intensified in the south-east, and 'took on the appearance of a class society' by the eve of the First World War, specific attributes commonly held typical of the Cardi were increasingly condemned, notably in the press and novels of the time.[94] The importation of police from the county during the industrial disturbances of 1911 inflamed this attitude.[95] Amid the many facets that comprised the image of the Cardi in the war and interwar years, that of being apart from a 'communal conscience' would prove central.[96] Contention between the champions of the county's cultural centrality and marginality increased in years covered in the following chapter.

[94] Hesgin, 'Y Cardis', *Y Fflam*, 1, 5 (1948), 24–5, 24; E. D. Lewis, *The Rhondda Valleys* (London, 1959), p. 236; Chris Williams, *Democratic Rhondda: Politics and Society, 1885–1951* (Cardiff, 1996), p. 24. Also see David Smith, 'Tonypandy 1910: definitions of community', *Past and Present*, 87 (1980), 158–84, 172–3, and *Pontypridd Chronicle*, 29 January 1881, 2.

[95] *Glamorgan County Times*, 28 July 1911, 5. See the comments of Allan Rogers, MP for the Rhondda, who said in 1998: 'back at the beginning of the century, my ancestors were called a lot of things by the Cardies who came in to join the then Glamorgan constabulary': *House of Commons Hansard Debates*, 26 January 1998 (pt 14), col. 52. Also see David Evans, *Labour Strife in the South Wales Coalfield, 1910–1911* (Cardiff, 1911), p. 257.

[96] For values located in the Welsh miner, see Hywel Teifi Edwards, 'The Welsh collier as hero: 1850–1950', *Welsh Writing in English*, 2 (1996), 22–48. For numbers of migrants entering Glamorgan in this period, see Brinley Thomas, 'The migration of labour into the Glamorganshire coalfield (1861–1911), *Economica*, 30 (1930), 275–94.

V

LIBERAL AND INDIVIDUAL, 1914–1945

An agricultural economic base and a declining population continued to influence the way in which Cardiganshire and the Cardi were located between and during the world wars.[1] New imperatives, however, altered the meanings attached to these structural features, thus ensuring that Cardiganshire retained its value in discourse. These included a modification of the dichotomy between rural and industrial Wales caused by the latter's ailing industries. There was all the more reason to deem Cardiganshire an agricultural county during this time as the woollen industry, which had given some parts a pseudo-industrial feel, declined. The sale of great estates after the First World War meant that there were more small landowners, yet this group did not receive as much commendation as it had during the late Victorian and Edwardian periods.[2] An emphasis on home-based food production during the wars, and a growing awareness of its importance between them, also directed assessments of the county. One Cardiganshire man recollected that during the First World War, miners from the south went about the county to entreat ('crefu') farmers for butter, eggs and bacon – in all likelihood, this seller's market accentuated the image of the shilling-accumulating Cardi. The founda-

---

[1] Between 1871 and 1881 the population declined by 4.32 per cent and between 1881 and 1891 it fell by 10.87 per cent. Furthermore, between 1921 and 1931 there was a decline of 9.36 per cent and between 1931 and mid-1939 there was an estimated slide of 6.4 per cent: John Williams, *Digest of Welsh Historical Statistics*, 2 vols (Cardiff, 1985), vol. 1, p. 12; see p. 122 for Cardiganshire's occupational structure at this time.

[2] J. Geraint Jenkins, *Life and Tradition in Rural Wales* (Stroud, 1991), pp. 105–6; John Davies, 'The end of the great estates and the rise of freehold farming in Wales', *Welsh History Review*, 7 (1974–5), 186–212, 212; Richard J. Moore-Colyer, 'Farming in depression: Wales between the wars, 1919–1939', *Agricultural History Review*, 46 (1998), 177–96. Still, the cultural value placed on farmers emerged in popular publications: see I. O. Evans, 'Cardiganshire', in S. P. B. Mais and T. Shephenson (eds), *Lovely Britain* (London, 1935), pp. 222–5, 222.

tion of the Milk Marketing Board in 1933 led the milking of cows to become more profitable for some farmers than the grooming of horses.[3]

Politics further distinguished the county. Liberal Party support continued to be robust in this period. At a time when the Liberal Party was faltering on the British stage – the party accumulated only forty seats in the 1924 election – this adherence was all the more salient. Meanwhile, Labour champions asserted that 'Liberalism and the Liberal party had now parted company and that true Liberalism lay in supporting the Labour party and progress'. Labour's claim to personify the future had consequences for the county's progressive image. Class tensions were articulated; the stitches of the Liberal banner, which held worker and employer together, were being gently unpicked by the rise of Labour. Although changes in class-consciousness happened in rural areas, such as Cardiganshire, where rural labourers' societies increased activity in the interwar years, the shift was greatest in the industrial regions of south-east Wales.[4] Cardiganshire's political complexion and its predominantly agricultural population drew sharp comparisons with industrial areas. Gwyn A. Williams's comment that the county exhibited 'a slow, inward looking and complacent Liberalism', is a relatively recent example of a socialist Welshman's judgement evoked by the county's muted radicalism. Contemporaries said much the same. When a Labour candidate, the Revd D. M. Jones, came bottom of the poll in 1932, he observed that the people of the county were not ready for the gospel of socialism yet.[5] Within the county, criticism of the individualistic, non-communal behaviour of Cardiganshire's farmers and its rural middle class shaped commentary about perceived Cardi characteristics in this period.

Notions of Welshness continued to play a part in Cardiganshire's representation. The 1921 census recorded

---

[3] Evan Jones, *Balchder Crefft* (Abertawe, 1976), p. 92; Richard Phillips, *Dyn a'i Wreiddiau: Hanes Plwyf Llangwyryfon* (Aberystwyth, 1975), pp. 86–7.

[4] Michael Bentley, *The Liberal Mind, 1914–1929* (Cambridge, 1977), p. 121; David A. Pretty, *The Rural Revolt that Failed: Farm Workers' Trade Unions in Wales, 1889–1950* (Cardiff, 1989), p. 111.

[5] Gwyn A. Williams, *The Making of a Unitarian: David Ivan Jones, 1843–1924* (London, 1995), p. 13; *CTA*, 30 September 1932, 1.

a decrease in adult Welsh speakers for the first time, and calls to preserve aspects of Welsh culture swelled. The formation of Plaid Genedlaethol Cymru, later Plaid Cymru (the Party of Wales), in 1925, together with the foundation of a youth movement, Urdd Gobaith Cymru (the League of the Hope of Wales), two years earlier, revealed a willingness to protect Welsh-speaking Wales. With its Welsh-speaking population never slipping below 80 per cent, according to the census returns of 1921 and 1931, Cardiganshire was an important geographical symbol.[6] This was especially so in the south-Walian context, where comparisons between east and west were common. No Plaid Cymru candidate stood in Cardiganshire – although one of the four seats contested by this party during the interwar years was for the University of Wales seat, whose voters included graduates of the Welsh colleges, and a county council seat (Talybont) was won by the Revd Fred Jones in 1928. Some of the party's leading figures, such as the historian William Ambrose Bebb and the dramatist James Kitchener Davies, came from the county. At this stage, cultural aspects dominated the party's agenda, and it was Cardiganshire's cultural potency as an emblem of Welshness rather than as any bastion of political nationalism that pervaded representations of the county. Distinctiveness in terms of Welshness combined with other facets of the county's individuality, its agricultural economic base, its immigrant tradition and the county's personification in the Cardi.

Technological innovations, notably motor transport and the cinema, induced and amplified representations of the county. By the late 1930s, for instance, a local commentator expressed concern that the county's distinctive dialects were being eroded because the motorbike enabled young men and women from opposite ends of Cardiganshire to form relationships. People from the county could read more about their area than before as newspapers included additional debate. They could see films depicting their home county; between

---

[6] J. W. Aitchison and Harold Carter, 'The Welsh language 1921–1991: a geolinguistic perspective', in Geraint H. Jenkins and Mari A. Williams (eds), 'Let's Do Our Best for the Ancient Tongue': The Welsh Language in the Twentieth Century (Cardiff, 2000), pp. 29–107, 34, 35–6.

1915 and 1920 three of Allen Raine's novels were adapted
to film. Scholars at Aberystwyth's university college culturally
located the county and its inhabitants through publications
and lectures. Beyond the county, groups of people from
Cardiganshire who lived in Cardiff and London formed societies, and their activities were relayed in the county's local
press.[7] Evan Evans of Llangeitho, a successful businessman in
London, demonstrated how modern means could enhance
contact with the home county when he arranged for a
plane to fly from the capital to his home village to enable
him to attend its agricultural show.[8] New sources emerged
that expressed opinions about the Cardi and the county.
The stream of writing emanating from south-east Wales,
long a source of impressions of Cardiganshire, offered new
perspectives. These were complemented by Caradoc Evans's
contentious *oeuvre*. Reactions to these portraits of the Cardi
reveal how locations of the county brought contrasting views
to light during a tense period that marked 'a struggle for the
hearts and minds of the Welsh people'.[9]

NAMING

Letters in the local press frequently signed off with the name
'Cardi'. More importantly, such correspondence alludes
to qualities associated with the area's inhabitants. These
included common sense, an eye for profit and a special
relationship with the land. During 1924, one correspondent
bemoaned recent failures to exploit the county's lead seams,
noting that only one mine was operating at that time. The
new, larger companies have, Cardi argued, wasted money by
not heeding the advice of one of the 'old school of Mining
captains [who] were invariably experienced' and made
profits even during the leanest times: 'Similar tales can be

[7] D. J. Morgan, 'Y sir: rhai o'i phobl a'i phethau', *Cymdeithas Ceredigion Llundain
Llawlyfr*, 3 (1936–7), 21–9, 27; David Berry, *Wales and Cinema: The First Hundred Years*
(Cardiff, 1996), pp. 66–72.

[8] T. I. Ellis, *Crwydro Llundain* (Abertawe, 1971), p. 26.

[9] Emyr Humphreys, *The Taliesin Tradition* (London, 1983), p. 224. Reactions to
Caradoc Evans's controversial collection of short stories, *My People*, are discussed
by John Harris in 'Caradoc Evans: my people right or wrong', *Transactions of the
Honourable Society of Cymmrodorion 1995*, new ser., 2 (1996), 141–55.

told of several others and within a few years, the whole of the expensive modern machinery was either left derelict or sold as scrap.'[10] In Cardi's summary of the state of mineral extraction in northern Cardiganshire, the practical, traditional and basic outsmart the theoretical, modern and complicated. There is, though, a note of powerlessness, originating in the locals' inability to provide the capital needed to conduct operations. Being an 'uneducated man', an old mining captain's sage advice was ignored. Although education was embedded in many representations of Cardiganshire's inhabitants, this tale challenges its inherent value. Such contradictions are overlooked in general comments about the Cardi and education, and this letter hints at another variant of 'Cardi-ness' that differed from the professional variety that dominates the written record.

Outsiders' comments complement self-definitions. A familiar, humorous use of the name found its way into a 1935 travel book written by Edmund Vale, who also wrote about architecture and heritage. Vale used the term 'Cardy Boys', which he noted is 'self-styled' and synonymous with the 'cheerful, optimistic, industrious inhabitants' of the county. On one level, this illustrates and perpetuates the supremacy of the male as a public symbol of Cardiganshire's inhabitants. The characteristics of the 'Cardy Boys' described by Vale suggest that they do not belong to the professional strata of Cardiganshire's residents or émigrés. Instead, this picture of sanguine and hard-working men contrasts with the industrial workers whose plight had necessitated the Depressed Areas Bill of 1934 which created special areas in receipt of government aid. In this instance of naming with its emphasis on 'can do', the county of Cardigan is a kind of reverse special area peopled by those who help themselves, as seen in the following 'local legend' about New Quay harbour: 'It is rather typical of the "Cardy Boys" that when the Government offered them the services of Rennie [a distinguished engineer] to build them a harbour . . . they chose to carry out the work themselves.'[11] Although the work was deemed inferior by Vale, who had a critical and informed eye on engineering

[10] CN, 24 October 1924, 3.
[11] Edmund Vale, The World of Wales (London, 1935), pp. 99, 131–2.

matters, their indomitable spirit and independence was something that Vale believed marked these people out, making the place a centre of desirable values.

Unlike the previous examples of naming, Caradoc Evans, who spent most of his childhood in southern Cardiganshire, associated the Cardi with less salubrious features. The publication of Evans's short stories, *My People*, in 1915 provoked outrage as its focus on unpraiseworthy characteristics tarnished the Welsh halo that had been repeatedly polished with respectability. In his 1930 novel, *Nothing to Pay*, Evans made one of his infrequent references to the name. He also informed his readers of his own definition of the name. Evans explained that the character Amos, who had just arrived at Carmarthen to begin work as a draper's assistant, was unaware that 'Cardi is a disparaging term, even among the Welsh'. Amos was depicted as a country dweller out of place in a large town, and Evans intimates poor education and rural simplicity when a fellow worker, Trots, remarks 'Fancy a Cardi can read!' as Amos notices the sign of his employer-to-be. Yet Evans challenged more than the image of the educated Cardi; he associated the name with deceit and acquisitiveness. Amos's new employer in Cardiff, Sam Samson, on being told that Amos hailed from Cardiganshire announced: 'Every Cardi are liars.' In Evans's book about the London Welsh, a character says 'like the old Welsh of Cardigan is your cunning'.[12] Dylan Thomas summarized features associated with the name, too, highlighting the importance that migrants from the county played in its definition. Thomas, who spent time at New Quay and Talsarn, touched on how the London Cardis contributed to the county-type at this time. In *Where Tawe Flows*, completed in 1939, Thomas associated the name with profit-minded London Welsh milk traders when a Mr Evans says: 'The Cardies always go back to Wales to die when they've rooked the cockneys and made a packet.'[13]

Naming did not always encase a simple stereotype extracted from a particular section thought to represent the

[12] Caradoc Evans, *Nothing to Pay* (London, 1930), pp. 78, 147; *idem*, *My Neighbours: Stories of the Welsh People* (New York, 1920), p. 240.

[13] D. Thomas, 'Where Tawe flows', in *Collected Stories*, ed. W. Davies (London, 1993), pp. 186–200, 197.

area. As the above examples show, the name could evoke various features. Nonetheless, there was a certain precision used when naming the inhabitants of Cardiganshire. In 1921 the rector of Llangeitho, D. Worthington, wrote two articles on the county's contribution to Welsh culture in the Church in Wales journal, *Yr Haul*. In this tribute, Worthington remarked that Cardis came in only two varieties. They were either saintly individuals like the Methodist preacher Daniel Rowland, or roguish characters like Twm Shon Cati – the early modern Welsh Robin Hood.[14] Either way, there was something definite about the Cardi, something about the name that could be attached to human qualities and, therefore, assume greater and symbolic significance. In addition to listing various county notables, Worthington was indirectly sketching the significance of a county-type that expressed archetypal aspects of human nature. He was implying that there is something genuine, unaffected in the type. A key part of the Cardi's rootedness was tradition. The qualities of the Cardi and the county had been located in the past before, but external and internal changes led to variations in emphasis that need to be explored if the county's complex relationship with the past is to be fully appreciated.

PAST

As the county's complexion was determined by contrast, value placed on Cardiganshire's proximity to the past increased as a consequence of social strife, industrial decline and techno-logical change. The plummeting fortunes of the coal industry added lustre to an imagined rural setting. Furthermore, personal associations influenced the location of tradition in Cardiganshire. These included the county's attributes being drawn upon in recollections of seemingly less complicated times. As in former periods, folklore contributed to this link with the past, but technological change now provided a sharper contrast. Works on Welsh folklore relied on the county for a disproportionate amount of their material. In

[14] D. Worthington, 'Enwogion Ceredigion', *Yr Haul*, Cyfres Dolgellau, 23 (1921), 161–2, 162.

addition, commentators noted discontinuities with the past. These perceptions emphasized the losses within the county, rather than celebrated the relative plenitude of residues. They identified a gap between Cardiganshire present and Cardiganshire past.

The memoirs of Thomas Jones, a civil servant whose consensus-mindedness can be seen in speeches he wrote for Stanley Baldwin, reinforced a particular mental location. Built on a contrast with contemporary class tensions, Jones's impressions located Cardiganshire in a partial past. Jones was born in Monmouthshire, but his father hailed from Cardiganshire and had moved to the south-east where he became the manager of a company shop. Differences between his father and other men demonstrate how Jones perceived the gap between old and new Wales: 'Debt and dishonesty were the bugbears of my father's life and indolence he could not abide. He had brought with him from his home in the country great physical strength, energy and self-reliance. He had not a lazy bone in his body.' Reminiscences of holidays during the 1880s on a farm between Tregaron and Pontrhydfendigaid also evoked tradition through descriptions of a simple lifestyle of peat cutting, family prayers and home-made clothes. No mention was made of tensions between parts of the rural community. It is peaceful, the train does not interrupt this quiet farm and the only aural intrusion comes from the 'yelling English hawkers' who provided the 'cheap cottons' that the author contrasted with the best 'homespun' clothes. Revealingly, given Caradoc Evans's publications, Jones sought to counter what he described as the current 'fashion to poke fun at the characteristics of the small peasantry'. Jones, who was a negotiator in many industrial disputes, clearly found something comforting in these recollections, in which the hard work 'was transfigured by the graceful acts and thousand decencies of daily life . . . the home had a simple beauty which in retrospect I find difficult to parallel in *my subsequent experience* [my italics]'.[15] Jones was

---

[15] Thomas Jones, *Rhymney Memories* (Newtown, 1938), pp. 115, 93. For more on his life, see E. L. Ellis, *T.J.: A Life of Doctor Thomas Jones, CH* (Cardiff, 1992). For similar reminiscences and opinions, see Glamorgan Record Office, William Jones, 'Memories of Llanafan School', D/DX 935/295; E. J. Saunders, *Rhamant y De* (Llanelli, 1933), pp. 86–7.

looking back (he was sixty-eight years old when the memoirs were published) but he was also defending the contemporary peasant population from ridicule.

There was a twofold conception – of Cardiganshire as pleasant past and industrial south-east Wales as unpleasant present – that permeated popular consciousness in the interwar years. Wolverhampton-born B. L. Coombes wrote accounts of his life as a miner in the south Wales valleys. In his abandoned novel *Castell Vale*, written in the mid-1930s – a time when many were fleeing the valleys' 'slough of despond', some with the aid of the Industrial Transference Scheme – Coombes introduced a character known simply as 'Jack's mother'. She was a woman sculpted by life in the open air; her 'face was still weather-beaten from many years of Cardigan's sun and wind'. Coombes related that Jack's mother's 'longing for her native Cardiganshire was still strong', and she did not find it easy mixing with others. Even her speech – the 'sibilant S's of the Cardigan dialect were very plain' – marked her as a *déracinée*. Her son, Jack, was also a product of the county's rural environment that bestowed specific characteristics: 'clean living and an early life spent on a farm had given him a strength that was unusual'. Jack also reads George Borrow's description of Cardiganshire – which enables him to 'see over the hills to my home' – and he is determined to return there with his mother. Like Thomas Jones's father, 'Jack's mother' stood for something different from the distressing present, the economic uncertainty and turmoil of the interwar coalfield; in the story industrial disputes had eaten away Jack's savings with which he intended to buy their old farm. Jack's mother's comments about the pointlessness of young men who used to be miners being taught how to be farmers – 'they'll never learn farming, it's got to be in the blood' – pointed towards the basic relationship with nature that she, her son and the county typified. Links between people and nature were valued by Coombes: they appear to offer something more than the vagaries of coalfield life, which he experienced during the lockouts of the 1920s. Cardiganshire's appeal was a personal one, an allure of past stability that extended, as Coombes illustrates, beyond those raised in the area. It must be remembered, however, that there were soup kitchens for needy children in Cardigan in the winter of 1934–5.[16]

The county was a portal to the past. This representation was amplified by the accessibility afforded by the car and other means of transport. Along with two other novelties espied in its 'Peeps through the window of the world', a 1935 Pathe newsreel featured postmen on horseback in the east of the county, a signal contrast to increased motorized transport.[17] Like this film, visitors' accounts did not embody the past in particular people such as those drawn upon by writers from south-east Wales; rather, it was expressed in a wide range of objects and symbols. A Liberal speaker who visited Cardiganshire during the lively 1921 by-election campaign, which set Liberal against Liberal, placed Cardiganshire firmly in the past. Writing under the name Gwytherin, the author assembled a collection of praiseworthy traditional features. In Aberaeron, for example, the parlour of an inn is described as being full of people, 'farmers and sea-faring folk', discussing politics. The selection of these occupations is significant as they epitomized long-established means of earning a living. Upstairs in the author's room there was a candlestick, whose unintentionally organic design Gwytherin described as being 'without handles, perfect in proportion, tender in their silver grey colouring, solid to the touch, with their shallow bowls curving upwards like the calyx of a flower. When shall we make, unconsciously, such things of beauty again, thought I.' This object and the weather-beaten people downstairs are deemed 'pearls', a word containing within it biblical connotations of purity. Most of the rooms in other places described by Gwytherin were lit by candle light or oil lamps, at a time – the early 1920s – that witnessed the swift advance of electricity.[18] Although the author mentioned

[16] B. L. Coombes, *With Dust Still in His Throat: An Anthology of Writing by B. L. Coombes*, ed. Bill Jones and Chris Williams (Cardiff, 1999), pp. 102–4; *CTA*, 29 March 1935, 1. For an investigation of the land's appeal at this time, see Pyrs Gruffudd, 'Back to the land: historiography, rurality and the nation in interwar Wales', *Transactions of the Institute of British Geographers*, new ser., 19, 1 (1994), 61–77.

[17] *Peeps through the window of the world* (no. 28), British Pathe, 4 April 1935. For a social history of the car, see Sean O'Connell, *The Car in British Society: Class, Gender and Motoring, 1896–1939* (Manchester, 1998).

[18] Gwytherin, 'Cardiganshire, February, 1921', *Welsh Outlook*, 8 (1921), 107–9, 107–8.

that he was born in Kent, the Cardiganshire he visited in 1921 took him back to his childhood. The past as a concept was located in the tanned faces and craftsmanship seen in Cardiganshire.

Past locations are most securely anchored by extant folk customs and beliefs. Two books published in the 1930s perpetuated the connection between the area and old beliefs that had existed more than a century earlier. In T. Gwynn Jones's *Welsh Folklore and Welsh Customs*, twelve of the forty-eight authorities consulted in the making of the book were from Cardiganshire, more than from any other county. The content of the book naturally reflects this, and may in part be accounted for by the Denbighshire-born author having resided in Aberystwyth for many years while working as a librarian and lecturer. One of the authorities cited by Jones was his friend Evan Isaac, a Wesleyan Methodist minister from northern Cardiganshire. In 1938, Isaac published his own collection of Welsh folk tales entitled *Coelion Cymru* (Welsh Beliefs). Even though his work was based on Welsh customs and beliefs as a whole, the north of the county supplied a disproportionate amount of material. Belief in spirits, Isaac observed, was an established feature of this part of Wales. Isaac's superstitious northern Cardis exuded individuality, a distinctiveness accentuated by their relationship with symbols of modern life. A section of Isaac's book is dedicated to the belief in curses, often used to explain anything strange. The distance between these superstitions and modern life is illustrated by examples from the 1920s and 1930s, one featuring two doctors' being told by an ill woman's husband that their diagnosis was incorrect and that her ailment originated from a curse, and the other concerned the author's motorbike being cursed by an elderly woman he had upset.[19] Cardiganshire harboured a remnant of the past in its least visited corners.

Yet this past location could be based on something more philosophical than quaint beliefs. The poet R. S. Thomas

[19] T. Gwynn Jones, *Welsh Folklore and Folk-Customs* (London, 1930), pp. xi–xii; Evan Isaac, *Coelion Cymru* (Aberystwyth, 1938), pp. 52, 134–6. For another past-focused work about old village characters Isaac had known, see *Yr Hen Gyrnol a Brasluniau Eraill* (Aberystwyth, 1935). Also see NLW, MS David Thomas (Aberystwyth), section B.

wrote an essay on 'The depopulation of the Welsh hill country', published in the journal *Wales* in 1945, that extolled isolated hill dwellers and hoped that modern life's 'desire for uniformity' would bypass 'these hardy and extremely individual people'.[20] Thomas referred to a category of people who lived in different parts of Wales but shared a link to the land about them. Cardiganshire's highlands contained a number of these people. So when there was a 'search for a cross-cultural primordial humanity' after the First World War, such areas were prioritized in discourse. As will be seen below, these examples of perceived essence also led to groups being identified as a hope for the future, particularly when many perceived 'modern civilization [as being] inevitably self-destructive'.[21]

Some, however, focused on the erosion of past landmarks. Paying attention to this aspect counters the simplistic notion of the county, or, rather, selected parts of it, as solely serving as a comforter in times of change. Instead, rapid depopulation around the turn of the century was thought to have changed Cardiganshire's character. An early example of this sentiment of loss can be found in the aptly entitled *Dail yr Hydref* (Autumn Leaves), written by Daniel Thomas and published in 1916. The First World War contributed to this sense of loss, but the darkening of the scene was primarily attributed to extractions from the area, not to importations that had detached the area from a recent, defining past. Out-migration, primarily to the south-east, had pulled the heart from the author's home village; Dôl-y-Bont was littered with empty and ruined houses. Foremost among those missed by the author were the craftsmen. There was, therefore, a qualitative loss in addition to a quantitative one. A section of the community – the tanners, tailors, cobblers and smiths – had been shed, leaving a place shorn of diversity.[22]

---

[20] R. S. Thomas, 'The depopulation of the Welsh hill country', *Wales*, 7 (1945), 75–80, 80.
[21] Frank Trentmann, 'Civilization and its discontents: English neo-Romanticism and the transformation of anti-Modernism in twentieth-century western culture', *Journal of Contemporary History*, 29, 4 (1994), 583–625, 602, 601.
[22] Daniel Thomas, *Dail yr Hydref: Sef Adgofion am Dol-y-Bont, Llanfihangel-Genau'r-Glyn, a Rhos-y-Gell* (Dinbych, 1916), p. 9.

Occupations help to shape regional representations, and the demise of occupational diversity was believed to have profound consequences for Cardiganshire's spirit. In the 1920s, an academic commented on the decline in the number of craftsmen. Richard Phillips remarked that more pastoral farming and a higher standard of living had attended the decline of arable farming and out-migration. Even so, he regretted the demise of the village artisan. Additionally, those who remained were the least vibrant: 'The area is now populated by people interested in agriculture only, and the absence of the tonic effect of other callings is a consider-able loss to the social life of the district.'[23] This way of life was not only being preferred to some external feature, but was deemed better than contemporary Cardiganshire, which had been denuded of its non-farming population. The loss of craftsmen, who rapidly became a symbol of the past, influenced conceptions of Cardiganshire between the wars, contributing a local rivulet to the stream of opinion that valued the past over change. Part of this was an admiration of independence and self-sufficiency. The distinctiveness of old communities was observed in their self-reliance. In a time of increased mass consumption, the memory of closely situ-ated trades interlinked in a village or market town setting had considerable potency. Words like 'independence' and 'skilful' were used to describe the work of craftsmen, and, more broadly, the non-specialists who made their own tools. The connection between the county and particular trades, such as basket making, added more poignancy to the account of their demise.[24] Part of the county's identity is thought to have wilted, and this sense of loss is a reminder that places that may epitomize the past for some are for others victims of change.

Changes had been afoot for some time but they multiplied during the wars and the interwar years and were magnified by commentators. Cardiganshire as a 'typical' country area was compared with the industrial areas to the east and with

[23] Richard Phillips, 'Some aspects of the agricultural conditions in Cardiganshire in the nineteenth century', *Welsh Journal of Agriculture*, 1 (1925), 22–8, 28.
[24] R. M. Evans, 'Folklore and customs in Cardiganshire', *Cardiganshire Antiquarian Society Transactions*, 12 (1937), 51–7, 51–2.

modern life in general, and could be used by those uneasy with aspects of the present. However, locating the past in rural areas and their inhabitants, present or long departed, existed alongside other portrayals of the Cardi and Cardiganshire that concentrated on the future – a future that contrasted with, or even offered a way out of, the problems besetting interwar Britain. A similarity between the two locations lies in the continued particularization of the county and its people.

FUTURE

Some comments about the county's potential concentrated on the need to improve its infrastructure. In 1924, an editorial warned that the county had two futures: 'It may develop into a holiday ground, or drop back into an indolent condition and support a small population on a small harvest of small potatoes. Nothing is so conducive to prosperity as good roads.'[25] Yet some projections drew on characteristics particular to this geographically peripheral area. These representations of Cardiganshire differed from those forward-looking features identified in the previous chapter because they did not include the optimism of democratic advance. There were, however, other missions requiring a progressive narrative that found inspiration in the county and its people. During this period county societies were especially active; their members saw Cardiganshire as a place where the individual could learn ways that would garner future success, and as a place with the potential to regenerate a fissured society. In doing so, they demonstrate how notions of progress reinforce the morality of the peripheral.

The county-type that valued education and sought opportunities elsewhere, first evident in the late Victorian and Edwardian period, continued to be deployed in the twentieth century. Thriving migrants lent the image greater potency as successful émigrés provided examples of the Cardi's reputed knack of climbing the ladder. Nevertheless, a humorous tale related in 1931 by Hugh Evans, an author and publisher from Denbighshire, noted a less sophisticated

---

[25] *CN*, 7 March 1924, 5.

native of Cardiganshire than the one who expounded the
area's virtues at county society meetings. It reveals, however,
that the association of the Cardi with individual progress
was not restricted to the more well-off members of society.
In the story, a group of English imperialists sought new land
to conquer and after a treacherous journey found an enormous wall at the end of the world on which they stuck the
Union flag. Some of the conquerors scaled the edifice, and
saw on the other side a Cardi sitting on his haunches, casually
smoking: an epitome of the pioneering spirit ahead and yet
at the same time part of the greatest empire of the world.[26]
Evans cited the north Pembrokeshire-born archdruid Evan
Rees (Dyfed) as the source of this comic story that indicates how far the climbing (literally in this case) Cardi had
entered collective reference by the interwar years. A traditional Glamorgan tune 'Cân y Cardi' (The Cardi's Song)
was first published in 1928: it celebrated a hardy man who
moved to the coal districts and ended up earning more than
his father, indicating how significantly migration contributed
to a generic county character.[27]

Traces left by these earthy figures point to a different kind
of Cardi from the persons who had moved to Swansea and
wore 'chic evening toilettes' at the 'Swansea and District
Cardiganshire Society's Dinner and Dance' in 1938.[28]
Nonetheless, they both fostered the notion of a distinct
people, marked by origins and advancement in the world.
They gave the symbol of the advancing Cardi, whether miner
or minister's wife, added resonance because they ensured
that it existed on more than one level. This potent combination of individual and county amplified the county's
character. Against a backdrop of interwar regional poverty
and class divides, a section of migrants from Cardiganshire
celebrated material and cultural advancements at annual
dinners. The stress placed on progress from agricultural
labourer to industrial worker is, the above mentioned song
aside, less well recorded; doubtlessly because it lost some of
its sheen at times when staple industries were suffering.

[26] Hugh Evans, *Cwm Eithin* (Lerpwl, 1931), pp. 4–5.
[27] *Y Darian*, 29 March 1928, 3.
[28] NLW, MS Mary Williams 1042, 'Bundle of newspaper reports of activities of the
Swansea and District Cardiganshire Society'.

Although there is evidence that people from the county met socially in the early years of the twentieth century, it was during the interwar period that these societies assumed prominence, prompting regular press coverage.[29] In the declarations of various worthies, from Swansea to London, it is possible to discern an eagerness to attach a group's activities to a name. They were not alone: there were Pembrokeshire, Devonian and Carmarthenshire societies in 1930s Swansea, for instance. Societies founded on links with Cardiganshire, however, could call upon a motif with accumulated cultural capital in the form of the Cardi. Shifts in expressions of identity are often propelled by 'the pursuit of political advantage and/or material self-interest'; this may well explain early associations between people from the same area in a new, urban environment.[30] Moreover, a group narrative of hard work and deserved reward could be used to justify material success. Put differently, expressions of group identity could sum up the group experience – write its story, so to speak – as well as satisfy immediate material needs through the pecuniary benefits of networking.

Highlighting their Cardi links identified these well-heeled migrants with a tale of deserved success. An account by 'A returned exile' in the *Cambrian News* demonstrates the selective nature of those chosen to represent the successful Cardi. The progress of those born in Cardiganshire was measured by their status outside the county. These people constituted a category of notables too numerous to be listed in a modern equivalent of the nineteenth-century publications about county figures, but these symbols of success were entered in newspaper columns. They often claimed that achievements were based on a character formed by the county. According to the 'returned exile', his fellow Cardis were, by 1924, to be found in worthy positions, in both 'Church and State', from Holyhead to Cardiff and beyond Wales. Indeed, few places

---

[29] According to one newspaper, the first reunion of 'Cardiganshire men and women' in Cardiff was on 7 March 1908: *WG*, 2 April 1908, 2. Increased interwar activity is demonstrated by the publication of the London Cardiganshire Society's first handbook in 1935, and the evidence left by Mary Williams (NLW, MSS 1037–1042) relates to county society activity in Swansea during the 1930s.

[30] Richard Jenkins, *Rethinking Ethnicity: Arguments and Explanations* (London, 1997), pp. 44–5.

have 'the misfortune to lack a Cardi among its estimable residents. Thus in Holyhead the Vicar, the Headmaster of the
County School, and the manager of the National Provincial
Bank all hail from Cardiganshire'.[31] Not only was a claim
being made for the Cardis' acumen, but there was a celebration of an ability to notch up a particular type of success, one
based on professions and the public acknowledgement that
often accompanied these positions.

The image of the county was central to many pronouncements made in speeches at society meetings. Cardiganshire's
lack of industry and poor soil made the trajectory of progress
sketched in these speeches appear all the more impres-
sive. Furthermore, a sense of deserved success was derived
from this reiteration of background want.[32] A revealing
example of these mores is provided by a report of the Cardiff
Cardiganshire Society's seventh annual dinner, presided
over by A. T. James, barrister at law, in 1923. During the
event, John Humphreys Davies, principal of the university
college at Aberystwyth since 1919, spoke of progress and
individual fortunes. While the past formed the subject of
many of the society's lectures, the reports and speeches dwelt
on contemporary success and individual progression. Davies
mentioned that the decline in lead mining and shipbuilding
led to dependence on a 'poor and bleak soil'. This forged
characteristics that insured that a man from Cardiganshire
'could succeed anywhere once he left his native county'.
As well as indicating the male-dominated narrative of the
Cardi diaspora, Davies's speech featured the related strand
of accomplishment in a career as a mark of Cardiganshire's
migrants. He also made a telling reference to the reception
given to these achievers that pointed to tensions about the
way the archetypal Cardi's ambition could lead to the group
being located away from communitarian qualities desired
by other sections of society. Such accomplishments, Davies
noted, 'perhaps accounted for the feeling of jealousy with
which he [the migrant Cardi] was sometimes regarded

[31] *CN*, 10 October 1924, 8.

[32] Jean Peneff observes that 'the myth of a poor childhood can be found in
almost all the better-off sections of society': 'Myths in life stories', in R. Samuel and
P. Thompson (eds), *The Myths We Live By* (London, 1990), pp. 36–48, 37.

by natives of more productive soil where a living could be gained easier'.[33]

In marked contrast with those employed in ailing industries, material advancement was experienced by other sections of society during the interwar years.[34] The pronouncements of the county societies used a county character to explain advancement at this time of contrast; a general shift was being particularized by these societies. Society members also identified opportunities to acquire wealth. A lecture given in 1935 on 'The sanctuary of Saint David and its future' ended with the plea to found a 'gliding centre' in eastern Cardiganshire – incidentally, the British Gliding Association had been formed five years earlier.[35] But the future focus of these societies is most noticeable in the praise bestowed on qualities possessed by individuals. In introducing the bishop of Llandaff, the chief guest, at the London Cardiganshire Society dinner, T. Bronant Jones remarked that: 'One can only conclude that there must be some peculiar quality in being "of Cardiganshire" which ensured success, for the church, the law, the arts, politics and big business.'[36] During the interwar years the idea of the excelling Cardi was reiterated by advocates in the press; one report from the *Western Mail* in 1939 mentioned the people exported from the county acting as 'leaven [for] the whole country'.[37] This focus overlooked other groupings from, or remaining in, the county. It would have aroused some resentment from those whose shared experience was poverty and uncertainty instead of success and personal progress.

David Evans, a lecturer in German at Aberystwyth, expanded upon this notion that people from rural areas were

[33] *CN*, 16 March 1923, 3. Also see *WG*, 2 February 1933, 4; similar points were made about the 'Yorkshire character', *The Times*, 5 May 1932, 11.

[34] John Stevenson and Chris Cook, *The Slump: Society and Politics during the Depression* (London, 1979), p. 18.

[35] NLW MS, Mary Williams 2749, G. Arbour Stephens's 'The sanctuary of St. David and its future', 13. Not all features of modern life, especially the decline of 'home-produced food', pleased Stephens, who was a medical man. Also see *WG*, 26 December 1935, p. 2. His double role as midwife of modernity and an embalmer of tradition is apparent in his call for Wales to have more airports: 'Rhaid i Gymru cael aeroplens', *Ford Gron*, 1 (1930–1), 5.

[36] *CN*, 22 April 1932, 8.

[37] *WM*, 17 February 1939, 8.

more successful than others in the world at large. His view
that virtues unique to rural areas needed to be acknowledged
and preserved was shared by many at this time – indeed, he
mentioned Benito Mussolini's policy of imposing penal-
ties on those migrating to urban areas. Rural depopulation
was causing concern in Cardiganshire, which was experiencing an interwar exodus. Based on the dictum 'Ar arall dir
tyf arall ddyn' (Different lands grow different men), Evans
emphasized that land formed character. More specifically,
he believed that the rural environment bred an interest in
all things, whereas life in urban areas was one dimensional.
This was a sentiment similar to one contained in a comment
by David Lloyd George that 'the country is much healthier
for brain and muscle and heart than the towns'.[38] Evans
compared the rounded education afforded by countryside
living with the training received in English public schools,
namely that it developed body and mind. This psychological
facet to rural superiority, noticeable in images of the Cardi,
complemented other types of praise bestowed on rural areas.
The advantages possessed by rural man can, Davies argued,
be seen in the success of people from the countryside in the
cities – he had already mentioned the London dairy men
from Cardiganshire – because they see the whole situation
and can work out the possibilities offered by various opportunities.[39] This modern, rural renaissance man was drawn
upon to explain business success or, as Maurice Jones of
Lampeter wrote, 'those outstanding qualities we associate
with the Cardi' could explain proficiency in the many duties
modern vicars were called on to perform.[40] In addition, some
occupants of the county were used to support visions that
extended beyond individual progress and offered hope in
unsettling circumstances.

The effect of the First World War on notions of progress
based on modernization resulted in some commentators

[38] Mary Meek Atkeson, *The Woman on the Farm* (New York and London, 1924),
p. 318.

[39] David Evans, *Y Wlad: Ei Bywyd, ei Haddysg, a'i Chrefydd* (Lerpwl, 1933), pp. 6,
65, 99.

[40] Maurice Jones, 'St. David's College', *Cymdeithas Ceredigion Llundain Llawlyfr*, 3
(1936–7), 14–20, 20.

proposing alternative conceptions of progress founded on the Celt. A letter published in the *Carmarthen Journal* during 1918 expressed the hope that the Celt would rejuvenate 'this war-weary world'.[41] This expectation was placed on a people whose spiritual and cultural heritage meant that they were supposedly less influenced by materialism than other groups. Many contemporaries were suggesting an alternative path to the future that avoided the less appealing features of progress. Cardiganshire, with a little assistance from anthropology and plant breeding, was a site where these ideas could locate themselves. Some academics took callipers to people's heads and proclaimed the existence of the past in flesh and blood. The work of the Aberystwyth anthropologist H. J. Fleure permeated much commentary at this time; even a biography of the early nineteenth-century preacher Christmas Evans referred to the county's racial types.[42] Despite an awareness of the risks involved in categorization, Fleure separated races – broadly Mediterranean, Alpine, Nordic and some earlier types – and linked them with particular traits. He identified a number of types in Wales. Sparsely populated, upland areas, however, presented 'a considerable survival of ancient types relatively unmodified'. In 1926, Fleure published findings on the head shape and colourings of men in Cardiganshire in the Antiquarian Society's journal. There were a variety of types in the county, but he concluded that dark long-headed people constituted a significant part of the population. Their cultural achievements and appearance were praised; the category 'draws up a good number of people of decided intellectual ability, and this has been noted among the women who are also often very good looking'.[43] Opinions like this effectively refashioned a 'primitive' stock into a group which could provide intellectual leadership.

These dark, long-headed people were held as exemplars for the future conduct of humanity by a number of

[41] *CJ*, 15 March 1918, 3.
[42] E. Ebrard Rees, *Christmas Evans* (London, 1936), pp. 23–4.
[43] H. J. Fleure, *The Races of England and Wales: A Survey of Recent Research* (London, 1923), p. 108; *idem*, 'The people of Cardiganshire', *Cardiganshire Antiquarian Society Transactions*, 4 (1926), 15–21, 21; *idem*, 'An outline story of our neighbourhood', *Aberystwyth Studies*, 4 (1922), 111–23, 115.

intellectuals. Speaking before the Shrewsbury Cymmrodorion Society in 1927, the geographer and anthropologist E. G. Bowen explained how the people of the Pumlumon area of Cardiganshire provided an example of the advantages of slow adaptation over revolutionary change. A colleague of Fleure, Bowen concluded that modern society was inherently unstable. As a result, a

> new vision which was not to be expected from those who were obsessed with the present system . . . was more likely to come from those who retained their rural roots . . . from the ranks of these people might come leaders with a world message in these days of strife.[44]

This alternative vision, broadcast by academics, was not limited to Wales. For instance, Patrick Geddes, who had collaborated with Fleure, felt that there was some 'visionary potential' in the everyday. This disenchantment and vision gave places a theoretical future importance; good citizenship came from attachment to place, a quality that the moorland folk encapsulated.[45]

Cardiganshire could satisfy diverse requirements: the Cardi embodied material progress, and the moorland type could realign the zeitgeist on a spiritual axis. Both emphasized the isolation of the area, and from this projected something different from the perceived norm. The playwright J. O. Francis, whose attention, like that of many others, was drawn to the 'mysterious county' during the 1921 by-election, detected both when he wrote 'it is both the dream and the business'.[46] Yet the two were expressed in terms of advancement, thus allotting an active role to ostensibly contrasting elements.

Material gain and cultural advancement were brought together by R. G. Stapleton's attempt to breed strains of grass suited to the British uplands. In doing this, Stapleton hoped

[44] E. G. Bowen, 'The people and culture of rural Wales', *Bye-Gones*, n.s. 1 (1925–7), 77–8, 78. Also see J. E. Daniels, 'The geographical distribution of religious denominations in its relation to racial and social functions' (MA thesis, University of Wales, Aberystwyth, 1928), 9, 83.

[45] David Matless, 'Regional surveys and local knowledges: the geographical imagination in Britain, 1918–39', *Transactions of the Institute of British Geographers*, 17, 4 (1992), 464–80, 466, 472.

[46] J. O. Francis, *The Legend of the Welsh and Other Papers* (Cardiff, 1924), p. 80.

to preserve and enhance the livelihood of the small pastoral farmer. His 1935 work, *The Land Now and To-morrow*, referred to the importance of 'self-reliance' and revealed little affection for what he termed the 'multitude'.[47] Individual development emerging from a 'long struggle of adaptation between man and his environment' was cherished by Stapleton, and the same qualities were applied to the nation. Self-sufficiency and freedom from foreign foodstuffs would benefit the nation as well as the small farmer. In the uplands of Cardiganshire, away from large-scale agriculture, Stapleton identified an environment where he saw evidence of 'the yeoman spirit'. By offering a vision of thriving uplands rendered economic by 'modern science', this project lent descriptions of the area a future focus.[48] Interwar visitors mentioned the Plant Breeding Station and praised the work carried out there, stressing its contribution to the British Empire.[49] The *Manchester Guardian*'s comments on the establishment of new buildings for the project illustrate how the activities of this project were couched in terms of progress: 'Aberystwyth's efforts bespeak the generous interest of all who feel the maintenance of our country's rural life is of primary importance for the future of Britain.'[50] Attempts to increase the fertility of upland Cardiganshire contributed to the area's status as a typically rural and character-building environment. Stapleton may have quoted Disraeli and spoken of the English spirit of the yeoman, but the concept he venerated could be transported to Cardiganshire, where the idea was reinvigorated with the promise of science.

Projections into the future were founded on features thought to characterize the county, most notably its economic

[47] R. G. Stapleton, *The Land Now and To-morrow* (London, 1935), p. 289. The relationship between progress and the countryside was explained by Stapleton in 'The changing countryside', *Welsh Review*, 3 (1944), 283–9.

[48] R. G. Stapleton, *The Way of the Land* (London, 1943), p. 86.

[49] For example, see S. L. Bensusan, *On the Tramp in Wales* (London, 1929), pp. 92, 102. Also see H. V. Morton, *In Search of Wales* (London, 1932), pp. 180–2, and the 1942 film *Wales: Green Mountain, Black Mountain* (1942), directed by John Eldridge. For more on this field of agricultural science, see Paolo Palladino, 'Science, technology, and the economy: plant breeding in Great Britain, 1920–1970', *Economic History Review*, 49, 1 (1999), 116–36.

[50] NLW MS, Benjamin Davies, box 19, 7; *Manchester Guardian*, 23 December 1936, 11.

structure and isolation. Authors of these projections were selecting some aspects as a means towards progress both individually and collectively. In combining an idea of the county with progress, these perspectives on the potential of Cardiganshire reflected both a tangible sense of difference and disenchantment with broader trends. At the same time, the county was a centre of values that accentuated contemporary contrasts.

CENTRE

Value is often ascribed to an area because it contributes materially or ideologically to the nation state; this explains why Stapleton's experiments were so highly regarded. Such 'parental' praise, particularly during war, became an important component of Cardiganshire's image. County pride and government recognition coalesced during the Second World War when the news magnate Lord Beaverbrook, then minister for aircraft production, suggested bestowing the county's old Welsh name (Ceredigion) on two Spitfires purchased from the county's Spitfire appeal.[51] If the nuances of the county are to be fully comprehended, more diffuse estimations of the area, which located some kernel of virtue in Cardiganshire, need to be investigated as well. Many positive qualities, such as virtue and Welshness, were, according to outsiders and inhabitants, concentrated in Cardiganshire. Those keen to encourage specific patterns of behaviour drew on the county extensively during the interwar years, possibly in order to encourage the greater political nation to absorb these principles. Significantly, this praise came at a time when criticisms of characteristics thought to typify the county were appearing in print. Some assertions examined here are, therefore, reactions to criticisms. More generally, class issues, changes in patterns of leisure and religious observance influenced the location of the county at this time vis-à-vis other places. As in earlier decades, issues elsewhere shaped depictions of Cardiganshire.

[51] *CTA*, 21 March 1941, 5.

During the First World War the personal habits attributed to the county's population garnered praise from those
in authority. From the autumn of 1916 to the war's end,
£618,534 was invested in government securities through the
Cardiganshire War Savings Committee, and members of the
county's associations numbered 12,085. This contribution,
hailed as 'a record, not only for Wales but for the United
Kingdom', was all the more momentous because 'the great
majority of the population is made up of small farmers and
labourers' working 'none too fertile uplands'. A reference to
the ability of joint secretaries of the county committee, David
Thomas and Jenkin James, to 'speak the Cardiganshire dialect
of the Welsh language' reinforced Cardiganshire's difference
while illustrating its loyalty. Most studies of nationalism dwell
on how governments bring groupings and regions together
through diverse means ranging from the press to ceremony,
in the 'blurring of distinctions'. Yet nations are often evoked
through the selection of a specific part, an ideal and often
atypical component.[52] Through painting the county as poor
but loyal, the government produced a portrait of sacrifice
that served a didactic purpose. The miners of south Wales,
their minds infected by political extremism and effected by
a lack of greenery, put sectional interests above those of the
nation, as demonstrated by wartime strikes.[53] By contrast,
Cardiganshire, a rural county far removed from hotbeds of
socialism, was portrayed as a centre of hard work and patriotism. It could be said that it echoed the ideal of the gallant
small nation, something that spurred support for the war.

Natives of the county expressed distinctions between
Cardiganshire and the industrial areas of south-east Wales.
In doing so they revealed cultural and economic, rather
than strictly political, tensions. A concentration of younger
people, relatively high wages and a greater range of leisure
activities in the south-east led to contrasts being drawn. In
these judgements, the west with its relative dearth of earthly
temptations was adjudged morally superior. Contrasts

[52] Geoffrey Cubitt, 'Introduction', in Cubitt (ed.), *Imagining the Nation*
(Manchester, 1998), pp. 1–20, 5–6.
[53] Ivor Nicholson and Trevor Lloyd-Williams (eds), *Wales: Its Part in the War*
(London, 1919), pp. 170–4, 72–3.

between these two regions in terms of wealth can be found from the late eighteenth century, but this period saw more factors attached to this long-standing polarization.[54] Values located in Cardiganshire at the time indicate how intense and prevalent this feeling of difference was. Cultural diffusion was accelerated as people from the south-east returned home or came to visit, bringing ideas and activities to the county. This encouraged many to further define and distinguish the county in symbolic terms.

The association of inhabitants of Cardiganshire with a morality derived from the county's deep Nonconformist tradition was, in the face of cultural transformation and social tensions within Cardiganshire, increasingly called upon during the interwar period. Internal representations of this defining respectability can be gleaned from reports and letters printed in local newspapers. Changing leisure patterns exaggerated this reputation. Greyhound racing and the football pools raised the profile of gambling, an activity incompatible with this Nonconformist image of Cardiganshire. A correspondent to the *Welsh Gazette* in 1921 stated that the habit of 'hap-chwareu' (games of chance) was entering the county as never before.[55] When noting that any Cardi worthy of the name would keep away from these pursuits, this letter instances how the name and the county were conflated with a type of behaviour. Young men returning to the area from the south-east were identified as the originators of the pursuit. Yet the correspondent also noted, with special sorrow, its prevalence among older people. By the interwar years, worries about working-class gambling had escalated – as demonstrated by evidence given to the Select Committee on the Betting Duty in 1923 – and 'the opposition from the ministry of both the established and dissenting churches was usually passionate'.[56] For the *Welsh Gazette*'s correspondent, gambling was morally repugnant because money could be acquired without work. For some, the divide

---

[54] Neil Evans, 'Gogs, Cardis and Hwntws: regions, nation and state in Wales', in Evans (ed.), *National Identity in the British Isles* (Harlech, 1989), pp. 60–72, 70.

[55] *WG*, 16 June 1921, 3.

[56] Ross McKibbin, 'Working-class gambling in Britain, 1880–1939', *Past and Present*, 82 (1979), 147–78, 176.

between Cardi and non-Cardi was not simply one of origins but of behaviour: in effect, those who gambled lost their right to the name Cardi. Cardiganshire was a county of mind and manners. The letter ends with a passionate plea that Cardis should reject such unwholesome outside influences.

Locations are based on more than one opposite. Contrasts with the Irish, noted in the previous chapter, continued in the interwar years. Ancient links and geographical similarities needed to be qualified by those who felt embarrassed by parallels. The transition from being a component of the British state to Irish Free State, in 1922, and then a sovereign Eire during 1937 surely influenced the perceptions of those who already disliked the Irish. An article on the parish of Llanwenog by D. J. Davies in the Cardiganshire Antiquarian Society journal for 1937 is a case in point. A colony of Gaelic Celts had, Davies asserted, existed there and, no doubt, many parish natives were descended from this branch of the Celtic family. Yet even such an early connection with the troublesome Irish had to be blurred by dissociation. Davies noted that the Llanwenog parishioners would 'very properly disclaim connection with the Irish of today, for they have by this time become acclimatized. They are eminently respectable and cultivate some of the finest acres in the parish.'[57] Two years earlier, during a visit to Tregaron, the county's high sheriff D. D. Williams responded to a comment made by the travel writer A. G. Bradley that Tregaron with its nearby bog had a hint of Ireland about it. Williams was quick to distance the town from Ireland, as indeed Bradley had been, by saying how it could 'boast of being tidy and clean, quite different from some of its Irish prototypes'.[58] Leading figures in the county wanted to distance Cardiganshire from anything potentially shameful. Some visitors' portrayals aided their efforts. W. T. Palmer, in his 1932 book on Wales, which was part of the 'Kit Bag' travel books series, noted that Tregaron has no signs of 'dilapidation' as Irish market towns have.[59]

[57] D. J. Davies, 'Llanwenog', *Cardiganshire Antiquarian Society Transactions*, 12 (1937), 31–50, 41.

[58] *WG*, 3 October 1935, 6.

[59] W. T. Palmer, *Wales* (London, 1932), p. 315.

Respectability was one centre; simplicity was another. An expression of *Schadenfreude* when the industrial areas hit hard times demonstrates how the ideal of simplicity was set against an area that had attracted many from the county during more prosperous times. A song entered in the 1935 Pentremawr colliery eisteddfod, Pontyberem, Carmarthenshire, provided a different perspective on the emigrant from the county who became a miner than did the celebratory 'Can y Cardi'. 'Can Crwt o Gardi' (The son of a Cardi's song) chides the aspirations of those who leave the land. A reckless young man spends all his pay on a motorbike and then suffers penury as the result of a strike. He forsakes mining and returns to his home county. There follows a summary of what Cardiganshire is not and what that area known as the 'works' ('Gweithe') is. Hallmarks of the industrial areas, such as margarine, smoke, noise and cinemas, are contrasted with the simplicity of country foodstuffs, notably *cawl*.[60] *Cawl* was associated with the area at the end of the nineteenth century, but was often referred to in the interwar years by those wishing to locate the county as an epitome of contemporary, simple living not so much as a symbol of the past. Physicians, including the county's medical officer Ernest Jones, expressed concern that there was an over-reliance on 'fabricated food' among cottagers in the county.[61] The county's culinary identity was at risk. A claim to be the part of Wales where *cawl* was most common allowed natives of Cardiganshire, such as Wyn Jones, Penmorfa, writing about *cawl* in the *Cardigan and Tivyside Advertiser*, to place their county at the heart of Wales. Further, this was a masculine Wales free of affectation in which a big bowl of *cawl*, disliked by women and over-refined Englishmen, together with a quarter of a loaf, could fuel a day's work.[62] This dish stood for particular notions of Welshness untouched by trappings of cultivation and consequently excluding those sections, identified as women and Englishmen, who thought port and whisky in tea to be more

---

[60]   *WG*, 26 December 1935, 3.

[61]   Ibid., 15 August 1935, 6.

[62]   *CTA*, 2 March 1934, 2. From the sentiments expressed in this poem it was possible that *cawl* could be set in contrast to another iconic meal – fish and chips – linked to urban life. J. K. Walton, *Fish and Chips and the British Working Class, 1870–1940* (Leicester, 1992).

appropriate for convalescing. At a time when people's diets were generally broadening to include more 'luxury' items, such as confectionery, the Spartan qualities of *cawl* were all the more apparent.[63] Therefore, praise bestowed on a meal that was no doubt thought of as peripheral, managed to place it and the county at the centre, not of fashion or taste, but of robustness and individuality.[64]

Locating the county at the core of Wales necessitated contrasts with places perceived as less Welsh. Claims were made that the Welsh language was, with due recognition of north-Walian assertions, at its purest here.[65] This distinction between the north and south of the country is important as, in a south-Walian context, Cardiganshire could and did claim to be the most Welsh of counties. Other observers, including the Carmarthenshire-born vicar David Davies, who had worked in the ports of Barry and Bristol, supported these claims. In his recollections of a visit to Cardigan, Davies observed that 'we were in the heart of Welsh Wales, where the Celtic tongue flourishes vigorously, and where the English language finds little root'.[66] Here, the centre of Welshness was founded on language – an important component in the constellation of values identified by commentators. Two accounts from the 1920s reveal how notions of the nation clustered around the area more than ever, and reflect how this impression of Cardiganshire depended on other places, primarily the south-east, being less Welsh. In tagging the county 'Little Wales beyond Wales', a contributor to the *Welsh Outlook* adapted the description of Pembrokeshire as 'Little England beyond Wales'. In addition to being eminently Welsh, Cardiganshire was a bastion of virtues that bred a 'strongly individualistic and adventurous type with a mind of its own and a will to enforce it'.[67] It was this blend of cultural and psychological distinction that made the county

[63] John Burnett, *Plenty and Want: A Social History of Diet in England from 1815 to the Present Day* (revised edn, London, 1979), p. 292.

[64] Also see Ffransis G. Payne, 'Pacmon yng Nheredigion', *Y Llenor*, 2 (1932), 90–8, 140–57, 145.

[65] A. T. Fryer, 'Edward Richard and Ystrad Meurig', *West Wales Historical Records*, 8 (1919–20), 67–81, 81.

[66] David Davies, *Reminiscences of My Country and People* (Cardiff, 1925), p. 238.

[67] Uwchaled, 'A holiday in the sweet shire of Cardigan', *Welsh Outlook*, 9 (1928), 264–9, 267.

conspicuous. Such accolades were, no doubt, stimulated by
a feeling of encroaching uniformity, like that expressed by
the political scientist Alfred E. Zimmern. Taking a popular
thermometer of culture, the third-class railway carriage,
Zimmern noted how topics of conversation changed as the
train moved westwards from London to Aberystwyth: 'Sport
retires into the background, and religion and politics, the
"two great interests of Cardiganshire" . . . are likely to take its
place.'[68]

However, this centrality was challenged in the publications of Caradoc Evans. Responses to his insights revealed
the tenacity with which notions of Cardiganshire as a respectable place were held. They also show how the county came
to represent Welsh-speaking rural Wales, as it had done in
the works of Allen Raine where the county's image was relatively far removed from the pillory. In Manchester, on Saint
David's day 1923, the county's MP, Captain Ernest Evans,
defended his constituents' reputation in the face of Caradoc
Evans's play *Taffy*. His reaction reveals how, in addition to
being a slight on all Welsh people, the work was interpreted
as a particular criticism of the county he represented, therefore magnifying the sense of betrayal. Captain Evans assured
his audience that he 'had not come across the type which
appears in this play' in all his years in the county, and the
playwright is accused of transforming this respected area
into 'an object of contempt' through 'exaggeration' and
'distortion'.[69] In view of Caradoc's revision of rural Wales's
respectability, attempts were made to re-establish the place
as a centre of good behaviour. A noteworthy example of this
came from the pen of a north Walian, J. T. Jones, who in 1924
sought to refute Caradoc's assertions that there existed an
ugly and avid materialism among rural folk; it was a criticism from one who saw seeds of independent action and
cooperation in the industrial south-east.[70] This champion of
rural respectability stayed in Rhydlewis, the village in which

---

[68] Alfred E. Zimmern, *My Impressions of Wales* (London, 1921), pp. 20–1.

[69] *CN*, 9 March 1923, 7. The reaction of another county notable, Lord Lisburne,
can be read in the *WM*, 15 May 1925, 12.

[70] See Caradoc Evans's description of 'The Welsh miner', in *idem, Fury Never
Leaves Us: A Miscellany of Caradoc Evans*, ed. J. Harris (Bridgend, 1985), pp. 154–6.

Caradoc had spent many of his early years, and reported its cardinal virtues. Like other places in the county, such as the iconic, isolated mountain chapel of Soar-y-mynydd to the east of Tregaron, which was described as a 'spiritual home' in the *Western Mail* over a decade later, Rhydlewis was rated as a place of cultural value.[71] To maintain its reputation, Jones was aware that spirit had to overshadow matter. Accordingly, he mentions that far from being the 'worldly, materialised people' of his opponent's books, culture 'is very life' for the people he met. In a similar vein to that of Zimmern and his train passengers, Jones cited examples of culture in everyday settings among labouring classes: 'I heard difficult questions of moral science discussed in the hayfield.' He then shifted attention from the village to the county, declaring that 'Cardiganshire people are renowned for their independence of spirit' in matters political and religious.[72]

Efforts to defend the county's position against allegations of miserliness continued during the Second World War. Claims that the county was a centre of good qualities sprang, once again, from learned quarters. In an outline of travellers' accounts of the county published in 1943, E. D. Jones emphasized instances of the 'generosity of Cardiganshire folk', something that one of the authorities called upon by J. T. Jones was also keen to underscore.[73] This was an attempt to impart qualities to the county's population that others felt they lacked. Such defensiveness could be retrospective. E. D. Jones took issue with disapproving comments made about Tregaron at the turn of the nineteenth century, claiming that the visitors had overlooked the fact that they were 'at one of the chief centres of a creative religious movement'.[74] In the same way, those who located the county as a centre of rural

---

[71] *WM*, 30 January 1935, 11.

[72] Ibid., 18 July 1924, 6.

[73] E. D. Jones, 'Some glimpses of Cardiganshire', *Journal of the Welsh Bibliographical Society*, 6 (1943–9), 5–27, 8. Other illustrations of defensiveness in the face of this negative image can be found in the *WM*, 19 July 1924, 6, which contains a quotation from an extramural teacher in Rhydlewis, Ifan ab Owen Edwards, son of O. M. Edwards, that the people of the area were 'not miserly' and were 'exceptionally kind and generous'. John Edwards, *Edwards Castellnedd* (Llandysul, 1935), p. 38, defends the reputation of the miserly Cardi ('Cardi cybyddlyd').

[74] Jones, 'Some glimpses', 27.

cooperation felt that accusations of greed were unfounded, and those who valued it as a centre of culture countered references to parochialism. As a result, the respectable Cardi and his champions could exude some confidence during the interwar years. Unlike those embodiments of the south-Walian miner and his north-eastern English counterpart, Shoni and the Geordie, the Cardi did not depend on a defining, declining industry.[75] Among intellectuals the symbolic status of the county, with its agricultural base and Nonconformist traditions, ensured its continuation as a cultural counter-balance. Yet at the same time criticism of this positive interpretation intensified, and a general feeling of disdain towards those sections of rural society that were thought representative of the county became more apparent. Instead of being at the centre of positive values, these critiques placed the county on the margins.

MARGIN

There was an unprecedented challenge to Cardiganshire's centrality during this era. Those who thought that comfortable assumptions about the qualities of the county and its inhabitants papered over class inequalities confronted positive depictions of Cardiganshire and the Cardi. Groups often taken to represent the county as a whole, above all farmers and shopkeepers, were condemned for putting sectional interests above those of the community. Some of the strongest of these criticisms were fashioned by the ideological convictions of Rhondda-born communist, Lewis Jones. His novels *Cwmardy* and *We Live* relate the turbulent history of a fictional mining community from the turn of the century to the end of the 1930s. Among the class enemies in the novels is a shopkeeper named Evans Cardi. This character, particularly in the second book covering the period from the General Strike to the Spanish Civil War, personified all that Lewis

[75] See Revd John Roberts's comment to the then prime minister, Ramsay MacDonald, that 'Sioni is dying', cited by T. Alban Davies, 'Impressions of life in the Rhondda Valley', in K. S. Hopkins (ed.), *Rhondda: Past and Future* (Ferndale, 1975), pp. 11–21, 16; Robert Colls, *Identity of England* (Oxford, 2002), p. 337; *idem, Collier's Rant: Song and Culture in the Industrial Village* (London, 1977), p. 183.

Jones thought disagreeable about Nonconformist, Liberal, respectable, petit-bourgeois Wales: namely, that it ignored the plight of the less fortunate. Although *Cwmardy* does not contain as sustained an attack upon the shopkeeper as that found in the second novel, we see Evans Cardi in a number of public roles that cast him as a man who is detached from his customers, including an appearance on the platform of a First World War recruitment meeting.[76]

Evans Cardi's characteristics refract the dominant positive image of the Cardi; virtues are twisted into defects. He owns shares in the pit, is a senior deacon and places excessive emphasis on his son's education. When the son becomes a communist, he is accused by his father of aligning himself 'to everything that is foreign to our people'. When a pregnant customer complains about the reduced wages the miners will receive on returning to work after a lockout, he remarks that 'hard work never hurt nobody'. Given that the novels feature deadly pit accidents, this statement appears all the more unsympathetic. The shopkeeper is adrift from the people because he adhered to values that put him on the wrong side in the clash between labour and capital. He is *in* the industrial community but not *of* it; although smitten by the strike's effect on business, the shopkeeper and his wife are too proud to accept parish relief, the spectre of poverty and the shame of having an 'infidel' of a son leads to his committing suicide after having, with her consent, slit his wife's throat.[77]

Other sources indicate that Lewis Jones was expressing, through the medium of fiction, opinions held by some communities.[78] As John Humphreys Davies inferred in

---

[76] Lewis Jones, *Cwmardy* (London, 1937), pp. 94, 27, 265. Also see David Smith, *Lewis Jones* (Cardiff, 1982), pp. 48, 55–6.

[77] Lewis Jones, *We Live* (London, 1939), pp. 64–5, 147–52. The contrast between bourgeois and proletarian values portrayed in *We Live* can also be found in Walter Greenwood's *His Worship the Mayor: or, 'It's Only Human Nature After All'* (London, 1934).

[78] For example, Leighton Stuart James argued that during the First World War 'the issue of food distribution also heightened the class-consciousness of the miners in south Wales' and referred to suggestions that shopkeepers were favouring their better-off customers: 'War and industry: a study of the industrial relations of the mining regions of south Wales and the Ruhr during the Great War, 1914–1918' (MSc Econ thesis, University of Wales, Cardiff, 1999), 43. According to others, this was nothing new: 'The grocer as industrial folk-villain is as old, at least, as the

his aforementioned speech to a Cardiganshire Society, conspicuous social climbing from proletariat to petit bourgeois aroused indignation. The affinity that migrants from Cardiganshire had with retailing did not apply to all who were either in or from the county. But there was enough of a link to foster ties that found expression in literature. While not as gruesome, melodramatic or underpinned by the same political drive as Lewis Jones, Jack Jones also separated 'the Cardies' from the bulk of the population of the mining valleys in his 1935 novel *Black Parade*, published seven years after he had left the Communist Party. Distinguished by thrift and 'saving', the former were the 'careful ones' who put aside what they earned in the mines, eventually becoming shopkeepers and 'leaving the hard work of the mines and steelworks to the natives again'. Religious adherence – they were 'the backbone of Welsh Nonconformity' – marked this particular group. A character called Glyn expresses a visceral opinion when he is described as having 'despised' the 'careful ones' who 'were picking their way through the main street, on which there were numerous drunken and rowdy natives, as though they were avoiding dogs' messes'.[79] The miner's reputation for being financially carefree highlighted the Cardi's fiscal caution.[80] This polarization of rural thrift and industrial or urban expenditure was part of many people's mental framework and was not limited to Cardiganshire and Glamorgan. However, these two counties provided useful symbolic means of expressing contending features of human affairs.

This type of peripherality, being divorced from desirable communal standards, was made in relation to other vocations connected with the county. A combination of disagreeable activity and geographical area conjured up the shadow image of the Cardi. Vicars and milk dealers were two examples

Merthyr Riots of 1831': Roger Stephens Jones, 'The Angry Summer: an essay on the structure of Idris Davies's poem', *Planet*, 37/38 (1977), 21–8, 28.

[79] Jack Jones, *Black Parade* (London, 1935), pp. 18–19.

[80] These perceptions were often influenced by the leisure activities available in the south-east, as seen in the memoirs of a Cardiganshire man who worked in a mining area during the First World War: the 'exhibition of thrift was seldom met with among the colliers. They squandered their money on sport and music': William Evans, *Journey to Harley Street* (London, 1968), p. 95.

of this category identified by the Welsh historian, barrister and Congregational minister, W. Watkin Davies.[81] Like A. G. Bradley before him, Davies noted with some surprise that this 'very decent type of man [the Cardi]' has 'come to be lightly regarded' by his fellow Welshmen. Unlike the earlier English visitor, however, Davies posited two reasons for this: the county's export of 'inferior parsons' and the many people from the county involved in the dilution of milk in London. Although the rest of his description of the county is favourable, this introductory comment indicated a tension between sections of society that occasionally flickers in accounts. A remark by the London-based author Rhys Davies suggests how inhabitants of Cardiganshire were distinguished from those in the rest of Wales in psychological terms. In a work of non-fiction in which he describes his travels around the country, the author approached Newcastle Emlyn, where he noted: 'We are getting quite close to the Cardiganshire tribe, where hardness, ruthlessness, and meanness are, the other tribes declare, the rule.'[82] Many believed that Cardiganshire people, whether home or away, displayed self-interested behaviour removed from the common weal.

Accounts in the local press reveal that the distance from collective behaviour attributed to the Cardi was, in fact, part of a more general criticism directed at individuals who neglected their social responsibilities. Individualism was the target bound up in the Cardi stereotype. Distance from desired behaviour was, for instance, noted among the county's farming community. Farmers' overriding concerns to make money, at the cost of the war effort, or their reluctance to part with it in commemoration of those killed in the war, stirred up anger in the local press. Around Aberaeron, the *Carmarthen Journal* remarked, there was a tendency among farmers to use land along the coast, well suited for wheat, in order to grow hay 'which in many cases is later on sold at good profits'. Erecting a war memorial at Lampeter did not attract money from those interested in lucrative investments. Farmers were not directly implicated here; it was

---

[81] W. Watkin Davies, *A Wayfarer in Wales* (London, 1930), p. 149. Also see H. W. J. Edwards, *The Good Patch* (London, 1938), p. 59.
[82] Rhys Davies, *My Wales* (London, 1937), p. 241.

a condemnation of those people 'possessing money' who invested in war bonds but did not sacrifice anything else either during the war or in order to commemorate the fallen.[83] The diatribe continued in a manner that echoed general criticisms made against the tight-fisted Cardi: 'Such men cannot take their money with them and yet they hoard every penny! They are professed Christians but what a flimsy thing their Christianity is after all.'

To counter such self-interested behaviour, critics summoned alternative ideals commonly linked to the county, thus illustrating how the county's noble image could be turned against members of the establishment. An editorial in the *Cambrian News* took issue with members of the county council, and particularly its education committee who advocated what was called 'economy'. Once again, farmers were the section of the county censured. This group, it contended, were not as poor as they claimed: 'the figures of the various banks prove this'. Moreover, this hoarding went against the national interests of the nation, because the education and health of the people suffered. Because of Cardiganshire's agricultural base, farmers symbolized the county, and many Welsh and British observers held that the farmer was a force for good. For instance, farming was described by the Pembrokeshire-born librarian and antiquarian Francis Jones as being the 'backbone of the nation', an opinion with which R. G. Stapleton would have no doubt concurred. Yet those with a more egalitarian agenda challenged this conception by appealing to higher ideals, not only to national efficiency but to the county's heritage: 'Is Cardiganshire content to be led by the nose by those who measure prosperity in £ s and d, and estimate the worth of a man by the figures in his bank book?' In answer to this, the editorial declared that the county 'has a soul above these things'. A month later the paper, reporting on a dispute between schoolteachers and a stringent education committee, invoked the county's educational tradition in defence of the teachers' claims.[84]

[83] *CJ*, 15 June 1917, 3; ibid., 3 October 1919, 2. For more on the erection of memorials commemorating this war, and the conflicts they engendered, see Angela Gaffney, *Aftermath: Remembering the Great War in Wales* (Cardiff, 1998).

[84] *CN*, 5 January 1923, 4; F. Jones, 'Two illustrious sons of Cardiganshire',

Nonetheless, those characteristics chastised in the *Cambrian News* were being taken as representative of the county rather than of just one part of it. This was partly due to the prominent nature of those who were seen to conform to the stereotype. One historian has identified the farmers as being 'the enemy of the farm labourers', the shopkeepers, 'a clan apart', and the 'Liberal public men', including chapel ministers, as being removed from the bulk of the population.[85] A similar gallery of villains emerges in the interwar period when public-minded individuals assailed their opponents. A native of the county living in Bristol asked whether any true Christian could remain a member of religious organizations when 'he knows the officers and leaders and members of the church for the most part are farmers who would not hesitate to dilute their produce . . . [and] shopkeepers who charge their fellow Christians to the uttermost farthing for inferior goods'.[86] When the condition of the people was placed in the foreground, the figureheads of Liberal Wales, and by default many from Cardiganshire, became tempting targets.

In addition to locating the county away from a desirable collectivist ethos, many continued to place the county's inhabitants far from the quality of good manners. Opinions like that of the poet Idris Davies, who while supervising evacuees in the county during the Second World War described the 'Cardi and his Carmarthen cousin' as 'especially' 'hard headed' though with a good 'sense of poetry', reveal the ambiguity and subtlety of mental locations.[87] They were seen as being rough, but at the same time cultured. By one standard, that of English inns frequented by Davies, the occupants of the Teifiside tavern were veritable bards. By another, that of genteel society, they were brazen. Both yardsticks were used to measure Cardiganshire's inhabitants in the past, but there were more instances in this period as travellers, politicians and newspapers contemplated a peripheral people. Some of

Cardiganshire Antiquarian Society Transactions, 13 (1938), 74–80, 74; *CN*, 9 February 1923, 4.

[85] David Smith, *Wales! Wales?* (London, 1984), pp. 19, 24, 27.

[86] *CTA*, 12 October 1934, 8. The tensions such issues evoked in Welsh religious circles are explored in Robert Pope, *Building Jerusalem: Nonconformity, Labour and the Social Question in Wales, 1906–1939* (Cardiff, 1998).

[87] NLW, MS 22412C, Idris Davies, miscellaneous prose, 'Teifyside', fo. 2.

these depictions came from within the county and show how the idea of peripherality, in terms of manners and knowledge, sprang from impressions of a particular, rusticated section of the county's population, far removed from the values cherished by cosmopolitan observers. These various sources reveal a type of Cardi that several people felt represented the county, an alternative to the businessman, teacher or preacher.

Isolation continued to influence descriptions of the county's population. Welsh commentators who championed the rural life, such as the folklorist Iorwerth C. Peate, were not immune from pointing out features thought to separate the area from the rest of the country. After noting that even at the time of writing, 1931, people often referred to three components of the country – namely, north Wales, south Wales and Cardiganshire – Peate speculated on the effects of this distinction on the county's people. The want of contact dulled aspects of their character as well as benefiting them in ways that Peate did not describe, possibly because these were taken as self-evident.[88] A specific example of how the distance between people from the area and those in more cosmopolitan places was expressed can be found in the musings of the author Gwyn Thomas, who had taught at Cardigan. Thomas tells of three introverted brothers from Cenarth who 'viewed talking pictures with a distrustful awe' and their experience of the Marx brothers film *Duck Soup* released in 1933. Due to their reverence for authority, they disliked their anarchic American counterparts. Thomas concluded that: 'Never had the Atlantic of the spirit that separates the Teifi from the Bronx been so neatly bottled.'[89] Contrasts such as this presented a people who were removed from many features of contemporary popular culture to be found in urban and industrial areas, and at the same time complemented the location of Cardiganshire as a centre of 'genuine' Welsh culture. Some, especially in the 1930s, would have found the reaction of these anti-Marx brothers praiseworthy.

Differences are readily communicated through the senses. People can cross the bounds of another group's acceptable

[88] Iorwerth C. Peate, *Cymru a'i Phobol* (Cardiff, 1931), p. 60.
[89] Gwyn Thomas, *High on Hope* (Cowbridge, 1985), pp. 43–4.

behaviour purely on the basis of their sensory impact. Evelyn
Lewes, who was related to the occupants of Gogerddan, one
of the county's main houses, drew a comparison between 'the
vivacious Cardiganshire folk' who 'have a tendency to shout
in the exchange of cheerful conversation', and the more
muted tones of Carmarthenshire. Even so, there was a place
for noisy chatter, but this was not, in Lewes's opinion, while
travelling by bus from Aberystwyth to Brecon. During this
journey, a man spoke so loudly that she asked him to quieten
down. A clergyman who was being addressed by the loud
man 'appeared shocked by my lack of appreciation of such
cheery company, and explained that the conversationalist's
shouting voice merely testified to the district from whence
he came. That district I presently discovered was none other
than my own county of Cardigan.' Owing to this mode of
transport, which could bring people from different classes
into close proximity, Lewes experienced a way of talking that
from a distance could be 'musical' but was 'inappropriate'
at close quarters.[90] The fact that a clergyman spoke up for
the boisterous passenger offers another example of the
aforementioned affection that ministers felt for the Cardi,
an inclination that may have been developed while studying
theology at Lampeter.

Representations are simplifications, but some contain
revealing ambiguities that are products of particular cultural
climates.[91] In a letter about party matters, the secretary of
the Liberal Central Association between 1917 and 1926,
Richard Humphrey Davies, admitted that he admired 'the
staunchness of these rough Cardis. [But] I prefer their
politics to their manners. There must be some sound hearts
beneath the rough exteriors.'[92] Roughness is not something that emerges in depictions of respectable or educated
Cardiganshire. Yet it would be a mistake to assume that the
suggestion that the Cardi was unsophisticated was confined
to those who occupied the upper reaches of society whose
polished manners were affronted by the earth-born Cardi.

[90] Evelyn Lewes, *Out with the Cambrians* (London, 1934), pp. 26–7.
[91] Zevedi Berbu, *Problems of Historical Psychology* (London, 1960), p. 63.
[92] NLW, MS E. Morgan Humphreys, A/584, undated letter from Richard
Humphrey Davies, fo. 1.

Local newspapers contain jokes about simple-minded people from out-of-the-way parts of the county that bear similarities to Irish Kerry-man jokes. An issue of the *Cardigan and Tivyside Advertiser* in 1932 included a joke about a 'farm labourer' who thought that the cost of an obituary in a newspaper, referring to inches of print, was in fact based on the height of the departed. Another took as its subject a maid from 'a remote part of Cardiganshire' who had little understanding of gas heating while working in Swansea and remarked: 'This gas is wonderful. I lit it the day before yesterday and it hasn't gone out yet.'[93] Of course, those who found such comic stories amusing would have thought of themselves as being more sophisticated than the subjects of the jokes, consequently achieving one of the functions of humour, 'a sense of superiority'.[94] This differentiation within the county points towards those sections of Cardiganshire deemed peripheral that may have filled the lenses of outsiders viewing what was still clearly identified as a distinctive county.

During the war and interwar years, the Cardi's individuality was criticized and complimented in equal measure. This chapter has demonstrated that these judgements were based on more than one criterion. Beyond what could, at first glance, be thought a crude stereotype there were many pressing questions that troubled contemporaries. The subsequent half-century would see the mutation of these points of view and the arrival of others as the county and its relationships were reconfigured by, among other things, continuing technical change, nationalism and heightened consumerism. A discussion of these changes will show how the Cardi and the county took on additional meanings at a time when many of their former defining features were being abraded.

---

[93] *CTA*, 2 September 1932, 1. Alun Lewis, a poet who was educated at Aberystwyth, tells the tale of an unworldly native of Cardiganshire in his short story 'Private Jones', in Jack Aistrop and Reginald Moore (eds), *Bugle Blast: An Anthology from the Services* (London, 1943), pp. 135–56.

[94] Henk Driessen, 'Humour, laughter and the field: reflections from anthropology', in Jan Bremmer and Herman Roodenburg (eds), *A Cultural History of Humour: From Antiquity to the Present Day* (Cambridge, 1997), pp. 222–41, 237.

VI

CONCERN AND JOKING, 1945–*c.*2000

The latter part of the twentieth century marked a considerable shift away from the characteristics that previously defined Cardiganshire and its people. It has been argued that there was a marked challenge to traditional notions of British national identity in the late 1950s and the 1960s.[1] Essentially, Britain was being relocated. Likewise, the cultural location of Cardiganshire was affected by Anglo-American culture, the changing roles of women and youngsters and a comparatively affluent, consumer society. Examining specific acts of location reveals how general trends like these were accompanied by particular expressions of resistance and compliance. As standards of living and the provision of welfare services generally improved, the Cardi's carefulness with money became a source of amusement. Conspicuous caution became all the more noticeable when consumption reached new heights.[2] The Cardi was swimming against stronger tides than before.

At the same time, local individuality became ever more cherished as perceptions of encroaching homogeneity increased.[3] Accompanying notions of individuality were anxieties about infection. Both of these influential themes, nurtured in earlier decades, were increasingly brought into play in the second part of the twentieth century.

Although the 1949 edition of the *Encyclopaedia Britannica* noted that the county possessed 'social and religious peculiarities', in the same year others were writing about the

---

[1] Richard Weight, *Patriots: National Identity in Britain, 1940–2000* (London, 2002), p. 211.

[2] Gwyneth Francis-Jones, *Cows, Cardis and Cockneys* (Borth, 1984), p. 55.

[3] For example, see Rob Shields's description of *Coronation Street* as being 'not primarily about working class community but about the assault upon the individual by institutions which are wholly other', in *Places on the Margin: Alternative Geographies of Modernity* (London, 1991), p. 227.

'canker' of anglicization on 'the fair face of Cardiganshire'.[4]
Assorted defining characteristics were fading. The institutional pillars of Nonconformity and the Liberal Party were
being simultaneously eroded.[5] Broader changes contributed
to this reformulation, notably occupational diversification.[6]
As the relative weight of these social features fluctuated, fears
that the Welsh language – an important part of religious,
political and farming life – was under threat multiplied.
The decline in Welsh speakers noted in the interwar years
continued and students took to the streets of Aberystwyth
during the Welsh-language campaign of the 1960s that was
crowned by the passing of the 1967 Welsh Language Act.
However, by 2001 the proportion of Welsh speakers in the
county had fallen from the 59 per cent recorded in 1991 to
52 per cent.[7] At the same time, political and cultural nationalism waxed, and the nationalist party captured the county
seat in 1992. By the twenty-first century a protest group, Llais
y Cardi (The Cardi's Voice), was formed to oppose council
plans to build some 6,500 houses in the county. The group's
position was that, although these developments were ostensibly for local first-time buyers, English incomers would be
able to purchase or rent these properties too, thus further
undermining the place of the Welsh language in the county.
This group's use of the nickname for the county's inhabitants in a serious manner contrasted with its usual association
with jokes in the latter part of the twentieth century.[8]

[4] *Encyclopaedia Britannica*, 24 vols (Chicago, 1949), vol. 4, p. 853; *CTA*, 14 October 1949, 6.

[5] David Jenkins, *The Agricultural Community in South-West Wales at the Turn of the Twentieth Century* (Cardiff, 1971), p. 278. For a sociological assessment of changes taking place in the 1960s, see F. A .B. J. Le Vay, 'The social and economic changes affecting farming communities in two contrasting Cardiganshire parishes, 1961–1971' (MSc thesis, University of Wales, Aberystwyth, 1972).

[6] D. I. Bateman, 'Cardiganshire agriculture in the twentieth century: an economic perspective', in Geraint H. Jenkins and Ieuan Gwynedd Jones (eds), *Cardiganshire County History*, vol. 3, pp. 113–34, 121. It is also noteworthy that links between religious vocations and farm life have been diminishing. One retired vicar from the county remarked how he must have been 'one of the last few clergy who was brought up on a farm' (ex inf. William H. Richards, 8 March 2004).

[7] National statistics statistical bulletin, '2001 census on population: first results on the Welsh language', *http://www.wales.gov.uk/keypubstatisticsforwales/content/publication/population/2003/sb22–2003/sb22–2003.pdf*, p. 3 (accessed 15 December 2003).

[8] A political party called Llais Ceredigion (Ceredigion's Voice) emerged from

Although ignorant people from the county were figures of fun in the past, printed jokes about another county type, the miserly rural dweller, burgeoned after the Second World War. The first book dedicated exclusively to this strain of joke was published in 1995.[9] These depictions indicate how images of the Cardi had become rooted in farming by the end of the twentieth century. As the occupations affiliated to the county narrowed, parsons, businessmen and migrants were supplanted by their agricultural counterparts. Both jokes and worries were, therefore, tied up in the name. Yet the two strands, noticeable at the start of the twenty-first century, took many forms in the years following the Second World War. On one side were anxieties about missing the fruits of progress. On another, change threatened to dilute the county's character. A debate in the county council over whether to permit the use of the county coat of arms on a tea towel to commemorate Cardiff's hosting of the British Empire and Commonwealth Games in 1958 illustrated this tension.[10] Pressures and compromises can be traced through the ways the county was located. The area could be redefined as a cultural counterweight to new features such as the Welsh capital, Cardiff, which had been officially granted the title in 1955, and various social incursions such as youth cultures. Its peripherality was repositioned in relation to changes elsewhere; indeed, much of west and mid-Wales was thought to be the poorer relation of a south-east Wales benefiting from the first Severn bridge, opened in 1966.[11] Praised or pilloried, the county kept its place in the popular consciousness throughout the late twentieth century. Referenda on Welsh Sunday closing and the second vote on devolution led to an increased awareness of the east–west divide in Wales.[12]

this pressure group. See 'End of the corporate body: monitoring the National Assembly December 2003 to March 2004', ed. J. Osmond, *http://iwa.org.uk/publications/pdfs/CorpBody.pdf*, p. 41 (accessed 1 August 2004).

[9] Brian John, *The Best Cardi Jokes* (Newport, Pembrokeshire, 1995). Also see Emyr Llywelyn, *Hiwmor y Cardi* (Talybont, 2006).

[10] *CTA*, 16 May 1958, 4; ibid., 18 July 1958, 1.

[11] On this, see G. Clare Wenger, *Mid-Wales: Deprivation or Development: A Study of Patterns of Employment in Selected Communities* (Cardiff, 1980). Mid-Wales Industrial Development Association was founded in 1957.

[12] John Osmond, *New Politics in Wales* (London, 1998), p. 7.

While firmly in the western camp, the county possessed its own symbolic impetus, a momentum driven by the diverse ways in which this county could be conceptualized and contextualized.

Many sources of opinion regarding the county, such as the press, grew, while others decreased; the flow of literature from the south Wales valleys became a trickle. New traces of representations are drawn upon in this chapter. These include the work of sociologists, political scientists and historians that stemmed from the expansion of academia in the years following 1945. Autobiographies, offering perceptions of the county at the time of publication, multiplied. The sheer range of material brings its own difficulties. Nonetheless, the variety does not prevent some signal changes in the categorization of the county from being detected; a few of these were subtle and others, such as those provoked by suggested changes to county boundaries and changes of name, were less so.

NAMING

A reorganization of local government in the latter part of the twentieth century meant that in 1974 Cardiganshire became part of Dyfed, which also comprised Carmarthenshire and Pembrokeshire. However, two years before the administrative merger, Ceredigion was decided upon as the name of the district council for the area within former Dyfed that was to correspond to the county of Cardigan.[13] When, in 1996, the three portions of Dyfed reverted to their former status as counties, there was extensive debate within the council about which name to adopt. This discussion was actuated by economic, cultural and political factors. Some, especially on the coast, feared that tourists would not recognize Ceredigion. On the other hand, there was considerable support for this name from Plaid Cymru, independent councillors and others, including many secondary school heads, who called for an appellation that conveyed the area's ancient heritage. Eventually, the district council name, Ceredigion,

---

[13]   *CTA*, 5 May 1972, 6.

was selected. The official adoption of a name originating in the early Middle Ages, pre-dating Cardiganshire, figuratively aligned the area with a Welsh historic kingdom, rather than a 'shire'. This decision to take a name that recalled a pre-conquest Wales was welcomed in the epilogue to the final volume of the county's official history – although the volumes were entitled Cardiganshire.[14]

Name changes from the 1970s may not have been to everyone's liking, but when the dismemberment of the historic county was suggested in the 1960s, there was an outcry. A county called 'Mid-Wales', composed of northern Cardiganshire and the eastern counties of Montgomery, Radnor and Brecon, was proposed by local government commissioners. Adverse effects on Welsh culture were cited as one reason against the alteration. Underlying this was a sense of the county being a centre of Welshness. The furore aroused by this suggestion also pointed towards an often unexpressed distinction between eastern mid-Wales and the areas on the western side of the Cambrian mountains, which contained a greater proportion of Welsh-speaking inhabitants. All the same, contemporaries continued to couch difference in terms of north and south. A councillor, E. Glyn Davies, spoke in defence of the retention of the county on the BBC current affairs programme Standpoint in 1963: 'The Cardis have a characteristic of their own. They do not seem to belong to North Wales or South Wales. They act as a bridge between North and South.' If the north of the county were amalgamated with English-speaking eastern areas it was feared a connection between Welsh-speaking parts of Wales would be lost. Another critic was baffled at how geographers, whose work on economic conditions suggested a connection between the parts of the proposed county, could overlook the topographical fact of 'ten miles of bare mountain between Ponterwyd and Llangurig'.[15] Cultural differences, preserved by this geography, had been overlooked. Reactions to the notion of a Mid-Wales county helped to define Cardiganshire as a physical and cultural entity.

[14] CN, 26 January 1996, 3, 6; ibid., 2 February 1996, 3; J. Kendal Harris, 'Epilogue', in Jenkins and Jones (eds), Cardiganshire County History, vol. 3, p. 618.
[15] WG, 21 March 1963, 1; ibid., 18 April 1963, 1.

As for the naming of people, there were less obvious shifts. Cardis did not become 'Ceredigs'. By the start of the twenty-first century, though, the Cardi had been replaced by 'a Ceredigion farmer' in a book of Welsh jokes published in the county.[16] In the period after the Second World War, the name Cardi remained and came to be increasingly related to farmers. It was no coincidence that both the author of the 'Farming notes and topics' section in the *Cambrian News* and the correspondent to the *Welsh Gazette* who expressed concern that the Welsh cob and pony were not represented at the 1949 Harringay horse show used the name.[17] Alliteration was adopted by D. J. Morgan, the county's agricultural organizer during the interwar and war years, to emphasize three symbols of the county: the Cardi, the cob and the corgi dog – Y tair 'C' Ceredigion (The three 'C's of Ceredigion). Evidently, pigs and pastors were not as pertinent as they had been in the nineteenth century. Agricultural achievements were central to county pride, and Morgan highlighted the accomplishments of farmers by contrasting their work with that of the miner, once again demonstrating the utilization of the neighbouring 'other' to the south-east. There were, he jested in the early 1950s, with the 1948 winter fuel crisis a recent memory, no strikes, absenteeism or shifts in farming.[18] When D. J. Morgan was described as a thorough ('trwyadl') Cardi, it was a compliment. This use of the name by people from the county as a badge of pride can be seen in the joy expressed by John Morris, MP for Aberavon in Glamorgan, on having received a telegram after he had entered the 1974 Labour Cabinet, as secretary of state for Wales, that congratulated him on being the first Cardi in the Cabinet.[19]

There were other perspectives on the name, however, that indicate how various meanings were attached to a seemingly straightforward label. Negative connotations possessed by the name were suggested by Daniel Parry-Jones in his book *Welsh Country Upbringing*, first published in 1948. The author dedicated a few paragraphs under the title 'Cardiganshire men' to a group that, like the men of Yorkshire and

---

[16] Dilwyn Phillips, *Welsh Jokes* (Talybont, 2002), p. 48.

[17] *CN*, 13 January 1950, 2; *WG*, 23 February 1950, 6.

[18] D. J. Morgan, *Pant a Bryn* (Llandysul, 1953), pp. 128, 56.

[19] *Cwysi Ceredigion: Cronicl Clybiau Ffermwyr Ifainc* (Felin-fach, 1974), p. 19.

Lancashire, have 'developed one quality in excess of the rest'. Parry-Jones, did not spell out this singular attribute, but praised the achievements of the type, noting the accomplishments of the Cardi in various fields. Yet, when he moved on to consider the 'Shoni', or miner from south Wales, he commented that this 'gregarious' type 'dislikes the individualistic Cardi with his preference for the lone hand'.[20] There is an echo of the conflicting ideas, noted in the last chapter, in this brief sentence written by a man who had been born on the Cardiganshire–Carmarthenshire border and worked in the Rhondda valley. As the twentieth century progressed, the sources of strain, political and economic, decreased and the name was applied more generally. Indeed, in Wales the term is currently commonly bestowed on anyone thought overly cautious with money. Other correlations between the area and character were wholly positive. In a book of recollections about life in interwar Cardiganshire, published in 2000, Lisa Pennant attached personal qualities to the name when she described the self-respect of the Cardi ('hunan-barch y Cardi'). Another recollection mentioned the emphasis every good Cardi placed on ensuring that their children were well educated.[21] Affirmative symbolic affiliations like these located many of the county's defining attributes in practices associated with the past.

PAST

Spurred on by the rapid technological and societal changes elsewhere, the relation of the place and its people to various pasts intensified. This application of time to space, of one place being traditional and the other modern, was a mixed blessing, especially given the prevailing spirit of the post-war years. In the late twentieth century, nations were becoming increasingly distinguished 'not by their heritage ... but by their pace of change'.[22] This trend, it could be argued,

[20] D. Parry-Jones, *Welsh Country Upbringing* (London, 1948), pp. 100–1.
[21] Lisa Pennant, *Tai Bach a Thai Mas: Y Cardi ar ei Waethaf* (Aberystwyth, 2000), pp. 7–8; Tom Herbert, *Herbert y Fet: Atgofion y Milfeddyg Tom Herbert* (Llandysul, 1989), p. 21.
[22] Daniel J. Boorstin, *Hidden History: Exploring our Secret Past* (New York, 1987), p. 308.

may be noticed in perceptions of smaller geographical units. Compared with other parts of Britain and Wales, Cardiganshire often found itself situated on the 'heritage' rather than 'change' side of the divide.

Features fashioned from the late eighteenth century such as Protestant religion, respectability and self-improvement were still identified with the county, but they were increasingly viewed as being characteristics of the past and not defining features of the present. Less overt emphasis on these themes rendered them even more distant than they were in the interwar period. When, in the mid-1980s, the former speaker of the House of Commons, Viscount Tonypandy, summed up the county, he picked out standard features that evoked past struggles and achievements: education treasured as escape, thrift to preserve the fruits of labour and religion rekindled by revivals.[23] Few would disagree with this selection. There were other stories of ignorance, tension and isolation, but these positive, affirmative qualities formed a widely held catechism, similar to that presented by county societies in the interwar years. The county's past cultural distinctions reverberated in descriptions at this time.

Towards the end of the twentieth century, rural chapel-dotted Wales was joined by industrial chapel-dotted Wales in the nation's mental archive. Yet, of the two, rural Wales was the most treasured deposit for much of the late twentieth century. The romantic novelist and biographer Elizabeth Inglis-Jones, who had spent much of her early life on the family estate of Derry Ormond near Lampeter, regretted the loss of the 'picturesque' aspects of farming in the early 1960s.[24] Mechanization might change the landscape, but it was the cultural landscape that was the inhabitants' primary concern. In comments made by those who had a more intimate relationship with the soil than Inglis-Jones, we can hear the felt dislocation between past and present.

Recollections are inclined to celebrate the past. Yet their criticisms and complaints regularly chimed with contemporary critiques of cultural uniformity. Loss is expressed and

[23] George Thomas, *My Wales* (London, 1986), p. 25.
[24] E. Inglis-Jones, 'Some impressions on revisiting Cardiganshire', *Cymdeithas Ceredigion Llundain Llawlyfr*, 16 (1960–1), 21.

it was only at this time, owing to the wealth of biograph-
ical publications, that a sizeable record of this sense of loss
is available. The county retained a comfortable majority
of Welsh speakers throughout the twentieth century, but
shifts in the use of English and the need to use it created
gulfs. In a National Eisteddfod-winning work looking back
on inhabitants of a southern part of the county, D. Emrys
Rees described how incomers ended up speaking the Welsh
language. However, something had changed by the early
1960s. Rees mentioned that there was little reason to use
English in the early 1900s, implying a greater need to use
it in everyday communication when his recollections were
published. It is this day-to-day sphere that is commonly given
significance because it was where cultural diffusion became
palpable. New farmers, from England and Poland, hastened
this process. Evan Jones's account of the Tregaron district,
published in 1967, expressed unease about the fate of Welsh
farm names given the origins of their new owners.[25] For
many, the maps were changing.

As with earlier periods, a consideration of how Cardiganshire was located in the past needs to include those who see a
living past in the area as well as people who saw the essence of
the county, that may have been fading gradually, as residing
in the past. Both perspectives prioritize aspects of the past,
giving little praise to more recent habits and developments.
Often remnants of the past detected in parts of the county
are used to criticize developments. This kind of selection can
occur in any area, but in one such as Cardiganshire, which
had a long-standing tradition of being judged traditional,
this evaluative process was heightened. Moreover, on occasion, the people of the county themselves were portrayed
as guardians of the past. A squabble over the 'Coffee Pot'
– an old bus that ran, irregularly, between Cardigan and
Newcastle Emlyn – dubbed 'antediluvian' by a 'sometime
traveller', included a comment that 'Cardis hold dear all

[25] D. Emrys Rees, *Cymdogion* (Aberystwyth, 1962), p. 71; Evan Jones, *Ar Ymylon
Cors Caron: Atgofion gan Evan Jones* (Aberystwyth, 1967), p. 92. Concerned witnesses
of late twentieth-century diffusion can also be heard in John Rees Jones, *Sôn am y
Bont*, ed. E. D. Evans (Llandysul, 1974), p. 64; John Williams and Eben Davies, *Fferm
a Ffair a Phentre* (Aberystwyth, 1958), pp. 17–18.

tradition and institution'.[26] The opinions of the critic were
seen as an attack on 'individuality' and a 'unique feature of
Cardigan'. The Coffee Pot debate illustrates how a relatively
recent entity was used to sum up an approach to life. It is
often such relatively recent features that prompt the location
of the area in the past. Therefore, it is a past to which feeling
was attached, whether loss or relief at finding a vestige of
something rare elsewhere. It is not so much the ancient
past as a past to which a commentator feels some emotional
attachment.

Comforting reassurances that some types of behaviour had
not been extinguished can be found in travellers' accounts.
These are examples of 'negative counterposition', when a
place is defined by what it is not.[27] Perhaps this designation is
all the more immediate because it originates from peoples'
conduct, a kind of animate heritage. As before, aspects of
the county provided a ready store of difference for those
disillusioned with changes and can, therefore, be a useful
measurement of unease with political and social transformations among those portions of the population that have
left a record. Some unnerving modern features within the
county were as Welsh as the soothing traditions. The pleasure that Anthony Bailey took in describing the hospitality of
a hill farmer near Talybont, who always laid out a table for a
possible visitor from over the hill, was implicitly contrasted
with an earlier meal in Tregaron that was upset by a nationalist waitress of punk-like appearance.[28] Forty years earlier,
S. P. B. Mais mapped tradition in a similar way, though
within a British framework. His concern at the eradication of
manners in a brash post-war world of levelled social relationships was eased somewhat by the habit of locals in south-west
Wales of 'instinctively' addressing him as 'Sir'.[29]

Depopulation and what was seen as gender-specific behaviour were touched upon in valorizations of the past. Loss was
nothing new, but expressions of unease were amplified

[26] *CTA*, 4 January 1946, 2.
[27] Doreen Massey, 'Places and their pasts', *History Workshop Journal*, 39 (1995),
182–93, 189.
[28] Anthony Bailey, *A Walk through Wales* (London, 1992), pp. 157, 123.
[29] S. P. B. Mais, *I Return to Wales* (London, 1949), p. 211.

during the first part of the period under consideration. The illustrated history of the county published in 1970, a copy of which was given to every secondary schoolchild in Cardiganshire, expressed anxiety about its declining population.[30] Underneath generally accepted reasons for this loss, however, there are others that illustrate how one foundation of the county's identity, that of a hard-working life on hill farms, was believed to be undermined by a female-led quest for comfort. Although far from being an Edenic environment, the rural Eve was implicated in the decline of a past way of life. While visiting the north of the county, the Canadian Thomas Firbank, then a hill farmer in Snowdonia, contemplated the reasons why people from the area were moving to towns. Central to his explanation was the figure of a woman who finds life hard. Male displeasure at inconvenience is not alluded to. It is instead the 'young bride', 'no longer willing to set up housekeeping with the amenities of a century ago', who precipitates the move.[31] Ten years later his perceptions were echoed in the autobiography of W. Jones-Edwards, published in 1963. Women, he claimed, were a fundamental reason why so many left the land: they were tempted by fish-and-chip shops and other amenities. Men, he stated, were more attached to the land but were nagged ('poenid') so much by their wives that they had to move to the south-east. He followed this description with a list of abandoned cottages.[32] A way of life was being eroded because women had been seduced by convenience. These descriptions absolve men from any part in the abandonment. They cast the past way of life as masculine and modern comforts as feminine. Changes in material conditions, notably opportunities for women to earn independent wages, encouraged the definition of the past as masculine. There are parallels here with the attitudes of those in the industrial south-east who, with the arrival of toy-making and confectionery industries after 1945, thought that 'Merthyr's gone cissy'.[33] A conflation

[30] W. J. Lewis, *Hanes Darluniadol o Geredigion* (Aberystwyth, 1970), p. 83.

[31] Thomas Firbank, *A Country of Memorable Honour* (London, 1953), pp. 165–6.

[32] W. Jones-Edwards, *Ar Lethrau Ffair Rhos: Atgofion Mwnwr* (Aberystwyth, 1963), pp. 53–5.

[33] R. G. Lloyd Thomas, *Welsh Odyssey* (Llandybïe, 1949), p. 24.

of gender, occupation, place and past could form part of an individual's *Weltanshauung.*

Given the attention the past has attracted at this time, it is no surprise to find older people from the county acquiring near iconic status. This was part of a broader tendency, by no means limited to Cardiganshire, but it became a crucial part in the definition and location of what was seen as the county's essence. The artist Kyffin Williams was interested in his own part of Wales, Anglesey and the mountainous north-west, but the worry that if the 'typical Welsh hill farmer' disappears 'part of Wales will go with him', is part of a twentieth-century apprehension primarily expressed by the literati and applied to many parts of the country. Thus, an aspect of society received enhanced symbolic status at a time when its physical continuation was felt to be under threat. The representation of the Cardi reveals how the traditional rural dweller was encased in the past. And the degree to which the past infiltrated depictions of the Cardi can be seen in the words regularly used in conjunction with the name. The Millennium edition of *Brewer's Dictionary of Phrase and Fable,* for instance, noted that Welsh people refer to 'an old Cardi'.[34]

The reception of Aneurin Jones's art demonstrates how those who feel attached to the county and rural Wales commonly located the roots of the area in farming, and it is telling that the subjects of his work are mainly older people. His paintings have been hailed as typifying a fading way of life, the victim of, in Peter Lord's view, 'a competing community intruding on the common ground'.[35] The artist, despite his having been born in Breconshire and having spent time teaching in north Pembrokeshire, is described as 'a true Cardi', and this shows how the term can be used to encapsulate the features of upland agricultural Wales.[36] In addition, the idea of place, people and past combined can be seen across a range of writing. In the former miner Ron Berry's novel *This Bygone* and his autobiography, people from the

[34] Kyffin Williams, *Drawings* (Llandysul, 2001), p. 82; *Brewer's Dictionary of Phrase and Fable Millennium Edition* (London, 2001), p. 204.

[35] Emyr Llewelyn (ed.), *Aneurin* (Talybont, 2000), p. 12.

[36] Welsh Arts Books, *http://www.welshartsarchive.org.uk/welsh_books.htm* (accessed 15 January 2003).

county are defined in relation to age.[37] Furthermore, there are often references to men being of 'Cardiganshire stock' or 'born and bred', denoting a historical attachment to and link with a particular, distinctive place or pedigree.[38] There is a sense in which the way of life epitomized by the county character, for good or ill, is out of step with the world. This is quite different from the assertive county image of a century earlier that was carried by the cultural and political streams of its day.

Conspicuous youth cultures, which emerged from the late 1950s onwards, provided a contrast to the Cardi. The advance of the Teddy Boys provoked a brief verse from John E. Morgan. Comparing two of his four-line poems (conforming to the *englyn* metrical form) provides an instance of how generational divides contributed to dominant locations of the Cardi. A 'Tedi Boy' is not a home-grown product, rather a 'rep' for rock and roll with a distinctive haircut and a liking for idols and images. There is a signal contrast with the following verse, 'Y Cardi', which describes a possessor of great faith and a knowledgeable farmer: hardly the idol-following youth but, rather, a person who possessed inner qualities instead of external trappings.[39] The county's heroes were, conversely, mainly drawn from the Victorian era.[40] A manifestation of increasing pluralism, these youth culture pioneers and consumers provided a modern contrast to the traditional Cardi. Although begetting generational polar-ization elsewhere, especially after the Mod versus Rocker clashes of 1964, a place with a firmly established county-type founded on the past could more convincingly fill an opposi-tional role.

In historical writing from the 1960s onwards the county-type has been depicted in a similar way, located in a past of hardship and struggle. The arrival of the Cardi in

---

[37] Ron Berry, *This Bygone* (Llandysul, 1996), pp. 9, 173; *idem, History is What you Live* (Llandysul, 1998), pp. 22, 34.

[38] For example, Meic Stephens (ed.), *Harri Webb, A Militant Muse: Selected Literary Journalism, 1948–1980* (Bridgend, 1998), p. 57; Gareth Williams, 'Sport and society in Glamorganshire, 1750–1980', in Prys Morgan (ed.), *Glamorgan County History*, vol. 4, *Glamorganshire Society* (Cardiff, 1988), pp. 381–400, 391.

[39] John E. Morgan, *Cerddi'r Eos* (Llandysul, 1967), pp. 25, 27.

[40] Daniel Davies, 'The county', *Cymdeithas Ceredigion Llundain Llawlyfr*, 16 (1962–3), 18.

historiography was, on the whole, a continuation of these celebratory, mainstream definitions. But at times a counter-image can be discerned. There is a hint of defensiveness in an explanation offered in the county's historical journal *Ceredigion* in 1963, for example. At the conclusion of an article about life in the first half of the nineteenth century, W. J. Lewis mentioned the Cardi's reputation 'for being tight-fisted' and explained that the hardship endured 'is in itself sufficient explanation for this state of mind. Had the Cardi not looked after every farthing, he might not have survived.' Later descriptions offer similar explanations.[41] Yet this repu-tation could only have been born of interaction with other groups that resulted in an interpretation of difference. The identification of the county's inhabitants with modes of behaviour has been a complicated process, influenced by numerous positions – including liberalism and socialism. In other words, the obvious explanation for the Cardi's reputa-tion for being cautious with money has been adopted and refracted, defended and attacked in ways that reflect funda-mental divisions as to how people should conduct themselves in society.

Two North American academics have offered their own brief interpretations of the county's distinctiveness based on a peculiar past, its 'small freehold farmers trying to eke a subsis-tence from marginal land'.[42] Welsh historians also defined the county by cultural features thought to typify an earlier period. An authority on rural crafts, speaking at Aberaeron in 1962, 'deplored the fact that by to-day [the] locality had ceased to be an economic unit' and that soon all places would be the same. Craftsmen were often 'men of culture and lead-ership', so their loss would result in more than a lack of material goods. In the 1980s another historian pronounced that the farmers and miners of the county's past were 'intel-

---

[41] W. J. Lewis, 'The condition of labour in mid-Cardiganshire in the early nine-teenth century', *Ceredigion*, 4, 4 (1960–3), 321–35, 333; Keith Robbins, review of *Cardiganshire County History*, vol. 3, in *English Historical Review*, 115, 460 (2000), 268.

[42] Peter Thomas, *Strangers from a Strange Land: The Voyages of the Brig Albion and the Founding of the First Welsh Settlements in Canada* (Llandysul, 1986), p. 9; Ann Kelly Knowles, *Calvinists Incorporated: Welsh Immigrants on Ohio's Industrial Frontier* (Chicago, 1997), p. 45.

ligent, sober and religious'.[43] Given this concentration of the county's essence in a Nonconformist culture with little mechanization, it was likely that, just as the Welsh philosopher J. R. Jones foresaw, features that previously defined areas would fade even though the language remained.[44] Elements of progress were embraced and defined in relation to the county. The need to improve material well-being was a fundamental component in Cardiganshire's desired and actual mental location. In some ways the county could claim to be modern; in others its long-standing traditions were challenged. This ambivalence pervaded perceptions of the county and can be readily discerned in conceptions of the future.

FUTURE

Fewer grand hopes were pinned to the county after the Second World War than during the interwar years. True, the work of Stapleton's Plant Breeding Station continued, but the decline of empire compelled a shift in rhetoric. Furthermore, the racially distinct moorland dweller, cherished by Fleure and Bowen, was less likely to be spoken of in a post-Holocaust world.[45] Grand themes of empire and race would not shed their light through Cardiganshire's prism as in the past. This did not mean that the area could not fill a space in people's conceptions of a better future, as the movement to the area of those in search of alternative lifestyles testifies. In the past, facets of Cardiganshire, most notably religion and liberalism, had been seen to guide, or have the potential to lead, other places. As the twentieth century proceeded, old vanguards did not offer much in the context of technological and secular change and became less relevant. Material concerns dominated as financial benefit was sought through contact with markets and the attraction of facilities. This was not in itself new, but the diversity of

[43] CN, 2 March 1962, 10; Ieuan Gwynedd Jones, 'The county and its history, 1909–1984', Ceredigion, 10, 1 (1984–7), 1–17, 9.

[44] Dewi Z. Phillips, J. R. Jones (Cardiff, 1995), p. 68. Also see The Times, 3 August 1954, 8.

[45] Amusing references to the anthropologist's legacy can be found in Roy Noble, Roy Noble's Wales (Cardiff, 1999), p. 185.

forms it took and the explicit emphasis placed on advertising certainly were. In the late 1950s, for instance, MPs stressed how the county contained sites where a nuclear power station could have been located. Growth was envisaged as moving along technological and material paths similar to those in the rest of the country. A past symbol of progress, the railway line between Carmarthen and Aberystwyth, was closed but there were many other potential ways to integrate this notoriously marginal place and draw in trade, tourists and technology.[46]

Science fiction is able to capture the tensions between visions of progress and feelings of stasis, and an example of this genre from Cardiganshire is provided by the remarks of 'a local visionary' who wrote a 'glimpse into future Cardigan' in 1946. The author, who awoke from a Rip Van Winkle-like sleep in 1972, described 'gyroplanes' and a broad road on which cars could travel four abreast. This twentieth-century equivalent of the 'Balladeer's Prophecy', discussed in chapter III, was no doubt stimulated by notions of urban planning prevalent in the post-war years. As with better-known science fiction, there was a contemporary satirical vein in this visualization that emerged when the visionary noted that the town's memorial hall was at last an accomplished fact. The issue of the memorial hall roused emotions some sixteen years later, and was felt to shame the county town, especially as other places had built such structures of remembrance.[47] This was a particularly local issue, but it was a variation on a theme of feared stasis that drew in other towns. Aberystwyth found itself, not for the first time, castigated for its dearth of theatres; a local academic argued that the theatre was, together with cinema and radio, vital for improving the mental health of the population.[48] The dread of being a stagnant pool rather than a progressive stream was nowhere more evident than in the discussions of those interested in attracting visitors, such as those at the Cardigan Bay Resorts Association meeting at Aberystwyth in 1955. For, indeed, it was in this sphere that the modern world, in the

---

[46] *The Times*, 1 February 1957, 4; *WG*, 22 August 1963, 1.

[47] *CTA*, 29 November 1946, 6; *CN*, 13 April 1962, 7.

[48] *CN*, 5 May 1950, 5; Cecil Price, 'Universities and the theatre', *The Welsh Anvil: Yr Einion*, 3 (July 1951), 35.

form of tourists wanting to go somewhere different and yet retain luxuries, met local services. Clifford Knight, a town councillor, put this in terms of food when noting that there would be little chance of retaining or attracting custom if Dover sole, a popular fish in English cooking, was not available in coastal cafes. An editorial in the *Welsh Gazette* weighed into the debate with an analysis that captured the need to advance, by getting rid of an 'archaic transport system' while maintaining an air of tradition. The 'modern coined phrase' that it pays to advertise was cited as a spur to promote the county, yet at the same time the need to retain 'old-world charm', like the coracles on the River Teifi, was underlined.[49] For those eager to draw visitors' money into the area, the somewhat paradoxical location of the county in both a modern and a traditional context would be needed in order to fulfill the county's potential as a tourist destination.

Discontent, hope and pride were framed in the language of temporality, in terms of a place being behind the rest of the world, alongside it or, in more positive tones, leading it. Hopes for advancement were founded on the development of improved communications. One of these aspirations, expressed in 1955, two years after the Korean War, which saw considerable deployment of the helicopter, called for helicopters to be utilized as a means of conveying people and materials. Though not one of the more successful examples among the 'proliferation of various forms of mobility and communications' characterizing the twentieth century, the interest in this form of transport demonstrated a desire to move forward and locate the county in a modern context.[50] Although part of the widespread desire to make the most of technological developments, the imperative for this part of Wales was related to the area's greater fear of being left behind. In 'the event of helicopters coming into commercial use', the county's planning committee undertook a survey of appropriate sites. Mental images of the county as a primitive land feature in the discussion of this potential boon. An editorial speculated on how some would think that this step

[49] *WG*, 31 March 1955, 1, 4.

[50] Amanda Root, 'Transport and communications', in A. H. Halsey and Josephine Webb (eds), *Twentieth-Century British Social Trends* (London, 2000), pp. 437–68, 463.

would be pointless in 'old-world Cardiganshire', and that 'Cardiganshire might be regarded in some quarters as being . . . a land where incredible mountain fables of giants and cave men still bear even more than a semblance of reality'. Unlike the more ambiguous blend of old and new needed to attract tourists, the benefits for industry of the anticipated helicopter revolution were described in an unmitigated modern light; the 'prosperity' that could result if this form of transport was adopted would be as 'resounding as the roar of the aero engines'. A desire to catch up and partake in the development of the light industry emerging in other places appears to have been based on the county having been 'written off' in the past and having its industrial potential 'strangled' by geography – the same geography that, in other contexts, was invoked as defining the county.[51]

The drive to build houses – a vision for the future espoused by politicians in the immediate post-war period – also touched the county. This was particularly important given the considerable loss of population from Cardiganshire between the wars. In 1947 the minister of town and county planning, Peter Scott, circulated a memorandum proposing a new town in the county. Lampeter was the favourite location, and the town council, which asked the county council for support and to exert pressure on the government to develop rural areas, welcomed the suggestion. Scott had intended to establish 'a first class dairy and vegetable growing area for supplying the needs of industrial towns'. A population of 20,000 was the aim – Lampeter's population in 1951 was 1,799.[52] Like the helicopter scheme, this vision did not come about, but it tells us how much was invested in the idea of moving the area forward, and how these notions were driven by external stimuli, in this case by what has been described as a nationwide post-war 'grandiose vision'. Appeals to external models of urbanization and industry did not negate local pride, however, as the foreword to a county council publication demonstrates. It contained the predictable invitation to tourists and a positive depiction of the county's inhabitants.

[51] *WG*, 10 March 1955, 1, 6. Another consideration of the proposal can be found in ibid., 5 May 1955, 1.
[52] *CJ*, 12 March 1948, 1; *CTA*, 18 November 1947, 1.

Yet it is noticeable that the Cardi is sketched as 'progressive' – in the handbook's Welsh version the Cardi was 'symudant gyda'r oes' (moving with the times). The British capital is the lodestar: there is 'a constant interchange of people and ideas between Cardiganshire and London', and this notion of a progressive native spirit places a different emphasis on the population to that noted by those who located the people in the past. In addition, migrants to the county are welcomed, 'even more so if they can bring their own light industry with them'. The invitation mentioned good educational facilities, electricity and water schemes in progress and 'a small reserve of ready workers'.[53]

Features noted in the 1961 handbook, including agriculture, formed a foundation that enabled the county to be positioned in a futuristic context. An inauguration ceremony to mark the Teifi Pools water scheme in 1958, which had been three years and £1.5m in the making, contained numerous references to the county's future; the Welsh secretary of the Ministry of Housing and Local Government, F. Blaise Gillie, pointed out that it constituted 'a step towards the future of Cardiganshire'. A newspaper reporter evoked a majestic scene: the crowd gathered at the rim of the mist-covered lake singing hymns. The occasion was marked by the chairman of the southern part of the county's water board, Cardigan alderman E. Glyn Davies, in a speech that highlighted conflicting positionings of the county. It is noteworthy that he selected the commencement of this visible mark of progress, which could be seen in some quarters as illustrating the county's belated entry into the modern world, to stress the county's home-grown achievements. Education was a fundamental part of the county's location in a progressive context. Alderman Davies appeared to use the county's educational tradition as a defence, to counter those who would portray Cardiganshire as a backward corner of a nation that was about to see its first portion of motorway

[53] Meryl Aldridge, *The British New Towns: A Programme Without a Policy* (London, 1979), p. 29; *Cardiganshire: The County Handbook* (Cheltenham and London, 1961), p. 7. The desire to attract light industry to the county is also illustrated in the *CN*, 6 October 1950, 5. Emphasis on the county's tendency to look beyond its borders, and a consequent refutation of any claims that it was backward, can be found in Margot James's novel, *The Cardi Comes Home* (London, 1956), p. 27.

opened at the end of the year. The county and its denizens were 'regarded to be the end of the pipeline and very much behind the times', but, he continued, 'even before the 1944 Act [R. A. Butler's Education Act] came into force there was a greater percentage of Cardiganshire children in grammar schools than in any other county in the country'.[54] Evidently, this public configuration of the county contained the message that a want of some attributes of modern life should not be equated with ignorance.

A blend of modern improvement and a statement of local progressiveness in education featured in the county's London Society publication. This journal was produced well into the 1970s – although declining membership after the war led to pleas in the press and a 50 per cent reduction in the membership fee.[55] The conveniences of modern life, piped water, baths and water closets, were notable for their absence from the 1951 census returns for the county. About half the houses in Cardiganshire had no water on tap, whereas the English and Welsh average was 17 per cent. Such circumstances would not, the educationalist Jac L. Williams assured his London Welsh readers, continue. Thanks to reservoirs and electricity projects, such as the Teifi Pools and Rheidol hydroelectric scheme, the county's inhabitants would not be behind for long. This process of going modern ('mynd yn fodern') would level up the quality of life for those living in the countryside to that experienced by the London Cardis, or enjoyed by holidaymakers in the best places in Aberystwyth. In a nod towards the notion of a 'classless society', Williams noted that even the road workers, who were among the least wealthy in the county, could now be seen driving to work. Yet Cardiganshire's educational tradition, popularly held to be rooted in the Cardis' belief in providing for their children's instruction, was once again articulated to illustrate the area's own contribution to individual development; this theme was backed up by statistics, such as those showing that over 13 per cent of 17–19 year-olds were in full-time education compared with 7 per cent in England and Wales as a whole. No doubt,

[54]   *CTA*, 9 May 1958, 1.
[55]   Ibid., 10 June 1949, 2.

these provided a cultural counterbalance to the indicators of deprivation.[56]

Contrasts between material circumstances and those of the mind – a division noted in various forms over the period covered by this study – were enhanced by education after 1945. In a number of respects, the county claimed precedence in educational matters and this is succinctly illustrated in an extract from the *Cardigan and Tivyside Advertiser* in 1946. Two men travelling in different directions meet on a bridge crossing the Teifi: the one heading out of the county assures the returnee that 'It's no use coming to Cardiganshire to make a living.' To which the other replies: 'I'm not coming to make a living. I'm coming to finish my education.' Of course, this did not reflect the reality of the educated who left the area in search of better opportunities, but it shows the association between a county marked by the river where the men met and an attitude to learning that existed in many minds. The importance of education in definitions of the county was repeated some thirty years later in the travel books of journalist Trevor Fishlock when he mentioned that the county sent a greater proportion of its schoolchildren to university than did any other.[57] Where once the old schools of Neuadd-lwyd and Castell Hywel or the universities were at the forefront, during the latter part of the twentieth century the numbers of Cardiganshire natives at grammar schools, undertaking post-16 education or studying at university and the county's swift adaptation of the comprehensive model of secondary schooling achieved prominence. Collections of statistics enabled this reputation to spread beyond local pronouncements: the geographers Coates and Rawstron, for example, found that the county led England and Wales in the number of awards given for students going to university in the late 1960s.[58] Indeed, this adjustment allowed Cardiganshire

---

[56] Jac L. Williams, 'Sut mae hi?', *Cymdeithas Ceredigion Llundain Llawlyfr*, 14 (1959–60), 12–13. Also see the comments of Ben Bowen Thomas, permanent secretary of the Welsh Department of Education in the *WG*, 20 January 1955, 6.

[57] *CTA*, 5 April 1946, 1; Trevor Fishlock, *Talking of Wales* (London, 1976), p. 60. In an earlier book Fishlock noted how 'in 1971 Aberystwyth became the first town in Britain to admit students to the policy making committee of its council': *Wales and the Welsh* (London, 1972), p. 130.

[58] B. E. Coates and E. M. Rawstron, *Regional Variations in Britain: Studies in Economic and Social Geography* (London, 1971), p. 266.

to be situated in a progressive context on a national scale as education became a watchword in political culture. The tradition was reinforced by greater attention paid to the Welsh language in education. By partaking in the revival of Welsh as a public language, and providing some pivotal educational institutions such as the Welsh nursery school movement (Mudiad Ysgolion Meithrin) in 1971, the county was at the confluence of an older progressive tradition of education and a newer one that asserted the Welsh language. Three political scientists studying the county's political trad- ition in the 1970s did not overlook this progressive feature and noted how, even though there was a general nationwide movement, the county possessed its own distinctive 'linguistic battles'.[59] The implementation of the compulsory teaching of Welsh from the ages of four to sixteen, initiated in 1958 by the local authority's county education committee, would, by twenty-first-century standards, appear vindicated and far sighted.

For most, agriculture was not as controversial as education. Yet progress in this sphere was also affirmed in a competitive manner. Much emphasis can be placed on an area's exports and the acknowledgement they receive, and this in turn heightens the originating locality's distinctiveness. Pride in supplying quality agricultural produce contributed to a sense of Cardiganshire's involvement in promoting Britain's well- being. This was expressed through a symbolic jostling for national importance between industry and agriculture. At an agricultural show at Llangwyryfon in northern Cardiganshire two years after the end of the Second World War, the coun- ty's Liberal MP Roderic Bowen spoke of how the county did not possess much industry and was 'somewhat off the map' in that respect. However, 'as far as agriculture was concerned, Cardiganshire was very much to the fore' and there was no 'talk of strikes or of a five day week'. This estimation of the farming community as a hard-working, uncomplaining contributor to the nation, 'the one British industry which has a better record than its rivals in Europe', was expressed on a British scale, particularly during years of trade union strife in

[59] P. J. Madgwick, Non Griffiths and Valerie Walker, *The Politics of Rural Wales: A Study of Cardiganshire* (London, 1973), pp. 118–21.

the late 1970s.[60] The comparison between, on the one hand, the industrial worker and disputes in that sector and, on the other, the farmer reveals how much was invested in asserting the contribution of the county and farming towards the healthy growth of individuals. Farming was being presented as a means of contending the importance of a place. Success at the Royal Welsh Show of 1973, the ninth at its permanent site at Llanelwedd, led to comments that conveyed the dynamism and worth of Cardiganshire. Winning the Harlech Television (HTV)-sponsored inter-county competition for the second year running prompted David Meredith, HTV press and publicity officer, to announce that the county not only had better products but 'better people', because the effort for one county with so small a population to win the award two years in a row reflected 'individual hard work'.[61] Commendations like this doubtless compensated somewhat for what was, in the latter part of this period, a decline in the social role of agriculture as illustrated by the fall in the number of agricultural jobs.

At the start of the twenty-first century the county proffers examples of 're-traditionalization' – where previous social and economic features related to the area take on new prominence in changed circumstances.[62] The Aberaeron Festival of Welsh Ponies and Cobs, begun in 2002 to celebrate the centenary of the Welsh Pony and Cob Society, is an example. This event illustrates how a county tradition – the breeding of horses – can fuse with broader tourist attractions; indeed, the assertion of a county tradition is here taken beyond those who are involved in breeding to a wider, often visiting, public and was inspired by Spanish horse festivals. It has contributed to that sometimes conflicting combination of agriculture

[60] *CTA*, 19 September 1947, 1; John P. Mackintosh, *Britain's Malaise: Political or Economic?* (Southampton, 1977), pp. 23–5, where the farmers' 'capacity for innovation' is praised. An earlier instance of praise for future-focused farmers can be found in the *WG*, 13 January 1955, 6.

[61] *CN*, 12 April 1974, 9.

[62] Barbara Adam, 'Detraditionalization and the certainty of uncertain futures', in Paul Heelas, Scott Lash and Paul Morris (eds), *Detraditionalization: Critical Reflections on Authority and Identity* (London, 1996), pp. 139–40. For an analysis of the place of the cob in the county today, see Samantha Hurn, 'The "Cardinauts" of the western coast of Wales: Exchanging and exhibiting horses in the pursuit of fame', *Journal of Material Culture*, 13, 3 (2008), 335–55.

and tourism that Cardiganshire-born Welsh Secretary John Morris identified in the mid-1970s as constituting the best hope for the county's future.[63] Some thirty years later the language of advancement is similarly focused on developing the 'resources of [Cardiganshire's] high quality environment'. Although the aim to provide opportunities 'for all to reach their full potential' indicates how individual progress still retains a place discourse, the 2004 Ceredigion Community Strategy was not linked to traditional Cardi qualities but was, to use the language of our times, inclusive not exclusive.[64] By the start of the twenty-first century, Cardi characteristics, which would have been seen as epitomizing an outdated morality, were not called upon.

CENTRE

Combining space with value generally involves a contrast between economic/political cores and a cultural/spiritual counterbalance. Changes in this period, such as the rise of the environmental movement from the 1970s, provided new ways in which the county could be used to counterbalance economic/political cores. Instead of a relatively homogeneous centre to be preserved, during the latter part of this period more commentators located the county as a heterogeneous centre that contained an energetic cultural force.[65] Toleration and inclusiveness are not limited to particular historical moments. They have been, however, stressed in positive portrayals of the county to a greater extent than at any other time, even among professed Welsh nationalists who see sympathetic migrants contributing to Welsh culture.[66]

[63] J. Morris, 'Sir Aberteifi', *Barn*, 162–3 (1976), 213.

[64] 'Strategaeth gymunedol Ceredigion community strategy: Ceredigion 2020', *http://www.ceredigion2020.org.uk/doc/040712ceredigionstrategy.pdf*, p. 1 (accessed 28 July 2004).

[65] Caustic comments in response to this diversity can be found in Colin Palfrey and Arwel Roberts, *The Unofficial Guide to Wales* (Talybont, 1994), pp. 41–2, and Geraint H. Jenkins, '"I will tell you a word or two about Cardiganshire": Welsh clerics and literature in the eighteenth century', *Studies in Church History*, 38 (Woodbridge, 2004), pp. 303–23, 317.

[66] See Gwyn Williams, *ABC of (D)GW* (Llandysul, 1981), p. 206. The relationship between migrants sympathetic to the Welsh language and the native Welsh has been pointed out by Neil Evans, Paul O'Leary and Charlotte Williams, 'Introduction:

This corresponds to changes in the make-up of the county, and a realignment of 'Britishness' elsewhere, and owes much to greater mobility; the percentage of Welsh-born people in the county fell from 64.2 in 1991 to 58.6 ten years later. In the latter year the average for Wales was over 75 per cent. In absolute terms, 31,038 of the county's population of 74,941 were born outside Wales.[67]

Despite their reflecting what constitutes a desirable diverse society, projections of the county situate it in the context of its own cultural traditions. In this way, the meeting of outside and inside is rendered mutually beneficial. A television programme aired in 2003 included comments from the county's Welsh Assembly Member Elin Jones who, against the backdrop of the Cardigan agricultural show, twice stressed the county's 'vibrancy' that resulted from the meeting of a rural Welsh-speaking culture and those attracted by its two university colleges. Additionally, the novels of Niall Griffiths, the Liverpool-born 'Welsh Irvine Welsh', who writes about those who 'just seem t'drift to' Aberystwyth, have captured the relatively cosmopolitan nature of twenty-first-century Ceredigion with his books' melange of accents and languages. A generation of those born to English people who moved to rural Wales from the 1960s is being joined by first-generation arrivals such as the subjects of Griffiths's novels, and this palimpsest, when combined with the large number of Welsh speakers, gives this part of the country an eclectic air. Poetry such as Gwen Palmer's 'Welcome, Saeson [English]', describing the arrival and settlement of people like Palmer, who originally hailed from Buckinghamshire, to the area captures this variety in a rural environment.[68] The cultural consequences of diversity, from environmental consciousness to poetry, have recently given the county another facet that allows it to be contrasted with urban areas.

race, nation and globalisation', in Neil Evans, Paul O'Leary and Charlotte Williams (eds), *A Tolerant Nation? Exploring Ethnic Diversity in Wales* (Cardiff, 2003), p. 10.

[67] 'Members research service 2001 census of population: key statistics for Assembly constituencies: Ceredigion, 2003', *http://www.wales.gov.uk/organipo/content/news/ceredigion.pdf*, p. 1 (accessed 15 June 2004).

[68] *The Counties of Wales: Cardiganshire*, HTV Wales, 6 November 2003; Niall Griffiths, *Grits* (London, 2001), p. 249; G. Palmer, '"Welcome, Saeson"', in Mid Teifi Arts Writers Group, *Teifi Whispers* (Llandysul, 2000), p. 62. Also see Noragh Jones, *Living in Rural Wales* (Llandysul, 1993), pp. 35–7.

When the 2001 census revealed that the population of Ceredigion had increased at a faster rate than that of any county in Wales, the *Western Mail* ran an article on 'God's county'.[69] The division running through the report is between built-up areas and rural ones; a person quoted in the article refers to an urban crime-ridden Cardiff and a less hectic Ceredigion. Apprehension about crime in modern Britain opens up another axis on which to contrast two ideas of place, but it is not a new one as mid-nineteenth century definitions of Cardiganshire and Glamorgan used the prevalence of crime to mark their differences. In this analysis, commercial centres lack not only the cultural sophistication – one of the county's redeeming features is that it is a place 'where people don't look at you blankly when you tell them you are a poet' – they also compel people to be louder in speech because they are living in a noisy environment. People in Ceredigion are, by contrast, described as 'quiet'. A core of decency and peace, reflecting the surroundings, is painted, and conflicts, whether the result of criminality or occupational struggle, are only found far away from its borders. One person interviewed for the article, the poet Menna Elfyn, an active and occasionally imprisoned Welsh-language campaigner, pointed out that the people of the county had 'not been conditioned by trade unions' as those from urban and industrial places were. The polarization of Glamorgan and Cardiganshire runs through the modern period, and these recent examples, touching on environmental and social issues, indicate that the cultural/commercial dichotomy continues to play a part in mental maps of Wales, although the decline of heavy industry has meant that the nature of the contrast has changed.

However, the post-1945 environment, with its bolder political divides – notably the arrival of a majority, reforming Labour government – evinced different divisions from those of half a century later. Compared with 1935, Labour's share of the vote in Cardiganshire fell in 1945, presenting an eddy against the substantial Labour victory. A programme of nationalization unnerved many. There was also a sense

---

[69] *WM*, 1 October 2002, 5.

of cultural upheaval, which saw a wealthier and educated working class portrayed as upstarts. For those uneasy with these changes, Cardiganshire could be alluded to as an alternative. A people who were not seeking to upset the way things were became a useful didactic tool. In his 1950 travelogue, Tudor Edwards's interpretation of 'the men of Cardiganshire' makes them stand up to contemporary opponents from outside: in this case, 'the current wave of Socialism' that has transformed the worker 'into a pampered and superficially educated work-shy, tawdry smart-Alec'. No other area in his book is used in such a confrontational way. Edwards, who wrote about travel and architecture, utilized the Cardi to make a political point, an echo of which can be heard in Elfyn's comment. Edwards's usage illustrates how the representation could be revived and adapted to meet new political and social circumstances, thus ensuring that the Cardi did not disappear as a symbol, despite its having passed its apex in terms of both the apparent volume of representations and their influence.[70]

A contemporary mood that 'posed something of a challenge to entrenched wealth and power' encouraged some politicians to call upon the assistance of the Cardi.[71] Comments made at the annual meeting of the county's Liberal Association in 1950 indicate how the county was thought to be a repository of common sense at a time when rash radical political philosophies were at hand. They show how, against the backdrop of the Cold War, a county character was evoked to counterbalance an encroaching state. Roderic Bowen praised 'a Liberal way of life' whose standards were opposed by 'socialist ideologies' and the impending 'bureaucratic state'. It was claimed that these bogies heralded the abolition of 'free enterprise' and, therefore, 'did not appeal to the Cardi'. Another speaker concurred:

---

[70] Tudor Edwards, *The Face of Wales* (London, 1950), p. 52. Another example of commendation can be found in David Raymond, *We Go to Wales* (London, 1954), p. 105, where 'Cardis' are described as 'awfully intelligent people'. Also see Glyn James, 'Cardi yn y Rhondda: ambell atgof Glyn James', in Hywel Teifi Edwards (ed.), *Cwm Rhondda* (Llandysul, 1995), pp. 334–5.

[71] Jim McGuigan, 'Cultural change', in Jonathan Hollowell (ed.), *Britain Since 1945* (London, 2003), pp. 279–95, 281.

'Socialism was quite foreign to the make-up and tempera-
ment of the Cardi.'[72] In a Wales that, in terms of seats won
and votes cast, was dominated by Labour, the Cardi was identified as a taproot of contrary values. Although a Marxist
critic of Clement Attlee's Labour government described it as
not having 'even taken a step' towards 'a socialist commonwealth', representations of the county and its inhabitants
in the late 1940s and early 1950s indicate that an intense
competition between ideas, that involved the evocation and
redeployment of ideal types like the Cardi, was taking place.[73]
Such juxtapositions may – with hindsight, especially after
the county elected a Labour MP (albeit a former member of
Plaid Cymru) in 1966 – appear unwarranted, but if the means
to which some people put representations of Cardiganshire's
inhabitants are to be fully appreciated, these concerns need
to be acknowledged.

The habit of saving continued to be attributed to the county's inhabitants during most of the period. Local papers
expressed pride that the county was ahead of other places
in saving schemes. Two examples, one from the late 1940s
and one from the early 1960s, demonstrate how the location of Cardiganshire as a hub of prudence and self-control
reaped representational dividends. Cardiganshire's tradition
of saving was, unsurprisingly, called into play during post-war
austerity. The chancellor of the exchequer, Stafford Cripps,
architect of Britain's austerity policy, was concerned that
money spent on imports and consumer goods had hamstrung
Britain's export trade. Cripps took an interest in the county's 'savings week'. In a demonstration of local pride, the
Cardigan and Tivyside Advertiser proclaimed that the scheme
was planned on 'its [the county's] own initiative' and was
the only such programme planned in the whole kingdom.
Recognition of the county's worth was assured when Cripps
and the organizers of the National Savings adopted this
'savings week' on a national scale. Acknowledgement
from outside, a crucial component of identity formation,

[72] *WG*, 12 October 1950, 5. Roderic Bowen described the county's 'hardcore of
Liberalism' in ibid., 23 February 1950, 6.
[73] David Coates, *The Labour Party and the Struggle for Socialism* (London, 1975),
p. 47.

could not have come from a higher source (though it was somewhat ironic in view of reservations expressed about Cripps's party); and, the paper added, 'full details of the Cardiganshire scheme were now being sent to every constituency in England and Wales'.[74]

The example from the early 1960s might be expected to prove less defining, but it still reveals the link between an activity, a widely recognized county character and the part the local press played in bringing it to the attention of the public. A headline in the *Cambrian News* during December 1962 announced that 'Cardis save £888,928 in six months'. This was part of the savings movement largely based on collections made at schools, thus combining two markers of Cardi identity, and it amounted to the highest figure per head for south Wales. It is important to note how this claim to centrality was filtered in an earlier instance. The county could not claim precedence in Wales as a whole, yet the context of southern Wales allowed the reputation of the Cardi for thrift to be alluded to with pride.[75] Still, this marker of 'Cardi-ness', despite being commonly used to this day as shorthand for a 'tight' person generally, became less pronounced as the period progressed. This was probably a consequence of the further development, in the late twentieth century, of a society where 'choice and credit are readily available'. These instances of a saving culture's being attached to the county illustrate how an earlier feature of the county's image persisted and was reinforced in a widely publicized way – something that was also done by a sociological study published in 1962 that mentioned cases of men doffing their caps when entering banks in Tregaron.[76]

At a time when definitions of Wales were being articulated to an increasing degree, claims that the county was the cultural heart of Wales became ever more noticeable in representations of the area. Such claims had been expressed

[74] *CTA*, 17 June 1949, 1.

[75] *CN*, 14 December 1962, 1; ibid., 8 June 1962, 12.

[76] John Benson, *The Rise of Consumer Society in Britain, 1880–1980* (London, 1994), p. 4; Emrys Jones, 'Tregaron: the sociology of a market town in central Cardiganshire', in Elwyn Davies and Alwyn D. Rees (eds), *Welsh Rural Communities* (Cardiff, 1962), pp. 65–117, 91–2.

before, yet after 1945 the debate entered new waters. A recent study has described Aberystwyth as being 'a hub and generator of Welsh nationalist discourse' from the 1960s onwards.[77] Yet the town's undeniably vital role hinged, in part, upon conceptions of the county. Commercial and urban growth in south-east Wales added a further dimension to the long-standing apposition of Glamorgan and Cardiganshire. Cardiff's acquisition of capital status was, in time, followed by the moving of many functions of the Welsh Office there from London and the setting up of the Welsh Assembly in 1999. There was, therefore, a rising political as well as commercial centre in the south-east. An assertion of the cultural over the material was the response. A conceptual boundary between a centre of power and a centre of sentiment was etched out again, with an appeal to an authority higher than economics or population density. The argument that intellectuals were inclined to champion the idea of the nation over that of the state – or cultural over polity– is supported by the background of those who located Cardiganshire as a centre of Welshness.[78] When, in 1952, the barrister Alun Talfan Davies introduced the first in a series of books each dedicated to a Welsh county, he wrote that Cardiganshire was a suitable county with which to open the series: 'Dyma ganol Cymru, ac i lawer o Gymry Llundain, dyma'i chalon hefyd.' (Here is the centre of Wales, and for many London Welsh the heart as well.)[79] Moreover, images of the area in publications designed for the tourist market reinforced perceptions of it as being more genuinely Welsh than other places.[80] This congruence amplified the impression of centrality.

Geographic centrality was only one reason for this judgement: others included cultural institutions, ways of life,

[77] Rhys Jones and Carwyn Fowler, *Placing the Nation: Aberystwyth and the Reproduction of Welsh Nationalism* (Cardiff, 2008), p. 203.

[78] M. Weber, 'Structures of power', in *Max Weber: Essays in Sociology*, ed. H. H. Gerth and C. Wright-Mills (London, 1948), p. 176.

[79] T. I. Ellis, *Crwydro Ceredigion* (Llandybïe, 1952), p. iii.

[80] For example, see Robert Kemp, *Colourful Britain* (Norwich, 1967), p. 29 (unnumbered), where, opposite a picture of New Quay harbour, Kemp outlines his impression of Wales. After describing 'cosmopolitan places' like Tiger Bay in Cardiff 'with its considerable number of coloured folk', Kemp remarked that 'Cardiganshire is one of the strongholds of the Welsh tongue', and noted that it 'is fitting' that the National Library of Wales is there.

language and dialect. In 1958, D. Gwenallt Jones concurred with the subject of his biography, the dramatist Idwal Jones, in his judgement that the dialect of central Cardiganshire lacked the extremes of both north and south.[81] Statements of linguistic centrality, a mid-point dialect, had significant potency among those who defined the Welsh nation in terms of language. The poet Wil Ifans (Edward Evans), three times crown-winner at the National Eisteddfod, noted in 1949 that Cardiff was 'claiming to be the capital of Wales'. He disputed this. The 'real wealth of the nation' was found in 'little fields' near Synod Inn and in chapel school rooms, like one in Llandysul where 'Art, music, and literature were being discussed . . . in the unpolluted Welsh of Ceredigion'.[82] These alternative centres, with their emphasis on culture and community, were ideals but their apparent fancifulness does not mean that they did not play a significant part in the creation of the public meaning of Welshness.

The sentiments of less notable people than Wil Ifans are rarely recorded in detail. However, an account of a visit to the 1966 National Eisteddfod held at Aberafan, including a description of nearby Port Talbot, by contributors to the first edition of the literary publication *Y Cardi*, captures something of the way in which the gap between Cardiganshire and the south-east was perceived by those who traversed it. Both the main awards that year went to men from the county, the chair and the crown to Dic Jones and Dafydd Jones respectively. Significant for county pride as these victories were, comments made about Port Talbot provide a greater insight into what Cardiganshire was defined against in the mid-1960s. In the words of Fredrik Barth, the steel boomtown, which had the honour of being the first town to Wales to have a casino and the first stretch of urban motorway in Britain, provided 'cultural materials' that the visitors deployed in ascribing characteristics to this industrial settlement and to their self image.[83] The visitors had crossed a boundary into

---

[81] D. Gwenallt Jones, *Cofiant Idwal Jones* (Aberystwyth, 1958), p. 88.

[82] Wil Ifan, *Here and There* (Cardiff, 1953), p. 6. In addition, he linked the county's 'canny Cardis' with literary accomplishment (p. 44).

[83] Fredrik Barth, 'Preface 1998', in Barth (ed.), *Ethnic Groups and Boundaries: The Social Organisation of Difference* (Prospect Heights, IL, 1998), p. 6. For a description

an area defined by an industry that cast its shadow ('cysgod') over the place – even the wealth is described as industrial money ('arian diwydiannol'). Excessive use of blond hair dye is referred to, but this artificiality is said to detract from the very fashionable clothes worn by the female inhabitants. Artificiality was the defining feature of Port Talbot in the eisteddfod-goers' eyes, as everything, including the gambling, depended on the steel works. The sightseers were keen to point out that industrial decline would swiftly smother this heady atmosphere; perhaps they had the interwar situation in mind. Certain features – untidy gardens and closed windows – were cited as evidence that this place was under the shadow of industry.[84] Port Talbot was thought to be far removed from values ranging from naturalness to security. This was quite the opposite of natural and cautious Cardiganshire, whose award-winning representatives were described as country poets ('beirdd gwlad').

Industry was not the sole 'other' used to define the visitors' home county, and the bundle of characteristics against which Cardiganshire could locate itself at the centre of decency can be noted from further sources of contact with perceived antitheses. Films, such as *Last Tango in Paris* (1972) and *Monty Python's Life of Brian* (1979), allowed representatives of the county to claim moral superiority, using language evoking ethical centrality. The county clerk, Eric Carson, asserted that by twice banning the former movie the county had 'demonstrated that it was an oasis in a desert of permissiveness' – even though the county was one of several dozen local authorities that refused to grant the X certificate advised by the British Board of Film Classification (BBFC) for *Last Tango in Paris*, a film it had already cut.[85] In the period considered in this

of this town, nicknamed 'Treasure Island', see Patrick Hannan, *The Welsh Illusion* (Bridgend, 1999), p. 75.

[84] Pat a Siân, 'Cysgod y gwaith', *Y Cardi: Cylchgrawn Cymdeithas Ceredigion*, 1 (1966), 11–12. Also illustrative of how many latter-day self-professed Cardis saw other parts of Wales is the account of a day trip to the Rhondda: Gwilym Thomas, 'Ar wib i Gwm Rhondda dydd Sadwrn 17 Mehefin 1995', *Y Cardi: Cylchgrawn Cymdeithas Ceredigion*, 23 (Gŵyl Ddewi, 1996), 29–31. The importance of local eisteddfodau in Cardiganshire in the early 1970s, in comparison with Glamorgan, struck one native from the latter county who moved to Cardiganshire (ex inf. James Marvin Morgan, 29 November 2002, p. 1).

[85] *CN*, 21 September 1973, 14. Incidentally, Carson was speaking at the annual

chapter there were shifts in the county's leisure landscape that, in time, undermined such claims to moral authority or distinctiveness; these can be detected during the *Last Tango in Aberystwyth* dispute when the pro-ban county council was opposed by the more liberal borough council. One traveller, for example, mentioned how Aberystwyth in the early 1970s was not the kind of place where you would find a nightclub. Less than thirty years later he would have found a chapel converted into a public house that opened on a Sunday – which itself only became possible in the county after 1989.[86] Some old defining oppositions had to be abandoned, therefore. Nonetheless, as seen at the start of this section, contrasts between the county and various external features were still drawn. Over time, however, those perceived qualities that had earned Cardiganshire a central position were eroded by a cultural shift detectable in activities and language. As the explicitly moralistic element of public discourse ebbed, so did the county's status as a moral centre.

By and large, the county's image has been a projection of cultural capital – education and cultural pursuits that were often inseparable from Nonconformity – onto a geographical canvas. In Cardiganshire, even the 'ordinary' people were cultured: barbers were poets and caretakers eagerly awaited the arrival of the library van.[87] Running alongside this, however, were other reputations that did not sit comfortably alongside those that saw the Cardi as an embodiment of culture and rectitude yet still contributed to the popular image of Cardiganshire. An abundance of cultural capital, whether perceived or actual, does not necessarily secure the reputation of a place or its people. Those who toyed with the image of the grasping Cardi assigned meaning to the county up until the end of the century.

luncheon of the Aberystwyth branch of Industrial Life Offices, and noted that 'saving' was also 'desirable even in this permissive age'. Also see ibid., 5 October 1973, 1.

[86] Fishlock, *Wales and the Welsh*, p. 129.

[87] Tom MacDonald, *Where Silver Salmon Leap* (Llandysul, 1976), p. 16. The county was the first in Wales and one of the first five in England and Wales to implement village library services after receiving money from the Carnegie United Kingdom Trust in the years following the First World War.

MARGIN

The butts of jokes are set apart from a behavioural norm. Everyday actions illustrate a group's supposed distance from conventional conduct, and demonstrate putative differences between groups. Jokes about the Cardi, such as the frontispiece of this book, generally point towards variations in what anthropologists call 'social judgements on spending'.[88] Parsimony intensified the closer you moved towards Cardiganshire. In one tale, reputed in 1969 to be an old story ('hen stori'), about the welcome received by a hypothetical tea-drinking guest, the quantity of generosity declined the further west the caller went. In Glamorgan the guest was given the sugar bowl, in Carmarthenshire an extra spoon of sugar was offered and in Cardiganshire the visitor was advised to stir the tea vigorously in order to make the most of a single spoonful.[89] Yet Cardi jokes, and accompanying impressions of this county-type as being removed from a much vaunted, 'traditional' Welsh quality of generosity, were not fixed in the late twentieth century. Social change meant that they underwent adjustments in their content and reception.

It was only in the post-1945 period that printed versions of these jokes proliferated. The less deferential atmosphere of the post-war years may well have hastened their appearance. With the arrival of books dedicated to Welsh jokes from the late 1970s, the Cardi joke found a more prominent spot in printed culture. A section on 'Welsh humour' in an Edwardian book did not allude to the Cardi.[90] Jokes at the expense of backward country dwellers, that appeared in the press from the interwar period, began to fade. Extended educational provision and facilities meant that misunderstanding could not be so easily attributed to origins in the county's remote hills. The field on which social interac-

---

[88] Mary Douglas and Baron Isherwood, *The World of Goods: Towards an Anthropology of Consumption* (2nd edn, London, 1996), p. 13.

[89] Brinley Richards, 'Manion', *Y Cardi: Cylchgrawn Cymdeithas Ceredigion*, 5 (1969), 10.

[90] David Macrae, *National Humour: Scottish, English, Irish, Welsh, Cockney, American* (Paisley, 1904), pp. 229–57. Neither does an interwar collection, T. Mardy Rees, *Hiwmor y Cymro* (Lerpwl, 1922), or a collection of nineteenth-century jokes in Welsh, Anon., *Hiwmor y Cymry: Hwyl o'r Bedwaredd-Ganrif-ar-Bymtheg* (Penygroes, 1976).

tions occurred had been transformed. Additionally, more hostile representations, which linked the Cardi to gross errors of character, grew fainter in this period. To come from Cardiganshire did not carry the same associations in kind or degree in, say, 2000 as they did in 1930 or earlier. The complexion of the county and the volume and nature of migrants from Cardiganshire had changed. Just as sayings and common phrases, such as to 'dial' a number of a push-button phone, continue after the physical origins disappear, so some reputations live on after the qualities that gave birth to them have waned.

Miserliness, which has been increasingly associated with Cardiganshire people since the praise of thrift became less noticeable, is still referred to by commentators today. Nevertheless, such observations are increasingly expressed in general, bantering ways. Take, for instance, the remarks overheard by the American travel writer Paul Theroux in Cardigan during his journey around the coast of the United Kingdom in 1982. A drunken woman from Swansea calls the Cardis 'tight', to which the hotel owner, a native of the town, agrees, boasting: 'Aye, we're tighter than the Scots.'[91] The meaning seems to have drifted from a precise category founded on frugality, most likely born of factors such as religious adherence and hardship, to a term applied in broad sweeps, even sometimes to people from beyond the area who might, for instance, not pay their way. This shift from the precise location of behaviour based on previous contrasts noted in earlier chapters to the general present-day survival confused the author of a 1989 guide book to Wales. After describing the legend surrounding Devil's Bridge in the north of the county, the author noted that the Cardis are 'held to be mean' by other Welsh people, yet he found no proof of this himself and thought that such 'legends die hard'.[92]

The persistence of these jokes probably owed much to the ostensible butts themselves who, like the Cardigan town hotel proprietor mentioned above, were not insulted by being put

[91] Paul Theroux, *The Kingdom by the Sea* (Harmondsworth, 1984), p. 166.
[92] Brian Bell, *Wales* (Singapore, 1989), p. 179.

in a category far removed from conceptions of generosity, especially when the emphasis was on a determination to bargain and on quick wittedness.[93] In the late 1980s, the journalist Keith Stevenson mentioned that the Cardis 'tell even ruder jokes about themselves'. But this was not always the case. The jokes, and equally importantly the attitudes from which many of them sprang, were more direct and sharply felt at the start of the period considered in this chapter. Indeed, the ambivalence towards jokes noticeable in the late twentieth century has partly obscured the antagonism of the interwar years towards the self-seeking Cardi. The sociologist Christie Davies cautioned those investigating jokes about particular groups against assuming that they all derive from hostility, and late twentieth-century Cardi jokes were rarely hostile.[94] There was little ill will towards the Cardi at that time, so jokes cannot always be a reliable index of tensions between groups. Even so, those who proffered negative characterizations of the Cardi, and their reasons for doing so, must not be obscured by a less contentious present.

Responses to what the *Cardigan and Tivyside Advertiser* described, in 1948, as a 'thrust' made by Dewi Emrys (David Emrys James), a Cardiganshire-born poet and Independent minister whose poems included one in praise of *cawl*, indicate how Cardi jokes were not always taken without complaint, even when uttered by a fellow county man. Many of the jokes printed in newspapers during this period could be taken as a slight towards the humanity of a Christian county. Emrys mentioned how people were afraid of being buried alive, but such fears were not present in Cardiganshire because every family had a gold sovereign that they put in the palm of the apparently dead relative. If a fist was not made around this coin the relative was declared deceased. The newspaper noted that 'Cardis are said to have taken exception' to this. It appears that Emrys, who was in his late sixties at the time,

---

[93] See the quip made by J. M. Davies in his memoirs, *O Gwmpas Pumlumon: Atgofion a Hanesion* (Aberystwth, 1966), p. 13. Also see Gerald Morgan, *Ceredigion: A Wealth of History* (Llandysul, 2005), p. 402.

[94] Keith Stevenson, *A Slice of Britain: A Light-Hearted Journey Across Seven Shires* (Ystrad Meurig, 1988), p. 170; Christie Davies, *The Mirth of Nations* (London, 2002), p. 17.

related a type of joke that had long been in existence, for
the newspaper ended its brief report with the comment
that 'Cardis, we believe, have learnt by now to laugh at jokes
against themselves.' And it appears that jokes about them
came from many directions. Emrys, who spent a number of
years in northern Pembrokeshire, may have picked up his
jokes about the Cardiganshire Lazarus from his time there; a
Pembrokeshire joke collector, Brian John, has suggested that
this part of Wales spawned such jokes.[95] Other areas, however,
such as industrial parts of Carmarthenshire and Glamorgan,
produced jokes that point towards the interactions that
inspired these humorous tales. In 1954, a Welsh-language
joke from Llanelli won a 5s. weekly prize for the best joke
in the *Carmarthen Journal*. It was entitled 'Trachwant y Cardi'
(The Cardi's greed) and tells of a man from Llanelli who
holidayed at a farm in Cardiganshire. On leaving the break-
fast table the maid saw something hanging from the visitor's
trousers and thought he had stolen a duster, although it
was in fact his shirt. The Llanelli man had the punchline
when he remarked that he had heard that Cardis were tight,
but he had never thought that they were so tight that they
would take your shirt.[96] People from the industrial area had
been taking holidays in Cardiganshire from the nineteenth
century, and the continuation of this opportunity to rub
shoulders and preconceptions with country cousins, many if
not most of whom would have been relatives, in the 1950s was
also touched on in an article in *The Times*.[97] For such jokes to
be generated there has to be contact between two different
world-views. Although the momentum may carry images of,
for example, money-hungry Jews to parts where a material
basis for the stereotype may not be found, the beginnings

[95] *CTA*, 19 November 1948, 1; Brian John, *Up Among the Mountain Men* (Newport,
Pembrokeshire, 1997), p. 4. However, Emrys's brief notes about the Cardi (NLW,
MS Dewi Emrys 11/1, fo. 1) make a point of stressing the positive qualities of the
type, noting that the reputation for being 'tynn am fargen' (driving a hard bargain)
is really another way of saying that they possess backbone and determination.

[96] *CJ*, 31 December 1954, 6. Another joke in this paper (10 December 1954, 8)
played with the Cardi's ambivalent reputation for materialism and religion when
a preacher in the middle of the county approaches a man who had been crying
during his sermon only to find that the farmer was grieving over his white mare
that had died.

[97] *The Times*, 17 September 1959, 12.

need some foundation through contact that breeds contesta-
tion, resentment or bemusement.

The caution, suspicion and covetousness identified in
these jokes were the other side of the thrift and carefulness
celebrated in accounts that described the Cardi as a paragon
of sensible behaviour. Contact through trade contributed to
this mocking interpretation of habits. A commercial foundation to a cultural phenomenon could then be interpreted
through various mental filters. This foundation, it could
be argued, indicates that the jokes served some compensatory purpose for those who found themselves having to buy
in a seller's market, whether from shopkeepers or farmers.
An example of the latter can be found in a Cardiganshire-
based newspaper from 1947. When a housewife complained
to a farmer about the size of the dozen eggs she had bought,
'the "Cardi" quickly recovered and answered: "Well I've
always noticed that new laid eggs are small."' Housewives'
apprehension about food was heightened during the 1940s,
against a backdrop of rationing, and this context would have
lent the tale greater resonance than it has when read today.[98]
Although this duel between buyer and seller illustrates the
role of trade in some Cardi jokes, it could also be taken as
evidence of the farmer's craftiness and thus celebrating this
quality. Alternatively, there were those who tried to sell products in Cardiganshire. In 1976, a former vacuum cleaner
salesman reflected on his time in the county and, contrary
to others' expectations, noted his productive period there in
the 1930s. Other voices in his account – those who warned
him that 'you will never sell one of those to a Cardi' – and
his final statement that 'I shall defend the thrift and integrity
of the Cardis on all occasions', show how trade contributed a strand to discourse about the county's reputation. It
appeared that a different kind of human nature was being
located in the county, and the former salesman's pledge to
counter criticisms of his previous customers implies how
widespread disparagement of the Cardi could be.[99]

[98] I. Zweiniger-Bargielowska, *Austerity in Britain: Rationing, Controls, and Consumption, 1939–1955* (Oxford, 2000), p. 113.

[99] *CTA*, 18 November 1947, 1; O. T. Morris, 'Salesman in the thirties', *Planet*, 32 (June 1976), 26–7. At a thank-you party to celebrate funds raised in Cardiganshire,

In the late 1960s, the pre-eminence of the parsimonious archetype was clearly not felt to be what it had once been. As a result, the features that compelled some to castigate the Cardi in the past were not as pressing. The south Pembrokeshire-born travel writer and horticulturalist H. L. V. Fletcher, in his brief sketch of the county, thought that: 'There is *still some* [my emphasis] of that hard unbending character that Caradoc Evans knew and pilloried in the Cardiganshire hills.' This implies the existence of a literally stubborn remnant, rather than the predominant ethos that Evans denounced. One aspect of that remnant, a reluctance to borrow money, came under attack in the early 1960s when groups like the Agricultural Credits Corporation Ltd noted that farmers were not using credit wisely. Their culture, which was described as containing 'a kind of morality' that made them 'loathe to borrow money', meant that they were not operating their businesses as well as they could.[100] To be a true *homo economicus* certain habits needed to be abandoned. Ways of life that once, and indeed might still at times, have placed them in a central position were now marginalizing them, even in the economic sphere, where the Victorian and Edwardian canny Cardi was once supreme.

Even during the late twentieth century, most descriptions of Cardiganshire and its inhabitants come from what could be broadly called the professional class, although jokes are able to offer some idea about the kinds of opinions held by those who were lower down the social scale. Reliance on accounts written by those who were from the middle or upper classes means that we hear only an echo of feelings evoked about the Cardi among other groups. At a time when the state assumed a greater role and religious tenets were becoming less prominent, it might be expected that those who disliked what the Cardi often stood for would continue to express their disdain until the traces of what this archetype represented disappeared. Hints of deep-seated opinions not substantially

the president of the county's branch of the Red Cross began her speech with: 'It makes me hit the roof to hear the Cardi described as mean.' This also illustrates how the marginal position accorded Cardis could raise ire: *CN*, 16 June 1972, 10.

[100] H. L. V. Fletcher, *The Coasts of Wales* (London, 1969), p. 98; *CJ*, 19 February 1960, 9.

articulated in print can be found in the brief account of the
inhabitants of Cardiganshire by the naturalist R. M. Lockley
in 1969; he defended this county-type whose 'natural thrift
. . . has given an unwarranted stigma of meanness to the
epithet "Cardi"'. Lockley then afforded an explanation based
on the justifiable 'distrust' with which the 'native Welsh'
viewed the English 'exploiters', thus overlooking the role
played by internal dynamics in establishing the county's reputation.[101] By the 1960s many felt that Wales had been treated
unfairly by England, and this sense of injustice, that no doubt
contributed to the election of Plaid Cymru's first MP in the
same year as Lockley's book was published, appears to have
influenced his assessment of the Cardi. All the same, the
recognition of a disputed undeserved reputation points to
the existence of harsher judgements in much the same way
as the vacuum cleaner salesman's reminiscences do.

Again, many of these negative impressions seem to be
founded on interwar experiences. Leslie Norris's short story
'The Girl from Cardigan', published as part of a collection in
1988, drew on the interwar theme of the high-achieving, yet
overtly 'other', Cardi who had migrated to south-east Wales.
Three brothers are described by the narrator, whose story is
thought to have been based on Norris's own experience of
working in local government in the 1930s. The brothers are
from Cardiganshire and have risen to positions of importance
in an industrial area of Monmouthshire. As well as this ability
to succeed, the other Cardi characteristics that marked them
out and divided them from others were a 'clannishness' and
an obsession with money.[102] Further evidence of this south-
eastern perception can be found in the 1951 memories of
a Monmouthshire man, William Williams, who noted that
Cardis, like the successful 'Mr David Jenkins, Manager' to
whom he dedicated a chapter, were and still are exceedingly
interested in money. This stereotype, which like so many is
an exaggeration of something rather than its concoction,

---

[101] R. M. Lockley, *Wales* (London, 1966), p. 129.
[102] Simon C. Baker, 'Keeping short boundaries holy' (MA thesis, University of
Wales Swansea, 1987), 3; Leslie Norris, 'The Girl from Cardigan', in Norris, *The Girl
from Cardigan* (Bridgend, 1988), pp. 13, 16.

could, in the opinion of a Glamorgan-born adopted Cardi, take the form of a monstrous, merciless Shylock.[103] The hostility expressed towards the county's populace by Johnny Powell, one of the 'Welsh tinkers of gypsy origin' with whom Cledwyn Hughes spent three months in the early 1950s, would seem out of place later in the century. Hughes, who became Lord Cledwyn of Penrhos in 1979, recorded that on entering the county 'Johnny thought all "Cardis" mean and hard natured', before adding his less passionate reading: 'and it is true that the people of this county have a reputation for thrift and care in money matters'. These different interpretations reveal a gap in experience as well as attitude. Evidently, Johnny felt he had more reason to resent the inhabitants of Cardiganshire than did the solicitor Hughes. Johnny's opinion illustrates the way generalizations about places were still expressed in a county framework, no doubt partially founded on occupational structure. In a review of his *festschrift*, J. D. Marshall noted that counties were 'fundamentally [a] top down creation'. Yet as examples in this section and others have shown, this product of administration could be used in the language of the disgruntled to encapsulate features they disliked.[104] Still, in time, the tinker's equation of county with character would lose its congruence. The references to Cardi today are by and large echoes of sentiments conceived from numerous slivers of interaction, tales and jokes. This is not to say that the money-cautious are extinct, but people who display such characteristics have not been able to attain the clarity of previous distinctions in popular perception.

At times a more wide-ranging condemnation was superimposed on the mean and avaricious image. This was one that touched on the area's provinciality in manners and beliefs. Such images match other critical portrayals and reveal how the general image of the county were to be used to express

[103] William Williams, (Myfyr Wyn), *Atgofion am Sirhywi a'r Cylch* (Caerdydd, 1951), p. 28; Dewi Eirug Davies, 'Atgof', *Cymdeithas Ceredigion Llundain Llawlyfr*, 13 (1956–57), 26; Michael Pickering, *Stereotyping: The Politics of Representation* (Basingstoke, 2001).
[104] Cledwyn Hughes, *West with the Tinkers: A Journey through Wales with Vagrants* (London, 1954), p. 142; J. D. Marshall, review of *Issues of Regional Identity*, *Journal of Regional and Local Studies*, 18, 2 (1998), 49–60, 50.

socio-political positions. Various expressions of the Cardi's ostensible behavioural marginality have been articulated, but for those who championed collectivism over individuality, the secular over established religious practice, or cosmopolitanism over insularity, the Cardi became convenient bête noire in the post-war period. Recollections of personal experiences, like those that compelled Goronwy Rees to paint a dark vignette of the Aberystwyth elite in the 1950s, often made use of Cardiganshire's negative template; a template that combined peasant greed with religious hypocrisy and had been in existence long before it was deftly applied by Caradoc Evans. The fact that this is a personal view should not distract from what is under investigation here. In this instance Rees, who resigned from his position as principal at Aberystwyth's university college during 1957 in the aftermath of disclosures about his friendship with the spy Guy Burgess, depicted an isolated, ossified town. His wife's unhappiness there provoked the criticism expressed in his biography. The place, and by implication the surrounding county, was full of the 'pettiness of provincial life' and constituted 'a Methodist cage'. The claim that the area was unsophisticated also entered an evaluation of the Cardiganshire-born Welsh nationalist W. Ambrose Bebb published in the late 1970s; this intellectual's support for the right-wing Frenchman Charles Murras is explained by their common roots in provinces, farming backgrounds and 'petit-bourgeois ideology'.[105]

The tendency to compare the distinctive marks of Cardiganshire's county-type with those of other groups increased after the Second World War. This feature of late twentieth-century commentary about the county indicates an extension of people's frame of reference. Goronwy Rees noted how many of the 'qualities' said to be possessed by 'Cardiganshire men', such as 'hypocrisy', which he stressed had not rubbed off on his grandfather who was a stonemason

---

[105] Goronwy Rees, *A Chapter of Accidents* (London, 1972), p. 243. It is also significant that an academic, John Harris, who has written about both Caradoc Evans and Rees, should express disdain at the 'social hierarchy and reputation' embodied in the memorial for Sir David James Pantyfedwen at Strata Florida, in 'Neighbours: Caradoc Evans, Lloyd George and the London Welsh', *Llafur*, 5, 4 (1983), 90–8, 92; G. Meils, 'Ambrose Bebb', *Planet*, 37/38 (May 1977), 70–9, 78–9.

in London, made this kind of person 'the Aberdonian of Wales'. Similarly, the Cardi was compared with the Jew in many jokes. Both Jew and Aberdonian – the latter often magnified into a Scottish type – share reputations for guile and business acumen. On rare occasions the frame is extended beyond the British Isles, to such as the Ibos of Nigeria (a comparison inspired by the tribe's reputation for social climbing).[106] These comparisons have emerged quite recently in the representational history of the Cardi, at a time when the type has lost much of its symbolic vigour. This is not to say that the county has been divested of distinctiveness by the start of the twenty-first century, rather, that the cultural functions of the place and its people are not tied to prominent, contending ideologies as they once were.[107] Having mapped the ways in which Cardiganshire and the Cardi have been located during the modern era, the following chapter compares the locus of this study with other examples of places and people that further our understanding of the process of location and the significance of the Cardi. A concluding assessment of similarly located places and people reveals some telling differences and similarities.

---

[106] Rees, *Chapter of Accidents*, pp. 4–5; Christie Davies, *Welsh Jokes* (Wrexham, 1986), p. 35, contains two definitions of a Cardi, one of which is 'A man who can buy an item from a Jew, sell it to a Scotsman and make a profit'; Fishlock, *Talking of Wales*, p. 46.

[107] Rainer Schulze, 'Region, industrialisation, structural change: a regional approach to problems of socio-economic change', in Schulze (ed.), *Industrial Regions in Transformation: Historical Roots and Patterns of Regional Structural Change – A European Comparison* (Essen, 1993), pp. 40–63, 56.

VII

CONCLUSION: DIFFERENT BUT SIMILAR

This study is an investigation of opinions: how Cardiganshire and the Cardi have been culturally located. It has explored the county's representational history; in other words, how the county's image has been constructed and received in the modern period. More, it has outlined and interrelated the key categories through which these judgements were expressed. Issues such as who made distinctions, the foundation of distinctions and how they changed over time are fundamental components in the figurative location of a place and its people. The factors from which these estimations have been composed form the categories deployed in this study: the processes of naming, locating a place relative to notions of the future and the past, and deeming a place a centre of qualities or distant from such a centre. Each needs to be considered when exploring the representation of places and people. The study has not reduced 'a complex set of relationships into an "other"' because it has engaged with a plurality of contrasts.[1] For example, although south-eastern Wales has figured prominently in the cultural location of Cardiganshire and the Cardi, it was not the only area of Wales to take on this role: representations from adjacent counties and those to the north contributed to the county's multifaceted image. These conceptual positionings are evident in the reflections of historical actors themselves as they engaged with and defined their settings. They also show how different world-views prompted clashes over what constituted the most prominent characteristic of a place or a people.

The inquiry has emphasized the discontinuities and continuities in the representational history of Cardiganshire and the Cardi. Periods when distinct interpretations arose

[1] P. Mandler, 'Problems in cultural history: a reply', *Cultural and Social History*, 1, 3 (2004), 326–32, 332.

were identified, and the roles of various contemporary interests in establishing locations have been assessed. Observers
prioritized different qualities at different times. An investigation of these acts of location enhances our appreciation of
commentators' understandings. The chronological structure
of the study highlighted the ascent and descent of different
locations, and identified their continuation in different
circumstances. The perception that Cardiganshire was the
quintessence of virtue can be found in many periods; yet its
exact meaning altered as different witnesses offered their
testimonies.

The reasons why people selected this county and its people
to convey particular ideas have been considered throughout
this investigation. All comparisons served a purpose and
were based on symbols. In the mid-nineteenth century,
for example, some observers keen to see every corner of
Britain contribute to the nation's industrial development
set the symbol of the industrious industrial worker against
the county. Additionally, the county and its inhabitants have
obtained symbolic status themselves. The inquiry demonstrated how such symbols were 'potent resources in the arenas
of politics and identity'.[2] However, despite the wide range of
materials drawn upon during this study, it does not claim to
address all uses of the county and the Cardi; the thoughts
of most witnesses go unheard. Although the representations
founded on locations and naming do not tell us everything,
they tell us something about the manner in which representations were established, replaced and politicized.

In this concluding chapter some notable differences and
similarities between representations of Cardiganshire and
other places will be presented. Similarly, the periods on
which this study has been based nurtured representations
that can be defined against earlier and later manifestations.
These comparisons identify the similarities between people
and places that have acquired prominence in discourse.
Contrasts between similar cultural positions shed light on
the elements involved in locating groups and places. Taken

---

[2] A. P. Cohen, 'Culture as identity: an anthropologist's view', *New Literary History*,
24, 1 (1993), 195–209, 196.

together, an appreciation of differences and similarities between these cultural phenomena reveal some underlying reasons behind the origins and power of symbolic locations.

THE IMPORTANCE OF NAMING

Naming, whether in the form of nicknames or the formal name of a place, brings into focus qualities thought to reside in the area and its population. This book has acknowledged the importance of naming in the categorization of groups and places; it often forms the tip of a representational iceberg. Over the last 240 years, the names conferred upon the county, now officially called Ceredigion, provide insights into the values placed on it. No place goes unnamed, but some names, such as Essex, achieve greater notoriety than others.[3] Such places have often held a well-defined place in popular consciousness and embody contemporary issues. Associations stemming from a proper name are conferred when people equated the county with some value, for instance, religion or ignorance. This investigation has demonstrated that the county received a series of names and associations throughout the modern period, each of which carried meanings founded on implicit or explicit contrasts with other areas.

The south-east of Wales played a recurring part in the naming process, both in the sense of ascriber and as a stimulus for people from Cardiganshire to define themselves. From descriptions of Cardiganshire as a barren, poor place – the Devil's Grandmother's Jointure – in the late eighteenth century, to later designations alluded to by Anglo-Welsh writers, the south-east has defined itself while defining the county to the west. Migrants from Cardiganshire – whether seasonal or permanent, agricultural or industrial, petit bourgeois or professional – evoked responses that surfaced in representations. This is not to deny that other parts, such as Herefordshire and London, contributed to the naming and

---

[3] The Essex man/boy/girl provides a recent example; see Anthony King, 'The night itself', in King et al. (eds), *New Labour Triumphs: Britain at the Polls* (Chatam, NJ, 1998), pp. 1–13, 13; Germaine Greer, 'Long live the Essex girl', *http://www. guardian.co.uk/women/story/0,,446451,00.html* (accessed 1 August 2004).

definition of the county's inhabitants. But the volume and intensity of representations produced from Glamorgan and Monmouthshire, the former industrial heartland and southern arable area of Wales that attracted many from west Wales, meant that these places contributed more representations than others. Where migrants went they met other cultures; here a boundary between groups was defined and naming took place. As Barth argued, 'identity is a matter of self-ascription and ascription by others in interaction'.[4] Therefore, areas where interaction took place, of which the south-east was one, generated names and gave them particular meanings.

Significantly, this study has shown how things that Cardiganshire was felt to exemplify were not peculiar to it. The county stood for characteristics thought typical of the Welsh countryside in general. The uncomfortable flannel clothes that people from the county were 'born into . . . and lived and died in', were not exclusive to the county.[5] The same is true when it came to the name most often connected with Cardiganshire: Cardi. Indeed, this illustrates the problem that the same name can mean different things as times change. Cardi, according to a number of south-eastern sources, was used to describe a person from an area that did not necessarily conform to the county boundaries. People who hailed from northern Carmarthenshire could fall into the category. The same applies to the attachment of particular characteristics to the name. A strong link between Cardiganshire and respectability meant that some were surprised to note any dissonance between behaviour and place of origin or abode.[6]

On another level, it has been noted that the county's name reflected and reinforced a sense of attachment or identification. This kind of naming occurred when county residents were involved with those from outside the county. Allotting a designation was the result of interaction, and the designa-

---

[4] Frederik Barth, 'Preface 1998', in Barth (ed.), *Ethnic Groups and Boundaries: The Social Organisation of Difference* (Prospect Heights, IL, 1998), pp. 5–7, 6.

[5] Rhys Davies, *Print of a Hare's Foot* (London, 1969), p. 41.

[6] See D. Parry-Jones's remarks when reflecting on seeing a marketplace trickster in 'A day in Newcastle Emlyn', *Carmarthenshire Historian*, 4 (1967), 55–65, 61.

tion becomes widespread when many migrate; the Okies, who vacated their impoverished land in interwar America, provide an example of this link between movement and naming.[7] Although the coming together of migrant and host community can explain the intensification of naming, each instance contains numerous, specific motivations some of which emerge from the migrant group themselves or from commentators beyond the point of contact.

This investigation has shown that the names attached to Cardiganshire and its inhabitants were at times drawn upon by those wishing to promote their own world-view. Often, the name 'Cardi' was not neutral but instead denoted pride or disdain. An illustration of how names gather meaning as a result of the namers can be seen in an expansion of the Cardi/ Ibo comparison made at the end of the previous chapter. The Nigerian tribe's name represented something positive in the eyes of many western commentators in the 1960s. In contrast with the summation of an interwar visitor that they were a people without 'determination and perseverance', later twentieth-century commentators praised them for the ostensible European characteristics that they, unlike the Muslim northerners, had acquired.[8] The similarity between Ibo and Cardi lies not only in their reputation for hard work and strong will but in their deployment by those who wished to exercise influence. The Ibo received praise because they corresponded to a particular perspective, just as the Cardi was utilized by Liberals opposed to Salisbury's Conservatives at the end of the nineteenth century or those wary of Attlee's Labour Party in the middle of the twentieth. We need to be aware of the reasons behind the underscoring of particular names.

THE PAST PUT INTO PLACE

Of all the locations, the past has attracted the most academic attention. Places or symbols considered representative of the

[7] James N. Gregory, *American Exodus: The Dust Bowl Migration and Okie Culture in California* (Oxford, 1991).

[8] George Thomas Basden, *Among the Ibos of Nigeria* (London, 1921), p. 137; Minabere Ibelema, 'Tribes and prejudice: coverage of the Nigerian civil war', in Beverly G. Hawk (ed.), *Africa's Media Image* (Westport, CT, 1992), pp. 77–93, 84.

past of a nation or region have often been examined and the underlying ideological uses made of them identified.[9] The past is seen as inculcating a sense of unity, a common heritage usually at the national level that leaves out more than it includes. This inquiry, however, did not prioritize this variety of location. In so doing, it has avoided a one-dimensional reading of the county's representational history. At the same time, the study illuminated some of the different forms that past locations may take.

First, a past location has not always been a boon. At times when progressive currents occupied a strong position in commentaries, especially in the years from the start of this period of inquiry to the latter part of the nineteenth century and again in the years immediately after the Second World War, features deemed old often detracted from a place's value – they hindered progress. Those who advocated change could be motivated by religious or secular reasons. Also, in the eighteenth and nineteenth centuries, these perceived undesirable pasts were not so much the historical past as a living past. Dead ideas did not inhibit progress, whereas old ideas in living people did so. Antiquaries chronicled standing stones while slighting beliefs deemed primitive. Therefore, it is important to distinguish the kind of past to which a place is being related. One issue addressed in this book was not whether or when past practices died out, but the way in which they were interpreted in the context of other currents, such as the 'march of intellect' that sought to extinguish superstitious survivals during the first three-quarters of the nineteenth century.

Secondly, value placed on the past was commonly derived from a relatively recent past.[10] Figures such as Nonconformist ministers and poets, from eras hardly shrouded in the mists

---

[9] For example, Felix Driver and Raphael Samuel, 'Rethinking the idea of place', *History Workshop Journal*, 39 (1995), pp. v–vii, where a 'radical local history' is outlined in response to more static, or closed, interpretations of place. Also see Matthew Kurtz, 'Re/membering the town body: methodology and the work of local history', *Journal of Historical Geography*, 28, 1 (2002), 42–62, for an investigation of 'sites of memory' on a 'small scale'.

[10] This tendency has been noted in the thought of J. B. Priestley whose ideal England was not a 'timeless rural England' but urban northern England before 1914: John Baxendale, '"I had seen a lot of Englands": J. B. Priestley, Englishness and the people', *History Workshop Journal*, 51 (2001), 87–111, 98.

of time, dominated mental chronologies of the area. This contrasts with other examples where considerable value was placed on a place's past, such as that of the English Germanist writer, Charles Kingsley, who stressed the part played by the Fenlands in resisting the Normans.[11] Indeed, in the case of Cardiganshire, it is the human connection, a link to movements and institutions experienced by some people, that surfaced in depictions of the place. Notably, Nonconformity and education constitute the area's dominant story.[12] Furthermore, less obvious embodiments of the past, not linked to any institution, have been identified in this study. Locating qualities of the place at a personal level in terms of human characteristics extends a place's usefulness by attaching it to perceived manners and attributes. This feature is shared by other locations where specific groups have been held up as personifying the past, particularly by artists.[13] From paintings capturing authentic country folk that appeared in the late twentieth century, to the more specifically defined character of the 'Cardiganshire butterman' from the latter part of the nineteenth century, there has been a succession of monuments to the past in the form of symbolic individuals. Nonetheless, different concerns particular to the time played a part in their composition – racial degeneration in the late 1800s and anxieties about overwhelming cultural uniformity in the late 1900s. Dismissing these as nostalgic obituaries overlooks their contemporary psychological usefulness for specific sections of society. Owing to its relative distance from main currents of change, Cardiganshire has served this purpose repeatedly over the years. It has been tapped into and consequently shaped peoples' image of the past. Peter Fowler argued that 'pastness does not come in a pure essence'.[14] Although factually correct, it is important to

[11] His stance was, in part, provoked by what he considered a disproportionate emphasis on the heroic qualities of Highlanders. See Billie Melman, 'Claiming the nation's past: the invention of an Anglo-Saxon tradition', *Journal of Contemporary History*, 26, 3/4 (1991), 575–95, 585.

[12] John Rees Jones, *Sôn am y Bont*, ed. E. D. Evans (Llandysul, 1974), pp. 15–16.

[13] Ysanne Holt, 'London types', *London Journal*, 25, 1 (2000), 35–51, 39; Bernard Deacon, 'Imagining the fishing: artists and fishermen in late nineteenth-century Cornwall', *Rural History*, 12, 2 (2001), 159–78, 166.

[14] Peter J. Fowler, *Then, Now: The Past in Contemporary Society* (London, 1992), p. 10.

note that some representations are, in fact, taken to be the 'pure essence' of the past.

Thirdly, an important component of a place's location in relation to the past occurs when features felt to define the county or a way of life are thought to be diminishing or to have disappeared – that is, where a place is seen as being dislocated from its past. These sentiments are noticeable in the recollections of individuals in the twentieth century and offer some idea of the relative value of what is lost. Although this sense of change and loss is widespread and occurs in many settings, from the Cardiff dockland of Tiger Bay to the disused coal mines of post-industrial valleys, rural west Wales offers a particularly potent pre-industrial resonance as it embraced both the language and the land. A sense of a place being measured against its own past and found wanting is usually present in the memoirs of those with knowledge of the area. Small indicators, or shifts, in the fabric of life reveal feelings of what was considered important. As this theme touches on such concepts as bureaucratization and aliena-tion, it continues in the protest of the small or marginal who feel that they have little control over their environment.

APPLYING THE FUTURE

The location of a place or people in relation to a desirable future is a potent rhetorical device and may provide a basis for self-definition and the judgement of others. As seen in this investigation, these are not straightforward estimations of advancement; rather, they are value-laden assessments about the place's contribution to any one of many progres-sive visions that can range from the technical to the spiritual.

An opportunity to transform what many conceived as a backward, peripheral region was a habitual theme in the future location of Cardiganshire. First seen in the schemes of late eighteenth- and early nineteenth-century agricultural innovators, these summations of the county mark the appli-cation of a general progressive yardstick to the place. Instead of simply detailing the unpleasant past, it presented a design for change, focusing on what must be done rather than what was wrong. To take one mid-nineteenth-century example, the potentiality of converting the county's many beaches into attractions along the lines of Aberystwyth was contrasted with their current non-commercial use by locals. Those who set Cardiganshire against a potential future aspired to integrate a county on the western edge of Britain into a commercial and communications network. Underpinning these locations there were notions of progress produced by particular world-views that relied on perceptions of classes and cultures thought to impede progress.

Over the period surveyed, numerous suggestions were made by those seeking to advance the county's fortunes. Even when they were not implemented, there is value in noting these potential developments. Taken together they provide an account of conceptions of material progress. The attempt to improve, that most often took an economic form – whether in terms of agriculture, industry or communications – could be described as the importation of innovation: the adoption of outside models and methods in order to progress. Industrial developments in Cardiganshire were noted with pride at a time when the British nation was defined by its industrial activities.

Yet there were other, generally spiritual or intellectual, matters in which the county could claim to be at the helm of improvement. This contrast between material striving and intellectual leadership contributed enormously to the perception of Cardiganshire. Just as certain objects and structures – railways or indoor plumbing – enter Cardiganshire's modern story, so ideas had central roles at specific times. A connection between the county and individual progress can be discerned, especially from the late nineteenth century. An expansion in commercial and educational opportunities was entwined with the county image as migrants wove their own life stories and attributed success to a Cardi background that disciplined their minds and instilled them with ambition. A similar selective vision radiated from interwar intellectuals who saw rural life as a source of individual fulfilment and, more mystically, believed that the answer to modern life's problems lay in the moorland folk.

Notions of political progress can foster a future location. Like the image of the sturdy miner in the north-east of England, the hardy and progressive tenant farmer of Cardiganshire could serve an ideological purpose.[15] He provided an icon of progress embracing ideas of self-help and independence – a kind of cultural melding of geographical area and personal prospects. At this point it is possible to discern a shift in the representation of the county. Although certain qualities had been praised in the late Georgian and early Victorian periods, the emphasis was not strictly progressive. An active image had not been fully formed, although the foundation in terms of religion and an emphasis on education was developing. Then, in the late Victorian and Edwardian periods, the county-type became very useful for those promoting a democratic and behavioural model. This was a facet of the 'entrepreneurial ideal'.[16] Just as Lancashire – or, more commonly acknowledged, Manchester – became a place with progressive connotations in the minds of Liberals, Cardiganshire was transformed from a generally static location, in political terms, to being a template.[17]

Representations of the Swabians of south-western Germany also yoked regional character and political, personal progress. The lower-middle-class, anti-militaristic democratic movement in late nineteenth-century Württemberg has been reckoned to embody 'the Swabian character'.[18] A correspondence between material scarcity and mental fecundity was said to characterize the Swabian. This work ethic is reflected in the Lutheran Swabian's 'canny' nature and in the fact that 'in their business dealings they are shrewd and tenacious'. The German author of these comments, penned between the wars, also noted the Swabians' educational achievements.[19] As a result, this way of life enabled individuals to progress in their lifetime.

[15] Robert Colls, *The Collier's Rant: Song and Culture in the Industrial Village* (London, 1977), p. 165.
[16] Harold Perkin, *The Origins of Modern English Society, 1780–1880* (London, 1969), pp. 221–30.
[17] For an example of the conflation of Lancashire with Manchester in a progressive world-view, see Donald Read, *The English Provinces, c.1760–1960: A Study in Influence* (London, 1964), p. ix.
[18] Alon Confino, *The Nation as a Local Metaphor: Württemberg, Imperial Germany and the National Memory, 1871–1918* (Chapel Hill, NC, 1997), p. 77.
[19] Eugen Disel, *Germany and the Germans*, trans. W. D. Scott-Robson (New York, 1931), pp. 115–17. The phrase in the title of Frederick Marquardt's review article, '"Schaffe, Schaffe, Hausle Baue": Hans Medick, the Swabians, and modernity',

The personalization of progress in a way of life could set apart a group from other, less ambitious or cautious populations that did not embody mobility: in the case of Swabia the opposite was often the Saxon, while the Cardi was contrasted with the industrial workers of Glamorgan. Cardiganshire's reputation for education and business aptitude is a key feature in its portrayal. As the comments of county societies in urban areas during the interwar years reveal, this sense of personal progress played a part in the ways in which people defined themselves and their home county.

THE PERIPHERY AS CENTRE

Dissonance and friction between beliefs can also be detected in contrasts that were not founded on measurements along a temporal axis. Throughout Cardiganshire's representational history, the county and its inhabitants have been set against several people and places. The potency of these positive locations is indicated by the diversity of those who subscribed to them. A feature of the later eighteenth century and much of the nineteenth century was the setting of Cardiganshire against places, notably the wealthier agricultural districts of England and the industrial areas of Wales, whose denizens were deemed troublesome or ungrateful. Visitors and those compiling government reports cited the value of a simple life without temptation, inordinate comfort or, especially at that time, the threat of rebellion. An image of the area, woven from selected material, gained credence. There was a shift from uncomplicated innocence to respectability in the late Victorian and Edwardian periods, as some inhabitants became part of the political nation and the small landholder acquired symbolic weight among those concerned with urban degeneration. Even political opponents of the Liberalism that contributed so much to Cardiganshire, such as Tory landlords and their supporters, occasionally praised the area for its lack of discontent in comparison with other parts of Wales and Ireland. Members of the Anglican

Journal of Social History, 32, 1 (1998), 197–207, translates as 'work, work, and build a house', and is a Swabian phrase encapsulating the region's reputed work ethic.

Church, outnumbered in a predominantly Nonconformist county, located values in the county character, too. As a type, the Cardi was not consistently the possession of one faction, as, for instance, the 'Protestant Boy' was in Ulster.[20] The place could be a centre of respectability, even for those who might not have shared the projections of their political or theological opponents. Even so, the agreement on what constituted desirable virtues should not obscure that which was left out of the representation. The study has shown how these locations were highly selective readings of the place and its people; they amounted to representations that were both the 'weapons and the stakes' of 'social conflict'.[21]

Attributes regarded as typical of the county were given greater emphasis during troubled times.[22] They could be called upon and made use of by those attempting to steer the state through troublesome waters. Areas elevated as an example to others would have, no doubt, mirrored and fed local pride. Two examples of times when the county's reputation for saving was called into play for a patriotic purpose have been noted in this study, one during the First World War and the other in the aftermath of the Second World War. It was not so much the principle of thrift on a personal level that was being stressed, as the way in which, during times of trouble, a locality could be praised by those in authority and, as a result, be placed on a dais as an example for others to follow. The intersection of local pride and congratulation from the seat of power is a phenomenon that featured in other contexts. Attributes thought representative of certain groups – like the pluck of the Cockney evacuee in the 1942 film *Went the Day Well?* – were accentuated during wartime and helped to evoke the sense of a disparate nation pulling

[20] D. G. Boyce, '"The marginal Britons": the Irish', in Robert Colls and Philip Dodd (eds), *Englishness: Politics and Culture, 1880–1920* (London, 1987), pp. 230–53, 243.

[21] Roger Chartier, *On the Edge of the Cliff: History, Language and Practices*, trans. Lydia G. Cochrane (Baltimore and London, 1997), p. 23.

[22] This supports the point that 'the representation of place is also necessarily a question of ideology'; Gillian Rose, 'The cultural politics of place: local representation and oppositional discourse in two films', *Transactions of the Institute of British Geographers*, new ser., 19, 1 (1994), 46–60, 46.

together.[23] Cardiganshire has evidently played its part in the symbolic repertoire of those in positions of influence, from the snuffing out of the shambolic French invasion of 1797 by the Cardiganshire militia to the shrewd post-1945 investor.

The quiescence and respectability beloved by some were concurrent with a location at the heart of independence and nonconformity, not so much in a religious as in a psychological sense. In this way the county shared something of Yorkshire's reputation for hard-headed individualism, although sporting prowess is notably absent in depictions of the Cardi, possibly because the county lacked large urban settlements or substantial industrial areas.[24] E. P. Thompson suggested that it was to the master clothier of the industrial revolution 'that the Yorkshire reputation for bluntness and independence may be traced'.[25] Yet this embodiment of a specific regional or county character in the form of one trade is problematic as, like the Cardi freeholder, its putative ideal characteristics appear to have permeated general conceptions of what epitomized a particular county and transferred these characteristics to other occupations. There must have been a desire to be related to these distinctive qualities, often abbreviated as 'the natural independence of the Yorkshire character', together with an inclination by others to use this geographical shorthand to identify particular attributes.[26] The location of virtues like naturalness and determination in both county-types was intended to contrast with artificiality and weakness.[27] In the Welsh context, the county had no rivals as the centre of qualities akin to those of the Yorkshire man.

Such qualities encouraged commentators to locate both counties at the heart of their respective nations.[28] There was, therefore, an added distinction: a double identity of an

[23] Ross McKibbin, *Classes and Cultures: England, 1918–1951* (Oxford, 1998), p. 446.

[24] M. C. F. Morris, *The British Workman: Past and Present* (Oxford, 1928), p. 141; Dave Russell, 'Sport and identity: the case of Yorkshire County Cricket Club, 1890–1939', *Twentieth-Century British History*, 7, 2 (1996), 206–30.

[25] E. P. Thompson, *The Making of the English Working Class* (London, 1963), p. 274.

[26] William Rothenstein, *Men and Memories: Recollections of William Rothenstein* (New York, 1931), p. 6.

[27] Charlotte Brontë, *Shirley* ([1849] Oxford, 1998), p. 152.

[28] Pam Morris, 'Heroes and hero-worship in Charlotte Brontë's *Shirley*', *Nineteenth-Century Literature*, 54, 3 (1999–2000), 285–307, 300.

outstanding county that added weight to the national Welsh or English identity. With this assemblage of centres, it is not difficult to see how the county attained such symbolic potency in the modern period. Centres, however, are not permanent. In the latter part of the twentieth century, in particular, there was reduction in the value attributed to many of the central features of the county and few politicians or journalists heaped praise on a distinctive county character as in the past. Even during the height of Cardiganshire's centrality, however, the county's image was turned around and located at the edge rather than at the centre.[29]

ON THE MARGINS

Cardiganshire and the Cardi have been located on cultural margins throughout the modern period. Broadly, there were two kinds of edge on which representative features of the county were located. First, there was a professed gulf between the county's inhabitants and certain norms. Secondly, there were features that, though rarely a threat to the social fabric, were reprimanded or mocked. Both clashed with the location of positive values in the area. Claims that the county was a cultural lodestar, for instance, were rendered less convincing by accounts noting rural ignorance. These inconsistencies demonstrate the provisional and often partial nature of claims to know the essence of the area. This informative dissonance was especially pronounced when the county and its designated representative type became prominent from the late Victorian period onwards. At this point a symbolic encounter was played out between the ascendant embodiment of individualistic principles and its antithesis – a socially conscious mentality. Issues such as the health of the county's poor were contrasted with the wealth of its migrants, and

[29] A similar modification in the attribution of value has been noted regarding the American Midwest. While 'wholesome, progressive people' predominated in the years before 1915, the region was, for various reasons, indicted for 'abdicating its role as the center of American nationalism': James R. Shortridge, 'The emergence of "Middle West" as an American regional label', *Annals of the Association of American Geographers*, 74, 2 (1984), 209–20, 217. Also see Nina Sibler, 'Intemperate men, spiteful women and Jefferson Davis: Northern views of the defeated South', *American Quarterly*, 41, 4 (1989), 614–35, 616.

religious observance was set against hypocrisy by commentators who stressed the need to rectify inequalities.

Besides the distinction between the two kinds of cultural periphery, it is important to stress how the values of outsiders and of those within the county often did not significantly differ. However, the people who made the criticisms shared similar backgrounds and we need to be aware that the judgements of groups – clerical or lay – would regularly concur on conditions believed to define the county. In the late eighteenth and early nineteenth centuries, both local notables and central government were worried about potential or actual trouble. During this time the place was seen to teeter on the verge of disorder, though this instability was the result of hunger and deprivation not revolutionary ardour. Equally, smuggling, a common practice at this time, contributed to the location of a sizeable portion of the county's population far from notions of responsible behaviour. Resting on these worrying distinctions were those related to diet, dress and demeanour that were less alarming but possibly more defining and set the place apart from refined standards. Moreover, as Jenkin Jones's diary revealed, local people of humble status were aware of the gap, and this difference influenced their interactions with others. Yet, in less than a hundred years, the place, while retaining some of the difference, lost much of its perceived inferiority.

Concerns about rebelliousness had abated by the latter part of the nineteenth century. But this metamorphosis did not result in universal praise for the people since new perspectives ascribed negative aspects to Cardiganshire and the Cardi. This change came about through alterations in the background and intentions of social commentators. Increasingly, interpretations of the area contained apprehensions about the behaviour of its leading figures. These were the professional and business classes who had come to represent the county, in both metaphorical and political terms, when they replaced the substantial landowners. The positioning of Cardiganshire's cultural and economic leadership on the edge of societal values was symptomatic of an age when collectivist ideas increasingly challenged the individualistic ethos of the Cardi. The objects of criticism, such

CONCLUSION: DIFFERENT BUT SIMILAR   249

as money-grubbing farmers and shopkeepers, were not new. Echoes of tensions between the poor, whose ability to purchase products at Cardigan market was restricted by high prices, can be found in the folk tales about Plant Rhys Ddwfn (The children of Rhys Ddwfn), for example.[30] In the first half of the twentieth century those thought to be displaying a lack of concern for the less fortunate members of society – who were now, incidentally, members of the political nation – came under increasing criticism. With this change in emphasis, the personification of the county in the form of the Cardi was frequently vilified. Then, as its actual and perceived influence declined, it was joked about.

There are resemblances between the way this distinct Welsh group was located and types in other countries. Like the Cardi, the latter were deemed representative of specific geographical areas and often viewed negatively. Such comparisons also identify common sources of friction based around buying and selling. The reputation of people from the mountainous Auvergne in south-central France for hard work, personified in Honoré de Balzac's character Graslin – an Auvergnat who arrived in Limoges a poor man only to rise to the position of bank manager – embodied ideas of personal progress and the value of thrift similar to those detected in the Swabian and the Cardi.[31] Conversely, the same attributes could be portrayed negatively. Frances M. Gostling, a lyricist and author of books on French regions, praised the Auvergnats but betrayed a critical attitude when she noted the impression of others that 'the Auvergnat is the closest-fisted man on earth, where the taking of money is concerned'. Nineteenth-century French cartoons personify this cupidity.[32] Both the Cardi and the Auvergnat have been compared with the Jew, sharing the dubious honour of being the epitome of covetousness. Similarly, both groups were

[30] Gwynionydd, 'Plant Rhys Ddwfn', *Y Brython*, 1 (1858–9), 110–11. These super-natural beings were thought to influence prices at Cardigan market. The tale mentions the 'gwanc' (greed) of the farmers. Also see David Davies, *John Vaughan and his Friends: Or More Echoes from the Welsh Hills* (London, 1897), p. 238.

[31] Honoré de Balzac, *The Village Rector*, trans. Katherine Prescott Wormeley (Boston, 1896), pp. 27–8.

[32] Frances M. Gostling, *Auvergne and its People* (London, 1911), p. 257; David Kunzle, *The History of the Comic Strip: The Nineteenth Century* (Berkeley, 1990), p. 168.

known to own shops in urban areas, the latter as cafe owners in Paris and the former in the industrial valleys of south Wales and London. It appears that the image of a grasping clan apart owed much to this contact between shop owner and customer. There were obvious differences between and within these regional groupings. For instance, the Cardi was a Protestant and so conformed to the Weberian entrepre-neurial model, while the Auvergnat was Catholic; and not all of these migrants had petit-bourgeois occupations. Even so, their location away from some general quality of generosity, that could at times acquire a political resonance, was used to identify both of them.[33]

All groups and areas have a representational history that is entwined in a socio-economic record. Even seemingly insignificant items, such as *cawl*, possess a dual history of materiality and meaning. Objects often contribute to the collection of meanings attached to groups and places.[34] This examination of locations in which the county and the people connected with it have been placed has primarily operated at the level of ideas; yet it has not treated these as floating free from social or economic moorings and has drawn atten-tion to the circumstances that stimulated ways of locating Cardiganshire. For a county, Cardiganshire has a particularly fecund representational history. Using the concept of loca-tion enabled the manner in which its representation has been manipulated to be brought to the fore. The significance of its deployment has been estimated through a consideration of the relationships between complementary and sometimes competing locations. Instead of focusing on a single 'image' of the Cardi or the county, this study has placed a plethora of symbols on a broad canvas and tracked their shifting config-urations over time. Complexity needs to be acknowledged and incorporated into considerations of the meanings

---

[33] There are parallels here with the Aberdonian and the Scot: C. Graham, 'Aberdeen', in David Daiches (ed.), *The New Companion to Scottish Culture* (Edinburgh, 1993), pp. 1–2; Roy Lewis and Angus Maude, *The English Middle Class* (London, 1953), p. 133.

[34] For example, see F. Miller Robinson, 'The history and significance of the bowler hat: Chaplin, Laurel and Hardy, Beckett, Magritte and Kundera', *Triquarterly*, 66 (spring/summer 1986), 173–98.

attached to places and people. An appreciation of a range of ideas, items and oppositions enables the symbolic richness of Cardiganshire and the Cardi to be comprehended. The appeal of Cardiganshire and the Cardi was, on the surface, simple. Within a British and Welsh context, both the county and its inhabitants were perceived as different and, therefore, drew praise, criticism and ridicule. Yet, as this study has shown, this difference took on or shed meanings only when interested parties drew upon the place and its people.

SOURCES AND BIBLIOGRAPHY

1. ARCHIVAL SOURCES

Bangor University Library (BUL)
Cerddi Bangor 24 (123–4), John Jones, 'Person Sir Aberteifi' [n.d.].
Cerddi Bangor 25 (145), Anon., 'Taith y Cardi o Landyssul i Lundain, yn ystod pa un y daeth i gyffyrddiad a'r Widw Fach Lan' (*c.*1904).

Carmarthenshire Archive Service (CAS)
CDX/632/2, manuscript copy of 'An Agricultural Survey of Cardiganshire' by Thomas Lloyd (1793).
MS Beckingsale 61/5, scrapbook.

Ceredigion Archives (CA)
ADX/168, 'Pocket book and farmers' diary, 1889, of Morgan Evans, J. P. Oakford, Llanarth'.
ADX 504 3/2, obituary Bethesda Chapel (1913).

Glamorgan Record Office
D/DX 935/295, 'Memories of Llanafan school' by William Jones.

Museum of Welsh Life
Evan Jones Collection, 2035/78, T. M. Jones, 'Can newydd sef achwyniad Sion Morris Griffith y Cardi, o herwydd iddo briodi gwraig anrefnus'.

National Library of Wales (NLW)

MS Aberpergwm (1), 903, Letter from W. Williams to Major Smith (1841).

MS Benjamin Davies, Box 19, 7, *Manchester Guardian*, 23 December 1936.

MS 22412C, Idris Davies, miscellaneous prose, 'Teifyside'.

MS Dewi Emrys, 11/1, 'Y Cardi'.

MS Glynne of Hawarden, B/57, A journal of a tour through south Wales and the border counties (1824).

MS E. Morgan Humphreys, A/584, undated letter from Richard Humphrey Davies.

MS 785A, Captain Jenkin Jones, 'Tours in England and Wales' (1819).

NLW, Baledi, J. D. Lewis, 'Casgliad o faledi' (1911).

MS 786A, Captain Lloyd, 'A tour in England and Wales' (1827).

MS 15467C, minute book of 'Cymdeithas Genedlaethol Cymry Manceinion, 1900–1911'.

MS Maybery, 1884, transcripts of John Lloyd, 'Cardy Carts' [*c.*1906].

MS Noyadd Trefawr 1678, letter from J. Paynter to Robert Lance (1770).

MS 16352D, Original MS of D. J. Saer's *The Story of Cardiganshire* (1912).

MS 933, Thomas Stephens, 'The working men of Wales' (1852).

MSS David Thomas (Aberystwyth) section B.

MS Mary Williams, 1042, bundle of newspaper reports of activities of the Swansea and District Cardiganshire Society.

MS Mary Williams, 2749, G. Arbour Stephens, 'The sanctuary of St. David and its future'.

MS 12165E, Richard Williams, 'Parturition in Cardiganshire'.

MS 687B, Richard Vaughan Yates, 'A Tour in Wales' (1805).

2. British parliamentary papers

BPP, XVI (1844), *Report of the Commissioners of Inquiry for South Wales* (London: HMSO, 1844).

BPP, XXVII (1847), *Reports of the Commissioners of Inquiry into the State of Education in Wales Part II* (London: HMSO, 1847).

BPP, LXXXIX (1852–3), *Census of Great Britain, 1851. Religious Worship. England and Wales. Report and Tables* (London: HMSO, 1853).

BPP, XIII (1870), *Commission on the Employment of Children, Young Persons, and Women in Agriculture Third Report* (1867) (London: HMSO, 1870).

BPP, XIV (1893–4), *Royal Commission on Labour: The Agricultural Labourer Volume II (Wales)* (London: HMSO, 1893).

BPP, XXXVII (1894), *Minutes of Evidence taken before the Royal Commission on Land in Wales and Monmouthshire Volume II* (London: HMSO, 1894).

BPP, XL (1895), *Minutes of Evidence taken before the Royal Commission on Land in Wales and Monmouthshire Volume III* (London: HMSO, 1895).

BPP, XXXIV (1896), *Second Report of the Royal Commission on Land in Wales and Monmouthshire* (London: HMSO, 1896).

BPP, XIV (1910), *Royal Commission of the Church of England and other Religious Bodies in Wales and Monmouthshire Volume I* (London: HMSO, 1910).
Hansard House of Commons Debates.

3. NEWSPAPERS AND JOURNALS

Aberystwith Observer
Archaeologia Cambrensis
Y Brython
Y Brython Cymreig
Bye-Gones
Cambrian
Cambrian Journal
Cambrian News
Y Cardi
Y Cardi: Cylchgrawn Cymdeithas
Ceredigion
Cardiff and Merthyr Guardian
Cardiff Times
Cardigan and Tivyside Advertiser
Cardiganshire Antiquarian Society Transactions
Carmarthenshire Historian
Carmarthen Journal
Cylchgrawn Cymdeithas Hanes y Methodistiad Calfinaidd
Y Cymmrodor
Cymru
Cymru'r Plant
Daily News
Demetian Mirror
Y Diwygiwr
The Druid
Y Drysorfa

Yr Eurgrawn Wesleyaidd
Y Fflam
Ford Gron
Y Geninen
Glamorgan Gazette
Goleuad
Yr Haul
Journal of the Welsh Bibliographical Society
Pontypridd Chronicle
Red Dragon
Seren Gomer
Silurian
South Wales Daily News
Swansea Boy
Tarian y Gweithiwr / Y Darian
The Times
Y Traethodydd
Wales (1894–7)
Wales (1911–14)
Wales (1939–60)
Welsh Gazette
Welsh Outlook
Welsh Review (1891–2)
Welsh Review (1939–48)
Welshman
Western Mail
Ymofyn(n)ydd

4. BOOKS AND ARTICLES

i. Biographies and memoirs
Alexander, D. T., *Glamorgan Reminiscences* (Carmarthen, 1915).
Cardi, 'Cofion Cardi', *Y Geninen*, 19 (1901), 191–4.
Davies, Dan and William Thomas Hughes, *Atgofion Dau Grefftwr* (Aberystwyth, 1963).
Davies, David, *John Vaughan and his Friends: Or More Echoes from the Welsh Hills* (London, 1897).

———, *Reminiscences of My Country and People* (Cardiff, 1925).

Davies, Dewi Eirug, 'Atgof', *Cymdeithas Ceredigion Llundain Llawlyfr*, 13 (1956–7), 26–7.

Davies, Hettie Glyn, *Edrych yn Ôl: Hen Atgofion Bentref Gwledig* (Lerpwl, 1958).

Davies, J. M., *O Gwmpas Pumlumon: Atgofion a Hanesion* (Aberystwyth, 1966).

Davies, Jonathan Ceredig, *Life, Travels and Reminiscences of Jonathan Ceredig Davies* (Llanddewi Brefi, 1927).

Davies, Rhys, *Print of a Hare's Foot* (London, 1969).

Edwardes, D., *Reminiscences of the Rev. D. Edwardes* (Shrewsbury, 1914).

Edwards, John, *Edwards Castellnedd* (Llandysul, 1935).

Edwards, Owen, *Clych Atgof: Penodau yn Hanes fy Addysg* (Wrecsam, 1933).

Ellis, E. L., *T. J.: A Life of Doctor Thomas Jones, CH* (Cardiff, 1992).

Evans, David, *Adgofion yr Hybarch David Evans, Archddiacon Llanelwy* (Llanbedr Pont Steffan, 1906).

Evans, Hugh, *Cwm Eithin* (Lerpwl, 1931).

Evans, Myra, *Atgofion Ceinewydd* (Aberystwyth, 1961).

Evans, William, *Journey to Harley Street* (London, 1968).

Ferris, Paul, *Dylan Thomas: The Biography* (London, 1977).

Francis-Jones, Gwyneth, *Cows, Cardis and Cockneys* (Borth, 1984).

Fryer, A. T., 'Edward Richard and Ystrad Meurig', *West Wales Historical Records*, 8 (1919–20), 67–81.

Griffith, John, 'Daniel Rowlands of Llangeitho', *Red Dragon*, 2 (1882), 1–8.

Griffiths, J., *Profiad ar y Môr* (Tonypandy, 1908).

Gruffydd, W. J., *Hen Atgofion* ([1936] Llandysul, 1964).

Herbert, Tom, *Herbert y Fet: Atgofion y Milfeddyg Tom Herbert* (Llandysul, 1989).

James, Glyn, 'Cardi yn y Rhondda: ambell atgof Glyn James', in Hywel Teifi Edwards (ed.), *Cwm Rhondda* (Llandysul, 1995), pp. 319–46.

Jones, D. Gwenallt, *Cofiant Idwal Jones* (Aberystwyth, 1958).

Jones, Dan, *Atgofion Llafurwr i Ieuenctyd Cymru* (Bow Street, 1956).

Jones, Evan, *Ar Ymylon Cors Caron: Atgofion gan Evan Jones* (Aberystwyth, 1967).

———, *Balchder Crefft* (Abertawe, 1976).

Jones, J. Islan, *Yr Hen Amser Gynt* (Aberystwyth, 1958).

Jones, John Rees, *Sôn am y Bont*, ed. E. D. Evans (Llandysul, 1974).

Jones, Owen, 'The land of his birth', in B. D. Thomas (ed.), *Frederick Evans D. D. Ednyfed: A Memorial* (Philadelphia, 1899), pp. 11–18.

Jones, Ruth, *Atgofion Ruth Mynachlog, sef Ruth Jones, Brynsilio, ger Synod, Ceredigion* (Llandysul, 1939).

Jones, Thomas, *Rhymney Memories* (Newtown, 1938).

———, *Leeks and Daffodils* (Newtown, 1942).

Jones-Edwards, W., *Ar Lethrau Ffair Rhos: Atgofion Mwnwr* (Aberystwyth, 1963).

Lewis, H. Elvet, *The Life of E. Herber Evans, D.D.: From his Letters, Journals, etc* (London, 1900).

Llewelyn, Emyr (ed.), *Aneurin* (Talybont, 2000).

Lockhart, J. G., *The Life of Sir Walter Scott* (London, 1906).

Moorman, Mary, *William Wordsworth: A Biography* (Oxford, 1957).

Morgan, D. J., *Pant a Bryn* (Llandysul, 1953).

Morgan, J. Myfenydd, 'Ioan Mynyw', *Y Traethodydd*, 55 (1900), 183–90.

Morgan, John Vyrnwy, *Kilsby Jones* (Wrecsam, 1897).

Morris, O. T., 'Salesman in the thirties', *Planet*, 32 (June 1976), 26–7.

Noble, Roy, *Roy Noble's Wales* (Cardiff, 1999).

Parry-Jones, D., *Welsh Country Upbringing* (London, 1948).

——, 'A day in Newcastle Emlyn', *Carmarthenshire Historian*, 4 (1967), 55–65.

Payne, Ffransis G., 'Pacmon yng Nheredigion', *Y Llenor*, 2 (1932), 90–8, 140–57.

Pennant, Lisa, *Tai Bach a Thai Mas: y Cardi ar ei Waethaf* (Aberystwyth, 2000).

Rees, D. Emrys, *Cymdogion* (Aberystwyth, 1962).

Rees, E. Ebrard, *Christmas Evans* (London, 1936).

Rees, Goronwy, *A Chapter of Accidents* (London, 1972).

Richards, Brinley, 'Manion', *Y Cardi: Cylchgrawn Cymdeithas Ceredigion*, 5 (August 1969), 10–12.

Richards, Tom, *Atgofion Cardi* (Aberystwyth, 1960).

Rothenstein, William, *Men and Memories: Recollections of William Rothenstein* (New York, 1931).

Smith, David, *Lewis Jones* (Cardiff, 1982).

Stephen, Leslie, *Life of Henry Fawcett* (5th edn, London, 1886).

Thomas, Daniel, *Dail yr Hydref: Sef Adgofion am Dol-y-Bont, Llanfihangel-Genau'r-Glyn, a Rhos-y-Gell* (Dinbych, 1916).

Thomas, Gwyn, *High on Hope* (Cowbridge, 1985).

Williams, David, *Y Wladfa Fach Fynyddig* (Dinbych, 1963).

Williams, Gwyn, *ABC of (D)GW* (Llandysul, 1981).

Williams, James, *Give Me Yesterday* (Llandysul, 1971).

Williams, John and Eben Davies, *Fferm a Ffair a Phentre* (Aberystwyth, 1958).

Williams, Rowland, *The Life and Letters of Rowland Williams D.D. with Extracts from his Note Books*, 2 vols (London, 1874).

Williams, William, *Atgofion am Sirhywi a'r Cylch* (Caerdydd, 1951).

ii. Fiction and poetry

Balzac, Honoré de, *The Village Rector*, trans. Katherine Prescott Wormeley (Boston, 1896).

Barnes, Julian, *England, England* (London, 1998).

Berry, Ron, *This Bygone* (Llandysul, 1996).

——, *History is What You Live* (Llandysul, 1998).

Brontë, Charlotte, *Shirley* ([1849] Oxford, 1998).

Coombes, B. L., *With Dust Still in His Throat: An Anthology of Writing by B. L. Coombes*, ed. Bill Jones and Chris Williams (Cardiff, 1999).

Davies, Rhys, *Sketches in Wales* (Brecon, 1875).

Evans, Caradoc, *My Neighbours: Stories of the Welsh people* (New York, 1920).

——, *Nothing to Pay* (London, 1930).

——, *Fury Never Leaves Us: A Miscellany of Caradoc Evans*, ed. John Harris (Bridgend, 1985).

Finnemore, John, *The Custom of the Country: An Idyll of the Welsh Mountains* (London, 1898).

Gaskell, Elizabeth, *North and South* ([1854] Harmondsworth, 1995).

Greenwood, Walter, *His Worship the Mayor, or, It's Only Human Nature After All* (London, 1934).

Griffiths, Niall, *Grits* (London, 2001).

James, Jenkin (ed.), *Gemau Ceredigion* (Caerdydd, 1914).

James, Margot, *The Cardi Comes Home* (London, 1956).

Jones, Jack, *Black Parade* (London, 1935).

Jones, Lewis, *Cwmardy* (London, 1937).

——, *We Live* (London, 1939).

Jones, Rees, *Crwth Dyffryn Clettwr* (Caerfyrddin, 1848).

Lewis, Alun, 'Private Jones', in Jack Aistrop and Reginald Moore (eds), *Bugle Blast: An Anthology from the Services* (London, 1943), pp. 135–56.

Lowellin, David, *The Admirable Travels of Messieurs Thomas Jenkins and David Lowellin through the Unknown Tracts of Africa* (London, 1786).

Mid Teifi Arts Writers Group, *Teifi Whispers* (Llandysul, 2000).

Morgan, John E., *Cerddi'r Eos* (Llandysul, 1967).

Norris, Leslie, 'The Girl from Cardigan', in Leslie Norris, *The Girl from Cardigan* (Bridgend, 1988), pp. 7–18.

Prichard, T. J. Llewelyn, *Twm Shon Catty* (Aberystwyth, 1828).

Raine, Allen, *A Welsh Witch: A Romance of Rough Places* (London, 1902).

——, *Where Billows Roll: A Tale of the Welsh Coast* (London, 1909).

Thomas, Dylan, *Collected Stories*, ed. W. Davies (London, 1993).

Wordsworth, William, *The Poetical Works of William Wordsworth*, ed. Thomas Hutchinson (Oxford, 1996).

iii. Travel writing and guide books

Aikin, John, *England Delineated; or, a Geographical Description of Every County in England and Wales* (3rd edn, London, 1795).

Anon., 'O Lanbedr i Lyn Teifi', *Yr Ymofynydd*, 3rd ser., 1 (1868), 265–9.

Anon., 'Siroedd Cymru: I Morgannwg', *Cymru'r Plant*, 8 (1899) 15–18.

Anon., 'Siroedd Cymru: II Ceredigion', *Cymru'r Plant*, 8 (1899) 47–51.

Bailey, Anthony, *A Walk through Wales* (London, 1992).

Barber, J. T., *A Tour throughout South Wales and Monmouthshire* (London, 1803).

Bell, Brian, *Wales* (Singapore, 1989).

Bensusan, S. L., *On the Tramp in Wales* (London, 1929).

Bingley, Revd W., *North Wales Delineated from Two Excursions* (2nd edn, London, 1814).

Borrow, George, *Wild Wales* ([1862]Llandysul, 1995).

Bradley, A. G., *Highways and Byways in North Wales* (London, 1898).

——, *Highways and Byways in South Wales* (London, 1903).

Camden, William, *Britannia . . . enlarged by Richard Gough*, 3 vols (London, 1789).

Cardiganshire: The County Handbook (Cheltenham and London, 1961).

Clarke, Gillian, *Banc Siôn Cwilt: A Local Habitation and a Name* (Newtown, 1998).

Cliffe, Charles Frederick, *The Book of South Wales, the Bristol Channel, Monmouthshire and the Wye* (2nd edn, London, 1848).

Cliffe, John Henry, *Notes and Recollections of an Angler* (London, 1860).

Cobbett, William, *Rural Rides*, 3 vols ([1830] London, 1930).

CYMRO, 'Cursory remarks on Welsh tours or travels', *Cambrian Register*, 2 (1799), 421–54.

Dark, Sidney, 'Middlesex', in C. E. M. Joad (ed.), *The English Counties Illustrated* (London, 1948), pp. 43–50.

Davies, Daniel, 'The County', *Cymdeithas Ceredigion Llundain Llawlyfr*, 16 (1962–3), 17–20.

Davies, Rhys, *My Wales* (London, 1937).

Davies, W. J., 'O Ddowlais i sir Aberteifi', *Yr Ymofynydd*, c.n., 11 (1886), 135–8.

Davies, W. Watkin, *A Wayfarer in Wales* (London, 1930).

Davies, William, *Llandeilo-Vawr and its Neighbourhood* (Llandeilo, 1858).

Disel, Eugen, *Germany and the Germans*, trans. W. D. Scott-Robson (New York, 1931).

Donovan, E., *Descriptive Excursions through South Wales and Monmouthshire*, 2 vols (London, 1805).

Dugdale, Thomas, *Curiosities of Great Britain*, 11 vols (London, 1845).

Edwards, H. W. J., *The Good Patch* (London, 1938).

Edwards, O. M., *Yn y Wlad: Troeon Crwydr Yma ac Acw yng Nghymru* (Wrecsam, 1932).

——, 'Stray leaves', *Wales*, 3 (1896), 1–6.

Edwards, Tudor, *The Face of Wales* (London, 1950).

Ellis, T. I., *Crwydro Ceredigion* (Llandybïe, 1952).

——, *Crwydro Llundain* (Abertawe, 1971).

Emerson, R. W., *English Traits* (Boston, 1856).

Evans, I. O., 'Cardiganshire', in S. P. B. Mais and Tom Shephenson (eds), *Lovely Britain* (London, 1935), pp. 222–5.

Evans, J., *Letters Written during a Tour through North Wales in the year 1798, and at Other Times* (London, 1800).

——, *Letters Written during a Tour through South Wales* (London, 1804).

Evans, Thomas, *Walks through Wales* (London, 1819).

Firbank, Thomas, *A Country of Memorable Honour* (London, 1953).

Fishlock, Trevor, *Wales and the Welsh* (London, 1972).

——, *Talking of Wales* (London, 1976).

Fletcher, H. L. V., *The Coasts of Wales* (London, 1969).

Freeman, G. J., *Sketches in Wales; or a Diary of Three Walking Excursions to that Principality* (London, 1826).

Gell, William, *A Tour in the Lakes 1797 by William Gell*, ed. William Rollinson (Otley, 2000).

Gostling, Frances M., *Auvergne and its People* (London, 1911).

Griffith, Owen, *Naw Mis yn Nghymru* (Utica, 1887).

Hall, Mr and Mrs S. C., *The Book of South Wales, the Wye and the Coast* (London, 1861).

Horsfall-Turner, E. R., *Walks and Wanderings in County Cardigan: Being a Descriptive Sketch of its Picturesque, Historic, Antiquarian, Romantic and Traditional Features* (Bingley, 1902).

Howell, J., 'Adgofion boreu oes, gan mwyaf yn fy nghysylltiad a Merthyr', *Y Geninen*, 19 (1901), 212–15.

Hughes, Cledwyn, *West with the Tinkers: A Journey through Wales with Vagrants* (London, 1954).

Jones, Alun R. and William Tydeman (eds), *Joseph Hucks: A Pedestrian Tour through North Wales in a Series of Letters* (Cardiff, 1979).

Kemp, Robert, *Colourful Britain* (Norwich, 1967).

Lewes, Evelyn, *Out with the Cambrians* (London, 1934).

Lewis, Samuel, *Topographical Dictionary of Wales*, 2 vols (London, 1833).

Lipscomb, George, *Journey into South Wales . . . in 1799* (London, 1802).

Lockley, R. M., *Wales* (London, 1966).

MacDonald, Tom, *Where Silver Salmon Leap* (Llandysul, 1976).

Mais, S. P. B., *I Return to Wales* (London, 1949).

Malkin, Benjamin Heath, *The Scenery, Antiquities, and Biography of South Wales* (London, 1804).

Marks, Jeannette, *Gallant Little Wales: Sketches of its People, Places and Customs* (London, 1912).

Mavor, William Fordyce, *A Tour in Wales and through Several Counties of England . . . Performed in the Summer of 1805* (London, 1806).

Meyrick, Samuel Rush, *The History and Antiquities of the County of Cardigan* (London, 1808).

Morton, H. V., *In Search of Wales* (London, 1932).

Murray, John [firm], *A Handbook for Travellers in South Wales and its Borders* (London, 1860).

Onwhyn, Joseph [firm], *Onwhyn's Welsh Tourist* (2nd edn, London, 1853).

Palfrey, Colin and Arwel Roberts, *The Unofficial Guide to Wales* (Talybont, 1994).

Palmer, W. T., *Wales* (London, 1932).

Parry, W. T., 'Dau ddiwrnod yng nghanolbarth Sir Aberteifi: yr ail ddiwrnod', *Cymru*, 21 (1901), 268–74.

Pat a Siân, 'Cysgod y gwaith', *Y Cardi: Cylchgrawn Cymdeithas Ceredigion*, 1 (1966), 11–12.

Pratt, Samuel Jackson, *Gleanings through Wales, Holland, and Westphalia*, 2 vols (London, 1795).

Prichard, T. J. Llewelyn, *The New Aberystwyth Guide* (Aberystwyth, 1824).

Raymond, David, *We Go to Wales* (London, 1954).

Rees, Thomas, *A Topographical and Historical Description of Cardiganshire* (London, 1810).

Roscoe, Thomas, *Wanderings and Excursions in South Wales* (2nd edn, London, 1854).

Rowlands, John, *Historical Notes of the Counties of Glamorgan, Carmarthen and Cardigan* (Cardiff, 1866).

Saunders, E. J., *Rhamant y De* (Llanelli, 1933).

Sikes, Wirt, *Rambles and Studies in Old South Wales* (London, 1881).

Simond, Louis, *Journal of a Tour and Residence in Great Britain during the years 1810 and 1811*, 2 vols (Edinburgh, 1815).

Smith, W. G., 'A holiday in Cardiganshire', *Bye-Gones* (1878–9), 111–12.

Spence, Elizabeth Isabella, *Summer Excursions through Parts of Oxfordshire . . . and South Wales* (2nd edn, London, 1809).

Stephenson, J., *The Aberystwyth Guide* (Aberystwyth, 1816).

Stevenson, Keith, *A Slice of Britain: A Light-Hearted Journey Across Seven Shires* (Ystrad Meurig, 1988).

Theroux, Paul, *The Kingdom by the Sea* (Harmondsworth, 1984).

Thomas, Edward, *Beautiful Wales* (London, 1905).

Thomas, George, *My Wales* (London, 1986).

Thomas, Gwilym, 'Ar wib i Gwm Rhondda dydd Sadwrn 17 Mehefin 1995', *Y Cardi: Cylchgrawn Cymdeithas Ceredigion*, 23 (Gŵyl Ddewi 1996), 29–31.

Thomas, R. G. Lloyd, *Welsh Odyssey* (Llandybïe, 1949).

Turner, Thomas, *Narrative of a Journey . . . July 31st to September 8th, 1837* (London, 1840).

Uwchaled, 'A holiday in the sweet shire of Cardigan', *Welsh Outlook*, 9 (1928), 264–9.

Vale, Edmund, *The World of Wales* (London, 1935).

Warner, Richard, *A Walk through Wales in August 1797* (2nd edn, Bath, 1798).

——, *A Second Walk through Wales* (Bath, 1799).

Wigstead, Henry, *Remarks on a Tour to North and South Wales in the Year 1797* (London, 1799).

Wilmot-Buxton, E. M., *Peeps at Many Lands: Wales* (London, 1911).

Wyndham, Henry Penruddocke, *A Gentleman's Tour through Monmouthshire and Wales in the Months of June and July, 1774* (London, 1775).

iv. Other published primary sources

Anon., 'Eisteddfod Aberystwyth', *Yr Haul*, Cyfres Caerfyrddin, 9 (1865), 336–8.

Anon., 'Etholiadau Ceredigion a Meirionydd', *Y Traethodydd*, 20 (1865), 488–512.

Anon., *Hiwmor y Cymry: Hwyl o'r bedwaredd-ganrif-ar-bymtheg* (Penygroes, 1976).

Ap Adda, 'The Cardiganshire butterman', *Red Dragon*, 2 (1882), 160–2.

——, 'The Cardiganshire herring dealer', *Red Dragon*, 5 (1884), 76–8.

——, 'The old stocking knitter', *Red Dragon*, 5 (1884), 271–3.

Atkeson, Mary Meek, *The Woman on the Farm* (New York and London, 1924).

Bowen, Emrys G., 'The people and culture of rural Wales', *Bye-Gones*, new ser., 1 (1925–7), 77–8.

Bruce, Henry Austin, *Lectures and Addresses by the Right Hon. Henry Austin Bruce* (London, 1901).

Carlyle, Thomas, 'Signs of the times', in Thomas Carlyle, *Selected Writing*, ed. Alan Shelston (Harmondsworth, 1971), pp. 59–86.

Ceredig (O. Ap Harri), *Y Dosbarth Gweithiol yng Nghymru* (Caerfyrddin, 1865).

Clark, John, *General View of the Agriculture of the County of Hereford* (London, 1794).

Cobbe, Frances Power [F.P.C.], 'The Celt of Wales and the Celt of Ireland', *Cornhill Magazine*, 32 (1877), 661–78.

Curtis, Mary, *The Antiquities of Langharne and Pendine* (London, 1871).

Cwysi Ceredigion: Cronicl Clybiau Ffermwyr Ifainc (Felin-fach, 1974).

D.J., 'The Gwyddyl in Cardiganshire', *Archaeologia Cambrensis*, 3rd ser., 17 (1859), 306–7.

Darlington, T., 'The Cymric element in the English people', *Wales*, 1 (1911), 361–8.

Davies, Christie, *Welsh Jokes* (Wrexham, 1986).

Davies, D. J., 'Llanwenog', *Cardiganshire Antiquarian Society Transactions*, 12 (1937), 31–50.

Davies, Evan, *Hanes Plwyf Llangynllo* (Llandysul, 1905).

Davies, J. H. (ed.), *The Letters of Lewis, Richard, William and John Morris, of Anglesey*, 2 vols (Aberystwyth, 1909).

——, 'Daniel Rowland: contemporary descriptions (1746 and 1835)', *Cylchgrawn Cymdeithas Hanes y Methodistiad Calfinaidd*, 1 (1916), 52–7.

—— (ed.), *The Letters of Goronwy Owen (1723–1769)* (Cardiff, 1924).

Davies, J. Llefelys, 'The diary of a Cardiganshire farmer, 1870–1900', *Welsh Journal of Agriculture*, 10 (1934), 5–20.

Davies, Jonathan Ceredig, *Folklore of West and Mid-Wales* (Aberystwyth, 1911).

Davies, Walter, *General View of the Agriculture and Domestic Economy of South Wales*, 2 vols (London, 1815).

De Quincey, Thomas, *The Confessions of an English Opium Eater and Other Essays* (London, 1906).

Duncumb, John, *General View of the Agriculture of the County of Hereford* (London, 1805).

Eden, Frederic Morton, *The State of the Poor*, 3 vols (London, 1797).

Edwards, G., 'Education in Wales and the proposal for founding a Welsh university', *Cambrian Journal*, 10 (1864), 73–104.

Edwards, J. Hugh, 'Interviews with Welsh leaders: Ellis J. Griffith MP', *Welsh Review*, 1 (1906), 19–21.

Evans, David, *Y Wlad: Ei Bywyd, ei Haddysg, a'i Chrefydd* (Lerpwl, 1933).

Evans, R. M., 'Folklore and customs in Cardiganshire', *Cardiganshire Antiquarian Society Transactions*, 12 (1937), 51–7.

Fleure, H. J., 'An outline story of our neighbourhood', *Aberystwyth Studies*, 4 (1922), 111–23.

——, *Races of England and Wales: A Survey of Recent Research* (London, 1923).

——, 'The people of Cardiganshire', *Cardiganshire Antiquarian Society Transactions*, 4 (1926), 15–21.

Fowler, Robert, *A Complete History of the Case of the Welsh Fasting Girl* (London, 1871).

Francis, J. O., *The Legend of the Welsh and Other Papers* (Cardiff, 1924).

Grose, Francis, *A Provincial Glossary with a Collection of Local Proverbs and Popular Superstitions* (2nd edn, London, 1790).

G.W., 'Superstition', *Cambrian Journal*, 7 (1861), 42–4.

Grosvenor, George, 'Statistics of the abatement of crime in England and Wales, during the twenty years ended 1887–1888', *Journal of the Royal Statistical Society*, 53 (1890), 377–419.

Gwenog, Ieuan, 'Dydd Calan yn Ngheredigion', *Y Brython*, 3 (1860), 10–13.

Gwynionydd, 'Plant Rhys Ddwfn', *Y Brython*, 1 (1858–9), 110–11.

Gwytherin, 'Cardiganshire, February, 1921', *Welsh Outlook*, 8 (1921), 107–9.

Harford, John S., *Address Delivered in the Assembly Room of Aberystwyth on October 18th, 1849* (Bristol, 1849).

Hassall, Charles, *General View of the Agriculture of the County of Pembroke* (London, 1794).

Hesgin, 'Y Cardis', *Y Fflam*, 1, 5 (1948), 24–5.

Howells, W., *Cambrian Superstitions* (London, 1831).

Ifan, Wil, *Here and There* (Cardiff, 1953).

Inglis-Jones, E., 'Some impressions on revisiting Cardiganshire', *Cymdeithas Ceredigion Llundain Llawlyfr*, 16 (1960–1), 20–2.

Isaac, Evan, *Yr Hen Gyrnol a Brasluniau Eraill* (Aberystwyth, 1935).

——, *Coelion Cymru* (Aberystwyth, 1938).

James, Jenkin, 'Education in Cardiganshire: elementary and higher', in J. Ballinger (ed.), *Aberystwyth and District: A Guide Prepared for the Conference of the National Union of Teachers, 1911* (Aberystwyth, 1911), pp. 232–44.

Jefferies, R., 'The labourer's daily life [1874]', in R. Mabey (ed.), *Landscape with Figures: An Anthology of Richard Jefferies' Prose* (Harmondsworth, 1983), pp. 40–63.

Jenkins, D. C. (ed.), *The Diary of Thomas Jenkins of Llandeilo, 1826–1870* (Bala, 1976).

Jenkins, Joseph, *Diary of a Welsh Swagman*, ed. William Evans (Victoria, 1975).

John, Brian, *The Best Cardi Jokes* (Newport, Pembrokeshire, 1995).

——, *Up Among the Mountain Men* (Newport, Pembrokeshire, 1997).

Johnes, Thomas, *A Cardiganshire Landlord's Advice to his Tenants* (Bristol, 1800).

Jones, Edmund, *A Relation of Apparitions of Spirits in the Principality of Wales* ([Trevecca (?)], 1780).

Jones, Griffith, *Enwogion Sir Aberteifi: Traethawd Buddugol yn Eisteddfod Genedlaethol Aberystwyth, 1865* (Dolgellau, 1868).

Jones, Maurice, 'St. David's College', *Cymdeithas Ceredigion Llundain Llawlyfr*, 3 (1936–7), 14–20.

Jones, Noragh, *Living in Rural Wales* (Llandysul, 1993).

Jones, T. Gwynn, *Welsh Folklore and Folk-Customs* (London, 1930).

Kenrick, G. S., 'Statistics of the population in the parish of Trevethin (Pontypool) and at the neighbouring works of Blaenavon, in Monmouthshire, chiefly employed in the iron trade and inhabiting part of the district recently disturbed', *Journal of the Statistical Society of London*, 3 (1840), 366–75.

Laws, Edward, *The History of Little England Beyond Wales, and the Non-Kymric Colony Settled in Pembrokeshire* (London, 1888).

Littlejohns, J., *Pamphlets for the People No.1: Black Glamorgan* (Swansea, 1901).

Llewelyn, Emyr, *Hiwmor y Cardi* (Talybont, 2006).

M.T., 'Aberporth ac addysg', *Yr Haul*, Cyfres Caerfyrddin, 12 (1868), 389.

Macrae, David, *National Humour: Scottish, English, Irish, Welsh, Cockney, American* (Paisley, 1904).

Malkin, Benjamin Heath, *Essays on Subjects Connected with Civilization* (London, 1795).

Morgan, D. J., 'Y sir: rhai o'i phobl a'i phethau', *Cymdeithas Ceredigion Llundain Llawlyfr*, 3 (1936–37), 21–9.

Morris, John, 'Sir Aberteifi', *Barn*, 162–3 (1976), 213.

Nicholson, Ivor, and Trevor Lloyd-Williams (eds), *Wales: Its Part in the War* (London, 1919).

Owen, Hugh (ed.), *Additional Letters of the Morrises of Anglesey (1735–1785)* (London, 1947).

P[ayne], E. W., *Memoir of David Lloyd of Hafod Fach, Cardiganshire* (London, 1849),

Peate, Iorwerth C., *Cymru a'i Phobol* (Cardiff, 1931).

Phillips, Dilwyn, *Welsh Jokes* (Talybont, 2002).

Phillips, Richard, 'Some aspects of the agricultural conditions in Cardiganshire in the nineteenth century', *Welsh Journal of Agriculture*, 1 (1925), 22–8.

Price, Cecil, 'Universities and the theatre', *The Welsh Anvil: Yr Einion*, 3 (July 1951), 29–35.

Price, T., *An Essay on the Physiognomy and Physiology of the Present Inhabitants of Britain* (London, 1820).

Rees, T. Mardy, *Hiwmor y Cymro* (Lerpwl, 1922).

Rees, Thomas, *Miscellaneous Papers on Subjects Relating to Wales by Thomas Rees, D.D.* (London, 1867).

Richard, Henry, *Letters on the Social and Political Condition of the Principality of Wales* (London, 1866).

St John, James, *Letters from France to a Gentleman in the South of Ireland*, 2 vols (Dublin, 1788).

Siencyn Ap Tydfil, 'Buchedd Gitto Gelli Deg yn yr wythnos gadw', *Seren Gomer*, 3rd ser., 3 (1820), 163–4.

Stapleton, R. G., *The Land Now and To-morrow* (London, 1935).

——, *The Way of the Land* (London, 1943).

——, 'The changing countryside', *Welsh Review*, 3 (1944), 283–9.

Stephens, G. Arbour, 'Rhaid i Gymru cael aeroplens', *Ford Gron*, 1 (1930–1), 5.

Stephens, Meic (ed.), *Harri Webb, A Militant Muse: Selected Literary Journalism, 1948–1980* (Bridgend, 1998).

Thomas, Edward, *Selected Letters*, ed. R. George Thomas (Oxford, 1995).

Thomas, R. S., 'The depopulation of the Welsh hill country', *Wales*, 7 (1945), 75–80.

Tout, T. F., 'Welsh shires: a study in constitutional history', *Y Cymmrodor*, 9 (1888), 201–26.

Trevelyan, Marie, *Glimpses of Welsh Life and Character* (London, 1893).

Vincent, J. E., *Letters from Wales* (London, 1889).

Wallis-Jones, W. J., *Welsh Characteristics* (Pencader, 1898).

Wilkins, Charles, *Tales and Sketches of Wales* (Cardiff, 1879).

Williams, Benjamin, *Enwogion Ceredigion* (Caerfyrddin, 1869).

Williams, E., 'Crime in Wales', in T. Stephens (ed.), *Wales To-day and To-morrow* (Cardiff, 1907), pp. 174–5.

Williams, Jac L., 'Sut mae hi?', *Cymdeithas Ceredigion Llundain Llawlyfr*, 14 (1959–60), 11–16.

Williams, Kyffin, *Drawings* (Llandysul, 2001).

Williams, Lucy, 'Factors in the culture of pre-railway Holyhead', *Anglesey Society and Field Club Transactions*, 8 (1940), 93–9.

Williams, R. E., *Glimpses of Wales and the Welsh* (Pittsburgh, 1894).

Worthington, D., 'Enwogion Ceredigion', *Yr Haul*, Cyfres Dolgellau, 23 (1921), 161–2.

Zimmern, Alfred E., *My Impressions of Wales* (London, 1921).

v. Secondary material and works of reference

Abrams, Philip, *Historical Sociology* (Shepton Mallet, 1982).

Adam, Barbara, 'Detraditionalization and the certainty of uncertain futures', in Paul Heelas, Scott Lash and Paul Morris (eds), *Detraditionalization: Critical Reflections on Authority and Identity* (London, 1996), pp. 134–48.

Aitchison, J. W. and Harold Carter, *A Geography of the Welsh Language, 1961–1991* (Cardiff, 1994).

——, 'The population of Cardiganshire', in Geraint H. Jenkins and Ieuan Gwynedd Jones (eds), *Cardiganshire County History*, vol. 3: *Cardiganshire in Modern Times* (Cardiff, 1998), pp. 1–18.

——, 'The Welsh language 1921–1991: a geolinguistic perspective', in Geraint H. Jenkins and Mari A. Williams (eds), *'Let's Do Our Best for the Ancient Tongue': The Welsh Language in the Twentieth Century* (Cardiff, 2000), pp. 29–107.

Aldridge, Meryl, *The British New Towns: A Programme Without a Policy* (London, 1979).

Appadurai, Arjun, 'The production of locality', in Richard Fardon (ed.), *Counterworks: Managing the Diversity of Knowledge* (London, 1995), pp. 204–25.

Applegate, Celia, 'A Europe of regions: reflections on the historiography of sub-national places in modern times', *American Historical Review*, 114, 4 (1999) 1157–81.

Atkins, P. J., 'The retail milk trade in London, *c.*1790–1914', *Economic History Review*, 33, 4 (1980), 522–37.

Barnes, David Russell, *People of Seion: Patterns of Nonconformity in Cardiganshire and Carmarthenshire in the Century Preceding the Religious Census of 1851* (Llandysul, 1995).

Barth, Fredrik, 'Preface 1998', in Fredrik Barth (ed.), *Ethnic Groups and Boundaries: The Social Organisation of Difference* (Prospect Heights, IL, 1998), pp. 5–7.

Basden, George Thomas, *Among the Ibos of Nigeria* (London, 1921).

Bateman, D. I., 'Cardiganshire agriculture in the twentieth century: an economic perspective', in Geraint H. Jenkins and Ieuan Gwynedd Jones (eds), *Cardiganshire County History*, vol. 3: *Cardiganshire in Modern Times* (Cardiff, 1998), pp. 113–34.

Batten Jr, Charles L., *Pleasurable Instruction: Form and Convention in Eighteenth-Century Travel Literature* (Berkeley, 1978).

Baxendale, John, '"I had seen a lot of Englands": J. B. Priestley, Englishness and the people', *History Workshop Journal*, 51 (2001), 87–111.

Belchem, John, '"An accent exceedingly rare": Scouse and the inflexion of class', in John Belchem and Neville Kirk (eds), *Languages of Labour* (Aldershot, 1997), pp. 99–139.

——, '"The playground of northern England": the Isle of Man, Manxness and the northern working class', in Neville Kirk (ed.), *Northern Identities: Historical Interpretations of 'The North' and 'Northernness'* (Aldershot, 2000), pp. 71–86.

Benbough-Jackson, M., 'Ceredigion and the changing visitor gaze, *c.*1760–2000', *Ceredigion*, 14, 3 (2003), 21–41.

Benson, John, *The Rise of Consumer Society in Britain, 1880–1980* (London, 1994).

Bentley, Michael, *The Liberal Mind, 1914–1929* (Cambridge, 1977).

Berbu, Zevedi, *Problems of Historical Psychology* (London, 1960).

Berger, Peter L. and Thomas Luckmann, *The Social Construction of Reality* (London, 1966).

Berkhofer Jr, Robert F., *Beyond the Great Story: History as Text and Discourse* (Cambridge, MA, 1995).

Berry, Christopher J., *Social Theory of the Scottish Enlightenment* (Edinburgh, 1997).

Berry, David, *Wales and Cinema: The First Hundred Years* (Cardiff, 1996).

Bewley, Marius, 'Temptations of the cultural historian', *The New York Review of Books*, 19 November 1964, 19–21.

Boorstin, Daniel J., *Hidden History: Exploring our Secret Past* (New York, 1987).

Borsay, Peter, *The Image of Georgian Bath, 1700–2000: Towns, Heritage and History* (Oxford, 2000).

Boswell, Laird, 'From liberation to purge trials in the "Mythic Provinces": recasting French identities in Alsace and Lorraine, 1918–1920', *French Historical Studies*, 23, 1 (2000), 129–62.

Bourdieu, Pierre, *Outline of a Theory of Practice*, trans. Richard Nice (Cambridge, 1977).

Boyce, D. G., '"The marginal Britons": the Irish', in Robert Colls and Philip Dodd (eds), *Englishness: Politics and Culture, 1880–1920* (London, 1987), pp. 230–53.

Brace, Catherine, 'Gardenesque imagery in the representation of regional and national identity: the Cotswold Garden of Stone', *Journal of Rural Studies*, 15, 4 (1999), 365–76.

——, 'Looking back: the Cotswolds and English national identity, *c.*1890–1950', *Journal of Historical Geography*, 25, 4 (1999), 502–16.

Braudel, Fernand, *The Identity of France*, vol. I: *History and Environment*, trans. Siân Reynolds (London, 1988).

Brewer's Dictionary of Phrase and Fable Millennium Edition (London, 2001).

Brigstocke, W. O., 'Welsh county councils', *The Welsh Review*, 1 (1891–2), 485–92.

Burke, Peter, *Varieties of Cultural History* (Oxford, 1997).

Burnett, John, *Plenty and Want: A Social History of Diet in England from 1815 to the Present Day* (revised edn, London, 1979).

Carter, Harold, 'The growth and decline of Welsh towns', in Donald Moore (ed.), *Wales in the Eighteenth Century* (Swansea, 1976), pp. 47–62.

Carter, Ian, 'The changing image of the Scottish peasantry, 1745–1980', in Raphael Samuel (ed.), *People's History and Socialist Theory* (London, 1981), pp. 9–15.

——, *Railways and Culture in Britain: The Epitome of Modernity* (Manchester, 2001)

Caunce, Stephen, 'Regional identity in Lancashire and Yorkshire: hunting the Snark', *Journal of Regional and Local Studies*, 20, 1 (1999), 25–50.

Chartier, Roger, *Cultural History: Between Practice and Representations*, trans. Lydia G. Cochrane (Cambridge, 1988).

——, *On the Edge of the Cliff: History, Language and Practices*, trans. Lydia G., Cochrane (Baltimore and London, 1997).

Cheyette, Brian, *Constructions of 'the Jew' in English Literature and Society: Racial Representations, 1875–1945* (Cambridge, 1993).

Childers, Joseph W., 'Observation and representation: Mr. Chadwick writes the poor', *Victorian Studies*, 37, 3 (1994), 405–32.

Childs, Peter, 'Places and peoples: nation and region', in Mike Storry and Peter Childs (eds), *British Cultural Identities* (2nd edn, London, 2002), pp. 35–72.

Clark, Charles Manning, 'Re-writing Australian history', in T. A. G. Hungerford (ed.), *Australian Signpost: An Anthology* (Melbourne, 1956), pp. 130–43.

Clark, J. C. D., *English Society, 1688–1832: Ideology, Social Structure and Political Practice during the Ancien Régime* (Cambridge, 1985).

Coates, B. E. and E. M. Rawstron, *Regional Variations in Britain: Studies in Economic and Social Geography* (London, 1971).

Coates, David, *The Labour Party and the Struggle for Socialism* (London, 1975).

Cobb, James C., 'An epitaph for the North: reflections on the politics of regional and national identity at the millennium', *Journal of Southern History*, 66, 1 (2000), 3–24,

Cohen, Anthony P., *The Symbolic Construction of Community* (Chichester, 1985).

——, 'Culture as identity: an anthropologist's view', *New Literary History*, 24, 1 (1993), 195–209.

——, *Self Consciousness: An Alternative Anthropology of Identity* (London, 1995).

Collini, Stefan, 'The idea of "character" in Victorian political thought', *Transactions of the Royal Historical Society*, 35 (1985), 29–50.

Colls, Robert, *The Collier's Rant: Song and Culture in the Industrial Village* (London, 1977).

——, *Identity of England* (Oxford, 2002).

—— and Bill Lancaster, 'Preface', in Robert Colls and Bill Lancaster (eds), *Geordies: Roots of Regionalism* (Edinburgh, 1993), pp. x–xv.

Confino, Alon, *The Nation as a Local Metaphor: Württemberg, Imperial Germany and the National Memory, 1871–1918* (Chapel Hill, NC, 1997).

Corrigan, Philip, and Derek Sayer, *The Great Arch: English State Formation as Cultural Revolution* (Oxford, 1986).

Cranston, Maurice, *Sartre* (Edinburgh, 1962).

Cubitt, Geoffrey, 'Introduction', in Geoffrey Cubitt (ed.), *Imagining the Nation* (Manchester, 1998), pp. 1–20.

Curtis Jr, L. P., *Anglo-Saxons and Celts: A Study of Anti-Irish Prejudice in Victorian England* (Bridgeport, CT, 1968).

Dahrendorf, Ralf, *Life Chances: Approaches to Social and Political Theory* (London, 1979).

Davies, Christie *The Mirth of Nations* (London, 2002).

Davies, D. J., *Hanes, Hynafiaethau, ac Achyddiaeth Llanarth, Henfynyw, Llanllwchaiarn a Llandyssilio-Gogo* (2nd edn, Caerfyrddin, 1930).

Davies, Dewi, 'The early years of the Turnpike Trust in Cardiganshire: evidence from the minutes of Aberystwyth District', *Ceredigion*, 14, 3 (2003), 7–19.

Davies, Hywel M., 'Wales in English travel writing, 1791–8: the Welsh critique of Theophilus Jones', *Welsh History Review*, 23, 3 (2007), 65–93.

Davies, John, 'The end of the great estates and the rise of freehold farming in Wales', *Welsh History Review*, 7 (1974–5), 186–212.

——, *The Green and the Red: Nationalism and Ideology in Twentieth-Century Wales* (Aberystwyth, 1982).

——, 'The communal conscience in Wales in the inter-war years', *Transactions of the Honourable Society of Cymmrodorion 1998*, new ser., 5 (1999), 145–60.

Davies, Leonard Twiston and Averyl Edwards, *Welsh Life in the Eighteenth Century* (London, 1939).

Davies, Owen, 'Newspapers and the popular belief in witchcraft and magic in the modern period', *Journal of British Studies*, 37, 2 (1998), 139–65.

Davies, Russell, *Hope and Heartbreak: A Social History of Wales and the Welsh, 1776–1871* (Cardiff, 2005).

Dawson, Richard, *The British Folklorists: A History* (London, 1968).

Deacon, Bernard, 'Imagining the fishing: artists and fishermen in late nineteenth-century Cornwall', *Rural History*, 12, 2 (2001), 159–78.

Deane, P. and W. A. Cole, *British Economic Growth, 1688–1959* (Cambridge, 1962).

Dearnley, Moira, *Distant Fields: Eighteenth-Century Fictions of Wales* (Cardiff, 2001).

Douglas, Mary and Baron Isherwood, *The World of Goods: Towards an Anthropology of Consumption* (2nd edn, London, 1996).

Driessen, Henk, 'Humour, laughter and the field: reflections from anthropology', in Jan Bremmer and Herman Roodenburg (eds), *A Cultural History of Humour: From Antiquity to the Present Day* (Cambridge, 1997), pp. 222–41.

Driver, Felix and Raphael Samuel, 'Rethinking the idea of place', *History Workshop Journal*, 39 (1995), v–vii.

Eastwood, David, *Government and Community in the English Provinces, 1700–1870* (Basingstoke, 1997).

Edwards, Hywel Teifi, 'The Welsh collier as hero: 1850–1950', *Welsh Writing in English*, 2 (1996), 22–48.

Edwards, O. M., *Wales* (London, 1901).

Eliot, T. S., *Notes Towards the Definition of Culture* ([1948] London, 1962).

Encyclopaedia Britannica, 29 vols (Cambridge, 1910–11).

Encyclopaedia Britannica, 24 vols (Chicago, 1949).

Evans, David, *Labour Strife in the South Wales Coalfield, 1910–1911* (Cardiff, 1911).

Evans, Huw and Marian Davies, *'Fyl'na Weden I': Blas ar Dafodiaeth Canol Ceredigion* (Llanrwst, 2000).

Evans, George Eyre (ed.), *Cardiganshire* (Aberystwyth, 1903).

——, *Lampeter* (Aberystwyth, 1905).

Evans, Neil, 'Gogs, Cardis and Hwntws: regions, nation and state in Wales', in Neil Evans (ed.), *National Identity in the British Isles* (Harlech, 1989), pp. 60–72.

——, 'Regional dynamics: north Wales, 1750–1914', in Edward Royle (ed.), *Issues of Regional Identity: In Honour of John Marshall* (Manchester, 1998), pp. 201–25.

——, Paul O'Leary and Charlotte Williams, 'Introduction: race, nation and globalisation', in Neil Evans, Paul O'Leary and Charlotte Williams (eds), *A Tolerant Nation? Exploring Ethnic Diversity in Wales* (Cardiff, 2003), pp. 1–13.

Febvre, Lucien, *A Geographical Introduction to History*, trans. E. G. Mountford and J. H. Paxton (London, 1925).

Fenyő, Krisztina, *Contempt, Sympathy and Romance: Lowland Perceptions of the Highlands and the Clearances during the Famine Years, 1845–1855* (East Linton, 2000).

Field, John, 'The view from Folkestone', in Raphael Samuel (ed.), *Patriotism: The Making and Unmaking of British National Identity*, vol. II: *Minorities and Outsiders* (London, 1989), pp. 3–8.

Fowler, Peter J., *Then, Now: The Past in Contemporary Society* (London, 1992).

Fraser, Maxwell, 'Sir Benjamin and Lady Hall in the 1840s. Part II: 1846–1849', *National Library of Wales Journal*, 14 (1965–6), 194–213.

Freeman, Michael, 'The industrial revolution and the regional geography of England: a comment', *Transactions of the Institute of British Geographers*, new ser., 9, 4 (1984), 507–12.

Gaffney, Angela, *Aftermath: Remembering the Great War in Wales* (Cardiff, 1998).

Giddens, Anthony, *Sociology* (Cambridge, 1997).

Giles, Judy and Tim Middleton, *Writing Englishness, 1900–1950: An Introductory Sourcebook on National Identity* (London, 1995).

Gilmour, Robin, 'Regional and provincial in Victorian literature', in R. P. Draper (ed.), *The Literature of Region and Nation* (London, 1989), pp. 51–60.

Giner, Salvador and Eduardo Sevilla-Guzman, 'The demise of the peasant: some reflections on ideological inroads into social theory', *Sociologia Ruralis*, 20, 1–2 (1980), 13–27.

Golby, J. M. and A. W. Purdue, *The Civilisation of the Crowd: Popular Culture in England, 1750–1900* (2nd edn, London, 1999).

Goldman, Lawrence, 'The origins of British "Social Science": political economy, natural science and statistics, 1830–1835', *Historical Journal*, 26, 3 (1983), 587–616.

Graham, C., 'Aberdeen', in David Daiches (ed.), *The New Companion to Scottish Culture* (Edinburgh, 1993), pp. 1–2.

Gray, John, *Post-Liberalism: Studies in Political Thought* (New York, 1993).

Gray, Peter, *Southern Aberrations: Writers of the American South and the Problems of Regionalism* (Baton Rouge, 2000).

Gregory, James N., *American Exodus: The Dust Bowl Migration and Okie Culture in California* (New York, 1991).

Gruffudd, Pyrs, 'Back to the land: historiography, rurality and the nation in interwar Wales', *Transactions of the Institute of British Geographers*, new ser., 19, 1 (1994), 61–77.

——, 'Prospects of Wales: contested geographical imaginations', in Ralph Fevre and Andrew Thompson (eds), *Nation, Identity and Social Theory: Perspectives from Wales* (Cardiff, 1999), pp. 149–67.

Gutman, Huck, Patrick H. Hutton and Luther H. Martin (eds), *Technologies of the Self: A Seminar with Michel Foucault* (London, 1988).

Handley, James E., *Scottish Farming in the Eighteenth Century* (London, 1953).

Hannan, Patrick, *The Welsh Illusion* (Bridgend, 1999).

Harris, J. Kendal, 'Epilogue', in Geraint H. Jenkins and Ieuan Gwynedd Jones (eds), *Cardiganshire County History*, vol. 3: *Cardiganshire in Modern Times* (Cardiff, 1998), p. 618.

Harris, John, 'Neighbours: Caradoc Evans, Lloyd George and the London Welsh', *Llafur*, 5, 4 (1983), 90–8.

——, 'Caradoc Evans: my people right or wrong', *Transactions of the Honourable Society of Cymmrodorion 1995*, new ser., 2 (1996), 141–55.

Harris, Jose, *Private Lives, Public Spirit: Britain, 1870–1914* (Harmondsworth, 1994).

Harvey, John, 'Introduction', in John Harvey (ed.), *The Appearance of Evil: Apparitions of Spirits in Wales* (Cardiff, 2003), pp. 1–38.

Hechter, Michael and Margaret Levi, 'Ethno-regional movements in the West', *Ethnic and Racial Studies*, 2, 3 (1979), 262–74.

Hobsbawm, Eric, 'Introduction: inventing traditions', in Eric Hobsbawm and Terence Ranger (eds), *The Invention of Tradition* (Cambridge, 1983), pp. 1–15.

Holt, Ysanne, 'London types', *London Journal*, 25, 1 (2000), 35–51.

Hood, Susan, 'The significance of the villages and small towns in rural Ireland during the eighteenth and nineteenth centuries', in Peter Borsay and Lindsay Proudfoot (eds), *Provincial Towns in Early Modern England and Ireland: Change, Convergence and Divergence* (Oxford, 2002), pp. 241–61.

Hopkin, David, 'Identity in a divided province: the folklorists of Lorraine, 1860–1960', *French Historical Review*, 23, 4 (2000), 639–82.

Hopkins, K. S. (ed.), *Rhondda: Past and Future* (Ferndale, 1975).

Horn, Pamela, 'The contribution of the propagandist to eighteenth-century agricultural improvement', *Historical Journal*, 25, 2 (1982), 313–30.

Howell, David W., *Land and People in Nineteenth-Century Wales* (London, 1977).

——, *The Rural Poor in Eighteenth-Century Wales* (Cardiff, 2000).

Hughes, R. Elwyn, *Dysgl Bren a Dysgl Arian: Nodiadau ar Hanes Bwyd yng Nghymru* (Talybont, 2003).

Humphreys, Emyr, *The Taliesin Tradition* (London, 1983).

Humphreys, Rob, 'Images of Wales', in Trevor Herbert and Gareth Elwyn Jones (eds), *Post-War Wales* (Cardiff, 1995), pp. 133–59.

Hurn, Samantha, 'The "Cardinauts" of the western coast of Wales: exchanging and exhibiting horses in the pursuit of fame', *Journal of Material Culture*, 13, 3 (2008), 335–55.

Ibelema, Minabere, 'Tribes and prejudice: coverage of the Nigerian civil war', in Beverly G. Hawk (ed.), *Africa's Media Image* (Westport, CT, 1992), pp. 77–93.

James, David B., *Ceredigion: Its Natural History* (Bow Street, 2001).

Jenkins, David, *The Agricultural Community in South-West Wales at the Turn of the Twentieth Century* (Cardiff, 1971).

——, '"Cardiff Tramps, Cardi Crews": Cardiganshire shipowners and seamen in Cardiff, *c*.1870–1950', *Ceredigion*, 10, 4 (1984–7), 405–29.

Jenkins, Geraint H., *The Foundations of Modern Wales: Wales, 1642–1780* (Oxford, 1993).

——, '"I will tell you a word or two about Cardiganshire": Welsh clerics and literature in the eighteenth century', *Studies in Church History*, 38 (Woodbridge, 2004), pp. 303–23.

Jenkins, J. Geraint, *Life and Tradition in Rural Wales* (Stroud, 1991).

——, *Ceredigion: Interpreting an Ancient County* (Llanrwst, 2005).

Jenkins, Richard, *Rethinking Ethnicity: Arguments and Explanations* (London, 1997).

Johnson, Richard, 'Educational policy and social control in early Victorian England', *Past and Present*, 49 (1970), 96–119.

Jones, Adrian, 'Word *and* deed: why a *post*-poststructural history is needed, and how it might look', *Historical Journal*, 43, 2 (2000), 517–41.

Jones, Aled Gruffydd, *Press, Politics and Society: A History of Journalism in Wales* (Cardiff, 1993).

Jones, David J. V., 'Distress and discontent in Cardiganshire, 1814–1819', *Ceredigion*, 5, 3 (1964–7), 280–9.

——, *Before Rebecca: Popular Protests in Wales, 1793–1835* (London, 1973).

——, *Crime in Nineteenth-Century Wales* (Cardiff, 1992).

Jones, David Lewis, 'Aberaeron: the community and seafaring, 1800–1900', *Ceredigion*, 6, 2 (1969), 201–42.

Jones, E. D., 'Some glimpses of Cardiganshire', *Journal of the Welsh Bibliographical Society*, 6 (1943–9), 5–27.

Jones, Emrys, 'Tregaron: the sociology of a market town in central Cardiganshire', in Elwyn Davies and Alwyn D. Rees (eds), *Welsh Rural Communities* (Cardiff, 1962), pp. 65–117.

——, 'Where is Wales?', *Transactions of the Honourable Society of Cymmrodorion 1994*, new ser., 1 (1995), 123–34.

——, 'The age of societies', in Emrys Jones (ed.), *The Welsh in London* (Cardiff, 2001), pp. 55–87.

Jones, Emyr Wyn, 'Medical glimpse of early nineteenth-century Cardiganshire', *National Library of Wales Journal*, 14 (1965–6), 253–75.

Jones, Evan, *Cymdogaeth Soar-Y-Mynydd* (Abertawe, 1979).

——, *Y Mynydd Bach a Bro Eiddwen* (Aberystwyth, 1990).

Jones, F., 'Two illustrious sons of Cardiganshire', *Cardiganshire Antiquarian Society Transactions*, 13 (1938), 74–80.

Jones, Gareth Stedman, 'The Cockney and the nation, 1780–1988', in Gareth Stedman Jones and David Feldman (eds), *Metropolis London: Histories and Representations since 1800* (London, 1989), pp. 272–324.

Jones, Glyn Lewis, *Llyfryddiaeth Ceredigion: A Bibliography of Cardiganshire*, 4 vols (Aberystwyth, 1967 and 1970).

Jones, Huw, *Cydymaith Byd Amaeth*, 4 vols (Llanrwst, 1999).

Jones, Ieuan Gwynedd, 'The county and its history, 1909–1984', *Ceredigion*, 10, 1 (1984–7), 1–17.

——, *Mid-Victorian Wales: The Observers and the Observed* (Cardiff, 1992).

Jones, Owain J., 'The Welsh church in the nineteenth century', in David Walker (ed.), *A History of the Church in Wales* (Penarth, 1976), pp. 144–63.

Jones, R. Merfyn, 'Beyond Identity? The reconstruction of the Welsh', *Journal of British Studies*, 31, 4 (1992), 330–57.

Jones, Rhys and Carwyn Fowler, *Placing the Nation: Aberystwyth and the Reproduction of Welsh Nationalism* (Cardiff, 2008).

Jones, Roger Stephens, 'The Angry Summer: an essay on the structure of Idris Davies's poem', *Planet*, 37/38 (1977), 21–8.

Jones, Sally, *Allen Raine* (Cardiff, 1979).

Jones, T. Llew and Dafydd Wyn Jones, *Cancer Cures or Quacks? The Story of a Secret Herbal Remedy* (Llandysul, 1993).

Jordanova, Ludmilla, *History in Practice* (London, 2000).

Kammen, Michael, *In the Past Lane: Historical Perspectives on American Culture* (New York, 1997).

King, Anthony, 'The night itself', in Anthony King et al., *New Labour Triumphs: Britain at the Polls* (Chatam, NJ, 1998), pp. 1–13.

Knowles, Ann Kelly, *Calvinists Incorporated: Welsh Immigrants on Ohio's Industrial Frontier* (Chicago, 1997).

Kunzle, David, *The History of the Comic Strip: The Nineteenth Century* (Berkeley, 1990).

Kurtz, Matthew, 'Re/membering the town body: methodology and the work of local history', *Journal of Historical Geography*, 28, 1 (2002), 42–62.

Lambert, W. R., *Drink and Sobriety in Victorian Wales, c.1820–c.1895* (Cardiff, 1983).

Langton, John, 'The industrial revolution and the regional geography of England', *Transactions of the Institute of British Geographers*, new ser., 9, 2 (1984), 145–67.

—— and R. J. Morris (eds), *Atlas of Industrializing Britain* (London, 1986).

Law, C. M., 'The growth of urban population in England and Wales, 1801–1911', *Transactions of the Institute of British Geographers*, 41 (1967), 125–43.

Lemire, Beverly, 'Second-hand beaux and "red-armed belles": conflict and the creation of fashions in England, *c.*1660–1800', *Continuity and Change*, 15, 3 (2000), 391–419.

Lewis, E. D., *The Rhondda Valleys* (London, 1959).

Lewis, Peter, 'Region and class: an introduction to Sid Chaplin (1916–86)', *Durham University Journal*, 85, 1(1993), 105–9.

Lewis, Roy and Angus Maude, *The English Middle Class* (London, 1953).

Lewis, W. J., 'The condition of labour in mid-Cardiganshire in the early nineteenth century', *Ceredigion*, 4, 4 (1960–3), 321–35.

——, *Hanes Darluniadol o Geredigion* (Aberystwyth, 1970).

Leyton, Elliott, 'Opposition and integration in Ulster', *Man*, new ser., 9, 2 (1974), 185–98.

Lloyd, John Edward, *The Story of Ceredigion* (Cardiff, 1937).

Lloyd, Thomas, Julian Orbach and Robert Scourfield, *The Buildings of Wales: Carmarthenshire and Ceredigion* (London, 2006).

Lord, Peter, *Words with Pictures: Welsh Images and Images of Wales in the Popular Press, 1640–1860* (Aberystwyth, 1995).

Lowerson, J. R., 'Editorial preface', *Southern History*, 1, 1 (1979), 9–10.

Mackintosh, John P., *Britain's Malaise: Political or Economic?* (Southampton, 1977).

Madgwick, P. J., Non Griffiths and Valerie Walker, *The Politics of Rural Wales: A Study of Cardiganshire* (London, 1973).

Maidment, Brian, *Dusty Bob: A Cultural History of Dustmen, 1780–1870* (Manchester, 2007).

Mandler, Peter, 'Problems in cultural history: a reply', *Cultural and Social History*, 1, 3 (2004), 326–32.

Marquardt, Frederick, 'Review essay: " Schaffe, Schaffe, Hausle Baue": Hans Medick, the Swabians, and modernity', *Journal of Social History*, 32, 1 (1998), 197–207.

Marshall, J. D., *The Tyranny of the Discrete: A Discussion of the Problems of Local History in England* (Aldershot, 1997).

——, review of *Issues of Regional Identity*, *Journal of Regional and Local Studies*, 18, 2 (1998), 49–60.

Massey, Doreen, 'Places and their pasts', *History Workshop Journal*, 39 (1995), 182–92.

Mathias, Peter, *Retailing Revolution: A History of Multiple Retailing in the Food Trades Based upon the Allied Suppliers Group of Companies* (London, 1967).

Mathiopoulos, Margarita, *History and Progress: In Search of the European and American Mind* (New York, 1989).

Matthews, Roy T., 'Britannia and John Bull: from birth to maturity', *Historian*, 62 (2000), 799–820.

Marx, Karl, *Capital: A Critical Analysis of Capitalist Production*, ed. Friederich Engels, trans. Samuel Moore and Edward Aveling, 2 vols (New York, 1901).

Matless, David, 'Regional surveys and local knowledges: the geographical imagination in Britain, 1918–39', *Transactions of the Institute of British Geographers*, 17, 4 (1992), 464–80.

McCullagh, C. Behan, *The Truth of History* (London, 1998).

McGuigan, Jim, 'Cultural change', in Jonathan Hollowell (ed.), *Britain Since 1945* (London, 2003), pp. 279–95.

McKibbin, Ross, 'Working-class gambling in Britain, 1880–1939', *Past and Present*, 82 (1979), 147–78.

——, *Classes and Cultures: England, 1918–1951* (Oxford, 1998).

Meils, Gareth, 'Ambrose Bebb', *Planet*, 37/38 (May 1977), 70–9.

Melman, Billie, 'Claiming the nation's past: the invention of an Anglo-Saxon tradition', *Journal of Contemporary History*, 26, 3/4 (1991), 575–95.

Messinger, Gary S., *Manchester in the Victorian age: The Half-Known City* (Manchester, 1985).

Mitchell, B. R. and P. Deane, *Abstract of British Historical Statistics* (Cambridge, 1962).

Moore-Colyer, Richard J., *The Teifi: Scenery and Antiquities of a Welsh River* (Llandysul, 1987).

——, 'Farming in depression: Wales between the wars, 1919–1939', *Agricultural History Review*, 46 (1998), 177–96.

—— (ed.), *Land of Pure Delight: Selections from the Letters of Thomas Johnes of Hafod, Cardiganshire (1748–1816)* (Llandysul, 1992).

Moran, Joe, 'History, memory and the everyday', *Rethinking History*, 8, 1 (2004), 51–68.

Morash, Christopher Chul, *Writing the Irish Famine* (Oxford, 1995).

Morgan, Gerald, *Ceredigion: A Wealth of History* (Llandysul, 2005).

Morgan, J. J., *The '59 Revival in Wales* (Mold, 1909).

Morgan, Kenneth O., *Rebirth of a Nation: Wales, 1880–1980* (Cardiff and Oxford, 1981).

——, 'Cardiganshire politics: the Liberal ascendancy, 1885–1923', in Kenneth O. Morgan, *Modern Wales: Politics, Place and People* (Cardiff, 1995), pp. 216–50.

Morgan, Prys, 'Wild Wales: civilising the Welsh from the sixteenth to the nineteenth centuries', in Peter Burke, Brian Harrison and Paul Slack (eds), *Civil Histories: Essays Presented to Sir Keith Thomas* (Oxford, 2000), pp. 265–83.

Morris, M. C. F., *The British Workman: Past and Present* (Oxford, 1928).

Morris, Pam, 'Heroes and hero-worship in Charlotte Brontë's *Shirley*', *Nineteenth-Century Literature*, 54, 3 (1999–2000), 285–307.

Myrddin Ap Dafydd (ed.), *Pigion Llafar Gwlad 4: Llysenwau* (Llanrwst, 1997).

Nisbet, Robert, *History of the Idea of Progress* (London, 1980).

Nussel, Frank, *The Study of Names: A Guide to the Principles and Topics* (Westport, CT, 1992).

O'Connell, Sean, *The Car in British Society: Class, Gender and Motoring, 1896–1939* (Manchester, 1998).

O'Leary, Paul, 'The languages of patriotism in Wales, 1840–1880', in Geraint H. Jenkins (ed.), *The Welsh Language and its Social Domains, 1801–1911* (Cardiff, 2000), pp. 533–60.

Osmond, John, *New Politics in Wales* (London, 1998).

Palladino, Paolo, 'Science, technology, and the economy: plant breeding in Great Britain, 1920–1970', *Economic History Review*, 49, 1 (1999), 116–36.

Payton, Philip, *The Making of Modern Cornwall: Historical Experience and the Persistence of 'Difference'* (Redruth, 1992).

Peneff, Jean, 'Myths in life stories', in R. Samuel and P. Thompson (eds), *The Myths we Live By* (London, 1990), pp. 36–48.

Perkin, Harold, *The Origins of Modern English Society, 1780–1880* (London, 1969).

Phillips, Dewi Z., *J. R. Jones* (Cardiff, 1995).

Phillips, Richard, *Dyn a'i Wreiddiau: Hanes Plwyf Llangwyryfon* (Aberystwyth, 1975).

Phythian-Adams, Charles, 'Introduction: an agenda for English local history', in Charles Phythian-Adams (ed.), *Societies, Cultures and Kinship, 1580–1850: Cultural Provinces and English Local History* (Leicester, 1993), pp. 1–23.

Pick, Daniel, *Faces of Degeneration: A European Disorder, c.1848–c.1918* (Cambridge, 1989).

Pickering, Michael, *Stereotyping: The Politics of Representation* (Basingstoke, 2001).

Pittock, Murray G. H., *Celtic Identity and the British Image* (Manchester, 1999).

Plonien, Klaus, "'Germany's river, but not Germany's border": the Rhine as a national myth in early nineteenth-century century German literature', *National Identities*, 2, 1 (2000), 81–6.

Pooley, Colin G., 'Welsh migration to England in the mid-nineteenth century', *Journal of Historical Geography*, 9, 3 (1983), 287–306.

Pope, Robert, *Building Jerusalem: Nonconformity, Labour and the Social Question in Wales, 1906–1939* (Cardiff, 1998).

Pretty, David A., *The Rural Revolt that Failed: Farm Workers' Trade Unions in Wales, 1889–1950* (Cardiff, 1989).

Price, Richard N., 'The other face of respectability: violence in the Manchester brickmaking trade, 1859–1870', *Past and Present*, 66 (1975), 110–32.

Read, Donald, *The English Provinces, c.1760–1960: A Study in Influence* (London, 1964).

Rees, D. Ben, *Hanes Plwyf Llanddewi Brefi* (Llanddewi Brefi, 1984).

Rees, Thomas and J. Thomas, *Hanes Eglwysi Annibynol Cymru*, 5 vols (Lerpwl, 1871–91).

Rich, Paul, 'The quest for Englishness', in Gordon Marsden (ed.), *Victorian Values: Personalities and Perspectives in Nineteenth-Century Society* (London, 1990), pp. 211–25.

Robbins, Keith, *History, Religion and Identity in Modern Britain* (London, 1993).

——, Review of *Cardiganshire County History*, vol. 3, *English Historical Review*, 115, 460 (2000), 268.

Roberts, Gwyneth Tyson, *The Language of the Blue Books: The Perfect Instrument of Empire* (Cardiff, 1998).

Rodger, R. G., 'The evolution of Scottish town planning', in George Gordon and Brian Dicks (eds), *Scottish Urban History* (Aberdeen, 1983), pp. 71–91.

Root, Amanda, 'Transport and communications', in A. H. Halsey and Josephine Webb (eds), *Twentieth-Century British Social Trends* (London, 2000), pp. 437–68.

Rose, Gillian, 'The cultural politics of place: local representation and oppositional discourse in two films', *Transactions of the Institute of British Geographers*, new ser., 19, 1 (1994), 46–60.

Rose, Michael E., 'Rochdale man and the Stalybridge riot: the relief and control of the unemployed during the Lancashire cotton famine', in A. P. Donajgrodski (ed.), *Social Control in Nineteenth-Century Britain* (London, 1977), pp. 185–206.

Royle, Stephen A., 'The development of small towns in Britain', in Martin Daunton (ed.), *The Cambridge Urban History of Britain*, vol. 3: *1840–1950* (Cambridge, 2000), pp.151–84.

Russell, Dave, 'Sport and identity: the case of Yorkshire County Cricket Club, 1890–1939', *Twentieth-Century British History*, 7, 2 (1996), 206–30.

Saer, D. J., *The Story of Cardiganshire* (Cardiff, 1912).

Sahlins, Marshall, 'Goodbye to tristes tropes: ethnography in the context of modern world history', in Robert Borofsky (ed.), *Assessing Cultural Anthropology* (New York, 1994), pp. 377–95.

Said, Edward W., *Orientalism: Western Conceptions of the Orient* (London, 1978).

Saler, Michael, 'Making it new: visual modernism and the "Myth of the North" in interwar England', *Journal of British Studies*, 37, 4 (1998), 419–40.

Schulze, Rainer, 'Region, industrialisation, structural change: a regional approach to problems of socio-economic change', in Rainer Schulze (ed.), *Industrial Regions in Transformation: Historical Roots and Patterns of Regional Structural Change: A European Comparison* (Essen, 1993), pp. 40–63.

Schama, Simon, *The Embarrassment of Riches: An Interpretation of Dutch Culture in the Golden Age* (London, 1988).

Scott, Derek B., 'The music-hall Cockney: flesh and blood, or replicant?', *Music & Letters*, 83, 2 (2002), 237–59.

Sheeran, George and Yanina Sheeran, 'Discourses in local history', *Rethinking History*, 2, 1 (1998), 65–86.

Sherrington, Emlyn, 'O. M. Edwards, culture and the industrial classes', *Llafur*, 6, 1 (1992), 28–41.

Shields, Rob, *Places on the Margin: Alternative Geographies of Modernity* (London, 1991).

Shortridge, James R., 'The emergence of "Middle West" as an American regional label', *Annals of the Association of American Geographers*, 74, 2 (1984), 209–20.

Sibler, Nina, 'Intemperate men, spiteful women and Jefferson Davis: Northern views of the defeated South', *American Quarterly*, 41, 4 (1989), 614–35.

Smith, David, 'Tonypandy 1910: definitions of community', *Past and Present*, 87 (1980), 158–84.

——, *Wales! Wales?* (London, 1984).

Smith, Robert, *Schools, Politics and Society: Elementary Education in Wales, 1870–1902* (Cardiff, 1999).

Snell, K. D. M. (ed.), *The Regional Novel in Britain and Ireland, 1800–1990* (Cambridge, 1998).

——, 'The culture of local xenophobia', *Social History*, 28, 1 (2003), 1–30.

Solomon, Maynard, 'Some romantic images of Beethoven', in Thomas Pfau and Robert F. Gleckner (eds), *Lessons of Romanticism: A Critical Companion* (London, 1998), pp. 225–43.

Spierenburg, Pieter, 'Imprisonment and the family: an analysis of petitions for confinement in Holland, 1680–1805', *Social Science History*, 10, 2 (1986), 115–46.

Stapleton, Julia, 'Political thought and national identity in Britain, 1850–1950', in Stefan Collini, Richard Whatmore and Brian Young (eds), *British Intellectual History, 1750–1950: History, Religion and Culture* (Cambridge, 2000), pp. 245–69.

Stead, Jennifer, 'Prodigal frugality: Yorkshire pudding and parkin, two traditional Yorkshire foods', in C. Anne Wilson (ed.), *Traditional Food East and West of the Pennines* (Edinburgh, 1991), pp. 143–86.

Stevenson, John and Chris Cook, *The Slump: Society and Politics during the Depression* (London, 1979).

Storm, Eric, 'Regionalism in history, 1890–1945: the cultural approach', *European History Quarterly*, 33, 2 (2003), 251–65.

Sweet, Rosemary, *The English Town: Government, Society and Culture* (Harlow, 1999).

Thomas, Brinley, 'The migration of labour into the Glamorganshire coalfield (1861–1911)', *Economica*, 30 (1930), 275–94.

Thomas, Peter, *Strangers from a Strange Land: The Voyages of the Brig Albion and the Founding of the First Welsh Settlements in Canada* (Llandysul, 1986).

Thompson, E. P., *The Making of the English Working Class* (London, 1963).

Thompson, F. M. L., 'Town and city', in F. M. L. Thompson (ed.), *The Cambridge Social History of Britain, 1750–1950*, vol. 1: *Regions and Communities* (Cambridge, 1990), pp. 1–86.

Trentmann, Frank ,'Civilization and its discontents: English neo-Romanticism and the transformation of anti-Modernism in twentieth-century western culture', *Journal of Contemporary History*, 29, 4 (1994), 583–625.

Trezise, Simon, 'The Celt, the Saxon and the Cornishman: stereotypes and counter-stereotypes of the Victorian period', *Cornish Studies*, 8 (2000), 54–68.

Turner, Frederick Jackson, *Frontier and Section: Selected Essays of Frederick Jackson Turner* (Englewood Cliffs, NJ, 1961).

Vaughan, Herbert M., *The South Wales Squires* ([1926] Carmarthen, 1988).

Walton, John K., *The English Seaside Resort: A Social History, 1750–1914* (Leicester, 1983).

——, *Fish and Chips and the British Working Class, 1870–1940* (Leicester, 1992).

Weber, Eugen, *Peasants into Frenchmen: The Modernization of Rural France, 1870–1914* (London, 1976).

Weber, Max, 'Structures of power', in *Max Weber: Essays in Sociology*, ed. H. H. Gerth and C. Wright-Mills (London, 1948).

Weight, Richard, *Patriots: National Identity in Britain, 1940–2000* (London, 2002).

Wenger, G. Clare, *Mid-Wales: Deprivation or Development: A Study of Patterns of Employment in Selected Communities* (Cardiff, 1980).

White, Eryn, 'The people called "Methodists": early Welsh Methodism and the question of identity', *Journal of Welsh Religious History*, new ser., 1 (2001), 1–14.

Williams, Chris, *Democratic Rhondda: Politics and Society, 1885–1951* (Cardiff, 1996).

Williams, D., 'Rhyfel y Sais bach', *Ceredigion*, 2, 1 (1952–5), 39–52.

Williams, Gareth, 'The disenchantment of the world: innovation, crisis and change in Cardiganshire, *c.*1880–1910', *Ceredigion*, 9, 4 (1980–3), 303–21.

——, 'Sport and society in Glamorganshire, 1750–1980', in Prys Morgan (ed.), *Glamorgan County History*, vol. 4: *Glamorganshire Society* (Cardiff, 1988), pp. 381–400.

Williams, Gwyn, *The Land Remembers: A View of Wales* (London, 1977).

Williams, Gwyn A., *The Making of a Unitarian: David Ivan Jones, 1843–1924* (London, 1995).

Williams, John, *Digest of Welsh Historical Statistics*, 2 vols (Cardiff, 1985).

Williams, Moelwyn, *The South Wales Landscape* (London, 1975).

Williams, Raymond, *Culture and Society, 1780–1950* (London, 1958).

Williams-Davies, John '"Merched y Gerddi": mudwyr tymhorol o Geredigion', *Ceredigion*, 8, 3 (1978), 291–301.

Wilson, Kathleen, 'The island race: Captain Cook, Protestant evangelicalism and the construction of English national identity, 1760–1800', in Tony Claydon and Ian McBride (eds), *Protestantism and National Identity: Britain and Ireland, c.1650–c.1850* (Cambridge, 1998), pp. 265–90.

Young, G. M., *Victorian Essays* (Oxford, 1962).

Zweiniger-Bargielowska, I., *Austerity in Britain: Rationing, Controls, and Consumption, 1939–1955* (Oxford, 2000).

5. Unpublished theses

Baker, Simon C., 'Keeping short boundaries holy' (MA thesis, University of Wales Swansea, 1987).

Birtwistle, Michael, 'Pobl y tai bach: some aspects of the agricultural labouring classes of Cardiganshire in the second half of the nineteenth century' (MA thesis, University of Wales, Aberystwyth, 1981).

Daniels, J. E., 'The geographical distribution of religious denominations in its relation to racial and social functions' (MA thesis, University of Wales, Aberystwyth, 1928).

Davies, A. M. E., 'Poverty and its treatment in Cardiganshire, 1750–1850' (MA thesis, University of Wales, Aberystwyth, 1968).

Davies, Andrew, '"The reputed nation of inspiration": representations of Wales in fiction from the Romantic period' (Ph.D. thesis, University of Wales, Cardiff, 2001).

James, Leighton Stuart, 'War and industry: a study of the industrial relations of the mining regions of south Wales and the Ruhr during the Great War, 1914–1918' (MSc Econ thesis, University of Wales, Cardiff, 1999).

Le Vay, F. A. B. J., 'The social and economic changes affecting farming communities in two contrasting Cardiganshire parishes, 1961–1971' (MA thesis, University of Wales, Aberystwyth, 1972).

Thomas, G. Ivor, 'The growth and decline of Cardiganshire shipbuilding from 1740–1914 with special reference to Llansanffraid', 2 vols (M.Phil. thesis, University of Wales, Lampeter, 1994).

6. Internet Sources

Greer, Germaine, 'Long live the Essex Girl', *http://www.guardian.co.uk/women/story/0,,446451,00.html* (accessed 1 August 2004).

'Members research service 2001 Census of Population: key statistics for Assembly constituencies: Ceredigion, 2003', *http://www.wales.gov.uk/organipo/content/news/ceredigion.pdf* (accessed 15 June 2004).

National statistics statistical bulletin, '2001 census on population: first results on the Welsh language', *http://www.wales.gov.uk/keypubstatistics-forwales/content/publication/population/2003/sb22–2003/sb22–2003.pdf* (accessed 15 December 2003).

Osmond, John (ed.), 'End of the corporate body. Monitoring the National Assembly December 2003 to March 2004', *http://iwa.org.uk/publications/pdfs/CorpBody.pdf* (accessed 1 August 2004).

'Strategaeth gymunedol Ceredigion community strategy: Ceredigion 2020', *http://www.ceredigion2020.org.uk/doc/040712ceredigionstrategy.pdf* (accessed 28 July 2004).

Welsh Arts Books, *http://www.welshartsarchive.org.uk/welsh_books.htm* (accessed 15 January 2003).

7. Film and Television

The Counties of Wales: Cardiganshire, HTV Wales, 6 November 2003.

Peeps through the window of the world (no. 28), British Pathe, 4 April 1935.

Wales: Green Mountain, Black Mountain, directed by John Eldridge, Strand Film Production for Ministry of Information, 1942.

INDEX